School Learning
and Instruction

School Learning and Instruction

HERSHEL D. THORNBURG

University of Arizona

BROOKS/COLE PUBLISHING COMPANY
MONTEREY, CALIFORNIA

A Division of Wadsworth Publishing Company, Inc.

SPECIAL ACKNOWLEDGMENTS

Dr. Terry Cornell, EPIC Diversified, Tucson, Arizona, for conceptualizing with me the need for presenting a systematic theory of instruction.

Dr. Robert Gagné, Florida State University, for supporting me in the further exploration of his hierarchical learning system, which is a dominant part of this text.

Dr. Glen Nicholson, University of Arizona, for preparing the draft of Chapter 9 on intelligence.

Dr. Dal Curry, University of Arizona, for preparing the draft of Chapter 11 on behavior modification.

Dr. Robert A. Karabinus, Northern Illinois University, for preparing the draft of statistical Appendix A.

ISBN: 0–8185–0081–6
L. C. Cat. Card No.: 72–92048
Printed in the United States of America
1 2 3 4 5 6 7 8 9 10—77 76 75 74 73

This book was edited by Jim Arntz, with production supervised by Sandra Mangurian. It was designed by Linda Marcetti. Technical art was drawn by Carl Brown. The book was typeset, printed, and bound by Kingsport Press, Kingsport, Tennessee.

To Ellen

Preface

For many years, the colleges and universities with programs for the preparation of future teachers have included a course in learning in their curricula. In many of these courses, however, students are introduced to the concepts and principles of the various learning theories but are not provided with the information and materials by which these principles can be applied in practical classroom situations nor with the typical problem situations that they will face as teachers. Rather, the actual application of learning theory is postponed until the students enter the teaching profession. And at this point, the new teachers are inevitably faced with many learning problems whose solutions are not readily apparent. The teachers then must either seek outside help or come up with appropriate solutions through a trial-and-error process.

The purpose of this book is to close the gap between the time when a student is introduced to learning theory and the moment when he will begin to formulate his theory of instruction. This is accomplished by defining the phenomena of learning on an operational or observational plane, as well as on a theoretical plane, and then providing the reader with problems to which he can apply the learning principles and instructional concepts he is studying. It is expected that this book could be used not only at the undergraduate and graduate levels of teacher preparation but by those teachers who are seeking ways to improve their approaches to instruction through a better understanding of the principles and practical applications of current learning theory. Above all, it should be noted that this book is intended to provide future teachers and teachers in the field with insights into their everyday methods in the classroom, and it is *not* intended to provide educators with insights into experimental laboratory research on learning processes. For this reason, the author readily admits that there may be many facets to the learning process which are not considered in this book.

When approaching a task of this scope, an author must rely on the supportive efforts of many others in helping the book become a reality. I would especially like to thank Dr. Glen Nicholson, of the University of Arizona, for his criticisms of the text during its formative stages. Special recognition should also be given to Mrs. Alice Schoenberger for the manuscript preparation, and to James McIntosh, of the Tucson Public Schools, for his invaluable grammatical assistance. Reviews by other psychologists most assuredly gave strength to this text, and I extend my appreciation to Carol Gray, of the University of Washington; Edmund T. Emmer, of the University of Texas, Austin; Meryl E. Englander, of the University of Indiana; Larry Goulet, of the University of Illinois; and Michal C. Clark, of Arizona State University, for their opinions and recommendations. I have always found the Brooks/Cole staff challenging to work with. Terry Hendrix, Bonnie Fitzwater, and John Estes deserve equal recognition for the confidence and guidance they gave me in developing this book, and Jim Arntz and Sandra Mangurian were invaluable in their assistance throughout production.

Hershel Thornburg
Tucson, Arizona

Contents

Learning and Instructional Theory

The teacher is discouraged. Regardless of the number of efforts he has made to teach his class the difference between a coordinating conjunction and a subordinating conjunction, the students do not do well in their work exercises. *Do we know enough today about how students learn, to help the teacher solve his problem?* (See page 165.)

The government instructor finds that his students remember why our nation enacted certain legislation but cannot remember when, or who introduced the bills. *Could the problem be that the student responses required here are on two distinct operational levels?* (See page 135.)

The music teacher feels that her students do not appreciate classical music, but she is uncertain as to the reasons and therefore stymied by the problem. *Could the goals of this teacher be better defined, and are the classroom instructional procedures applicable here?* (See page 37.)

The students in a geometry class have difficulty distinguishing different geometric shapes. Although they all know a triangle, they do not always correctly identify quadrilaterals, pentagons, hexagons, octagons, and decagons. *What type of learning is involved here, and how can the material be more effectively taught?* (See page 133.)

The communications teacher wants his students to have an understanding of the forms of speech. *Can he maximize learning by moving sequentially from a relatively unstructured internal "speech" to such highly structured forms as debate, oratory, or choral reading?* (See page 207.)

The history teacher finds that her students are more successful in recognizing important dates in a matching exam than they are in completion statements.

1

What learning and retention principles may explain this finding? (See page 75.)

In his daily teaching strategy, the geography teacher tries to provide information feedback for each student's response. Eventually, he finds the procedure to be both burdensome and impractical. *"Is this technique really that crucial to learning?"* he asks. (See page 93.)

Of course, numberless instructional questions and problems arise in a classroom setting, and although experimental research in human learning allows us to answer these few sample questions, we should not conclude that there is a "cookbook" solution to every classroom situation. On the other hand, certain theoretical principles based on our knowledge of learning can provide the teacher with many practical solutions and, more important, can establish the foundations and framework from which instructors can build their own repertoire of problem-solving principles and techniques.

The eight chapters in Part 1 concentrate on learning theory. Chapter 1 establishes the historical precedents from contemporary learning theory. Chapter 2 advances an instructional theory, or a systematic teaching procedure, based on these learning principles and applicable to classroom settings. Chapter 3 stresses the concepts of transfer and retention because of their practical importance to classroom situations. Research on transfer has pointed to the practicality of structuring learning situations so that the acquisition of one learning task facilitates the acquisition of subsequent tasks. Retention is, of course, of comparable concern, and ways in which to ensure the longevity of learning are explored. Chapters 4 through 8 present the hierarchical learning model advanced by Robert Gagné, who believes that each person learns at different levels of complexity and in a successive, sequential manner. These chapters also feature a series of classroom applications that show how Gagné's hierarchy functions in the classroom. Chapter 8 is entirely an application chapter; a number of typical classroom problems illustrate how learning principles and instructional theory work in harmony. This chapter also confirms the basic instructional and learning principles advanced in Chapters 2 through 7.

The Relationship of Psychology to Education

Psychology is built on the assumption that there is consistency in behavior. Generalizations and hypotheses about behavior are derived from data accumulated in the course of systematic observations of behavioral patterns. Although psychological phenomena have been studied for several hundred years, psychology has evolved as a science only during the past 80 years, primarily through animal experimentation. One of the earliest experimenters in animal psychology was E. L. Thorndike. His classic studies with animals (1898) provided the basis for his studies of human learning and, subsequently, of learning in school situations (1903, 1913, 1932a). Today, educational psychology is more directly concerned with describing and explaining observable *human* behavior, but most psychologists attribute its beginnings to Thorndike's animal studies because of their later applicability to classroom learning.

DEFINITION OF EDUCATIONAL PSYCHOLOGY

Educational psychology comprises two areas: an understanding of how a child develops and learns, and an understanding of how the teacher perceives and instructs the child. As a science and a branch of the general field of psychology, educational psychology concentrates on the fields of learning, motivitation, cognition, perception, development, personality, affectivity, measurement and evaluation, and research and statistics. Although it is based on experimentation, educational psychology cannot be as exacting a science as experimental psychology, in which the variables among animals can be controlled. The psychologist working with human beings must deal with many variables in attempting to assess and predict the course of behavior. The particular strengths, weaknesses, and temperaments of each person make prediction difficult for the scientist; rarely can he state conclusively that if a certain thing is done to or by an individual, a certain thing will result.

Like the educational psychologist, the teacher must recognize that he is working with many individuals, all of whom will respond differently to some extent to his methods. Thus, the more theories of learning and instruction the classroom teacher knows, the more likely he will be able to provide consistently effective teaching strategies for *all* of his students.

DEFINITION OF LEARNING

Learning is thought of generally as a relatively permanent change in behavior that results from the interaction (experiences) of an individual with his environment. Learning is inferred by the student's ability to demonstrate knowledge and skills when given the opportunity to do so. It may result directly from the student's response to the teacher's instructional behavior. English and English (1958) define *learning* more formally as "a highly general term for the relatively enduring change, in response to a task demand, that is induced directly by experience; or the process or processes whereby such change is brought about" (p. 289). We know that learning results primarily from *reinforcement,* which is some form of feedback so that the student becomes aware of the correctness of his response.

Beyond this very general definition, when we ask the question "How do we learn?" it becomes necessary to respond with theoretical statements. *Theory* has been defined as "a general principle, supported by considerable data, proposed as an explanation of a group of phenomena" (English & English, 1958, p. 551). On the basis of theory, we can go on to establish *hypotheses* ("if . . . then" assumptions), which may then be tested in practical experiments to evaluate the validity of the theories. In short, a theory of learning states general laws or principles that describe the conditions under which learning may or may not take place.

Lindgren (1967) lists the following requirements of an adequate theory of learning for teachers:

1. It must help us understand all processes of human learning.
2. It must extend our understanding of the conditions or forces that stimulate, inhibit, or affect learning in any way.
3. It must enable us to make reasonably accurate predictions about the outcomes of learning activity.
4. It must be a source of hypotheses, clues, and concepts that we can use to become more effective teachers.
5. It must be a source of hypotheses or informed hunches about learning that can be tested through classroom experimentation and research, thus extending our understanding of the teaching–learning process [pp. 248–249].

Since the days of the early theoretical contentions of Thorndike (1903) and Koffka (1924), psychologists have tried to show that their particular persuasion was most applicable to the conditions necessary for classroom learning. This has resulted in several modifications in learning theory up to the present-day mind-substance theories. The remainder of this chapter is devoted to these developments.

ASSOCIATIONISTIC THEORIES

In psychology, *association* refers to "ideas, feelings and movements . . . connected in such a way as to determine their succession in the mind or in the actions of an individual, or . . . the process of establishing such connections" (Drever, 1964). Thus, *associationism* is "any general theory within which it is assumed that learning starts with irreducible elements and the process of learning is one of combining these" (Bigge & Hunt, 1962, p. 277).

Although many psychologists trace associationism back to Aristotle, the work of John Locke, the seventeenth-century English philosopher, gave rise to the notion that the individual's understanding is influenced by his previous experience. Locke rejected the faculty-psychology idea that man was innately good or bad and proposed that the mind was blank at birth. According to his theory, know as *tabula rasa,* the mind is highly impressionable, and the nurturing environment rather than heredity is the basis for learning. Locke saw knowledge, morality, and values as derived from sense experience. From such experiences, and through internal reflection, complex ideas are formulated and learning takes place.

Locke's considerations gave rise in the nineteenth century to Johann Herbart's concepts of *apperception* (associationism), in which newly perceived ideas relate to and are added to the aggregations of ideas already in the mind. As the learner entertains new ideas, these ideas find their way to his consciousness and strive to maintain themselves. This maintenance was facilitated by two principles the German philosopher Herbart postulated: (1) the *principle of frequency,* which held that the more often ideas entered the consciousness, the greater were the chances of their remaining; and (2) the *principle of association,* which suggested that when several ideas gather in the mind, the combined strength of the ideas determines the associations that will subsequently enter the consciousness.

Working from the ideology that the primary objective of education was morality, Herbart devised a set of theoretical considerations designed to make children good. His theory is much like Locke's idea of the mind, with two distinguishable differences: (1) Locke viewed the mind as blank and impressionable at birth and ideas as the result of sense experience and internal reflection. Herbart also accepted that there were no innate ideas in the newborn mind, but he insisted that an idea is learned only when it is perceived in the conscious mind and associated with other ideas. (2) Locke viewed the associations of ideas as passive; Herbart saw ideas as dynamic and moving, struggling with one another for a place in the consciousness.

Apperception, or *Herbartianism* as it is frequently called, went virtually unnoticed until after Herbart's death in 1841. Some years later, German philosophers expounded it; and in the 1890s, when some American students returned from studying in Europe, apperception spread throughout the United States and became overwhelmingly influential in teacher education. Herbart's ideas were further explored in the more formal theories of learning advanced in the early 1900s.

STIMULUS–RESPONSE (S–R) THEORIES

Connectionism

Thorndike undoubtedly influenced American learning theory more than any other man. In his research with cats, he was astonished by the overwhelming effect of reward on a cat's behavior, an observation he discussed in *Animal Intelligence* in 1898. His theoretical position, which incorporated several elements of associationistic psychology, became known as *connectionism,* the term he used to indicate that a relationship between a stimulus (S) and a response (R) had taken place.

According to connectionism, now more widely known as *S–R bond theory,* learning is a process of "stamping in" or forming connections in the mind. Because the cats in his research appeared aimless and random in their attempts to solve problems in a puzzle box, Thorndike came to view learning as a trial-and-error process. He found that when the cats came upon the correct response and were rewarded for it, the reward invoked a *satisfied condition* and thus reinforced (strengthened) the stimulus–response bond. The terms *satisfiers* and *annoyers* are essential to understanding the S–R laws of learning. "By a satisfying state of affairs is meant one which the animal does nothing to avoid, often doing things which maintain or renew it. By an annoying state of affairs is meant one which the animal does nothing to preserve, often doing things which put an end to it" (Thorndike, 1913, p. 2). Thus, attainment of a satisfier strengthens the connection between the stimulus and the response made just prior to the existing satisfying state of affairs.

From this basic principle, Thorndike formulated his most significant law of learning—the *law of effect*—which states:

> Of several responses made to the same situation, those which are accompanied or closely followed by satisfaction to the animal will, other things being equal, be more firmly connected with the situation, so that when it recurs, they will be more likely to recur; those which are accompanied or closely followed by discomfort to the animal will, other things being equal, have their connections with that situation weakened, so that, when it recurs, they will be less likely to occur [Bolles, 1967, p. 435].

Thorndike's second law—the *law of readiness*—incorporates the importance of attention and motivation for learning, employing the term *conduction unit* for the elements of the nervous system involved in establishment of S–R bonds. When a conduction unit is in readiness to conduct, to do so is satisfying for the learner. Thus, the law of readiness is closely related to the law of effect in that readiness is the physiological prerequisite for the law of effect. In other words, readiness is a preparation for action, which is commonly expressed by educators in such terms as "reading readiness," "spelling readiness," and so on.

Thorndike's third law of learning—the *law of exercise*—states simply that connections, or S–R bonds, are strengthened with use and weakened by disuse. In Thorndike's words (1913), "exercise strengthens the bond between situation and response" (p. 127). The term *strength* is used here to mean the probability that a certain response will occur when the appropriate stimulus is given; the term *weakness* indicates a lesser probability of response due to disuse or lack of practice.

Although Thorndike developed several subordinate laws, none had the serious implications for learning of his first three. And, after 30 years of scientific analysis, his three primary laws of learning and his theory of connectionism underwent several modifications, some of which he reports in *The Fundamentals of Learning* (1932a) and *The Psychology of Wants, Interests, and Attitudes* (1935). The most important of these modifications:

1. In his *law of effect,* annoying states (punishment) were no longer thought to weaken bonds. "Rewarding a connection always strengthened it substantially: punishing it weakened it little or not at all" (Thorndike, 1932a, p. 58). Thorndike found that if punishment influenced learning at all, it forced the learner to try *alternative* responses rather than to halt altogether the response to a particular stimulus. Thus, only reward truly brought about a focused response and learning.
2. Thorndike disavowed his third law, the *law of exercise,* because he could find no virtue in use or practice alone. Since learning resulted from reward, practice could be effective only if accompanied by reward. Practice itself was meaningless.
3. Thorndike formulated a new law, the *law of belongingness,* which had to do with the "fitness" of the S–R bond. If the stimulus and response belonged together in some natural or circumstantial order of things, the connection could be more easily made. For example, Thorndike illustrated "belonging" in terms of understanding the relationships between elements of a sentence. If each successive word in the sentence fits in some observable or logical way, the learning of the entire sentence will be facilitated.

Contiguity

During the period of Thorndike's research, Russian physiologist I. R. Pavlov was working with dogs in his laboratory. Combined with the work of the American psychologist J. B. Watson in 1914, Pavlov's research gave rise to the theory of *contiguity,* which was a basic modification of Thorndikean theory. Just as with connectionism, the contiguity theorists regarded learning as a matter of habit-forming or pairing of stimulus and response: "A connection is formed between sensations (stimuli or situations) and behavior (response) when elements of the two occur in close temporal proximity to each other" (Perkins, 1969, p. 344). The major difference between the two theories was a matter of timing. The contiguity theorists proposed that the individual learns best when there is an almost simultaneous occurrence of a stimulus and response. They also suggested that much learning results simply from a person's doing something at the time that an *unrelated* stimulus is provided. Whatever the person was doing may then become a habituated response to that indirect stimulus. We should look at Pavlov's original *classical conditioning* studies for a better understanding of this idea.

Classical conditioning. In Pavlov's view, the formation of an association between a stimulus and a *reflex* (response)—the primary learning process—was dependent for its effectiveness on the time proximity between the stimulus and response. He first demonstrated this notion in 1902, with his study of dogs. Pavlov noticed that a dog presented with meat powder would salivate. He interpreted the flow of saliva as an unlearned response, labeling it an *unconditioned response (UCR)* and the presentation of the meat powder an *unconditioned stimulus (UCS)*. He used the term *conditioning* because he was dealing with the unlearned "state of being" of the subject and was attempting to elicit the inherent responses of that state without the stimulus (the meat powder) instinctively associated with those responses.

Working with this unlearned S–R connection existing in the dog, and persuaded that any response pattern could be learned with appropriate and nearly simultaneous stimuli, Pavlov set up experimental conditions to get the dog to salivate when presented with a *neutral* stimulus—something other than the meat powder. Using such sensory stimuli as a tuning fork, a bell, or a flash of light as the *conditioned stimulus (CS),* Pavlov would present the conditioned stimulus and then follow it with the meat powder, the unconditioned stimulus (UCS). Within precisely the same time sequence after the sensory stimulus and the presentation of the meat powder, the dog salivated. And after several trials (usually eight or nine), the dog began salivating at the sensory stimuli (CS) even before the meat powder was presented. Thus, learning occurred, and this type of learning became known as a *conditioned response (CR)*. Such learning has since been referred to as *respondent conditioning* by B. F. Skinner (1938) and as *signal learning* by Robert Gagné (1965, 1970a).

Behaviorism. J. B. Watson was the first to reflect the Pavlovian influence in the United States. He accepted Pavlov's conclusions that learning is a process of conditioning reflexes (responses) through the substitution of one stimulus for another but rejected the Pavlovian idea that learning involved only that behavior which was externally observable. Watson proposed that learning is the process of associating relevant stimuli to the existing innate responses of man; and viewing man's emotional responses—primarily fear, love, and anger—as innate, he (1914) set out to show that emotional conditioning patterns existed among men.

In his most famous experiment, Watson conditioned a young child (reportedly eight or nine months old) to fear a white rat (Watson & Raynor, 1920). In a child this age, the sound of a loud noise (UCS) would trigger an unconditioned fear response (UCR); so Watson set up his experiment in much the same way as Pavlov's classical conditioning experiments with dogs. He paired a conditioning stimulus (the white rat) with an unconditioned stimulus (the loud noise) in order to substitute a conditioned response (fear of the rat) for the unconditioned one (fear of the noise). In just seven trials spaced over a one-week interval, Watson was able to establish a fear response in the child.

In addition to his study of emotional learning, Watson attempted to describe learning according to the *principles of frequency* and *recency.* His principle of frequency states that the more frequently the organism makes a given response to a given stimulus, the more likely the organism will give that same response to that same stimulus again. Similarly, the principle of recency says that the more recently an organism has made a given response to a given stimulus, the more likely the response will occur again. In light of these two principles, Watson maintained that reward is not necessary for learning, and he regarded the notion of reward as an illogical scientific explanation for the establishment of S–R bonds.

Extended contiguity.   Another American, E. R. Guthrie, extended the Watsonian theories to all types of learning. In addition, he rejected the connectionist ideas of Thorndike's law of effect (Guthrie, 1940). He suggested that rather than Thorndike's juxtaposition of timing, rewards, satisfying states, and annoying states, learning may be explained in one simple *law of association:* "A combination of stimuli which has accompanied a movement will on its recurrence tend to be followed by that movement" (Guthrie, 1952, p. 23). Thus, in Guthrie's view, if an organism responds to a contiguous stimulus, it will likely respond in the same way on subsequent stimulus presentations. In other words, when a conditioned stimulus and a conditioned response are paired, they are learned.

Guthrie went even further in revising earlier theories of contiguity. In his brief statement (1942): "A stimulus pattern gains its full associative strength on the occasion of its first pairing with a response" (p. 30), he proposes (1) that learning takes place in one trial; (2) that learning is not improved with practice; and (3) that no reinforcement (reward) is necessary for learning to take place. Guthrie contended that an individual learns by doing and that associations with reward have nothing to do with whether an individual learns correctly or incorrectly. Associations are made only in the initial one-trial stimulus and response, and reward does not strengthen the learner's subsequent responses in any way.

Guthrie agreed with Thorndike in only one area: The best time to teach something is when the learner appears ready to learn—which is Thorndike's law of readiness. In summing up Guthrian advice to teachers regarding readiness, another educational psychologist, B. R. Bugelski (1964), states: "The teacher must be in charge. He does not try to teach when he is not in charge, when he has reason to believe that the behavior he is looking for will not occur" (p. 105).

Reinforcement theory

The most prominent American learning theorist during the 1930s was Clark Hull. He was a connectionist who accepted and used Thorndike's law of effect as a basic part of his learning theory and is therefore referred to as a *reinforcement theorist.* His system is centered on *habit* as a factor in learning behavior. He held that learning takes place through conditioning and reinforcement, and he rejected Guthrie's ideas of the need for contiguity of stimulus and response and the probability of one-trial learning.

Two interesting contributions evolved from Hullian theory: (1) *Primary reinforcement* and (2) the *habit-family hierarchy.* Hull's law of primary reinforcement is basically a restatement of Thorndike's law of effect. Reinforcers, which Hull specified in terms of the reduction of a *drive* (a basic physiological need), strengthen the stimulus–response behaviors (Thorndike-satisfiers) they accompany, while responses not accompanied by reinforcers are not strengthened and in fact may be weakened (Hull, 1943). Out of this law comes two conditions to learning: (1) It is necessary for a drive to be reduced. If drive reduction does not take place, no reinforcement and therefore no learning takes place. (2) The drive does not have to be eliminated, only diminished to some extent. In fact, the continuing drive serves as a motivator, and motivators are fundamental to learning. In brief, Hull maintained that when drive-stimulus conditions exist, they facilitate responses, which in turn reduce the drive and thereby reinforce the response and bring learning. At the same time, the diminished drive continues, motivating the search for further S–R behaviors and for learning.

Hull's concept of habit-family hierarchy (1934) views the organism as being born with a family of inherent responses *(habits)* that, when certain biological needs arise, are more likely to occur than other, lesser responses. His "hierarchy" is the ordering of the variety of probable responses (habits) that may occur with any given stimulus. The greater the need or drive, and the more likely a particular response will reduce that need, the higher that response ranks on the habit-family hierarchy. Bugelski (1964) makes the following comments about Hull's habit-family hierarchy.

In teaching an organism, we do not usually try to teach the most probable response: that already is most likely to happen. Education itself really involves only those situations where society has decided that some less likely response should be performed.

Learning would amount to reinforcing the selected lower member of the hierarchy until it gained superiority over the several other members, eventually exceeding the most natural in potency.

In short, education consists of changing relative positions in a hierarchy. Note that the originally most likely behavior is not lost. It is merely displaced [pp. 74–75].

The role of reinforcement in the Hull hierarchy is vital. The original hierarchy of inherent responses is rearranged in relation to the reinforcement received in the course of life experiences, with those responses leading to reinforcement increasing in probability, and, thus, gaining more strength on the hierarchy. The responses that are not reinforced decrease in probability and tend to assume lower positions on the hierarchy. It becomes clear, then, that in Hull's scheme the *frequency* of reinforcement is directly related to habit strength on the hierarchy.

A simplified version of Hullian theory was presented by Neal Miller and John Dollard (1941). Based on the idea of drive reduction, they defined the four components in the learning process: *drive, cue, response,* and *reinforcement (reward). Drive* is the Miller and Dollard term for the aroused state of the organism. This state is stimulated by internal and external conditions that compel or motivate the organism to act. *Cue* is the stimulus that elicits a response from the organism. The nature or specificity of the cue directs the appropriate response from the organism. In other words, drive, or the compulsion to act, triggers activity (readiness) in the organism, and the cue, or stimulus, determines the response. The *response* is some type of behavior elicited by a stimulus and enacted as a means of drive reduction. As with Hull, the Miller and Dollard "response" tends to reduce the drive, and the reduction in the strength of the drive then *reinforces* the response which immediately preceded the drive reduction so that learning of the response will take place. Thus, recurring stimuli continue to elicit those responses that have previously tended to reduce or eliminate a drive.

Like Hull, Miller and Dollard also held to response hierarchies. They felt that if a response is elicited frequently, it is easy to *reward* that response and thereby increase its frequency of occurrence. This position was delineated in Miller and Dollard's advancement of three hierarchical models: *initial hierarchy, resultant hierarchy,* and *innate hierarchy.*

While Miller and Dollard generally feel that hierarchical arrangements of responses are the outcomes of learning, they also contend that man has some responses that are not determined by learning but are a result of heredity. These responses comprise an innate hierarchy. For example, an infant may cry in response to environmental situations because of his inability to verbalize. This cry would be an innate response. Later, he may say "no," an initial hierarchical response.

Still another Hullian theorist was Kenneth Spence, who was a contemporary of Clark Hull and undoubtedly did more than any other theorist to maintain the significance of his work. Although Spence's theory was a modification of Hull's, the two were so much alike that their two positions have commonly been referred to as the Hull–Spence theory of learning (Logan, 1959).

Initially, Spence was convinced that the Thorndikean law of effect (Hull's reinforcement principle) applied to both cognitive and affective learning, but his research experiments at the University of Iowa in the 1940s (Spence & Lippitt, 1940, 1946; Spence, Bergmann, & Lippitt, 1950) caused him to modify his ideas so that they contained elements of both reinforcement theory and contiguity theory.

Spence (1956) defined conditioning with his own *empirical* law of effect: "Responses accompanied or followed by certain kinds of events (namely, reinforcers) are more likely to occur on subsequent occasions, whereas responses followed by certain other kinds of events (namely, nonreinforcers) do not subsequently show a greater likelihood of occurrence" (p. 33). For Spence, learning behavior is based on *excitatory potential*—the strength of the tendency in an organism to give a specific response to a specific stimulus. This potential is facilitated by the variables of *habit strength* (the frequency of prior S–R bond associations and the permanency of learning), the primary motivation of *drive,* and the secondary motivation of *incentive.* Like Hull, Spence proposed that habit strength depends exclusively on the number of times a response occurs. However, in contrast to Hull's statements, Spence stated that the initial response must be contiguous with the presentation of the stimulus. He also suggested (1951) that reinforcement is *not* necessary for the establishment and strengthening (habit strength) of stimulus–response bonds. Rather, the function of reinforcement is to implement incentive motivation. Thus, in Spence's view, reinforcement serves motivation and subsequent additional learning, rather than the strengthening of already established S–R bonds.

Operant conditioning

In perhaps the greatest shift in emphasis in learning theory since the Hullian approach, the systematic and pragmatic views of American psychologist B. F. Skinner (1938, 1953) came to the fore. Still writing within the Thorndike tradition of reinforce-

Photo courtesy of B. F. Skinner.

ment theory, Skinner emphasizes two types of conditioning—*respondent* and *operant.* In Skinner's theory, respondent conditioning is that behavior which is elicited by some *identifiable* stimulus. The learning condition required within respondent conditioning is *contiguity,* which is effective only if the emission of a response occurs within the presence of the stimulus. The associative strength of the S–R bond depends on this relationship of the response and the stimuli.

Watson and Raynor (1920) demonstrated the same principle when they found that the nine-month-old child would cry or show fear when being subjected to a loud sound and that the child could be conditioned with the stimulus of the noise to respond similarly to the appearance of a white rat. It is the contiguous pairing of the white rat (CS) and the loud sound (UCS) with the child's fear and crying (UCR, then CR) which is respondent conditioning. Bijou and Baer (1961, 1965) consider such conditioning the primary form of learning behavior during infancy.

While respondent conditioning is basic to Skinner's theory of learning, his concept of operant conditioning is a departure from previous theory and is most important to contemporary learning theory; for operant conditioning is a most useful explanation for the process by which most human learning occurs. Operant conditioning is simply a response by the person to his environment. In contrast to respondent conditioning, no specific or identifiable stimulus consistently elicits operant behavior. Skinner views most human behavior as operant: We *emit* varying responses to various stimuli situations; they are not elicited from us (respondent conditioning) by some specific and inherent grouping of S–R associations.

The likelihood of recurring operant responses, or learning, is found in Skinner's concept of *reinforcement.* If behavior is reinforced, it tends to be repeated and, thus, becomes learned behavior. Skinner (1953) prefers to use the term *reinforcement* rather than *reward.* He feels that *reward* carries with it the connotations of a pleasurable event (Thorndike's satisfier), whereas he views reinforcement as neutral and prefers to think of it as merely increasing the *probability* of response rather than ensuring that response. Skinner (1953) does not see any real problem in reinforcing human behavior. Simply to tell the learner that he has made the right response or even the learner's own knowledge of the results (the rightness) of his response are sufficient reinforcement.

Skinnerian theory has made a great contribution to classroom learning. For example, his *knowledge of results* principle is a highly useful theory of reinforcement for classroom learning; for in many learning situations, the reinforcement does not necessarily have to come from the teacher—just knowing that the right response has been emitted is satisfactory enough for the learner. Another highly effective part of this theory relates to contiguity of reinforcement—the immediacy with which reinforcement can occur. Because it can occur within a short period of time after the response, the learner can continually progress in his learning in a logical, sequential way. We can see the practical incorporation of Skinner's theoretical principles in the teaching machine (1958) and programmed textbooks.

Because of the impact of Skinner on learning theory, you can find his principles underlying the discussion throughout this text. His theory, built in the tradition of both associationism and S–R research and more appropriately labeled *reinforcement,* aligns itself well with contemporary learning practice. Considerable emphasis on Skinnerian theory will be found in Chapters 2, 4, and 9.

A theory of hierarchical learning conditions

The most recent significant work in the field of learning theory is that of American psychologist Robert Gagné. Following in the S–R tradition, Gagné deals primarily with the prerequisite *conditions* of different types of learning (1970a), proposing (1964) a *hierarchy of learning types,* or *levels,* from simple to complex and relying heavily on the cumulative and orderly effects of overall learning to support his theory. While he writes within the S–R tradition, Gagné does not view all learning as the same. It is the complexity of human learning that brings Gagné to consider a hierarchy of cumulative learning. He states (1965), "The attempt is made to show that each variety of learning begins with a different state of the organism and learning begins with a different capability for performance" (p. 60). He proposes (1970a) eight types* of learning that are considered cumulative because each more complex level of learning depends on the prerequisite knowledge or learning of a lower level of performance.

> *Level 1, Signal learning.*   The individual learns to make a reflexive response to some external and specific, identifiable stimulus. The type of learning represented here is the same as Pavlov's classical conditioning and Skinner's respondent conditioning.
>
> *Level 2, Stimulus–response learning.*   The learner discriminates among different stimuli and acquires a specific response to a specific stimulus. The response is voluntary (unlike level 1) and is the same as Thorndike's S–R connection and Skinner's operant conditioning. This level may also be termed *single discrimination learning.*
>
> *Level 3, Motor chaining.*   The individual learns to combine a number of already acquired S–R connections into a sequential *chain* of psychomotor behaviors.
>
> *Level 4, Verbal associations.*   The learner acquires a chain of responses that are verbal. Basically, the conditions resemble those for chaining in motor learning (level 3). However, the presence of language makes this a special type of response because the facilitating links in learning the chain may be provided internally by the learner from his repertoire of language.
>
> *Level 5, Multiple discrimination.*   The individual learns to discriminate among —make differently identifying responses to—two or more different stimuli which have a similar appearance or similar characteristics.
>
> *Level 6, Concept learning.*   The learner acquires a capability of identifying and making a common response to an entire class of stimuli (objects or events) that may differ from each other widely in physical appearance. His understanding of the objects or events is based on the abstract properties of the stimuli and/or on verbal definitions.
>
> *Level 7, Rule learning.*   A *rule* is a chain of two or more *previously learned* concepts that are combined by the learner into a verbal principle that explains or determines behavior, events, or relationships. The learning of a rule always infers a capability to act on that rule. This type of learning must be carefully distinguished from learning the mere verbal statement of a rule which is a level 4 response (a chain of verbal responses).
>
> *Level 8, Problem solving.*   Two or more previously acquired rules are combined to produce a new, higher order rule which can be applied in resolving previously unencountered problems.

Gagné (1970c) also suggests that the current shift of views toward learning from the older notion of connectionism—establishing S–R bonds—to a computer-based notion of *information processing* has some important implications for instructional

* Gagné refers to *types* in his hierarchy, but we shall use the term *levels* as a reminder to the reader of the hierarchical concept.

strategies. Gagné's idea that stimuli are "processed in quite a number of different ways by the human central nervous system, and that understanding learning is a matter of figuring out how the various processes operate" (1970c, p. 468) can be related to instructional procedure in the following ways:

1. Each learner enters a new learning task with a different set of prerequisite skills. For effective instruction, the teacher must take into account what the learner does and does not already know. This means diagnostic testing.
2. The most important guide to assessing student needs for a behavioral objective is the related prerequisite skills and information that the student has not yet mastered.
3. Well-planned periodic reviews of materials should be given to ensure retention.
4. Students should be taught strategies of *coding*. This involves presenting material so that the student can transform it into a form that makes it easier to remember at a later time.

Since Gagné's model accounts for the various levels of classroom learning more so than other contemporary learning theories, many of his concepts will be basic to both the learning and the instructional theory in this book.

THEORIES OF LEARNING—A SUMMARY

Beginning just over 70 years ago with experimentation on animals, Thorndike (1898) provided educational psychology with the basis for stimulus-response theory as an explanation of learning processes. Throughout this chapter we have traced the development of this theory and the major contributors to that development. In summary, they are

E. L. Thorndike	Connectionism
I. P. Pavlov	Contiguity (classical conditioning)
J. B. Watson	Contiguity (behaviorism)
Edwin R. Guthrie	Contiguity (extended contiguity)
Clark L. Hull	Reinforcement theory
Neal Miller and John Dollard	Reinforcement theory
Kenneth W. Spence	Reinforcement theory
B. F. Skinner	Operant conditioning
Robert M. Gagné	Theory of hierarchical learning conditions

Each psychologist has advanced the field of stimulus–response psychology in some way, often borrowing and building from the leading theorists of his era. Yet, the most

TABLE 1.1. *The Evolution of Thorndike's Law of Effect*

Psychologist	Law	Definition	Source
Thorndike	Original law of effect	"When a modifiable connection between a situation and a response is made and is accompanied or followed by a satisfying state of affairs, that connection's strength is increased; when made and accompanied or followed by an annoying state of affairs, its strength is decreased."	Thorndike, *Educational psychology, vol. II: The psychology of learning,* 1914, p. 12.
Thorndike	Truncated law of effect	"Rewarding a connection always strengthened it substantially; punishing it weakened it little or not at all."	Thorndike, Reward and punishment in animal learning. *Comparative Psychological Monographs,* 1932b, **8** (39), p. 58.
Hull	Primary reinforcement	"Whenever a response is closely followed by the reduction of a drive stimulus, there will result an increment in the tendency for that stimulus on subsequent occasions to evoke that reaction."	Hull, *Principles of behavior,* 1943, pp. 68–83.
Spence	Empirical law of effect	"Responses accompanied or followed by certain kinds of events (namely, reinforcers) are more likely to occur on subsequent occasions, whereas responses followed by certain other kinds of events (namely, nonreinforcers) do not subsequently show a greater likelihood of occurrence."	Spence, *Behavior theory and conditioning* 1956, p. 33.
Skinner	Operant conditioning	"If the occurrence of an operant [response] is followed by presentation of a reinforcing stimulus, the strength [of the response] is increased."	Skinner, *The behavior of organism,* 1938, p. 21.

profound contribution remained that of its originator, E. L. Thorndike. Through many decades and many S–R psychologists, the validity of Thorndike's basic law of effect has been largely maintained. As can be observed in Table 1.1, the law of effect has been modified somewhat into today's idea of reinforcement theory. Yet all of the psychologists represented in Table 1.1* indicated, with Thorndike, (1) the necessity of reinforcement for learning, (2) the greater effect on learning that positive reinforcement (rewards, satisfiers, drive reduction) has over negative reinforcement (punishment, annoyers), and (3) the weakening of a response tendency if no reinforcement occurs.

SUGGESTED READINGS

Bigge, M. L.   Representation theories of learning and their implications for education. *NEA Journal,* 1966, **55,** 18–19. Reprinted in H. D. Thornburg (Ed.), *School learning and instruction: Readings.* Monterey, Calif.: Brooks/Cole, 1973, chap. 1.

Bitterman, M. E.   Thorndike and the problem of animal intelligence. *American Psychologist,* 1969, **24,** 444–453.

Brody, N., & Oppenheim, P.   Tensions in psychology between the methods of behaviorism and phenomenology. *Psychological Review,* 1966, **73,** 295–305.

Hill, W. F.   Does learning theory apply to education? *Psychology in the Schools,* 1964, **1.** Reprinted in H. D. Thornburg (Ed.), *School learning and instruction: Readings.* Monterey, Calif.: Brooks/Cole, 1973, chap. 1.

Hoffman, D. T.   The reinforcement principle of behavior and the human adult. *Educational Technology,* 1971, **11,** 52–54. Reprinted in H. D. Thornburg (Ed.), *School learning and instruction: Readings.* Monterey, Calif.: Brooks/Cole, 1973, chap. 1.

Kantor, J. R.   Behaviorism in the history of psychology. *Psychological Record,* 1968, **18,** 151–166.

Rogers, C. R.   The place of the person in the new world of the behavioral sciences. *Personnel and Guidance Journal,* 1961, **40,** 442–451.

Seligman, M. E. P.   On the generality of the laws of learning. *Psychological Review,* 1970, **77,** 406–418.

Skinner, B. F.   The technology of teaching. *Proceedings of the Royal Society,* 1965, **162,** 427–443.

Skinner, B. F.   Contingency management in the classroom. *Education,* 1970, **90** (2), 93–100. Reprinted in H. D. Thornburg (Ed.), *School learning and instruction: Readings.* Monterey, Calif.: Brooks/Cole, 1973, chap. 1.

Wittrock, M.   Focus on educational psychology. *Educational Psychologist,* 1967, **4** (7), 17–20.

* The theorists mentioned in this chapter but not included in Table 1.1 either rejected Thorndike's law of effect or did not employ it in their theory.

2

A Theory of Instruction

For some time now, there has been concern among educators that theories of learning are of only limited usefulness for improving the teaching–learning process. While the theories have been extremely successful in defining the processes by which an individual learns, they have not delineated the ways in which a teacher can ensure that such learning will take place. Of course, this is not the function of learning theories; yet the serious need remains, and, in consequence, separate theories of instruction are currently receiving increasing emphasis in educational psychology in the hope of providing the teacher with procedures which will improve learning.

A theory of instruction may be simply defined as *the way in which the teacher influences a pupil to learn.* Bruner (1966) adds that a theory of instruction is *prescriptive,* because it establishes rules concerning the best way to teach knowledge and skills; *normative,* because it "sets the criteria and states the conditions for meeting [these rules] . . ." (p. 40); and *descriptive,* because it tells us what has happened in the instructional process. In short, a theory of instruction provides procedures by which teachers may ensure the learning function.

INSTRUCTIONAL MODELS

Several models of instructional theory have been advanced in the past few years. These models vary considerably because of widely differing opinions on what constitutes a theory of instruction. Jerome Bruner's book *Toward a Theory of Instruction* (1966) states four components of an effective instructional theory:

1. "A theory of instruction should specify the experiences which most effectively implant in the individual a predisposition toward learning . . ." (p. 40). Within this view, Bruner contends the *interpersonal relations* between the teacher and the learner affect the learning situation the most.
2. "A theory of instruction must specify the ways in which a body of knowledge should be structured so that it can be most readily grasped by the learner" (p. 41). Bruner contends that the optimal structure for a body of knowledge (a) simplifies information, (b) generates new propositions, and (c) increases the manipulability of the material.
3. "A theory of instruction should specify the most effective sequences in which to present the materials to be learned" (p. 41). There is, of course, no universal instructional sequence for all learners; rather, the sequence may depend on the prior learning and the developmental stage of the learner, the nature of instructional materials, and individual differences.
4. "A theory of instruction should specify the nature and pacing of rewards and punishments in the process of learning and teaching" (p. 41). Bruner sees the "nature" of reward as knowing when to shift emphasis from extrinsic teacher-provided reinforcement to an intrinsic, self-reinforcement system. The pacing of rewards is knowing when to shift from immediate reward to deferred reward.

N. L. Gage (1964) contends that we should not search for one theory of instruction because teaching includes too many processes, activities, and behaviors to be narrowed down into a single model. He suggests, instead, that the various elements of teaching be analyzed and categorized and that these categories, separately and as a whole, can serve as instructional models. Gage proposes four broad categories for analysis:

1. *Types of teaching activities.*   Here Gage describes the teacher activities of explaining, demonstrating, guiding, housekeeping, record keeping, assignment making, curriculum planning, and so on.
2. *Types of educational objectives.*   These types are classified as cognitive, affective, and psychomotor. Gage suggests that teaching processes can also be classified according to the objectives—cognitive, affective, and psychomotor—to which they seem most relevant.
3. *Types of learning.*   Gage contends that if learning can be analyzed into basic elements, then the obverse components of teaching can be similarly analyzed.
4. *Types of learning theories.*   Gage observes that some learning theories conceive learning to be a matter of conditioning, with punishment or rewards serving as primary or secondary reinforcements of independent or response-dependent stimuli. We have seen the evolutionary development of this type of theory in Chapter 1. Other theorists, such as Bandura (1962), emphasize that learning consists of the learner's identification with a model, a position to be discussed more fully in Chapter

11. Gage believes that each of these families of learning theory can suggest a corresponding theory of teaching.

A more well-known theory of instruction is that advanced by Robert Glaser (1962). Glaser conceptualizes the teaching process in two ways: what the learner brings into the teaching–learning situation, and what the teacher must do within the situation. Thus, his teaching model, Figure 2.1, is concerned with both learner variables and teacher variables. The four components of that model provide a rather concise, uncomplicated overview of the teaching–learning process. The first component within Glaser's model—the *instructional objectives*—both defines the learning that a student should acquire on completion of an instructional unit and initiates the teaching process itself.

The second component of Glaser's model—*entering behavior*—is his most striking feature. Entering behavior is the assessment of student ability that must take place prior to instruction. In describing entering behavior, Glaser focuses on intellectual ability and motivation, but we might also include the assessment of academic attainment as well. (It should be pointed out here that the assessment of student entering behavior need not be a difficult and complex process for the teacher. Most teaching is sequential, with one concept or unit being built on another. Thus, after completing one unit and assessing its effectiveness, a teacher can readily ascertain the readiness of students to advance to another unit of learning.)

The third component of Glaser's model—*instructional procedures*—describes the actual teaching process. Effective instructional procedures result, of course, in student learning. In commenting on this third component of Glaser's model, DeCecco (1968) emphasizes that this component should not be thought of as teaching strategy. Rather, teachers must use different strategies for teaching skills, language, concepts,

FIGURE 2.1. Glaser's Instructional Sequence Model

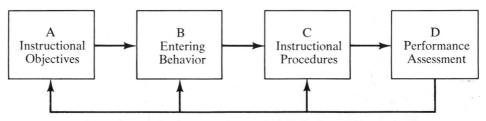

Adapted from Glaser, R. Psychology and instructional technology. In Glaser, R. (Ed.), *Training Research and Education*. New York: John Wiley & Sons, 1965, pp. 1–30.

principles, and problem solving. This is not unlike Gagné's instructional strategies, which will be referred to extensively throughout the remainder of this book.

The fourth component of Glaser's model is *performance assessment.* This phase of instruction is designed to test and observe how well the student has accomplished the initial educational objectives.

John Carroll (1963) has developed yet another instructional theory. Of the five major components of Carroll's model, three are comparable to Glaser's idea of entering behavior, since they are concerned with conditions within the learner prior to the actual teaching process. Carroll's first component is *aptitude,* which refers to the amount of learning time that the student requires to reach an instructional objective. The second component of *perseverance* represents the *willingness* of the student to spend the time necessary to attain an instructional objective. Carroll's third component is *comprehension*—the ability to understand instruction—which refers directly to the general intelligence of the learner.

The two remaining components of Carroll's teaching model refer to instructional procedures. One, stated as the *opportunity to learn,* refers to the time available for learning within the teaching situation. The other component, *quality of instruction,* is the way in which material is organized for learning to be acquired by the student. This latter component is, of course, highly dependent on the teacher's adaptation to the individual needs and differences of students.

A PROPOSED INSTRUCTIONAL MODEL

Several parts of the following proposed model of instruction do not differ significantly from other existing models. However, in using and elaborating elements from other models, this proposed theory of instruction offers, in the author's opinion, a more complete and pragmatic framework for effective teaching and learning. The model comprises four parts:

1. Identifying student needs.
2. Stating student behavioral objectives.
3. Developing a teaching strategy.
4. Assessing student behavioral change.

This model is most like Glaser's (1962), although there is one important difference. Although Glaser's *instructional objective phase* is comparable to the author's second component, *stating student behavioral objectives,* and although this phase of Glaser's model does not preclude an identification of student needs, the author feels that instructional or behavioral objectives should be written on the basis of *both* student needs and teacher-desired objectives. Thus, the author proposes a distinctive step, *identifying student needs,* as the initial phase of the teaching model.

The remaining two steps of the proposed teaching model follow Glaser's model. The third step, *development of a teaching strategy,* is similar to Glaser's *instructional procedures.* Because proper management of this component is the basis of learning, the teaching strategy or procedure must be constructed on a foundation of sound learning theory. The final step in the proposed model is, like Glaser's model, *assessment of student behavioral change* (Glaser's *performance assessment*). Through the use of teacher-made tests, standardized tests, and teacher observation, some measure of student learning must be made.

In the remaining pages of this chapter, we shall explore these four components of the proposed teaching model, briefly examining both the principles and the practical application of this instructional theory. Then, in Chapters 3 through 8, we shall seek a clearer understanding of each of the concepts introduced here. As we proceed through these chapters, the importance of proposing a theory of instruction and a theory of learning simultaneously will become increasingly clear. The integrative aspects of both of these theoretical considerations will give the teacher a more operational framework for his classroom.

Identifying student needs

The consideration of student needs is closely related to the teacher's determination of the behavioral objectives for the student, and, in fact, these two components of instruction are treated as the same procedure by some writers (Gagné, 1970c; Kibler et al., 1970; Lefrancois, 1972). However, there is an important distinction between the two procedures. The identification of student needs refers to the teacher's attempt to judge whether the student has the necessary learning prerequisites for the ensuing behavioral objectives—the intellectual skills or tasks—that will be expected of him. In other words, the student *needs* referred to here are *performance needs*—the deficiencies or sufficiencies of the accumulated knowledge and skills that the student brings to the classroom. The *primary* student need of basic ability is, of course, implicit in the performance needs; for regardless of the student's basic ability, the classroom teacher's task remains the same—to assess current student attainment and to determine the needs of that student if he is to meet the behavioral objectives of the classroom. The importance of identifying student needs *prior* to stating *final* behavioral objectives should be clear. The very nature of the objectives requires that they reflect the assessed student performance needs; for without this assessment, the objectives would be arbitrary and, probably, meaningless and ineffective as well. What emerges, then, from this first step of identifying performance needs is a decision about instructional procedures and objectives that is based on knowledge of both student needs and teacher goals, rather than simply on teacher goals.

One of the most important requirements of the identification of student performance needs is an *ongoing* evaluation by the teacher of the relevance and effectiveness of his objectives for the student. There are many teaching–learning conditions in which the student fails to perform at the designated expectancy level. If the student is not learning the material being taught, a need deficiency is probably at fault, and the behavioral objectives must be reevaluated in terms of the student deficiency rather than the original learning expectancies. Of course, this often means that a teacher must modify the stated objectives, since these objectives are no longer applicable to student performance within the immediate teaching–learning context. On the other hand, the reevaluation may reveal that the student's need deficiency can be easily remedied with supplemental instruction or a different instructional strategy, and the behavioral objectives can remain unchanged.

In summary, the purpose and the procedures of identifying student needs are the following:

1. The teacher appraises prerequisite student learning to determine if it meets the requirements for the performance needs necessary to the tentative behavioral objectives of the class.
2. After considering student performance needs and teacher goals, the teacher writes final student behavioral objectives that specify desired learning outcomes.
3. If need deficiencies exist, the teacher instructs the student in the supplemental skills necessary to meet the required prerequisite learning and the final behavioral objectives.
4. The teacher maintains ongoing assessment of performance needs. When it is apparent that student performance is below the stated objectives, reevaluation of the objectives in terms of student needs is necessary.
5. To align student needs and teacher goals, it may be necessary to restate objectives in more realistic behavioral terms designed to reduce need deficiency and allow the learner eventually to realize the original performance goal. Or, further supplemental instruction or a change of strategy may be sufficient to meet the original goal.

Assistance in writing objectives in both the affective and cognitive domain is given in the instrumentation charts in Appendix B on pages 357-362.

Stating student behavioral objectives

The use of behavioral objectives in the classroom is becoming more recognized. Many educators and psychologists advocate their use because the objectives help clarify the teacher's course of action in realizing student learning. Simply stated, a behavioral objective is a statement that describes what students will be able to do on completion of a teaching unit or particular instructional materials. More specifically, a *behavioral objective* may be defined as a statement that describes (1) the learning behavior that is expected of the student, (2) the expected proficiency level of each student in accomplishing the behavior, (3) the time needed by each student to achieve the behavior, and (4) the means by which the behavior is to be measured.

The various objectives will belong to one of three behavioral domains: *cognitive, affective,* or *psychomotor* learning behavior.

Cognitive.   Those objectives that emphasize remembering or reproducing something that has been learned and those that involve the solving of intellectual tasks in which the essential problem must be determined and then the given material must be reordered or combined with ideas, methods, or procedures previously learned. In short, cognitive objectives vary from simple recall of material to highly original and creative ways of combining and synthesizing new ideas and materials. Since the primary orientation in most classrooms is academic, the cognitive objectives tend to be used most frequently.

Affective.   Those objectives that emphasize an emotion, an appreciation of tone or quality, or a value judgment. Affective objectives range from simple attention to selected materials or phenomena to the attainment of complex and consistent qualities of character, conscience, or criticism. The affective objectives are used most commonly in the teaching of fine and performing arts and in observation of natural phenomena.

Psychomotor.   Those objectives that emphasize muscular or motor skills, manipulation of material and objects, and neuromuscular coordination. These objectives are most frequently related to handwriting, speech, physical education, and trade or technical courses.

The more detailed discussion that follows explicates specifically the different behavioral domains and the increasingly complex levels of objectives within each domain.

The cognitive domain.   Within an instructional model, it is useful to have an understanding of the various levels of cognitive objectives that might be required of a student. Bloom et al. (1956) list the cognitive behavioral objectives at six operational levels: (1) *knowledge,* (2) *comprehension,* (3) *application,* (4) *analysis,* (5) *synthesis,* and (6) *evaluation.*

> I. *Knowledge.*   Includes those behaviors and test situations which emphasize the remembering, either by recognition or recall, of ideas, material, or phenomena [p. 52].

One aspect of Bloom's *knowledge* is the recall of specific and isolable bits of information. Such knowledge operates at a very simple level. Most commonly, the objectives requiring this kind of knowledge are (1) *terminology* (familiarity with meanings of words) and (2) *specific facts* (dates, events, persons, places, and so on), particularly those pertaining to one's culture.

The other aspect of the knowledge level of Bloom's taxonomy is more complex. It deals with ways and means of using terminology and specific facts. The objectives requiring this kind of knowledge include (1) awareness of correct English form and usage; (2) understanding of the processes, directions, and generalizations that dominate any subject field; (3) awareness of the criteria by which facts, principles, opinions, and conduct are tested or judged; and (4) knowledge of the methods of inquiry and other techniques and procedures necessary to evaluate particular social problems and events.

> II. *Comprehension.*   Includes those objectives, behaviors, and responses which represent an understanding of the literal message contained in a communication. When students are confronted with a communication, they are expected to know what is being communicated and to be able to make some use of the material or ideas contained in it [p. 89].

Three basic functions occur within the objectives included in Bloom's comprehension level: *translation, interpretation,* and *extrapolation.* Translation refers to the ability to paraphrase material or to render it into a form of communication other than the original. Interpretation is the explanation or summarization of a communication; for example, the ability to analyze and explain data (Krathwohl et al., 1964). Extrapolation is the rational extension of evidence or ideas that are apparent in the communication but are not directly supported by the data.

III.   *Application.*   Includes those behaviors in which the student is applying the appropriate abstractions to a given situation without having to be prompted as to which abstraction is corrrect or without having to be shown how to use it in that situation. It is also the use of abstractions in particular and concrete situations [p. 120].

At the application level of Bloom's taxonomy, the objectives would be the use of abstractions as general ideas, rules, or methods that help the learner to understand or resolve a problem or situation. Bloom illustrates this process with the diagram in Figure 2.2. Elsewhere, Moore and Kennedy (1971) have shown the use of application in the area of language arts. First, they describe *functional application,* which refers to "the production of oral and written compositions which have as their primary purpose the dispensing of information" (p. 411). In addition, there is *expressive application.* This is the "production of creative or expressive oral and written compositions. This behavior is limited to oral and written expression which is intended solely for the purpose of expressing original and creative thought, taste, views, etc." (p. 413).

IV.   *Analysis.*   Emphasizes the breakdown of the material into its constituent parts and detection of the relationship of the parts and of the way they are organized [p. 144].

Bloom's three major subheadings at the analysis level are *elements, relationships,* and *organizational principles.* The primary objective in analysis of elements is the separation and identification of the various elements in a communication; for example, distinguishing facts from hypotheses or, in a story, theme from plot. The analysis of relationships is the detection of the connections and interactions between the elements of a communication. Bloom describes much of analysis of relationships as dealing with the consistency of elements. The analysis of organizational principles involves the understanding of the structure and the system that hold the communication together. Bloom illustrates this process as the ability to analyze, in a work of art, the relation of materials and means of production to the elements (color, line, and so on) and to the organization (composition). Another example: The ability to infer from an author's work his purpose, point of view, or characteristics of thought and feeling.

V.   *Synthesis.*   Includes those behaviors in which the student puts together elements and parts so as to form a whole. This is the process of working with elements, parts, etc., and combining them in such a way as to constitute a pattern or structure not clearly there before [p. 162].

FIGURE 2.2. The Application Level of Cognitive Behavioral Objectives

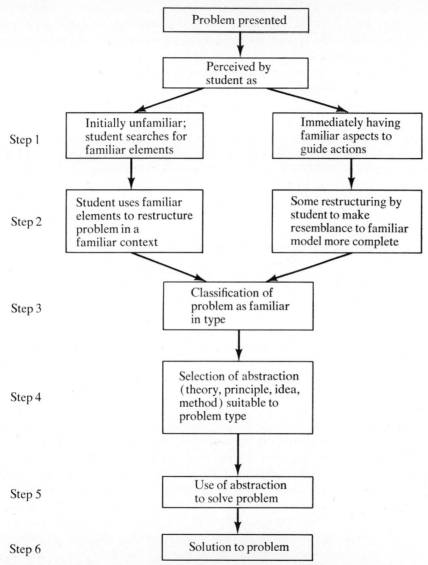

From Bloom, B. S., et al., *Taxonomy of educational objectives, Handbook I, Cognitive domain* (1956). Reprinted by permission of David McKay Company, Inc.

The synthesis level of cognitive objectives is considered by Bloom in three subheadings. First is the *production of a unique communication*—the development of a communication in which the writer or speaker attempts to convey his ideas, feelings, and/or experiences to others. This process may be stated as the behavioral objectives of (1) skill in organizing and writing, (2) ability to tell a personal experience effectively, or (3) ability to make effective extemporaneous speeches (Krathwohl et al., 1964).

The second element of synthesis is the *development or proposal of a plan of operations;* for example, the ability to propose ways of testing hypotheses, or the ability of a high school student to use several rules of good writing in the production of an essay. Bloom's third subheading for synthesis is the derivation of a set of abstract relations, such as the ability to make mathematical discoveries and generalizations or to formulate appropriate hypotheses based on analysis and then to modify such hypotheses in the light of new factors and considerations (Krathwohl et al., 1964).

> VI. *Evaluation.*   Defined as the making of judgments about the value, for some purpose, of ideas, works, solutions, methods, material, etc. It involves the use of criteria as well as standards for appraising the extent to which particulars are accurate, effective, economical, or satisfying. The judgments may be either quantitative or qualitative, and the criteria may be either those determined by the student or those which are given to him [p. 185].

Bloom's evaluation level may be thought of in two ways. The first involves *judgments in terms of internal evidence.* This process consists of an evaluation of the accuracy of a communication from such direct evidence as logical accuracy, consistency, and other internal criteria. Bloom suggests that the objectives for this type of evaluation might be the ability to apply given criteria to the judgment of a work or the ability to indicate fallacies in arguments.

The second type of evaluation involves *judgments in terms of external criteria,* which is the process of evaluating material with reference to selected or remembered criteria. A frequent use of this cognitive level is the comparison of major theories, generalizations, or facts about particular cultures. Bloom proposes other objectives for this type of evaluation, including the achievement of skills in recognizing and weighing the values involved in alternative courses of action or the ability to identify and appraise the judgments and values that were involved in a *choice* of a course of action.

It is generally recognized and not at all surprising that the cognitive domain is the most useful and frequently used in the teaching–learning process; for academic materials have the predominant and more formal place in existing school curricula. Equally significant is that most theories of learning are applied only to the cognitive domain. This emphasis will, of course, be reflected in this book, but the author would be remiss if the roles and significance of the affective and psychomotor domains were not discussed at least briefly.

The affective domain. The affective domain of behavioral objectives involves emotion, appreciation, or value judgment and applies to categories of learning encompassing sensitivities, interests, appreciations, attitudes, values, and beliefs (Loree, 1970). Bloom and Krathwohl, the same educators who prepared the cognitive domain structure in 1956, advanced an affective domain structure in 1964. The levels they propose for the affective domain are as follows:

I. *Receiving.* At this level, we are concerned that the learner be sensitized to the existence of certain phenomena or stimuli; that is, that he be *willing* to receive them. In receiving, the learner is aware of, or at least passively attending to (listening or seeing), the materials. For example, the student pays attention to what is being said about margins, indentations, and other information in language arts class.

II. *Responding.* This level is concerned with responses; it goes beyond simply perceiving the stimuli or phenomena. The learner is motivated and committed to actively attend or, perhaps, to prepare to do. It is still a low level of commitment, however, and one would not say that the learner is expressing or internalizing a value. Responding occurs once one begins acting toward some perceived stimulus in his environment. This may be as simple as getting up from an easy chair and taking a beer out of the refrigerator because an advertisement on television promoted the behavior, or it may be as complex as acting out the drama that one feels in a poem or play.

III. *Valuing.* At this level, the learner assigns worth to a stimulus or phenomenon, displaying responsive behavior in situations in which he is not forced to comply or obey. His concept of worth is in part a result of his own valuing or assessment, but it is much more a social product that the learner has gradually internalized, accepted, and used as his own criterion. For example, a teacher is looking for valuing responses when he asks students to express their attitudes about science and the pursuit of a scientific career. This might be in the form of an open-ended response device or an attitudinal questionnaire.

IV. *Organization.* As the learner successively internalizes and expresses values, he encounters situations for which more than one value is relevant. Thus the necessity arises for (1) the organization of his values into a system, (2) the determination of the interrelationships among them, and (3) the establishment of the dominant and pervasive values. This internally consistent system of values is built gradually and is subject to change as new values are incorporated. Listening to the opinions expressed by others about a topic on which one has information is an example of organizing affective behavior.

V. *Characterization by a value or value complex.* At this level of internalization and expression, the values have affected the behavior of the learner for a sufficient time that he routinely and consistently bases all his affective responses on them. In other words, characterization, in this context, describes an individual's philosophy of life, which always strongly affects his behaviors.

The psychomotor domain. There has been considerably less work and agreement about behavioral factors that constitute the psychomotor domain. Armstrong et al. (1970) have listed three psychomotor variables:

I. *Frequency.* The rate or number of times an individual performs a psychomotor skill.
II. *Energy.* The amount of strength or power an individual needs to perform a psychomotor skill.
III. *Duration.* The length of time an individual needs to perform a psychomotor skill.

While this is a plausible taxonomy of general behavioral objectives, it deals only with the learner's ability to perform the psychomotor skills; it does not define the actual skills involved.

Kibler et al. (1970) have also worked on the psychomotor domain and have classified behaviors at four levels: (1) *gross bodily movements,* (2) *finely coordinated bodily movements,* (3) *nonverbal communication behaviors,* and (4) *speech behaviors.* While this taxonomy lists the actual skills or movements involved in the psychomotor domain of behavioral objectives, it is not advanced here in lieu of a newly devised and more complete classification by Dave (1963):

I. *Imitation.* Imitation begins with an internal rehearsal of the muscular system in response to an inner urge to duplicate an observed action. This appears to be the starting point in the growth of a psychomotor skill. The overt performance of the action and the capacity to repeat that imitation then follow. However, the performance and its repetitions lack neuromuscular coordination or control and therefore are generally crude and imperfect.
II. *Manipulation.* At this stage, the learner is capable of performing an action according to instruction rather than on the basis of observation only, as in the case of imitation. The emphasis at this level is on the development of skills in following directions, in performing selected actions, and in fixing the performances through practice.
III. *Precision.* The proficiency of performance reaches a higher level of refinement at this level. Here the objectives of accuracy and proportion become significant.
IV. *Articulation.* This level emphasizes the coordination of a variety or a series of actions. Establishing an appropriate sequence and accomplishing harmony and consistency among different actions are the objectives.

V. *Naturalization.*   At this stage, the skill of performance attains its highest level of proficiency and the act is performed with the least expenditure of psychic energy. The objective here is to make the action so routine that it results in automatic and spontaneous response.

Applications of the behavioral domains.   To reiterate, the understanding and use of student behavioral objectives—what students will be able to do upon completion of a teaching unit—is the second phase of the proposed instructional model. These objectives can be categorized as either cognitive, affective, or psychomotor learning behavior, and each of these categories can, in turn, be subdivided into several levels of learning behavior, from the simplest to the most complex.

The primary behavioral domain used within the school is, of course, cognitive. Examples of practical applications of the cognitive objectives, using Bloom's et al. (1956) subdivisions, include the following:

Knowledge: The student will be able to match correctly the dates and places of historic battes of American wars.

The student will learn units of measurement in science content.

The student will learn factorial symbols in mathematics.

The student will recognize performance categories in the field of art.

The student will be able to recite stanzas from *Morte d'Arthur.*

Comprehension: The student will be able to transfer data from a line chart to a bar graph.

The student will be able to give more than one meaning for the word "perceive."

The student will learn to translate visual symbols of works of art into verbal terms.

The student will gain the ability to read and interpret a problem in math class.

The student will be able to translate fables learned in school to real-life situations.

Application: The student will be able to use simple, compound, and complex sentences in writing an essay.

The student will be able to apply mathematical rules to classroom math problems.

The student will be able to apply cultural information to the themes and plot of a work of literature.

The student will be capable of making proper entries into an accounting ledger.

The student will apply the kinetic theory of gases in postulating that gases are composed of particles.

Analysis:

The student will be able to identify simple, compound, and complex sentences in a written passage.

The student will be able to compare the consistency and inconsistency in a series of logical statements.

The student will be able to see the relationships among elements in a sentence by looking at a diagram of the sentence.

The student will be able to analyze the puns in a work of literature to explain their meaning and purpose.

The student will be able to analyze a rule to find its constituent concepts.

Synthesis:

The student will be able to develop a theory about student activism in the 1960s.

The student will be able to write a term paper with bibliographic references.

The student will develop skill in writing, using proper organization of ideas and statements.

The student will be able to make scientific discoveries and generalizations.

The student will be able to propose a research design for testing hypotheses.

Evaluation:

The student will be able to identify the major characteristics of democracy according to the criteria presented in class.

The student will be able to support the Freudian psychoanalytic view as a means of explaining human development.

The student will develop the ability to formulate judgments about political figures.

The student will gain the ability to recognize artistic quality in contemporary works of art.

The student will be able to determine if the data support the conclusions in a research study.

There are some occasions in which the teacher will want to elicit affective learning. Examples of practical applications of the affective objectives, using Krathwohl's (1964) subdivisions, include the following:

Receiving: The student will learn to attend to teacher directions.

The student displays an interest in joining a club at school.

The student enrolled in music appreciation will, through classroom presentations of musical works, become aware of different styles of music.

Responding: The student will voluntarily seek to be helpful to other members of an organization to which he belongs.

The student learns to enjoy writing through the experience of reading and writing.

The student voluntarily reads magazines that are of interest to him.

The student likes to engage in conversation about music.

Valuing: The student will learn to recognize the value in freedom of expression.

The student will learn to value the proper care of books.

The student will learn that his school experiences are a basic part of his social maturation.

Organization: The student will develop techniques for channeling aggression into socially acceptable patterns.

The student sees that reading books about social problems helps him determine his attitudes toward the problems.

The student will judge the quality of his musical performance ability.

The student will learn to appreciate skills in others which he himself may not possess.

Characterization: The student will arrive at some consistency between his values and his behaviors.

The student will develop an ethical sense based on democratic ideals.

The student will see that his philosophy of life provides him with a sense of direction.

The psychomotor domain is used in a learner's earliest experiences and throughout his education. Using Dave's (1963) categories, examples of practical applications of the psychomotor domain include the following:

Imitation: The student will be able to copy letters of the alphabet as the teacher illustrates them on the board.

Manipulation: The student will write the alphabet in response to teacher dictation.

Precision: The student will be able to demonstrate good tumbling form.

Articulation: The student will be able to demonstrate a variety of gymnastic exercises.

Naturalization: The student will learn to routinely use a T-square in mechanical drawing class.

Developing a teaching strategy

The third phase of the proposed instructional model is the actual teaching process itself—the development of a teaching strategy. The identification of student needs (phase one) and the stating of behavioral objectives (phase two) are also strategies of a kind and are essential forerunners to instruction, but it is the actual instructional process that finally determines the extent of student learning. Several theorists have attempted to apply their theories of instruction to specific instructional strategies, and two of these men—B. F. Skinner and Robert Gagné—present especially thorough and useful models, some phases of which are presented in the following sections.

Skinner's teaching machine.   Some educators argue that Skinner's theory of instruction is in reality a theory of learning. Regardless of the merits of that argument, Skinner uses his basic laws of learning to program his teaching machine, which is unquestionably a way of instruction.

Skinner distinguishes six major components of his theory which could be built into a teaching machine and ensure learning:

1. *Operant conditioning.*   Skinner (1953) suggests that responses followed by some kind of immediate reinforcement are most likely to be learned. Thus, as applied to

The music teacher feels that her students do not appreciate classical music, but she is uncertain as to the reasons and therefore stymied by the problem. *Could the goals of this teacher be better defined, and are the classroom instructional procedures applicable here?*

If the primary goal of the teaching situation is for the student to learn an appreciation for classical music, the teacher, through the use of Krathwohl's taxonomy of affective behavioral objectives, can identify the appropriate level of affective learning behavior for her goal and then specifically state the desired student objectives in terms of the behavior that can be expected at that age level. In this example, the desired student behavioral objective seems to be at the *valuing* level of the taxonomy. The teacher might state the objective, then, as follows:

> The student will attend to the presentation of classical music,
> forming some response as to his like or dislike of it.

There are actually three levels of affective functioning within this stated objective. First, the student must attend, or *receive*. Second, the student must react, or *respond*. Finally, the student must sort out his responses on a like/dislike continuum *(valuing)*. Thus, although this final behavior determines the level of student response desired by the teacher, the other two, less complex affective levels should be realized first. Moreover, although many teachers will stress affective learning in music, most music has cognitive components as well. And if the teacher can successfully relate *knowledge* about music to the expected affective responses, he will have established a stronger basis for the student to learn value in music.

Consider the following cognitive objective that can be related to affective goals:

> The student will learn the source of origin for classical music
> and its role in contemporary American music.

Making the student aware of classical music information allows an affective response to be made not simply at an attitudinal level but at an intellectual level as well, and this combination makes a student's valuing response more meaningful and therefore more likely.

teaching, operant conditioning is the arrangement of contingencies of reinforcement which facilitate learning (1968). In other words, by arranging proven means of reinforcement, which will be discussed below and later in this book, the teacher can control the teaching–learning situation.

2. *Reinforcement.*   When a student emits a response to material (a stimulus), the teacher can introduce a new stimulus that will serve as reinforcement so that learning occurs. Particularly with students, Skinner (1953) strongly feels that simple knowledge of correct results is an adequate reinforcer, although he also recognizes other reinforcing techniques, such as money, food, grades, and honors (1968). Presumably, Skinner sees such reinforcement as providing the learner with the satisfaction that he has made the appropriate response and has learned the material at hand. In addition, while many students may initially begin learning something through teacher-provided reinforcement and motivation, the students may eventually internalize reinforcement (knowledge of results) and, thus, be self-motivated to pursue learning further.

3. *Immediate reinforcement.*   A reinforcing stimulus must be given shortly after a response is emitted if learning is to occur. Experimentally, this reinforcement is thought to be necessary within five to 30 seconds after the response is emitted. There is evidence, however, that school reinforcement occurring within 24 hours, or at a subsequent class session, can be considered as immediate reinforcement (Markle, 1961).

4. *Discriminated stimulus.*   Generally, the teacher wants students to make and learn certain specific responses under specific conditions (that is, specific stimuli). Thus, when a specific stimulus (2 + 2 =) is the condition on which a specific response (= 4) is followed by reinforcement, we may say that *discriminated learning* has taken place. Therefore, in presenting stimuli to students, the teacher must make each stimulus so specific that only one response is correct. In addition, reinforcement must always be contingent on the student's emitting that correct response.

5. *Extinction.*   When reinforcement does not occur, a response becomes less and less frequent until it is no longer meaningful or learned. Skinner calls this process *operant extinction* (1953). Thus, the teacher's role is to withhold reinforcement when the student emits an incorrect response. This may force the student into another response; and if that response is correct, then reinforcement should follow. The effect is that a nonreinforced response becomes extinct (lack of reinforcement) and a reinforced response becomes established, or learned.

6. *Shaping.*   Much school learning consists of chains or series of S–R bonds which, taken together, equal a whole concept or solution or structure that could not be learned as a single operation. Indeed, the learning of each of the single components of a series significantly increases the learner's grasp of each of these components as well as the concept or structure that is the sum of the series. *Shaping* is Skinner's term for the process whereby the teacher directs student learning toward the final response in a series, individually reinforcing each step in sequence from first to last. This process of shaping gives significance to a series of sequentially emitted S–R bonds and ensures that the bonds and their sum are learned.

As we noted, Skinner used these six components in developing his teaching machine—which is to say that he was successful in incorporating his learning principles into the teaching process. Thus, in Skinner's teaching machine, the learner is required to compose an answer *(operant conditioning)* and the substance of that answer (the response) is controlled by the question *(discriminated stimulus)*. If the learner's response is correct, he is *reinforced immediately*. If the answer is incorrect, there is no reinforcement, so *extinction* occurs. After a series of such processes, the learner attains the learning end *(shaping)*.

There is no component within Skinner's teaching machine that cannot also be carried out by the classroom teacher. Let us take a classroom example:

> After a lecture on a mathematical concept, the students are asked to work through a series of math problems so that they may learn the concept before the next lecture period, when a related concept will be introduced. As the students compose their answers, they are learning *(operant conditioning)*. Because of the specificity of the problems, the student responses are limited *(stimulus discrimination)*. The teacher has made available on her desk the answers to each problem so that the students may check their answers as they go (*reinforcement* and *immediacy* if desired). When a student makes a mistake, there is no corresponding answer *(extinction);* thus, the student must recompose his answer or discuss the problem with the teacher (again, *reinforcement*). As the students work through all the problems, they are not only learning but preparing for the next lecture session *(shaping)*.

Gagné's events of instruction. In his most recent book, *The Conditions of Learning* (1970a), Gagné set forth nine specific functions, which he describes as the *events of instruction.* These events of instruction are highly consistent with his learning-hierarchy model and describe the desirable components of an instructional strategy.

1. *Gaining and controlling attention.* An environmental stimulus arouses appropriate attention.
2. *Informing the learner of expected outcomes.* Communication, usually verbal, tells the learner what he will be able to do after he has learned.
3. *Stimulating recall of relevant prerequisite capabilities.* The learner is reminded of the *relevant* skills and knowledge he has previously acquired.
4. *Presenting the stimuli inherent in the learning task.* The particular stimuli to which the newly learned performance will be directed are displayed.
5. *Offering guidance for learning.* The learner's thinking is directed by prompts or hints, usually verbal, until the desired performance is achieved.
6. *Providing feedback.* The learner is informed of the correctness of his newly attained performance.

7. *Appraising performance.*   Opportunity is provided for the learner to verify his achievement in one or more new situations.
8. *Making provisions for transferability.*   Additional examples are used to establish a broader applicability for the newly acquired performance.
9. *Ensuring retention.*   Provisions are made for further practice and use of the new capability so that it will be remembered.

A proposed teaching strategy.   In advancing an instructional model, the author acknowledges that much of his thinking has been influenced by the work of Gagné and Skinner. The proposed teaching strategy has six components:

    I. Student preparation
   II. Stimulus presentation
  III. Student response
  IV. Reinforcement
   V. Evaluation
 VI. Spaced review

I. Student preparation.   The first step is simply to begin preparing the student's mind for the learning situation to be presented. In most cases, this means gaining student attention in some way. Gaining attention may require no more than the teacher's description of the tasks to be learned, or the teacher may wish to make comments that trigger interest and motivation within the students. Whatever the procedure, the essential task for the teacher is to elicit interest in the immediate teaching–learning situation.

Not all teachers find it easy to gain such attention and interest from students. The following suggestions may assist them in this initial phase of the teaching strategy:

1. *Restatement of behavioral objectives.*   On some occasions, it is beneficial to bring students back to the general learning objectives at hand. A restatement of teacher–student goals often engages the student's interest and helps him in his line of pursuit as well.
2. *Warm-up.*   Students learn the task at hand more readily if the preceding assignments are highly similar in form or content; for the student transfers learning from one task to the next. Thus, a good way to use the warm-up effect is to draw the student's attention to the previously learned intellectual skills that will facilitate the acquisition of the skill at hand. This procedure directs the student's thought, familiarizes him with the content, and gives him a working basis for positive transfer to the ensuing learning situation. Several research studies (Hamilton, 1950; Irion, 1949) have shown warm-up to be effective on both learning and retention.
3. *Readiness for learning.*   By *readiness* is meant the degree to which the students have the prerequisite knowledge for new learning. Craig (1966) suggests that teachers ask

two questions: (1) "What must a student need to know or be able to do before he can learn this new thing in the way I plan to teach it? (2) To what extent do my students possess the prerequisite knowledge and abilities?" (p. 5). The author would ask a third question, "Does my proposed plan of instruction fall within the range of my student's ability as indicated by his prerequisite knowledge?" Gagné (1970c) also believes that diagnostic testing of the student is necessary before the teacher can know what course of instruction to take.

II. Stimulus presentation.   Classroom learning is based primarily on the successful presentation of stimuli (teaching) which elicit the desired responses from students (learning). Thus, one cannot stress enough the importance of the teaching function of preparing and presenting stimuli in a way that will maximize appropriate student response. The manner of stimulus presentation is partly determined by the behavioral objectives set up for the learning situation and by the prerequisite student knowledge. However, the most important factor in stimulus presentation is the *level of response* required of the student, which is discussed in step III of this instructional strategy. As required responses become increasingly complex, the manner of presenting stimuli must also change appropriately. For example, if you want the students' response to be a simple fact, then your stimulus statement may be something like, "How far is it from Chicago to St. Louis?" On the other hand, if you want a rule response, the stimulus must be capable of evoking it, such as, "State the formula for finding a square root."

Regardless of the level of instruction, the following three techniques of stimulus presentation will help direct the learner to the desired objective:

1. *Sequential stimuli.*   The greater the similarity from stimulus to stimulus, the more likely students will learn the materials presented.
2. *Discriminated stimuli.*   Specific, selected stimuli for specific responses will significantly reduce the likelihood that the student will learn inappropriate responses.
3. *Teaching devices.*   Teaching machines and programmed textbooks are designed to take a learner through a specific learning sequence, using sequential and discriminated stimuli. In devising the teaching machine, Skinner (1958) was especially concerned about (1) eliminating distracting stimuli and (2) removing negative reinforcement from the classroom. In using such devices, the teacher should make them an integrated part of his planning and teaching strategy.

III. Student response.   The teacher must always give students the opportunity to respond. Unless he has some deliberate plan of providing feedback to their responses, the teacher can never know if the students are *learning* and, in the case of discriminated stimuli, if they are learning the appropriate responses. The response system is inherently tied to the stimulus system in that as the teacher presents different stimuli, he will expect different responses that are comparable to the stimuli. This equivalence of the stimulus–response systems can best be illustrated by reviewing the different stimulus-presentation levels within Gagné's hierarchy (p. 16) and then noting the expected response at each level.

1. Stimulus presentation at the *stimulus–response, motor,* and *verbal association* levels (levels 2–4) are the same; the teacher presents a specific stimulus which evokes a response from the student. At level 2, it may be a simple multiplication correlate, while at level 4, it may be reeling off the multiplication tables. In either case, the responses are controlled by the stimuli and are mechanistic in nature.

2. Stimulus presentation for *multiple discrimination* (level 5) is more complex. Here the teacher must present the student with several similar stimuli which must be differentiated by the student in his responses. The learner must be given the opportunity to verbalize the differences he sees.

3. In *concept learning* (level 6), the stimulus presentation is not tied to discriminatory differences but to conceptual categories or classes. The teacher presents the concept of a category—for example, the class "balls"—and then the objects (stimuli) that represent that class. The student response should be at a conceptual level; that is, he can observe several different appearing objects, called "balls," and recognize that they are all representative of the concept category "balls." The student will then be able to generalize his understanding of this concept to any new ball that may be introduced to him. The teacher's role is to provide a wide range of stimuli within the class of stimuli being studied so that the student has many opportunities to respond conceptually to that class.

4. The stimuli that are presented for rule learning (levels 7 and 8) are, typically, verbal. The student is presented with a statement "$A = l \times w,$" for example, which is not only a verbal representation of several related concepts but also infers that if the student uses the stated formula to solve a problem, his response will be appropriate and successful. Thus, the verbal formula represents a rule, which, by its nature, operationally produces appropriate student responses. Gagné (1970a) contends that the major part of academic content is represented via verbal communication.

IV. Reinforcement.   Reinforcement is usually described in the terms of "positive" and "negative." By *positive reinforcement* we usually mean adding praise, knowledge of results, recognition, reward, and so on to the learner's response, thus increasing the probability of the response recurring upon subsequent elicitation. *Negative reinforcement,* often referred to as *aversive control,* may similarly *strengthen* a response, although the probability is less. Negative reinforcement should not be confused with punishment. Contrary to commonly held opinion, negative reinforcement has never been successfully used to extinguish or eliminate a response. Therefore, a classroom teacher should not believe that negative reinforcement of undesired student responses will eliminate such subsequent behavior.

What is important for the teacher to remember is that reinforcement strengthens S–R bonds and that positive reinforcement is more likely to strengthen than negative reinforcement (see Table 2.1). Therefore, it is important in a teaching strategy for the teacher to plan the use of positive reinforcement in the classroom to increase student learning. The following comments should prove useful:

1. *Continuous reinforcement.* This concept involves providing feedback to the learner at the time a response is made. In individualized instruction, this can be done rather easily; and in group instruction, it can be done if all students are learning the same material. Continuous reinforcement is important when students are learning material for the first time.

2. *Intermittent reinforcement.* In intermittent reinforcement, the learner is rewarded only part of the time for his responses. Because of a crowded curriculum and limited time in the classroom, this type of reinforcement is often most advantageous to the teacher. While research indicates that initial learning is somewhat poorer with partial reinforcement than with continuous reinforcement, studies also show that responses learned under partial reinforcement are less likely to become extinct than those learned under continuous reinforcement (Kimble, 1961). Much of school learning is shaped by partial reinforcement.

3. *Knowledge of results.* This concept, originally advanced by Skinner (1953, 1968), may be used in two ways: (a) It may be similar to continuous reinforcement in that the teacher provides fairly immediate feedback to the student as to the *correctness* or *incorrectness* of his response. (b) It may be a system of self-reinforcement, in which the teacher makes the correct responses available to the student so that he can internalize the reinforcement and therefore be self-motivated to continue to pursue the learning tasks at hand. Gagné (1970a) also points out that in complex learning, such as concepts and rules, feedback need not always come externally but may arise from the learner's satisfaction at knowing other related concepts or rules that aid him in solving the problem or explaining the situation. While the teacher does not control this type of reinforcement, it may well be the best form of feedback for more complex learning.

4. *Negative reinforcement.* Negative reinforcement *increases* the probability of a response because the undesirable behavior (the response) is followed by the removal, termination, or avoidance of the particular stimulus that the learner is unable or unwilling to deal with. Examples of positive reinforcement in the classroom are giving a child a pat on the head when he is courteous, acknowledging a student's correct answer in front of his classmates, or complimenting a student for doing extra-credit work. Examples of negative reinforcement are discontinuing close supervision of a reading group once they begin reading, writing negative remarks on homework, or removing annoying students from the classroom. The removal or

TABLE 2.1. Effects of Reinforcement

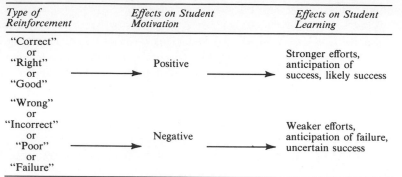

Type of Reinforcement	Effects on Student Motivation	Effects on Student Learning
"Correct" or "Right" or "Good"	Positive	Stronger efforts, anticipation of success, likely success
"Wrong" or "Incorrect" or "Poor" or "Failure"	Negative	Weaker efforts, anticipation of failure, uncertain success

avoidance of an unpleasant state of affairs increases the likelihood of an undesirable response occurring again in a similar situation. Thus, reinforcement may increase the likelihood of a response recurring by the addition of a pleasant event (positive) or the removal of an unpleasant event (negative).

5. *Nonreinforcement.*   If the teacher does not include reinforcement in his teaching strategy, two consequences may occur: (a) Without any reinforcement, the student cannot be certain of the accurateness of his responses. While he may suspect that he is responding correctly, he may, in fact, be attending to incorrect responses. Technically, a failure to reinforce means no learning takes place (extinction). (b) If a teacher has been giving continuous reinforcement and then begins withholding it, student performance may be drastically reduced. This is especially true when original learning is going on, rather than repetitive or more complex learning. Once a student has mastered certain skills through reinforcement, the teacher ought not to withhold reinforcement. On the other hand, it may be advantageous to shift from continuous to intermittent reinforcement as the teaching proceeds to more complex skills.

Stimulus presentation, student response, and reinforcement—steps II, III, and IV of this proposed teaching strategy—most often occur as simultaneous functions in a teaching–learning situation. In fact, the teaching strategy is usually best facilitated by presenting materials in such a way that the student response is recognized and some method of reinforcement is given. The following example illustrates how all three processes can occur within the same context:

The teacher presents a student with several small colored cards. The colors represented are blue, red, green, orange, and brown. The student is asked to select among the cards those which are colored blue. (It is clear that the expected level of response is appropriate to the nature of the stimulus.) If the student correctly selects the blue cards, the teacher acknowledges the correctness of the response so that the student is reinforced and the response is learned.

Now, let us assume that the teacher is interested in a more advanced response from the student, in which case the student must be presented with a more advanced stimulus. Therefore, the teacher presents several cards that are different shades of blue, and the student is asked to identify each card according to a known category of the color blue. (Again the expected response is comparable in difficulty to the stimulus presentation.) The student responds with royal blue, sky blue, navy blue, cobalt, turquoise. The student recognized the discriminated properties of the cards by making five different responses. Recognition of the student's correct responses serves to reinforce his learning.

It is possible, of course, for a still more complex level of stimulus presentation. The teacher verbally presents the category "blue." The introduction of blue as a category makes the expected student response a conceptual one. Therefore, to respond adequately, the student must know certain identifiable characteristics of the color blue that he can apply to any color stimulus within the range of the category "blue." In other words, he must go beyond the recognition of blue and learn what blue is all about. Knowledge of solid color, hue, tint, brilliance, and saturation are some of the responses that will help demonstrate an understanding of blue. The crucial factor for the teacher while teaching any concept is to provide the learner with a variety of objects that represent the concept presented.

If the teacher wanted the student to pursue his understanding of blue even further, he could present the student with rules governing the color blue. These rules would, of course, be based on previously acquired concepts regarding color and, specifically, the color blue. Once the rules are learned, the student can apply them to any relevant learning problems he encounters. Although intermittent reinforcement is always beneficial in helping to maintain student learning, the demands for reinforcement here are not as great as in the earlier stages of the example. Most reinforcement at the rule level comes from the student's use of already known concepts; that is, he is exercising a self-reinforcing system.

V. Evaluation. One of the most important aspects of the teaching strategy is the evaluation of student progress. This step commonly occurs after the teacher has presented a series of problems or a unit. Evaluation serves two essential functions:

1. *Student appraisal.* Perhaps the most crucial function of evaluation is providing the learner with feedback as to his general progress. If the learner has some idea of the

performance expected of him (behavioral objectives), he can evaluate his own response level to a certain extent. However, periodic teacher-provided evaluations are essential for guiding the learner and for motivating him toward additional learning. Evaluation does not mean the student must receive a letter grade; tests or exams serve this purpose. Evaluation is used here in the sense of simply providing frequent assessments and guidance to the learner.

2. *Teacher analysis.* The teacher needs spaced evaluations of student progress in order to change his teaching strategy according to the needs of the students. If a teacher withholds evaluation until the end of a unit of work, it may then become apparent that if a different teaching strategy had been used, the results of the teaching–learning process might have been more productive. Making frequent evaluations allows greater teacher flexibility throughout the teaching unit and facilitates teacher–learner goals.

VI. Spaced review. * This final phase of the teaching strategy—the review of learned materials—is important to ensuring retention of learning. Students become better in performing some skills with increased practice *(review)*. However, it has been demonstrated that continuous practice will lead to fatigue and loss of efficiency. Thus, by *spacing* the times in which the student is presented with additional review materials, the teacher may avoid this negative effect. Spaced review also allows the teacher to recall previous student learning, and such *recall–reinforcement* may serve to strengthen that learning and its retention. As the student moves from simple to complex learning, the practice effect seems to become less valuable. As Gagné has pointed out, "if a concept or rule has been completely learned, it is entirely possible that conditioned practice may have no appreciable effect on its retention" (1970a, p. 319).

If the teacher plans his evaluations of student progress in conjunction with the reviews of learned materials, it is possible for him to implement both steps of the teaching strategy simultaneously. The classroom teacher might also consider the following suggestions in providing the learner with spaced reviews:

1. The nature of the learning task should determine the extent of practice. If the student has learned *new* material, several spaced reviews might be helpful in ensuring retention. In the case of already well-established materials, less frequent review will be necessary for the learner.
2. In a review, the relating of learning to life situations adds meaning to the task. If the teacher can provide fresh and practical situations for applying the material under review, it is more likely that the practice will have positive effects.

* After Gagné, Some new views of learning and instruction. *Phi Delta Kappan,* 1970, **51,** 468–472.

TABLE 2.2. *The Proposed Teaching Strategy Model*

Step I: *Student preparation*

The teacher directs the students' minds toward the learning tasks at hand.

Step II: *Stimulus presentation*

The deliberate presentation of specific, identifiable stimuli will ensure more discriminated responses by the students.

Step III: *Student response*

Two crucial factors in teaching are giving the students time to compose a response to a stimulus and giving them feedback (reinforcement) as to the acceptability of the response.

Step IV: *Reinforcement*

Planning for reinforcement, preferably positive, will strengthen the tendency for students to learn a response and to maintain that response when it is subsequently elicited.

Step V: *Evaluation*

Some assessment of the quality and rate of learning should be undertaken by the teacher. This provides both the student and teacher with awareness as to the effectiveness of the teaching–learning environment.

Step VI: *Spaced review*

A crucial step in the teaching process is the periodic presentation of stimuli that will trigger previously learned responses. Such review ensures retention.

3. Occasionally, homework (essentially review on student time) is beneficial to the learner. If homework assignment is to be used for a review, the teacher must provide feedback—that is, check the papers in class—during the following class session.

Table 2.2 summarizes the six steps of the proposed teaching strategy model.

Assessing student behavioral change. When students complete a teaching unit, their work should be formally assessed by observation and examination to determine whether the behavioral objectives of the unit were met. Such assessment, of course, provides the teacher with data from which to grade, but assessment is also important within a theory of instruction for other reasons.

First, an evaluation based on the explicit behavioral objectives for a unit provides the teacher with specific criteria by which to determine student learning. If the ultimate performance level of the student is in line with these criteria, or stated objectives, then the student has *learned,* and the teacher does not need to measure that student's performance against the performance of the other members of the class *(norm-referenced measurement)* in order to determine individual learning and the success of the unit.

Second, assessment based on criteria and objectives provides the teacher with data on the effectiveness of his teaching theory and strategy in meeting the teacher–student goals. Such feedback will help the teacher in future planning as well as in assessing the effectiveness of the completed unit.

Three activities, then, are necessary in assessing student learning:

1. *Observing behavioral change.* Through evaluation with exams and/or observation, the teacher can detect whether the student is progressing toward the goals specified within the instructional objectives. If the student is progressing, then the teacher can conclude that the behavioral objectives were realistic and that the teaching strategy based on these objectives was effective. If the teacher finds that student progress is inadequate, then the teaching strategy (or the objectives) must be analyzed for its deficiencies. The ways in which causes of failure can be discovered are discussed in point 2.
2. *Analyzing learning deficiencies.*
   a. *Prerequisite-learning deficiencies.* It could be that students did not have the prerequisite skills necessary to learn the material. In such cases, the teacher may have written inappropriate behavioral objectives or failed to do adequate diagnostic testing in order to determine readiness.
   b. *Instructional deficiencies.* It could be that the teaching strategy was not designed well enough for the students to learn the specified materials. By diagnosing teacher behavior, the effectiveness of each phase of the strategy can be assessed in terms of student learning.
3. *Analyzing instructional theory.* As we have noted, the teacher's analysis of prerequisite learning deficiencies and of deficiencies in his teaching strategy can have an important bearing on the immediate teaching–learning situation. A third form of assessment—an analysis of teaching theory in regard to student learning—will be most important in future teaching–learning situations. Thus, the teacher may find through self-analysis that he can modify and improve his instructional procedures and thereby increase the success of student learning. Modifying instructional theory may involve no more than recognizing that reinforcement was not properly given through a particular teaching unit. The teacher would rethink the role of reinforcement in his teaching—how he failed to use it effectively in the completed unit, and how he might use it more advantageously in subsequent teaching–learning situations. Such an ongoing analysis of one's teaching behavior increases the potential for greater teaching effectiveness and better student learning.

THE PROPOSED INSTRUCTIONAL MODEL— A SUMMARY ILLUSTRATION

The instructional model proposed in this chapter includes the following points:

1. Identifying student needs
2. Stating student behavioral objectives
3. Developing a teaching strategy
   a. Student preparation
   b. Stimulus presentation
   c. Student responses
   d. Reinforcement
   e. Evaluation
   f. Spaced review
4. Assessing student behavioral change

To see the interrelationships of these points within a classroom situation, the following illustration is presented:

General subject:	Verb tenses.
Specific task:	Learning the perfect tenses of verbs.
Prerequisite skills:	Knowing the present, past, and future tenses of verbs.

1. Identifying student needs

To determine if the students are ready to learn perfect-tense verbs, the teacher must find out if the necessary prerequisite skills have been learned. If there has been a time lapse between the learning of the necessary prerequisites and the immediate learning task, then a diagnostic test would be helpful. Some of the items that could be part of such a test are as follows:

DRAW TWO LINES UNDER THE VERB IN EACH OF THE FOLLOWING SENTENCES. IN THE BLANK IDENTIFY ITS TENSE.

_____ The smallest of the three boys swam farthest.

_____ He had written his congressman.

_____ Willy is the best player on the softball team.

_____ The show will conclude today.

_____ Every person in the room questioned the waiter.

_____ Has he played that song before?

_____ Both runners were safe on an error by the catcher.

_____ Are the Munson twins your nephews?

_____ My mother will have purchased the album before we arrive.

_____ The museum will be closed Memorial Day.

_____ Where was the key to the house?

2. Stating student behavioral objectives

(1) The students will learn the meaning of the present perfect tense.

(2) The students will learn the meaning of the past perfect tense.

(3) The students will learn the meaning of the future perfect tense.

(4) The students will learn to conjugate verbs according to the perfect tenses.

(5) The students will be able to recognize perfect-tense verbs in sentences.

(6) The students will be able to demonstrate correct usage of the perfect tense.

3. Developing a teaching strategy

a. Student preparation.   The teacher can point out that some verbs are used to represent action that occurs at an indefinite time before the present (present perfect), or that occurred at a fixed point in time in the past (past perfect), or that will occur before a fixed point in time in the future (future perfect). When verbs express one of these times, they are called perfect-tense verbs, in contrast to the already learned verb forms of simple present, past, and future. Once the teacher has given some rationale for the continued study of verb tenses, he may begin presenting stimuli. The stimuli must be carefully related to the specified behavioral objectives for the student.

b. Stimulus presentation.

(1) The teacher introduces the concept "present-perfect tense." He gives a definition for it and illustrates it by providing the student with contrasting examples of the present-perfect and the past tense.

Definition: Use the present-perfect tense to show that something which began in the past is still going on at an indefinite time before the present.

Illustration:

Past Tense:	Marcelo *held* the No. 2 position among tennis players in Bolivia for two seasons. (He is no longer the No. 2 player.)
Present Perfect Tense:	Marcelo *has held* the No. 2 position among tennis players in Bolivia for two seasons. (He is the No. 2 player now.)
Past Tense:	Patty *called* Mr. Marshall about a summer job. (Something she did.)
Present Perfect Tense:	Patty *has called* Mr. Marshall about a summer job. (It is uncertain as to when in the past Patty actually called.)

(2) The teacher introduces the concept "past-perfect tense," following the same general procedure used in point (1).

(3) The teacher introduces the concept "future-perfect tense." (By the time this material is illustrated, the teacher will see that the first three behavioral objectives have been met.)

(4) The teacher is now ready to teach the students to conjugate verbs in the perfect tenses. To be able do this, they must have already learned the auxiliary verbs that specify the time of the perfect tenses. Therefore, the teacher presents the following information:

Present-perfect tense:	has or have + the past participle of verb.
Past-perfect tense:	had + the past participle.
Future-perfect tense:	shall have or will have + the past participle.

Four of the verb tenses have helping (auxiliary) verbs. Knowing these signs will help you recognize the tense in which the verb is being used. They are shown in the following conjugation of the six tenses:

Present tense	I choose	I go	I write
Past tense	I chose	I went	I wrote
Future tense	I shall choose	I shall go	I shall write
Present perfect	I have chosen	I have gone	I have written
Past perfect	I had chosen	I had gone	I had written
Future perfect	I shall have chosen	I shall have gone	I shall have written

c. Student response.   The stimuli presented here constitute all the necessary new information that the student needs in order to learn the concepts of present-perfect tense (objective 1), past-perfect tense (objective 2), future-perfect tense (objective 3), and how to conjugate each of these three verb tenses (objective 4). It is now necessary for the teacher to plan for providing opportunities for student response.

Generally, it is best to plan for student responses with each stimulus presentation. Therefore, after presenting the necessary information to learn objective 1, the teacher should not assume that his teaching has brought about learning but should give the student a chance to respond, to confirm his understanding of what is being taught. When originally presenting the material on the present-perfect tense, the teacher gave comparative examples of the past and the present-perfect tenses. Now, he might allow the students to supply these examples. The continued presentation of similar stimuli to which the students have the opportunity to respond tells the teacher if the concept has been learned.

It would be equally necessary to provide the students with an opportunity to conjugate verbs. This can be done once the student has learned the auxiliary verbs and has seen such verbs used operationally. Therefore, the teacher's task of providing for student responses is simply to supply new verbs which the students can conjugate.

Behavioral objectives 5 and 6—the ability to recognize perfect-tense verbs in sentences and to demonstrate their correct use—can be realized within this response component of the teaching strategy. These objectives are best accomplished by giving the students problems, work sheets, exercises, and so on, which provide them ample opportunity to apply the materials they have learned. An example of such an exercise is the following:

DRAW TWO LINES UNDER THE VERBS IN EACH OF THE FOLLOWING SENTENCES. IN THE BLANK IDENTIFY ITS TENSE.

_____ This morning Kris told me that she and her mother had decided to see Hamlet.

_____ Since Diane had looked at television all morning, she went for a bicycle ride after lunch.

_____ Stanley hasn't taken out the trash yet.

_____ Ever since Marchel went to the rodeo, she has talked about becoming a cowgirl.

_____ Steve will have played several games of basketball before next weekend.

_____ Susan has already sent one dollar for the special cosmetic kit.

_____ That's the third time in a row that Konried has beaten you at checkers.

_____ Since Marcia was six years old, she has wanted to be a ballerina.

Behavioral objective 6 can be realized by providing the students with a series of perfect-tense verbs and requiring them to compose sentences in which they use the verbs correctly.

d. Reinforcement.　Once the student has responded, the basis for reinforcement exists. It is likely that simply providing the students with knowledge of results as to the accuracy of their responses will be sufficient reinforcement. Since the teacher will probably move from one student to another for responses, it is a good idea for him to reinforce each student's response. Once the teacher sees that all of the students have learned one of the concepts, it may then be advantageous to move from continuous-reinforcement procedures to intermittent ones. This is easily accomplished by allowing the students to work independently on the materials.

e. Evaluation.　This phase of the teaching strategy is an ongoing process. Once the teacher has presented the designated stimulus material (such as information on the present-perfect tense) and has allowed the students to confirm their learning through responses, the teacher may want to evaluate the quality of learning that has occurred before he moves to new materials. If on the basis of the evaluation the teacher has reason to believe that a student or students have not learned the material adequately, additional teaching should go on at this point before moving to the new materials. The teacher must also find out where inadequate teaching or learning is occurring and correct the problem before presenting additional stimuli which might be highly dependent on previous learning.

For illustration purposes, let us assume that the students learned the present-perfect tense and past-perfect tense adequately but were unable to consistently respond to verbs of the future-perfect tense. The teacher must then (a) analyze the difficulty that the students are having, (b) attempt to extinguish any inappropriate learning which may have occurred, (c) restructure the lesson and reteach the concept of future-perfect verbs, (d) allow for student responses once again, and (e) reinforce the student responses more carefully. At the point in the reteaching phase that the teacher is sure that learning has been accomplished, it is beneficial to confirm such learning by providing additional classroom problems to which the student must respond.

f. Spaced review.　To ensure retention, the the teacher would plan, on subsequent teaching situations, to give the students the opportunity to review and use the learning that has taken place. This review could occur one day later, one week later, or even several months later. Perhaps at the end of all the work on verb tenses, the teacher would assign a general exercise or test in which the student would have to know all six verb tenses.

4. Assessing student behavioral change

The teacher may use this phase of the instructional theory to accomplish three things. First, a general examination may be given to determine how well the students have learned as well as to provide the teacher with some objective grading information. Second, the teacher could analyze those parts of the examination that were consistently difficult for the students in order to determine what learning deficiencies existed. Third, the assessment of learning deficiencies should tell the teacher whether he has been effective in his instruction and whether the behavioral objectives were realistic. On the basis of this assessment, the teacher might modify his strategy and/or objectives for subsequent classes.

SUGGESTED READINGS

Cleaver, T. J.   Inquiry objectives in curriculum development. *The American Biology Teacher,* 1970, **32,** 476–479.

Cook, H., Hill, C., & Wittrock, M.   Two instructional sets in children's learning. *Journal of Educational Research,* 1969, **63,** 78–80.

Cornell, T. D.   *A systematic approach to needs assessment.* Tucson, Ariz.: EPIC Evaluation Center, 1970.

Ebel, R. L.   Command of knowledge should be the primary objective of education. *Today's Education,* 1971, **60,** 36–39. Reprinted in H. D. Thornburg (Ed.), *School learning and instruction: Readings.* Monterey, Calif.: Brooks/Cole, 1973, chap. 2.

Gage, N. L., & Unruh, W. R.   Theoretical formulations for research on teaching. *Review of Educational Research,* 1967, **37,** 358–370. Reprinted in H. D. Thornburg (Ed.), *School learning and instruction: Readings.* Monterey, Calif.: Brooks/Cole, 1973, chap. 2.

Gagné, R. M.   Some new views on learning and instruction. *Phi Delta Kappan,* 1970, **51,** 468–472. Reprinted in H. D. Thornburg (Ed.), *School learning and instruction: Readings.* Monterey, Calif.: Brooks/Cole, 1973, chap. 2.

Gall, M. D.   The use of questions in teaching. *Review of Educational Research,* 1970, **40,** 707–721.

Knief, L. M.   Aspects of learning: Toward a theory of instruction. *Educational Horizons,* 1970, **48,** 117–123.

Macdonald, J. B., & Wolfson, B. J.   A case against behavioral objectives. *Elementary School Journal,* 1970, **71,** 119–128.

Miles, D. T., & Robinson, R. E.   Behavioral objectives: An even closer look. *Educational Technology,* 1971, **11** (6), 39–44. Reprinted in H. D. Thornburg (Ed.), *School learning and instruction: Readings.* Monterey, Calif.: Brooks/Cole, 1973, chap. 2.

Rosenshine, B.   Evaluation of classroom instruction. *Review of Educational Research,* 1970, **40,** 279–300.

3

Transfer and Retention

Two considerations basic to learning theory are the concepts of *transfer* and *retention*. Simply stated, transfer is the effect of previous learning on present learning, and retention is the strength and longevity of learning. Both concepts are experimentally proven phenomena of learning. There has been little doubt in most researchers' minds that learning in one situation will transfer to subsequent situations and that retention of conditioned response patterns is dependent on several variables in the learning process, including scheduling of reinforcement and meaningfulness of the learning behavior to previous learning and to the present teaching–learning situation.

But what about classroom practices? What is the functional role of transfer and retention within the classroom? The ensuing pages focus on three considerations: (1) the theoretical bases for transfer and retention; (2) the relationship of transfer and retention to the learning hierarchy; and (3) the practical applications of the concepts of transfer and retention within the classroom.

TRANSFER

Whether learning is motor or verbal, previous acquisition tends to influence subsequent acquisition. In most cases, previous learning facilitates additional learning; in some cases, however, it hinders it. The classroom teacher can determine a teaching strategy which utilizes transfer to its fullest extent to facilitate new learning. It is important, then, that the teacher know the various theories of transfer, so that he can incorporate the ideas into his instructional theory and strategy.

56

Transfer theory

Out of the traditional, Aristotelian-based views on learning evolved the nineteenth century concept that the mind was like a muscle, and with continuous and vigorous exercise, it could be strengthened. The *mental-discipline* theory emphasized the teaching of subjects, such as mathematics, Latin, and Greek, not so much because each would be functionally used in life or in other learning situations but because they were rigorous disciplines which strengthened the mind. It was not until the research of Thorndike and Woodworth in 1901 that serious doubts about mental-discipline theory arose. The research of these men conclusively demonstrated that it was not the rigorousness or lack of it that made learning transferable but, rather, the common or *identical elements* between two learning situations. This is not to say that the study of mathematics was irrelevant to the individual, but such study could not be assumed to necessarily increase an individual's general cognitive ability.

Theory of identical elements. As proposed by Thorndike, the theory of identical elements posited that "training in one kind of activity would transfer to another as long as certain features, such as aims, methods, and approaches, were identified in [the] two tasks" (Ellis, 1965, p. 63). Thorndike emphasized the stimulus in a learning situation as the important condition of identifiability and transfer. He suggested that there must be some kind of similarity of properties between stimulus 1 and stimulus 2 if transfer is to take place. The following examples focus on this point:

Learning $2 + 2 = 4$ will facilitate $II + II = IV$.

Learning $2 + 2 = 4$ will facilitate $2 + 4 = 6$.

Learning $4 + 4 = 8$ will facilitate $8 - 4 = 4$.

The major concern with Thorndike's theory was its specificity. How could a teacher ensure such a high degree of stimulus similarity in actual classroom practice? Are the Thorndikean demands for transfer so specific that the theory is nonfunctional? Those who tried to answer this question concluded that the theory was not generally applicable and was an insufficient explanation of the phenomenon of transfer. Therefore, a search for a less stringent, more practical theory was made.

Theory of generalization. The first researcher to question identical elements was Charles Judd (1908), who contended that transfer was based on an understanding of *general principles* rather than upon a recognition of identical elements. Judd proposed that the learner acquires a general principle and, upon subsequent stimulus presentations, then responds to the principle involved and not to the specific stimulus. This theory of generalization may be illustrated as:

Learning $\ 3 \times 3 = 9$ facilitates $\ 7 \times 8 = 56$.

Learning $15 \div 3 = 5$ facilitates $96 \div 16 = 6$.

Learning $4\frac{7}{8} - 3\frac{1}{2} = 1\frac{3}{8}$ facilitates $37\frac{3}{10} - 19\frac{1}{3} = 17\frac{29}{30}$.

In the mutiplication problem, the general principle "multiply" transfers to the new stimulus. Similarly, the principle "divide" the learning of the new division problem. And these two principles facilitate transfer in the third problem, which involves the multiplication and division of mixed numbers to find the remainder.

Judd's experiment involved two groups of boys who were to throw darts at a target placed under water. The experimental group was taught the principle of refraction prior to their behavior, while the control group was not. In the initial trial, both groups performed comparably, with knowledge of the principle of refraction being of no apparent value to the experimental group. However, when Judd increased the depth level of the target in a second trial, the experimental group performed more efficiently. Judd concluded that it was knowledge of the general principle which transferred successfully in the experimental group's second trial, whereas the identical elements of the two trials had no bearing on the performance of the control group's second trial.

It is important to remember that the source of departure for generalization theory was the theory of identical elements. Judd's research was essentially an attempt to develop a more general and functional theory of transfer, but he did not completely break from the notion of identical elements. His theory merely stresses that transfer may occur as well under less optimal and stringent conditions than those set forth in Thorndike's theory. However, some 30 years after Judd's experiment, two psychologists replicated the original study (Hendrickson & Schroeder, 1941) and concluded that an understanding of a principle transferred to new learning situations and that the more complete the theoretical principle, the more effectively it transferred. The findings supported Judd's original theory of the effectiveness of principle learning in transfer, and no other theory of transfer has since been theorized that is any more operational in the classroom.

Transposition theory. Transposition theory originated with Gestalt psychologists in the 1930s and emphasized that transfer was the *perception* by the learner of *relationships* between general principles and specific situations (Ausubel, 1968). In other words, if a learning situation can be seen and understood by the learner in its appropriate means–end relationship, the learning is transferable; and the better this relationship is understood, the greater the transfer. This theory is a refinement of Judd's principle, in that if an individual is to hit the deeply underwater target with a dart, he must perceive the situation in terms of the relationships among the previously acquired principles of refraction, water depth, and darts and targets.

This theory, in combination with the others, fits readily into Gagné's view of the hierarchical nature of learning and the importance of prerequisite conditions to each level of learning; for a learning hierarchy has transfer implicitly built into it. Since each level of hierarchy requires prerequisite knowledge, transfer is logically and readily used in the acquisition of new responses.

Hierarchical transfer. Two terms, *lateral transfer* and *vertical transfer,* are mentioned in the work of Gagné (1965). Lateral transfer may be described as a "kind of generalizing [of knowledge] that spreads over a broad set of situations at roughly the *same level of complexity*" (p. 231). This type of transfer is general and does not apply to hierarchical arrangements of learning so much as it does to capability in the broader life experiences. In other words, when new stimulus situations arise in the general environment, the individual can generalize his comparable previous learning to these situations and respond to them. Thus, lateral transfer is a general ability the individual acquires and internalizes through the expression of knowledge in a variety of situations. Teachers can attempt to broaden the learner's capability for lateral transfer through the presentation of a wide variety of different learning situations in which the student must use his previous knowledge and experience in more generalized ways.

Vertical transfer is the most significant underlying concept in the idea of a learning hierarchy. It may be defined as the acquisition of new responses contingent on the learning of prerequisite subordinate capabilities. The learner operates from two reference points when learning in a hierarchical manner. First, for any transfer to take place, original learning must be established; it is not possible to learn at a particular level on the hierarchy unless the prerequisite skills have been learned. These skills serve as an internal reference point (knowledge and vertical transfer) for the learner. A second, external reference point is provided through the instructional strategies of the

FIGURE 3.1.   Vertical Transfer: The Hierarchy of Prerequisite Conditions Essential for Each Level of Learning

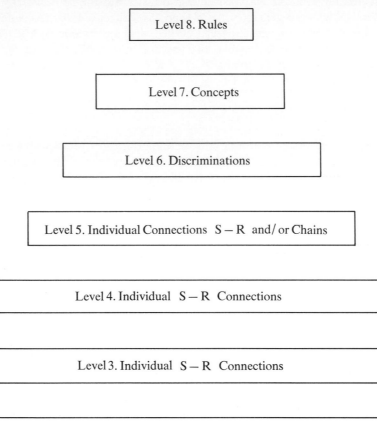

teacher as he guides the learner into more advanced learning stages. Thus, a verbal chain (level 4) in Gagné's hierarchy) may be learned because the stimulus–response bonds (level 2) necessary to the chain have previously been established. Figure 3.1 presents the prerequisite conditions essential to the subsequent learning of responses at different levels in Gagné's hierarchy.

Vertical transfer may be examined by working through an example of a student learning German verbs:

Learning Level	*Prerequisite Capability (Verbal Transfer)*
Level 2: Stimulus–response learning. The student learns to sight German verbs and to recognize and pronounce German sounds.	Apprehension of stimuli (level 1) and S–R connections (level 2) for English verbs and sounds.
Level 4: Verbal chains (associative learning). The student learns German and English verb equivalents.	S–R connections (level 2) for German verbs and sounds.
Level 5: Multiple discrimination. The student learns to discriminate among similar German verbs and among the conjugated forms of the verbs.	S–R connections (level 2) for German verbs and chaining (associative learning, level 4) of German–English verb equivalents.
Level 6: Concept learning. The student learns the functions of conjugated German verbs based on an understanding of English verb usage.	S–R connections (level 2) for English verb usage and multiple discrimination (level 5) of German forms.
Level 7: Rule learning. The student develops rules for conjugating German verbs according to their use.	Concept learning (level 6) of German verb conjugation and usage.
Level 8: Problem solving. The student translates a paragraph from English to German using appropriate verb forms.	Rule learning (level 7) of German verb conjugation according to use.

Thus, vertical transfer, as used by Gagné (1965, 1970a), facilitates the transfer of relevant skills up the learning hierarchy. If all classroom stimuli are presented in a logical, sequential, and meaningful manner, then prerequisite knowledge will inevitably become relevant (vertically transferable) to the learning task at hand. It should also be noted that lateral transfer may function in a classroom learning situation. For example, it is quite possible that a learned intellectual skill is (1) generally applicable to a variety of classroom contexts at a particular learning level (lateral transfer) as well as (2) serving as prerequisite knowledge for a more advanced skill. Figure 3.2 illustrates this point.

Lateral transfer occurs whenever something learned, regardless of the level of learning, is transferable to a variety of comparable classroom situations. Vertical transfer occurs whenever learning at one level in the hierarchy facilitates learning at a higher level.

FIGURE 3.2.   *Vertical and Lateral Transfer in Classroom Learning*

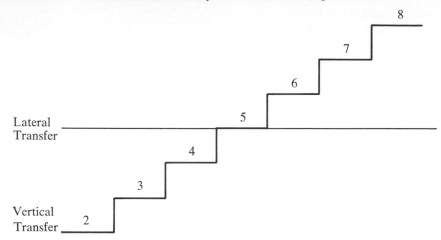

Transfer in the classroom

In its application to classroom situations, transfer is generally categorized as *positive, negative,* or *neutral* (zero), as well as *specific* and *nonspecific.*

1. *Positive transfer.*   If task 2 is facilitated by the learning of task 1, positive transfer is occurring. Thus, when the learning of two concepts (level 6) facilitates the learning of a rule (level 7), positive transfer occurs.
2. *Negative transfer.*   If task 1 inhibits the learning of task 2, negative transfer occurs. This phenomenon is also referred to as *proactive inhibition* or *interference.* In other words, the learning of a new task becomes difficult because of prior learning. Thus, when the learning of a concept inhibits its combination with another learned concept for the emergence of a rule, negative transfer exists.
3. *Neutral (zero) transfer.*   Zero transfer exists when the learning of task 1 neither facilitates nor inhibits the learning of task 2. This happens most often when students move from one type of material to new material that is totally unrelated. Although the situation of encountering new experiences that are completely novel or free from past association is relatively uncommon, it is still possible that diverse stimulus situations will generate little, if any, transfer.
4. *Specific transfer.*   When task 1 and task 2 are linked by similarities in specific components or properties and these similarities are invoked by the teacher in the teaching of task 2, specific transfer is occurring. Early experiments tended to equate

this phenomena with positive transfer (Bruce, 1933; Hamilton, 1943; Wylie, 1919), but more recent research indicates that similarity from one task to another may bring either positive or negative transfer, depending on the meaningfulness of the material to the learner (Jung, 1963).

5. *Nonspecific transfer.*   When the learning of task 1 affects the learning of task 2, but the transfer between the tasks does not involve any specific stimulus situation in these tasks, the transfer is effected by general principles which are broadly applicable to the nature of the task. Learning mathematical sets is an example of nonspecific transfer (Harlow, 1949; Duncan, 1960, 1964), in that general mathematical principles not specifically tied to the sets nevertheless facilitate understanding and learning.

Now, consider the following motor-learning situation, in which the various types of transfer are illustrated:

A high school senior decides to try out for the golf team at his school. His primary reasons are (1) an interest in the sport from watching it on television, (2) a belief that he can play the game well, and (3) a growing disinterest in baseball, which he has played well in his previous three years of high school. In the process of learning the techniques of golf, the student has no trouble understanding and learning the basic strokes, ball placement, body and foot position, and so on. However, in actual practice, the student develops trouble in consistently driving the ball well. He has (acquires) the tendency to hook the ball when driving.

On close analysis, the coach observes that the player has good foot position, tees the ball correctly, selects the right clubs for distance, and keeps his eye on the ball when driving. In these instances, positive transfer is occurring; that is, he successfully applies the techniques he has learned to actual practice. Yet, his problem with hooking the ball persists. Eventually, the coach detects that the new player turns his shoulder away from the ball when swinging, an action that is similar to his batting stance as a baseball player. This is an indication of negative transfer; the technique of swinging that he had learned for baseball inhibits his learning of the proper swinging technique for golf. The difficulty of overcoming this problem depends on (1) how strong the baseball habit is, and (2) how good the corrective instruction is.

Examples of nonspecific transfer in this situation are the general traits of the player's physical prowess and athletic skill and his interest and desire to do well, which are transferable from the skill already learned (baseball) to the task he now faces (golf), although they are not specifically tied to either learning situation. No specific transfer is found in the movement from baseball to golf.

Our prospective golfer may spend much time on the driving range working on *not* hooking the ball before he begins playing competitive golf on the course. In this commonsense action, he will be invoking an important and highly functional concept involved in the application of transfer in the classroom. This concept, which has become known as the *warm-up* or *practice effect,* is simply the idea that transfer of skills or knowledge may be enhanced through preliminary practice of the skills. The baseball pitcher warms up his arm before the game starts, and the pianist plays scales before performing a concert. In the same manner, the teacher will give exercises that require recall of learned material before introducing new information. The advantage of warm-up is to call upon existing information as a preparatory activity for subsequent learning.

RETENTION

Retention is the maintenance of a learned response over an extended period of time. It stands in direct contrast to forgetting, which is, of course, the tendency of a learned response to fail and disappear over an extended period of time. Retention has been equated by Gagné (1970a) to a *storage phase* within an individual in which learned material is retained until subsequently emitted. Recall or recognition of the previously learned responses represents the *retrieval phase.* Figure 3.3 illustrates this

FIGURE 3.3.   *Sequence of Events in Learning—Storage and Retrieval*

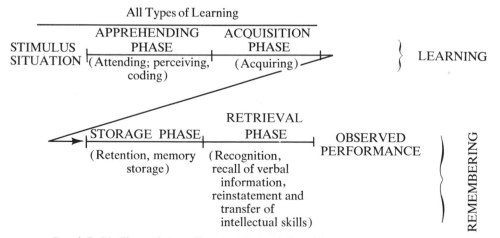

Gagné, R. M. *The conditions of learning.* (2nd ed.) Copyright © 1965, 1970 by Holt, Rinehart and Winston, Inc. Reprinted by permission of Holt, Rinehart and Winston, Inc.

sequence of events in learning and remembering. Note that in the figure Gagné gives equal stress to retention and acquisition in illustrating the events of learning. This suggests two points basic to the discussion here. First, this emphasis on retention should not lead one to lose sight of the importance of the original learning, because the most crucial variable in retention is the quality of original learning. Second, the obvious importance of retention in learning affirms the need for classroom teachers to know and use instructional techniques designed to ensure retention.

Research on retention

The first study on retention was conducted by Ebbinghaus in 1885. After mastering a set of nonsense syllables, he plotted the percentage of the syllables that were retained over a period of a month (see Figure 3.4). Upon measuring retention after only 19 minutes, Ebbinghaus found that only 58 percent of the learned responses could be recalled. There was a gradual decline in retention after the drastic drop during the first 24 hours, and at the end of 31 days 21 percent of the original learned list was

FIGURE 3.4.   Ebbinghaus Curve of Retention with Nonsense Syllables

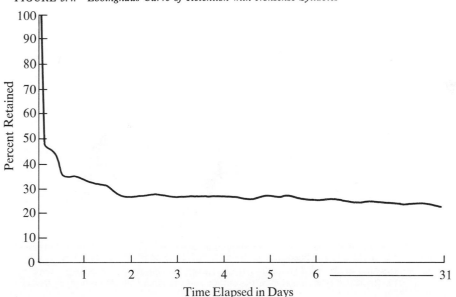

retained. The retention rate then seemed to plateau at 21 percent. Similar studies focusing on nonsense material were conducted throughout the early part of this century, and in most cases, the retention curves were basically the same.

Figure 3.5 is one example of this later research, which further confirmed the immediate loss of learning with nonsense syllables while demonstrating the higher retention rate of more *meaningful* material. By *meaningfulness,* we mean familiar material or material that can be put into relational or conceptual frameworks for which

FIGURE 3.5.   *Typical Retention Rates for Different Kinds of Material*

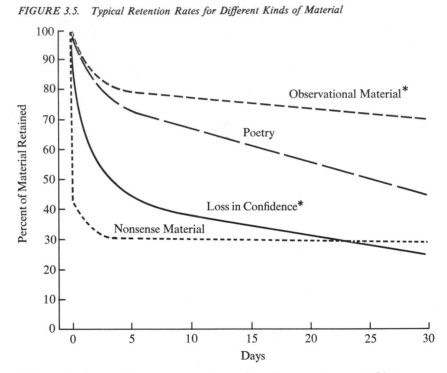

* *Observational material* was based on a picture of an office scene. *Loss in confidence* was based on the subject's certainty as to the correctness of his responses.

Gilliland, A. R. The rate of forgetting. *Journal of Educational Psychology,* 1948, **39,** 23. Reprinted by permission of the author and the American Psychological Association.

the learner sees some purpose. Hardly anyone will disagree with this, but it still remains to be investigated what learning variables facilitate retention and what do not. One would question that if learned material is sufficiently meaningful that no forgetting may occur as has been suggested elsewhere (Stephens, 1956). Rather, it is likely that some meaningful material will be forgotten, although material presented by the classroom teacher is usually better retained. That is, upon the single presentation of classroom materials more meaningful material is better learned than less meaningful material, and the retention rate is higher.

McGeoch and Whitely (1926) tested recall of observed material, which was a sheet of cardboard displaying two photos, a penny, a white button, a one-cent postage stamp, and a red and white label. Immediate recall was almost 100 percent, and the researchers found that even after 15 days, there was 95 percent recall. The retention of the observed material seemed to level off at about 65 percent after a period of 100 or more days. Gilliland (1948) investigated the same phenomenon and found that his subjects still retained 80 percent of the observed material after 25 days.

Retention curves for poetry also indicate a much higher rate than for nonsense syllables but a lower rate than for the simpler learning of observed material. Whitely and McGeoch (1928) investigated recall of learned stanzas of poetry. Within the first 30 days after learning, retention dropped sharply, with just over 40 percent recall, although it leveled off at that point. Gilliland's similar study (1948) showed a 50 percent retention rate in poetry after 30 days.

Dietze and Janes (1931) tested recall of factual material which had been read only once. Each subject was presented with a short article and was subsequently asked to recall through a series of multiple-choice questions (a procedure not unlike existing classroom practice). The immediate loss of learning was 30 percent (a 70 percent retention rate), with a gradual decline of retention throughout the first 30 days. Beyond that time, the subjects tended to maintain the learning at a 55 percent retention rate.

Bower and Clark (1969) investigated recall of 12 lists of nouns, which were presented to a group of college students with the instructions to learn each list and then to make up a story using the nouns in the list. Another group of students were given the same lists to learn but were not required to compose a story using the nouns. The effects of *immediate* recall of each list appeared to be the same for both groups; they retained 99 percent of the nouns after each list was learned. However, the cumulative effects of recall were markedly different for the two groups. When asked to recall all 12 lists, the group that had used the nouns in stories retained 93 percent of the nouns in the lists. In contrast, only 13 percent of the nouns in the 12 lists were retained by the other group of students. Presumably, the practical use of the nouns in stories increased their meaningfulness for the first group. This research is especially significant in that it closely approximates the type of learning behavior characteristic of the classroom.

In an unpublished study conducted by the author (Thornburg, 1967), the retention rate of emotionally loaded words* was measured for 84 students enrolled in undergraduate education courses. The students were given the following list of 15 words and asked to write a definition for them: attempt, bureau, just, kill, divide, industry, moment, notice, prepare, peace, trust, static, should, order, union. In five testing periods at varying intervals of 7, 9, 12, 14, and 21 days, or a total time lapse of 63 days, the retention of the students was measured. Table 3.1 indicates the retention rate:

TABLE 3.1.   *Retention Rate for 15 Emotionally Loaded Words Defined by the Subjects*

Testing intervals	7 days	9 days	12 days	14 days	21 days
Number of words recalled	6.03	7.04	6.96	6.90	6.14

Note that the retention rate after 7 days (about 40 percent) is virtually the same as the rate 63 days later. The slight rise in words recalled from 7 days to 9 days is probably attributable to the reinforcement effect of the first recall test. The fact that mastery of the list was not required most decidedly had an effect on retention (compare the higher rates for the comparable material in the Bower and Clark research). On the other hand, the practical use of the words in constructing definitions gave the students a meaningful context which undoubtedly facilitated recall.

In summarizing this and other research on retention, the following conclusions can be drawn:

1. Meaningful materials can be retained better than nonsense materials.
2. Highly meaningful material is better retained than less meaningful material. For example, the retention rate for poetry, which is usually learned by the association of words rather than by the *meaning* of the words, is lower than the rate for materials learned on the basis of their contextual meaning.
3. Contextual materials or lists of words with associative strength seem to be retained better than materials or words with little internal similarity or meaning.

* The words were selected from Thorndike, E. L., & Lorge, I., *The teacher's word book of 30,000 words.* New York: Columbia University, Bureau of Publications, Teachers College, 1944.

4. Practical uses of learned material result in better retention than with materials that are merely memorized.

Types of retention

Nonconceptual and conceptual retention.   Chapters 4 through 8 suggest that learning is hierarchical in nature; that is, prerequisite learning becomes a necessary condition as one begins to acquire more complex and involved tasks. Within the hierarchy proposed by Gagné (1965, 1970a), two types of learning, *nonconceptual* and *conceptual,* occur, and the recall or retention of that learning can be similarly categorized.

As we have seen, the works of Gagné suggest that stimulus–response learning (level 2), or single S–R connections, builds the base for subsequent learning at the higher levels. As several S–R bonds are learned, they may be organized into logical, associative sequences, or chains. If these associative series of learned responses are physical, they become motor chains (level 3); if they are verbal, they become verbal chains (level 4). Eventually, the learner must learn to distinguish among similar S–R connections on the basis of their discriminatory properties (multiple discrimination learning—level 5). For the learner to proceed from level 2 to level 5 learning, two conditions are necessary. First, as we have noted, each successive learning level must have the prerequisite learning at lower levels for its base. Second, each level of learning, from level 2 to level 5, is tied to the learner's ability to make specific responses to specific single stimuli. Thus, while learning becomes increasingly complex, it is characterized by the control or limitation of a single stimulus and is, in that sense, somewhat mechanistic. In other words, such learning (levels 2 to 5) must be characterized as *nonconceptual;* it is limited to the recall of specific stimulus situations previously learned and re-presented to the learner. This does not mean that what is being learned is not meaningful. In fact, the meaningfulness of the material facilitates the retention of responses *(nonconceptual retention)* and allows them to transfer from one level to the next on the hierarchy.

Conceptual retention is the recall of material learned at the concept learning (level 6), rule learning (level 7), and problem solving (level 8) levels of the hierarchy—the learning levels in which some abstract understanding (conceptualization) occurs. At these levels, a learner responds, not to the presentation of a specific stimulus, but, rather, to a *general* learning-problem situation to which he can apply relevant abstract concepts and principles based on his conceptualization of numerous specific S–R connections. Conceptual retention, then, focuses on the learner's understanding of the material he has learned and his ability to use such understanding in many new and different learning contexts. Because this form of learning has high-level meaningfulness, it also has, at least theoretically, the highest retention rate.

Short-term retention.   Our discussion of retention thus far has been concerned with *long-term memory* or *retention*—the ability to recall learned responses over an extended period of time. Yet, there are many learning situations in which we are required to retain responses for only a brief period of time. Looking up a phone number and remembering it long enough to dial the phone; remembering outstanding plays in a football game; recalling the names of streets just passed in an unfamiliar town; a waiter's ability to take orders for a large party and subsequently serve each person what he ordered; a card player's recall of all the cards that have been played from hand to hand in a game; remembering someone's name throughout the evening at a party —all are examples of *short-term retention.* This type of learning and retention functions well for its purpose, but it is quite obvious that this is not the type of retention that is typical of learning in the classroom. These latter forms of retention are long-term and their implications for learning are more diverse than those for short-term retention.

Little is known about the acquisition, retention, and transfer of short-term learning or about the distinctions between short-term and long-term retention. The theory of *trace decay* was advanced by Brown (1958) as an explanation of short-term memory. Essentially, he holds that after a short-term learning stimulus, such as a phone number, is received by the individual, it forms a cerebral memory trace, which has the characteristic of decaying rapidly. If the individual does not use that number again quite soon, the trace will disappear. If, however, the phone number is frequently used, the trace will be maintained throughout the period of use and, often, for a relatively brief time after its use ceases.

In trying to equate the phenomena of short-term and long-term retention, some researchers have attempted to explain short-term learning as subject to the same processes of forgetting and extinction as long-term learning. For example, one investigator concluded that a type of interference termed *retroactive inhibition* operated in both long-term and short-term memory (Murdock, 1961). That is, the amount of new learning intervening between the original use (learning) of material and its subsequent recall is a variable that affects forgetting. Thus, after one phone number is learned, the learning of several new phone numbers and the infrequent use of all of them will undoubtedly interfere with the retention of the original number. Other researchers, specifically Underwood (1964a), have indicated that short-term memory is not even a function of retention but is, rather, a simple type of original learning that is neither internally encoded (storage) nor strengthened by use. Instead, this learning simply carries over from use to use and must be relearned if use becomes infrequent.

Retention in classroom learning

The interference theory of forgetting.   As we have seen, *interference* is said to occur when one learned response inhibits the learning of another. Rather than attributing forgetting primarily to weakly formed original responses or to an inevitable function of time, most theorists believe that certain conditions of new learning affect a learner's previous or subsequent rates of response. Two terms are used to describe this phenomenon of interference: *retroactive inhibition* and *proactive inhibition*.

1. When the learning of task 2 interferes with the retention of task 1, retroactive inhibition occurs.
2. When the learning of task 1 interferes with the retention of task 2, proactive inhibition occurs.

The theory of retroactive inhibition was first advanced by John McGeoch in the 1930s. Later studies caused McGeoch (1942) to propose that forgetting does not occur unless something interferes with the original learning. Thus, if a person learns a list of words, he should be able to recall that list indefinitely, unless *similar* new learning takes place between the time of the original learning and its recall and thereby *interferes* with the recall.

Assume that a teacher has taught one class the intellectual skills necessary for acquiring the concept "proper fractions." He subsequently teaches them the skills necessary for acquiring the concept "improper fractions." After having learned both concepts, the students are given a test on proper fractions. Experimentally, the learning task would look like this:

Learns task 1	*Learns task 2*	*Retention test (recall)*
Proper fractions	Improper fractions	Task 1, proper fractions

Much to the teacher's surprise, the students do not do well on the test, and, in some cases, their answers are improper fractions instead of proper fractions. The phenomenon operating here is that the learning of task 2, improper fractions, is interfering with the retroactive recall of task 1, proper fractions.

Now assume that the teacher instructs another class in the same material but gives the students the retention test on proper fractions prior to their learning the concept "improper fractions." Experimentally, we have

Learns task 1	*Retention test (recall)*	*Learns task 2*
Proper fractions	Task 1, proper fractions	Improper fractions

The teacher finds that students in the second class do much better on the test. The lack of retroactive inhibition from the introduction of similar additional learning results in significantly better student recall.

Research studies conclusively show that the more similar task 2 is to task 1, the greater the interference level (Jensen & Anderson, 1970). Thus, a similar teaching situation,

Learns task 1	*Learns task 2*	*Retention test (recall)*
Proper fractions	Mixed numbers	Task 1, proper fractions

would not be likely to show such a high degree of interference. For in learning the concept "mixed numbers," the students would be dealing with the combination of a *whole number* and a *proper fraction,* the former entirely different from the original learning and the latter identical to it. Task 2 would therefore provide little interference in the recall of task 1. Table 3.2 illustrates these various teaching conditions and their potential for retroactive inhibition.

Proactive inhibition exists when an initially learned task interferes with the recall of a similar subsequently learned task. This phenomenon, which was first emphasized by Underwood (1949), signifies the type of forgetting that is characteristic of everyday life; for we typically acquire new responses that are highly similar to previously acquired responses, and upon recall of the new responses, components of the first learning situation are often recalled along with or instead of components in the second learning situation. To illustrate, if a class first learns the concept "proper fractions" without an opportunity for recall and then learns the concept "improper fractions,"

TABLE 3.2. *Retroactive Inhibition*

	Learning Conditions			Interference Effect
Class 1	*Learns task 1* Proper fractions	*Learns task 2* Improper fractions	*Retention test (recall)* Task 1, proper fractions	strong
Class 2	*Learns task 1* Proper fractions	(Does not learn task 2 prior to retention test)	*Retention test (recall)* Task 1, proper fractions	none
Class 1	*Learns task 1* Proper fractions	*Learns task 2* Mixed numbers	*Retention test (recall)* Task 1, proper fractions	mild
Class 2	*Learns task 1* Proper fractions	(Does not learn task 2 prior to retention test)	*Retention test (recall)* Task 1, proper fractions	none

proactive inhibition will likely affect the recall of the improper fractions in a retention test on that subject.

Learns task 1 Proper fractions	*Recalls task 1* No opportunity	*Learns task 2* Improper fractions	*Retention test (recall)* Task 2, improper fractions

As was true in the case of retroactive inhibition, the similarity or dissimilarity of the two learning tasks is a major variable in the strength of the proactive inhibitory effects (Table 3.3 illustrates this point). Another variable affecting proactive inhibition is *time*. For example, assume task 1 and task 2 were learned to the same level of performance. Studies show that if a retention test on task 2 comes within a few hours after learning that task, very little proactive inhibition occurs (Koppenaal, 1963; Underwood, 1948). However, if the task is recalled one day, two days, or a week later, there is increasingly stronger interference from the learning in task 1. In other words, as time passes before the recall of task 2, the clarity of the task diminishes and operationally becomes more like task 1.

Ceraso (1967) contends that this phenomenon does not result merely from

TABLE 3.3. *Proactive Inhibition*

		Learning Conditions			Interference Effect
Class 1	*Learns task 1* Proper fractions	*Recalls task 1* No opportunity	*Learns task 2* Improper fractions	*Retention test (recall)* Task 2, improper fractions	Strong
Class 2	*Learns task 1* Proper fractions	*Recalls task 1* Immediate and frequent opportunities	*Learns task 2* Improper fractions	*Retention test (recall)* Task 2, improper fractions	None
Class 1	*Learns task 1* Mixed numbers	*Recalls task 1* No opportunity	*Learns task 2* Improper fractions	*Retention test (recall)* Task 2, improper fractions	Mild
Class 2	*Learns task 1* Proper fractions	*Recalls task 1* Immediate and frequent opportunities	*Learns task 2* Improper fractions	*Retention test (recall)* Task 2, improper fractions	None

losing parts of task 2 or failing to discriminate task 1 but, rather, from a cerebral interaction of the two tasks which does not exist immediately upon the learning of task 2 but increasingly occurs with the passage of time before task 2 is recalled and strengthened. This is an important point for the classroom teacher to remember. The proactive interference does not occur at the *learning* of task 2 but during the retrieval (recall) stage. Clearly, the implication for instruction is to plan ways in which similar responses can be recalled shortly after each is learned and then frequently thereafter, so that the responses become strong and well discriminated.

A recent study by Ausubel, Stager, and Gaite (1969) indicates that *highly meaningful verbal material* does not appear to exhibit these proactive inhibitory effects. The study presented learners with portions of meaningful verbal materials rather than with the usual lists of serial or paired-associate verbal tasks to be learned by rote. The experimental learning task (task 2) was material regarding ZenBuddhism. The "inhibitory" learning materials (task 1) covered two topics: Buddhism and drug addiction. The similarity and relevance of task 1 to task 2 should be apparent. After the learning of the two tasks had taken place, the students were given both *immediate* and *delayed* retention tests on the ZenBuddhism material. When the data were analyzed, the researchers found no evidence of proactive inhibition effects in the students' recall of the

ZenBuddhism materials in either test situation. If additional research finds this result to be true—that previously learned, highly meaningful verbal materials may not have interfering effects with the recall of similar and subsequently learned, highly meaningful verbal materials—the classroom teacher may consider the meaningfulness of verbal materials in planning teaching strategies for the control of proactive inhibitory effects.

The history teacher finds that her students are more successful in recognizing important dates in a matching exam than they are in completion statements. *What learning and retention principles may explain this finding?*

This is not an uncommon phenomenon in the classroom; it is generally more difficult for a student to recall and *provide* information than simply to recognize and select the appropriate response. However, there is a crucial principle of retention to consider here as well. Retention is always affected by original learning. If the student has learned something well, he is more likely to be able to recall it without aids. And, as we have seen, strength in original learning is best facilitated by putting learning in a *meaningful* context and by providing immediate and frequent opportunities for recall of that learning.

Intelligence and retention.   Several early retention studies (Lyon, 1916; Mulhall, 1917; Achilles, 1920; and Dietze, 1931) clearly demonstrated that retention increases as chronological age (CA) and mental age (MA) increase. As chronological age increases, retention strengths are affected by development. Mental age may vary from chronological age. If an individual has an intelligence quotient of 100, his CA and MA are the same. As he moves upward from 100, his MA increases, and his retention rate is more affected by his MA than by his CA. The growth in mental age increases information-storage facilities and enhances the learning and recall potential of the individual. While these studies reflect logical biological maturation patterns, they do not allow for the variable of individual differences in basic capability, or intelligence, and its effects on retention of learning. Klausmeier, Feldhausen, and Check (1959), measured retention rates among children with low, average, and high intelligence. When given the same material to *learn,* the students with lower intelligence learned less than those with more intelligence, a factor attributable to basic acquisition ability. However, there was no proportional difference between the acquisition and retention rates of the students of low, average, or high intelligence (see Figure 3.6). Each subgroup recalled the materials they were able to learn at a proportionally similar rate of retention. In another investigation by Shuell and Keppel (1970), the same finding occurred. Fast (more intelligent) learners acquired more than slow learners but were unable to recall any more responses from their learning. These results held true under the conditions of immediate recall, 24-hour recall, and 48-hour recall. The authors of both studies concluded that while there were substantial differences in the rate of learning for various levels of intelligence, there were no significant proportional differences in rate of retention.

The research that has been done on the relationship between intelligence and

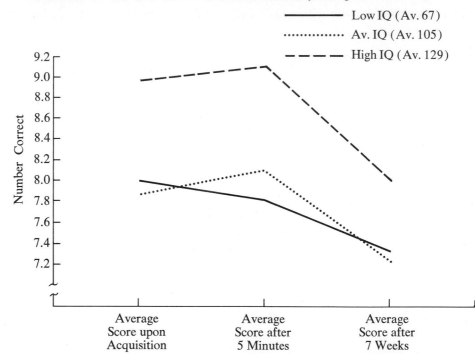

FIGURE 3.6. *Retention Rates in Subtraction Problems, by Intelligence*

Klausmeier, H. J., Feldhausen, J., & Check, J. *An analysis of learning efficiency in arithmetic of mentally retarded children in cooperation with children of average and high intelligence.* U.S. Office of Education Cooperative Research Project No. 153. Madison: University of Wisconsin, 1959, **12,** 69. Reprinted by permission of the authors.

retention has implications for the teacher regarding this variable of intelligence. Since studies show that the retention rates of most learners are proportionately the same, the teacher's primary concern involves original learning. By making sure that his students have the time necessary to respond to teaching, the teacher is in effect increasing the amount of learning that might occur. The student's recall is then related to the amount of information he has learned.

Strategies for increasing retention rate. Of practical consideration to the classroom teacher are ways in which retention can be increased. Three such possibilities are discussed here: *original learning, overlearning,* and *spaced review.* Regarding original learning, we have continually stressed the importance of the initial conditions of learning and their effect on recall and retention. If the teacher hopes to impart intellectual skills that will be retained over long periods of time, he must consider the following strategies:

1. Be sure the complexity of the desired response is within the range of the learner's capabilities and previous learning.
2. Provide for some warm-up or practice if the response may be affected positively by the transfer.
3. Make each stimulus situation clear and specific enough so that the learner will give and learn the desired discriminatory response.
4. Insert as much relevancy and meaningfulness into the learning situation as possible.
5. Reinforce the learner's response to confirm his accuracy and to strengthen the S–R bond.

When the skill is properly learned, the strategy of *overlearning* should come into play. Overlearning is the *practice* of a learned response *beyond* the point of mastery. Its importance rests in the fact that overlearned (frequently recalled) responses tend to be retained for longer periods of time than those responses that are not used after mastery. Figure 3.7 illustrates the results of a study (Kreuger, 1929) conducted to determine the effects of overlearning. Kreuger was able to demonstrate that those students who proceeded beyond the point of mastery (100 percent learning) to further confirm their responses had higher retention rates. Therefore, teachers should consider the following strategies:

1. Overteach materials that appear to be inherently difficult to learn.
2. Once mastery has been assured, provide additional meaningful stimulus situations in which the student can recall and confirm his newly mastered intellectual skill.

FIGURE 3.7. *Effects of Overlearning on Retention*

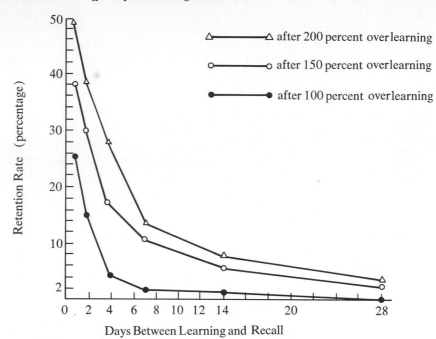

Kreuger, W. C. F. The effect of overlearning on retention. *Journal of Experimental Psychology,* 1929, **12,** 71–78. Reprinted by permission of the American Psychological Association.

A related but significantly different and equally important strategy in facilitating increased retention is the idea of *spaced review.* Spaced review should not be considered synonymous with overlearning, or additional practice. In spaced review, previously learned material is periodically re-presented and essentially *relearned,* with opportunities for the learner to recall and reuse the learned responses. Such relearning reestablishes the conditions of the original learning, thus strengthening the learning in the storage and retrieval stages (retention). The teacher should consider the following strategies:

1. Provide spaced review conditions periodically and systematically throughout a teaching unit or semester.

2. Provide additional teaching–learning situations in which the student not only is learning new material but is required to recall previously acquired responses as well.
3. Use opportunities provided in new teaching situations to interelate relevant existing learning.

SUGGESTED READINGS

Anders, T. R., Fozard, J. L., & Lillyquist, T. D.   Effects of age upon retrieval from short-term memory. *Developmental Psychology,* 1972, **6,** 214–217.

Andrews, T. G., & Cronbach, L. J.   Transfer of training. In W. S. Monroe (Ed.), *Encyclopedia of Educational Research.* (Rev. ed.) New York: Macmillan, 1950. Reprinted in Thornburg, H. D. (Ed.), *School learning and instruction: Readings.* Monterey, Calif.: Brooks/Cole, 1973, chap. 6.

Ausubel, D. P., Stager, M., & Gaite, A. J. H. Proactive effects in meaningful verbal learning and retention. *Journal of Educational Psychology,* 1969, **60,** 59–64.

Davidson, R. E., Schwenn, E. A., & Adams, J. F.   Semantic effects in transfer. *Journal of Verbal Learning and Verbal Behavior,* 1970, **9,** 212–217.

Deno, S. L., Jenkins, J. J., & Marsey, J.   Transfer variables and sequence effects in subject-matter learning. *Journal of Educational Psychology,* 1971, **62,** 365–370.

Emmer, E. T.   Transfer of instructional behavior and performance acquisition in simulated teaching. *Journal of Educational Research,* 1971, **65,** 178–182.

Gillman, S. I.   Retroactive inhibition in meaningful verbal learning as a function of similarity and review of interpolated material. *Journal of General Psychology,* 1970, **82,** 51–56.

Loftus, G. R., & Wickens, T. D.   Effect of incentive on storage and retrieval processes. *Journal of Experimental Psychology,* 1970, **85,** 141–147.

Shuell, T. J., & Keppel, G.   Learning ability and retention. *Journal of Educational Psychology,* 1970, **61,** 59–65. Reprinted in H. D. Thornburg (Ed.), *School learning and instruction: Readings.* Monterey, Calif.: Brooks/Cole, 1973, chap. 5.

Sturges, P. T.   Information delay and retention: Effects of information in feedback and tests. *Journal of Educational Psychology,* 1972, **63,** 32–43.

Tulving, E.   Organized retention and cued recall. *Journal of Experimental Education,* 1968, **37** (1), 3–13.

Underwood, B. J.   Interference and forgetting. *Psychological Review,* 1957, **64,** 49–60. Reprinted in Thornburg, H. D. (Ed.), *School learning and instruction: Readings.* Monterey, Calif.: Brooks/Cole, 1973, chap. 6.

4

Initial Learning

As we have learned in Chapters 1 and 2, there are generally considered to be two basic forms of learning, or conditioning—respondent and operant. Respondent conditioning dates back to the works of Pavlov, of course, while operant conditioning has its roots in Thorndike and is articulated by Skinner. These two types of learning, which constitute the lowest levels of Gagné's hierarchy of learning behavior, are explored in greater depth in this chapter to aid the reader in understanding their implications for learning and teaching.

RESPONDENT CONDITIONING (GAGNÉ'S SIGNAL LEARNING)

Respondent conditioning is considered to be the simplest type of learning known to man. Through laboratory experimentation with dogs, Pavlov (1927) determined that there is present in organisms a strong, involuntary stimulus–response relationship, which he called *reflexive* behavior. The components of this untrained relationship, or pairing, were termed the *unconditioned stimulus (UCS)* and *unconditioned response (UCR)*. An unconditioned stimulus is any stimulus that has the ability to elicit a response in an organism on a *regular* and *measurable basis* and *without prior training*. An unconditioned response is the behavior exhibited by the organism in reaction to the stimulus situation just described.

Pavlov's famous learning procedure, which became known as *classical conditioning,* involved substituting a *controllable* stimulus for the unconditioned stimulus. The controllable stimulus, which he called the *conditioned stimulus (CS),* was one that did not originally elicit a response from the organism but came to do so by being paired with the unconditioned stimulus (UCS). In Pavlov's experiments, the pairing of the two stimulus events occurred with the CS (a sound) first and the UCS (food) just momentarily delayed. After several pairings of the UCS (food) with the previously neutral CS (a sound), Pavlov noticed that the subject would respond (salivate) to the auditory stimulus (CS) without the presence of the food (UCS). Pavlov called this new response and pairing the *conditioned response (CR)*. The response is considered conditioned because the dog learned a new response or behavior that is *conditional* upon the presentation of the previously neutral stimulus, now the CS. In effect, the CS signals the organism that the UCS is about to appear. The dog salivated when seeing the CS because he anticipated that the UCS (reinforcement) was immediately forthcoming. The dog then learned to salivate in response to the CS. Pavlov demonstrated that reflexive (involuntary) responses could be conditioned—that is, could be learned in relation to new stimuli.

Two models of this learning phenomenon of respondent conditioning, or signal learning, are shown in Figure 4.1. Generally, such conditioned responses are learned within ten trials. On the average, Pavlov's dogs took nine trials to learn the CS–CR relationship, while Watson's (1919) conditioned-emotions experiment with a child took seven trials. The learned CS–CR response tends to be retained so long as it is useful and/or the UCS–CS association remains strong within the organism or individual.

The focus of the idea of respondent conditioning, particularly for human learning, is, of course, more on the CS–CR relationship than on the UCS–UCR relationship. Early in development, the infant demonstrates certain reflexive responses that arise out of physiological needs. When a physiological need exists, such as hunger or physical discomfort, some automatic, involuntary response (usually crying) is made in order to alleviate the physiological crisis; for example, the sound of an alarm clock could accompany an infant's morning hunger pangs or the discomfort of wet diapers. Such events may then become associated with the unconditioned response (crying), so that the child will later respond in the same way to the secondary event (the sound of the alarm), regardless of whether the physiological need exists. Thus, the child establishes a CS–CR relationship.

While signal learning tells us that man has the capability of pairing responses to conditioned stimuli, it is not the most common type of learning experienced by children in a classroom situation, or for that matter, in most life situations. Usually, respondent conditioning occurs within a formal school setting only in relation to emotional-conditioning experiences, such as the association of the morning bell with

FIGURE 4.1. Respondent Conditioning

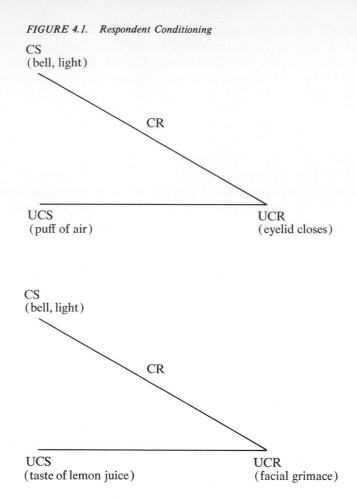

fear and anxiety, or the association of the teacher's touch with security and well-being. Most such learning goes on without teacher awareness, although, of course, the teacher should try to avoid instilling any negative associations in students. The initial, knowledge-building type of learning that does occur in the classroom (and in most human learning) is at the next level of Gagné's learning hierarchy.

Photo courtesy of Robert Gagné.

OPERANT CONDITIONING (GAGNÉ'S STIMULUS–RESPONSE LEARNING)

Operant conditioning, the second level of Gagné's learning hierarchy (discriminated stimulus–response learning), was first described by Thorndike. From his early experimentation with cats, Thorndike found that after exploring various possibilities of escape from a puzzle box, a cat would finally hit on the solution to the door latch and escape. Thorndike maintained that this operation was a result of blind, mechanical chance, and he termed it *trial-and-error learning.* With continued experimentation, however, Thorndike noticed that the more frequently a cat was confronted with the puzzle box, the quicker it tended to find and unlatch the door and escape. Out of such behavior, Thorndike developed his *law of effect,* which states that when a connection is made in the organism between a stimulus and a response and is followed by a satisfying state of affairs, that connection is strengthened and eventually becomes habituated, or learned. The cat's escape (response) from the box (stimulus) produces a satisfying state of affairs (reward or reinforcement) for the animal, thus increasing the likelihood of the response's recurring under the same stimulus conditions. Essentially, the cat is stamping a specific response to a specific stimulus into its mind.

How does this type of learning differ from respondent conditioning, or signal learning? First of all, although operant, or discriminated stimulus–response, learning may result from the stimulus of a basic physiological need as does signal learning, the response in operant learning is *voluntary,* not reflexive. That is, the response in operant learning depends on what the organism selects to do. Second, stimulus–response learning is often *suggested* to an organism, as in the case of a teacher providing the student with stimuli, whereas signal learning is invariably elicited as an involuntary response to an external stimulus. Third, and perhaps the most important contrast in the two types of learning, the manner in which the response is acquired differs. In Pavlovian-type learning, the CS is paired with the UCS and a response is made until, after several trials, the response becomes associated with the CS and the UCS serves then as reinforcement. In Thorndikean-type learning, a stimulus elicits a response and then reinforcement (reward) occurs to create an associative bond for that stimulus and response. Thus, in Thorndikean learning, reinforcement is contingent on the emission of the response, whereas in Pavlovian learning, the response is made in anticipation of reinforcement.

Recognizing this important difference—that reinforcement is contingent on the response—Skinner elaborated on Thorndike's law of effect, calling this type of learning *operant conditioning.* Skinner used the word *operant* to indicate that the organism "operates" on the environment (stimulus), altering it in some way by the selection and emission of a response. Once the response is made, the organism's behavior is reinforced either by the "satisfaction" of the altered environment or by another, independent stimulus presentation (that is, a new stimulus that is not directly associated with the original stimulus). In contrast to earlier S–R theorists, Skinner advances this idea of a second, *reinforcing* stimulus. He states that when an emitted response is followed by a stimulus, this stimulus reinforces the immediately preceding response, thus significantly increasing the probability of the response on subsequent presentation of the initial stimulus. Skinner (1938, 1953) also clearly states that respondent conditioning is relatively unimportant to human behavior and that operant conditioning is the better explanation of human learning patterns; for, because operant responses are voluntary and nonphysiologically based, the range of learning possible in such a situation is limited only by the capabilities and interests of the person at a given time.

Gagné places operant, or S–R, conditioning at a higher hierarchical level than signal learning, not because the latter is more complex but, rather, because it is more generally applicable to human learning and more typical of classroom learning. At this level, Gagné is not describing a type of learning that is in any significant way different from the Thorndike or Skinner models. He (1970a) classifies this second level as *stimulus–response learning* to emphasize that (1) "such learning concerns a single connection between a stimulus and a response . . . and (2) the stimulus and the response appear to become integrally bound together in such learning, in a way that does not happen with signal learning" (p. 104).

Perhaps a look at the paradigms Gagné uses in describing the first two types of learning on his hierarchy will help clarify his distinctions between the two types. In signal learning, the paradigm is S——R, which is an abbreviation or simplification of the classical-conditioning models presented in Figure 4.1. The S in Gagné's model represents the pairing of the UCS and CS to elicit the response (CR, stated as R in Gagné's model). The —— indicates the generalized, environmentally controlled *reflexive* connection of the stimulus (a flash of light, for example) and the response (the muscular contraction of the eyelid). In contrast, Gagné suggests that operant, or stimulus–response, learning is more representative of the paradigm S_s——→R. S_s is used to indicate that the encountered stimulus (S) is accompanied by internal psychological or physiological stimuli ($_s$) that do not determine the response, but merely assist the stimulus (S) in evoking the organism's selection and emission of the response. In contrast, all signal-learning responses are involuntary; that is, they are evoked only by such internal sensory stimuli ($_s$). The ——→ also indicates the specificity of the stimulus in this type of learning. The ——→ shows that the stimulus demands a *discriminated* (selected) response. If the response is inappropriate for the stimulus, then no connection is made and learning does not take place. If the response is appropriate and is reinforced in some way, then the learner builds a discriminatory S_s——→R bond and learning takes place.

Gagné suggests that the phenomenon of discrimination is particularly significant at the two levels of learning that serve as the primary basis for subsequent higher levels of learning. The first level of learning to significantly exhibit discrimination is Gagné's stimulus–response learning (level 2), which is described in this chapter. At this level, the S_s——→R bond involves the learning of what is called a *single discriminate*. In addition, Gagné suggests that in multiple discrimination learning (level 5), the learner is able to differentiate *(discriminate)* among a number of *similar* single S——→R connections, or single discriminates. Typically, multiple discrimination cannot be learned in one trial, whereas single-connection learning can be learned (Gagné, 1970b). Because of this and other aspects of level 5 learning which make it more complex, Gagné places multiple discrimination at a higher level in his hierarchy. Multiple discrimination will be discussed in detail in Chapter 6.

SIGNAL AND STIMULUS–RESPONSE LEARNING IN THE CLASSROOM

Two characteristics of signal learning should be reiterated at this point: (1) Most signal learning occurs prior to a child's entrance into school. (2) Since signal learning has a physiological basis, it is difficult for a teacher to control or even be aware of learning of this type. Two additional points are conjectured: (3) Most school learning experiences require specific, recall-type, emitted responses, whereas signal learning involves more generalized and contiguous involuntary responses and is, therefore, less applicable to school learning. (4) Learning in school is primarily a matter of accumulating a large and diverse repertoire of responses, while signal learning can only increase the number and diversity of stimuli for a response.

In short, stimulus–response learning is more characteristic of school learning. The student is typically required to acquire much basic information that will be important to his learning over a long period of time. The reinforcement of discriminated stimuli–response associations within the pupil appears to be the simplest and most durable manner in which such information can be acquired. Such learning is transferable, or cumulative, and the learner may successively build his knowledge and capability from simple to more complex tasks. Thus, as Gagné (1968) demonstrates, those who have not learned to accomplish a level 2 task generally cannot acquire a related higher level capability. (See the relationship of the first two levels in Gagne's learning hierarchy to the higher levels, as illustrated in Figure 4.2.)

Acknowledging that stimulus–response learning is most descriptive and the basis of classroom behavior, we must then be concerned with the manner in which $S_s \longrightarrow R$ connections will take place with the greatest efficiency. The following previously discussed learning phenomena are essential to an understanding of classroom learning and the planning of an effective teaching strategy.

Contiguity

The greater the temporal proximity between the stimulus and the response, the greater is the likelihood that the desired response will be emitted and learned.

FIGURE 4.2. *Gagné's Learning Hierarchy—Levels 1 and 2*

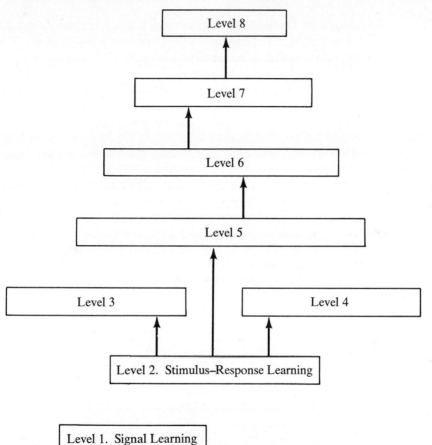

The two lowest learning types are represented in this way to indicate that, generally, level 1 precedes level 2 but is not prerequisite to it or to subsequent levels, whereas the more complex levels rely wholly on level 2 task learning.

Stimulus generalization

Beginning with Pavlov's work, it has been repeatedly demonstrated that two highly similar stimuli may evoke the *same* conditioned response (Razran, 1951; Guttman and Kalish, 1956; Kimble, 1961). In signal learning, this phenomenon of stimulus generalization readily occurs as the organism seeks to reduce a physiological need (basic drive). For example, stimulus generalization might occur in the case of a young child who is taken to the doctor's office, where he receives a painful injection. The UCS (needle entering the arm) elicits a UCR (withdrawal and crying), and the sight of the doctor (CS) may in future contacts elicit these same fear reactions of withdrawal and crying (CR). In addition, other stimuli that are in some way similar—the sight of dentists, lab technicians, nurses, and other people in white coats—may also elicit the fear reactions. This example of stimulus generalization is illustrated in Figure 4.3.

In stimulus–response learning within the classroom, it is quite common for the teacher to present similarly appearing but not identical stimuli to which the student must learn to make the same response. To illustrate, in learning lower- and upper-case letters, such as "b, B," the student is expected to be able to recognize and respond to both forms of "b" as the same letter.

The phenomenon of stimulus generalization may also occur without teacher

FIGURE 4.3. *Stimulus Generalization in Signal Learning*

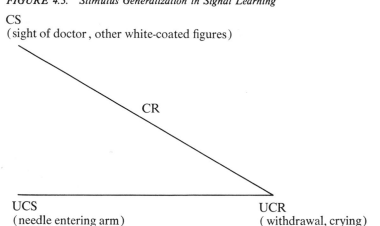

planning, of course. For example, if a student is presented with a red apple and responds that it is an apple, the student is also likely to respond "apple" when presented with a yellow apple. The two stimuli are similar enough to trigger the same response.

The important variable to remember is that generalization can occur with stimulus–response learning only when stimuli are closely related in appearance or characteristics. It is also important to remember that this phenomenon will often produce counterproductive effects in classroom learning, as, for example, when the learner mistakes the letter "d" for "b" or responds in the same way to two different but similarly appearing geometric figures. A failure by the teacher to present *discriminated* stimuli can result in poorly defined and diffuse or incorrect responses by the learner.

Discrimination

Early experimentalists found that the learned responses of an organism could be discriminatory as well as generalizable. In early Pavlovian experiments (signal learning), laboratory dogs learned to emit responses to specific, discriminated stimuli. In stimulus–response connections, the same phenomenon occurs. Indeed, the specificity of a stimulus invariably determines the rapidity and accuracy with which a response is learned. The phenomenon of discrimination also means that an individual can learn to react to differences in similar stimuli, just as he reacted to their similarities within the phenomenon of generalization. As we have seen, in most teaching situations, it is desirable to build discriminatory learning in the student. Discrimination is most likely to occur when the teacher presents the student with a specific stimulus and reinforces only if the student emits the correct response. Upon repeated presentations of this stimulus, the student will then give the same discriminatory response.

Recurrence of the stimulus

Once an S–R connection has been established, it may be strengthened by additional selected stimulus situations in which the learner is required to make the same discriminated response.

Reinforcement

The phenomenon of reinforcement is the major condition for most learning. Pavlov (1927) found it to be essential in signal learning, and Thorndike (1911), Hull (1952), Spence (1956), Dollard and Miller (1950), Skinner (1953), Gagné (1970a), and many others have demonstrated it to be the primary mechanism for the establishment of a desired S–R connection. Although all of the theorists agree generally that some kind of reinforcement must occur with the emission of an S–R bond if learning is to occur, there has been considerable research on (1) the effects on learning of different schedules of reinforcement (Skinner, 1938; Ferster & Skinner, 1957), and (2) the most appropriate types of reinforcement scheduling for different levels of learning (Gagné, 1970a). Gagné's proposals are presented as each level of learning in his hierarchy is discussed in Chapters 4 through 7. The conclusions of the Ferster and Skinner research on reinforcement scheduling are summarized as follows:

1. *Continuous reinforcement.* The effect of reinforcement for each response by a learner is usually an accelerated rate of responses in subsequent presentations of the stimulus. *Extinction* (the disappearance of a S–R bond due to lack of reinforcement) can occur relatively quickly when the connection was established under continuous reinforcement.
2. *Fixed interval reinforcement.* The initial response is reinforced after a fixed and considerable interval of time with this schedule. Telford and Sawrey (1968) cite regular paychecks or school grade cards as examples. The effect of this schedule is that the closer the learner gets to the time that reinforcement will be forthcoming, the more likely the response rate will increase. There is a greater resistance to extinction in responses established under this schedule than there is with responses made under continuous reinforcement.
3. *Variable interval reinforcement.* Reinforcement is random—neither constant nor on a fixed interval of time. In some cases, a learner may be reinforced several times within a very short time period; in other cases, the learner may go for an extended time period without any reinforcement. The effect of such a schedule seems to be a greater stability of response and learning than with either of the other previously described schedules. An indication of this stability is the fact that extinction is slow and very gradual in responses learned under this schedule.
4. *Fixed ratio schedule.* The learner is reinforced after a fixed number of responses are emitted. If a person is reinforced on every fifth response, for example, we would say that the reinforcement ratio is 5:1. The distinction between a *ratio* schedule and an *interval* schedule is that ratio is based on number of responses while interval is based on time. In a fixed ratio schedule, the reinforcement serves to strengthen the preceding responses and to motivate the subsequent five responses that must be emitted before the learner is reinforced again. Ferster and Skinner (1957) have

demonstrated that responses can be maintained under this schedule at very high ratios, even at 1000:1. Extinction is very slow to occur here, as it is with variable interval reinforcement.

5. *Variable ratio schedule.* The ratio is randomly set around an arbitrary mean so that the number of responses show the highest maintenance response and greatest resistance to extinction.

On the basis of this research, it is clear that the use of reinforcement in the classroom is important in the establishment and maintenance of learning, particularly in teaching situations in which timing and/or numbers have significance for the learning behavior. As we proceed through the next few chapters, the type of reinforcement scheduling thought most applicable to each level of learning will be presented.

In stimulus–response learning (level 2), which is the main subject of this chapter, the reinforcement should be *frequent* and as *immediate* after the response as possible. This usually means that the teacher must provide the student with some knowledge or subsequent satisfying activity that tells him that his emitted response is accepted and that he may proceed to emit additional responses in the same way.

Extinction

This principle, which originated with Pavlov, can be described as the continued presence of the conditioned stimulus without reinforcement until the conditioned response eventually diminishes and disappears. In signal learning, a response quickly becomes weaker if reinforcement is withheld. You will recall in Pavlov's experiments that the UCS (meat powder) served as reinforcement to the CR (salivation). Without the continuation of this reinforcement, the basic need (hunger) of the dog is not reduced by the CS (tuning fork), and the CS soon ceases to elicit the CR.

Usually, both classical (level 1) and operant (level 2) conditioned responses are maintained over a considerable period of time unless reinforcement is withheld. Skinner's pigeons maintained their conditioned pecking response for four years (1950) with continued reinforcement, and students, of course, will retain material presented in the classroom for extended periods of time with intermittent reinforcement. If a student is emitting an undesirable response, the teacher may implement a strategy of nonreinforcement that will facilitate extinction of the undesired response (see Table 4.1). Essentially, that is what behavioral modification attempts to do (Bandura, 1969; Wenrich, 1970).

TABLE 4.1.   *Extinguishing a Conditioned Response*

(Conditioning)	1.	CS——————→CR——————→Reinforcement (well-established)
(Extinction trials)	2. 3. 4.	CS——————→CR CS——————→CR CS——————→CR CS——————→CR CS——————→CR
(Extinction)	5. 6. 7.	CS——————→no response CS——————→no response CS——————→no response CS——————→no response CS——————→no response
	8.	Time lapse
(Spontaneous recovery)	9.	CS——————→CR
(Extinction)	10. 11.	CS——————→no response CS——————→no response CS——————→no response CS——————→no response

Telford, C. W., & Sawrey, J. M. *Psychology as a Natural Science.* Copyright 1972 by Wadsworth Publishing Company, Inc. Reprinted by permission of the publisher, Brooks/Cole Publishing Company, Monterey, California.

With stimulus–response learning (level 2), two variables may effect extinction of learned responses:

1. *No reinforcement.*   If a response was never originally reinforced, extinction invariably and quickly occurs (Skinner, 1938). Indeed, we cannot conclusively say that learning even occurred.
2. *Original reinforcement.*   The more strongly a response is originally reinforced, the more resistant it is to extinction when subsequent responses are not reinforced.

Spontaneous recovery

A related phenomenon to extinction is *spontaneous recovery,* which is the recurrence of a response after extinction has occurred. This phenomenon also was first observed by Pavlov. Kimble (1961) defines it as "the return in strength of a conditioned response, whether partial or complete, brought about by lapse of time following its diminution by extinction" (p. 483).

If an undesired response does recur in a classroom situation, then extinction procedures may be used again to reextinguish the response (see Table 4.1). After some time, the probability of spontaneous recovery decreases, and the response will not recur. Sometimes, a *desired* response recurs—for example, a student remembers a fact or formula that he had earlier forgotten (extinction). In such a situation, the teacher should strongly reinforce the recovered response with a show of approval, so that the S–R bond will be strengthened within the student.

In his daily teaching strategy, the geography teacher tries to provide information feedback for each student's response. Eventually, he finds the procedure to be both burdensome and impractical. *"Is this technique really that crucial to learning?"* he asks.

It is important to remember that reinforcement is proven to be a crucial factor in learning. However, the work of Ferster and Skinner (1957) suggests that reinforcement does not have to be continuous but may be *intermittent,* an idea they call *schedules of reinforcement.* Thus, if the student is emitting a response for the first time, it is most advantageous to reinforce; but on subsequent occasions, it may not be necessary to reinforce. Students who learn under intermittent reinforcement schedules do not become dependent upon reinforcement for every response. This teacher should try, then, to reinforce each original response and intermittently reinforce thereafter. The schedules of reinforcement which may be effectively used by the classroom teacher were discussed on pp. 90–91.

SUGGESTED READINGS

Boyles, E. E.   The idea of learning as development of insight. *Educational Theory,* 1952, **2,** 65–71.

Bruner, J. S.   Learning and thinking. *Harvard Educational Review,* 1959, **29,** 184–192.

Burgess, R. L., & Akers, R. L.   Are operant principles tautological? *Psychological Record,* 1966, **16,** 305–312.

Cradler, J. D., & Goodwin, D. L.   Conditioning of verbal behavior as a function of age, social class, and type of reinforcement. *Journal of Educational Psychology,* 1971, **62,** 279–284.

Franklin, C. W., Jr.   Toward a clarification of operant principles in human interaction. *Psychological Record,* 1970, **20,** 489–494.

Freeman, N. C. G., & Suedfeld, P.   Classical conditioning of verbal meaning: The roles of awareness, meaningfulness, and evaluative loading. *Psychological Record,* 1969, **19,** 335–338.

Hamilton, M. L.   Vicarious reinforcement effects on extinction. *Journal of Experimental Child Psychology,* 1970, **9,** 108–114.

Spence, K. W.   Cognitive vs. stimulus–response theories of learning. *Psychological Review,* 1950, **57,** 159–172.

Vogler, R. E.   Awareness and the operant conditioning of a cooperative response. *Journal of Psychology,* 1968, **69,** 117–127.

5

Learning Chains

The combination of a *series* of learned responses is the consideration of this chapter. Gagné (1970a) refers to this type of learning behavior as *chaining,* which is a term for describing a sequence of simple S–R bonds. In the classroom, the student is frequently called upon to emit learning chains, which vary in difficulty and length from the simple learning of the alphabet to the complex understanding and explanation of a chemical formula. Indeed, some type of chaining is involved in almost every circumstance of teaching and learning in the classroom.

Gagné divides learning chains into two types—*motor* and *verbal*—both of which he defines as arrangements of component tasks and sequences of responses within a larger learning task. Motor chaining (level 3) will be discussed first, since in most cases such learning occurs before verbal chains (level 4) are acquired.

MOTOR CHAINS

When the organism functions at the level of respondent learning behavior, the motor-learning chain is reflexive (Skinner, 1938). In other words, upon presentation of the stimulus, the chain of motor responses is elicited involuntarily. For example, consider the motor-chain reflex behavior in a newborn child. When stimulated, the infant's responses are (1) throwing his arms out to the side, (2) extending his fingers, and (3) bringing his arms and hands to the midline as if he were embracing someone.

The conditions for operant motor-learning behavior are not the same. Here the learner *voluntarily* emits a series of responses to a stimulus to develop a desired motor skill. In operant learning of motor chains, each S–R connection in the chain must be learned as a distinct individual bond for a sequential emission of the series, or chain, of S–R connections to take place. In addition, the strength and maintenance of the motor chain is highly dependent on positive reinforcement. Operant learning of motor chains is our primary concern, of course, since the type of learning behaviors most commonly emitted in the classroom are operant.

According to Gagné (1970a), the following four conditions appear to be necessary for motor chaining:

1. Individual links in the chain must have been previously learned.
2. The series of links must be learned contiguously—that is, in sequence and as a unit.
3. The final link of the chain must be followed by a satisfying state of affairs (positive reinforcement).
4. When the above three conditions are fully met, the acquisition of the chain is likely to occur in a single trial.

In addition, Gagné points out that although verbal cues (usually, verbal commands) provide external stimuli for the learning of chains of motor reponses, the need for the external verbal cues may diminish as the chains are repeated until, finally, the external cues become internalized and the chains therefore become self-directed in the learner.

Figure 5.1 illustrates a motor-learning chain. Note the significant conditions of this motor-learning chain:

1. Each link in the motor chain is the performance of an act that the learner already knows how to do.
2. At the end of any one link or any combination of links, the existing S–R connections set the conditions for the next link in the chain to occur in an orderly sequence.
3. Each link therefore consists of appropriate and meaningful behavior for the whole sequence of responses, thus increasing learning efficiency.
4. The final link serves as a terminal satisfaction and positive reinforcement, strengthening the whole chain.

Regarding the last point, note that with a learning chain only the final link need be reinforced. Skinner (1953) views any stimulus as a reinforcer if it increases the probability of response. And since each response within a chain must serve as the stimulus for the next response, thus increasing the probability of that response, each response in a chain has reinforcing strength within it. In other words, reinforcement is provided to the learner from one response to the next so that the reinforcement or satisfaction provided to the learner at the completion of a chain will strengthen the entire chain.

FIGURE 5.1.   Analysis of a Motor-Learning Chain

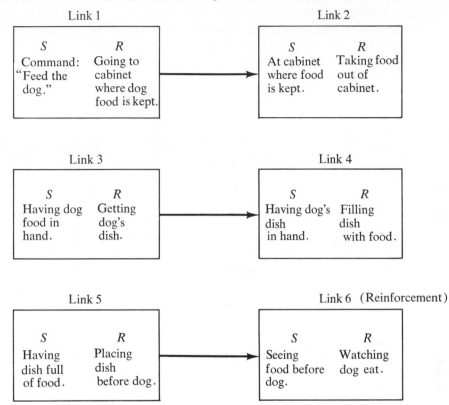

The unlearning, or extinction, of a chain may occur in the same way as it does in a single S–R connection—by a failure to reinforce. Thus, the final S–R link in the chain is not reinforced, resulting in a lack of reinforcement for the entire chain and subsequent failure by the learner to emit the chain again. An example of the use of extinction with a motor chain is described by Guthrie (1942). A girl who never hangs up her coat until her mother nags at her is made to go back outdoors, come in the house again, and go to the closet to hang up her coat. This action proves effective because the chain of stimuli now occurring when the girl comes into the house is associated with the desired response of hanging up the coat. The previous chain of responses, provided by the mother's stimulus of nagging, is now extinct.

Just as a single verbal cue ("feed the dog") may set off a chained motor-learning activity, several verbal cues or instructions may also be used to direct the learner through each link or sequence of a behavior. This technique for cuing a learner through each S–R link of a motor chain is especially useful in three situations: (1) when a learner does not know how to build a chain in a sequential order, (2) when there is an option as to the order that the links may occur in the chain, and (3) when the learner must learn to emit the links in a specific order.

In the first situation—building a motor chain in a sequential order—the following illustration is typical: A driving instructor tells the learner that there are three things a good driver must do after getting in the car and before turning on the ignition. Those three motor responses are (1) adjust the seat, (2) adjust the rear-view mirror, and (3) fasten the seat belt. In other words, the driving instructor desires to teach the learner a three-link motor chain that will prepare the driver to turn on the ignition with maximum safety. The following verbal instructions might accompany the teaching of the chain: "The first thing you should do when you get into a car is to adjust the driver's seat so that your feet meet the foot pedals properly. Now that you are in an appropriate driving position, you can adjust your rear-view mirror so that you will have good vision and fasten your seat belt so that it is snug and comfortable."

The purpose of these instructions is, of course, to provide the learner with verbal cues or instructions that will cause him to respond in a sequential way to the initial stimulus of getting into the driver's seat. A model of the motor chain would look like this:

S_1 Adjust the driver's seat. R_1 Driver's seat is adjusted.
S_2 With driver's seat adjusted. R_2 Adjust the rear-view mirror.
S_3 With rear-view mirror adjusted. R_3 Fasten the seat belt.

The final act in the sequence was to fasten the seat belt, which sets the condition for reinforcement to occur—in this case, being ready for the ignition of the car.

For the second motor-learning situation in which link-by-link verbal cues are useful—selecting among optional orders for a motor chain—let's go back to "feeding the dog" to illustrate. A six-link motor chain was presented in that example, with the verbal command "feed the dog" serving as the stimulus to link one of the chains. Let's look at the first three links in the chain again:

S_1 "Feed the dog." R_1 Going to cabinet where dog food is kept.
S_2 At cabinet where food is kept. R_2 Taking food out of cabinet.
S_3 Having dog food in hand. R_3 Getting dog's dish.

Now note a possible *optional order* in these three links:

S_1 "Feed the dog." R_1 Getting dog's dish.
S_2 Having dog's dish in hand. R_2 Going to cabinet where dog food is kept.
S_3 At cabinet where food is kept. R_3 Taking food out of cabinet.

The use of verbal instructions throughout this chaining situation would tell the learner how to respond in the desired sequence. And since the learner is capable of performing the chain in either order, with the same terminal behavior, the verbal instructions will increase the probability of one sequence being followed in preference to the other. Reinforcement would follow the terminal link.

The third learning situation in which several verbal cues are helpful—learning a motor chain in a specific order—can be illustrated as follows: The teacher's goal is to teach a high school age student the necessary steps for preparing to knit. The chain can be accompanied with both verbal instructions and visual aids (see Figure 5.2).

S_1 Verbal cue: "Let's prepare to cast on." R_1 Make a slip loop at the end of the yarn.

S_2 With slip loop at end of yarn. R_2 Place loop on needle.

S_3 Loop on needle. R_3 Pull ends of yarn.

S_4 With yarn pulled. R_4 Place needle between thumb and first finger.

S_5 Needle between thumb and first finger. R_5 Place yarn loosely over first finger.

S_6 With yarn over first finger. R_6 Place yarn under second finger.

S_7 With yarn under second finger. R_7 Place yarn over third finger.

S_8 With yarn over third finger. R_8 Place yarn under fourth finger above middle joint.

S_9 With yarn under fourth finger. R_9 Check hand position.

The teacher would now verbally provide reinforcement to the student for achieving the right position to begin knitting. If the learner is to emit and learn this motor chain properly, he must do it precisely as he is instructed by the verbal cues and visual

FIGURE 5.2. Visual Cues for Learning a Motor Chain in Specific Order

Steps in Preparing to Knit

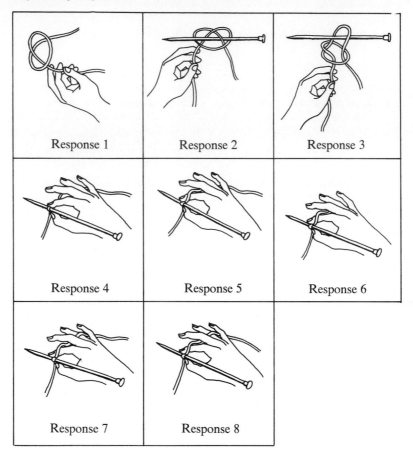

instructions. The importance of such cues in this type of motor-chain learning is obvious—they ensure that the learner will select the correct links for the chain.

In all three situations of learning a motor chain through several verbal cues, the instructions serve as stimuli that ensure the occurrence of the correct or preferred linking responses rather than incorrect or undesirable ones. Regarding this technique of verbal cuing, Gagné (1965) points out three highly important considerations:

1. After the first set of verbal instructions is administered to the learner, they may not be necessary on successive trials. As stated earlier, Gagné insists that when the two conditions of prior learning of the individual links of the chain and contiguity in the presentation of the links are met, the chain can be learned on a *single* occasion. Thus, when a person learns a chain that has been facilitated throughout by verbal cues, no verbal cues are likely to be necessary the second time a learner goes through the chain.
2. Verbal instructions may become self-administered. Gagné contends that verbal instructions are merely accompaniments to the initial establishment of the chain and are not a part of the chain itself. Therefore, after the first trial or two, the cues "may simply become unnecessary, because the stimuli from one link of the chain provide a suitable stimulus for the occurrence of the next link" (p. 90). In other words, as we noted earlier, the external cues become internalized, and the chain becomes self-directed.
3. Some learners, like animals or very young children, may not be able to respond to verbal cues. If a child is not able to understand verbal cues, then pictures, gestures, or some other mode of communication must be used to present cues. Again, it is necessary to cue the child only initially in order to facilitate learning of the desired chain.

A logical question at this point is "How does the individual make use of motor-learning chains both before and during his academic experiences?" The following list, broken into developmental periods, will answer that question and suggest many other examples of this simple and elemental learning phenomenon:

Infancy (0–2 years)	Drinking from a baby bottle
	Crawling, walking
	Grasping objects
	Climbing stairs
	Toilet training
Preschool (2–5)	Talking
	Running
	Pulling a wagon

	Brushing teeth
	Riding a tricycle
	Eating
	Opening doors
Primary grades (6–8)	Writing
	Tying shoelaces
	Riding a bicycle
	Drawing
	Throwing a baseball
	Cut-and-paste constructions
	Building
	Playing simple musical instruments
	Marching
	Constructing diagrams, etc.
	Drawing maps
Intermediate grades (9–11)	Working a combination lock
	Bat-and-ball coordination
	Gymnastics
Junior high school (12–14)	Executing sports strategies
	Home-economics skills
	Woodworking
	Household-maintenance tasks
	Drawing geometric figures
Senior high school (15–18)	Mechanical drawing
	Art
	Sports, gymnastics, dancing
	Driving
	Newspaper layout
Adulthood	Assembling do-it-yourself kits
	Refinishing furniture
	Occupational tasks
	Household tasks

In motor chaining, we find that most chains tend to be retained for a long time. Individual links within a chain may occasionally be forgotten, but they may also be recovered with very little difficulty. The retentive strength of motor chains rests ultimately on the use of the chain. A person who has not ice skated for a lengthy period of time may initially have some difficulties in the performance, whereas the individual who ice skates regularly will maintain indefinitely and without effort all the essential links in this motor chain.

VERBAL CHAINS

Verbal chaining, which Gagné (1965) calls *verbal association* (level 4), is vocalized learning—the learner's capacity to respond verbally. From the time an individual begins developing vocabulary, verbal chaining begins in its simplest forms, and, subsequently, almost all classroom and adult learning is acquired through verbal chains.

The conditions for learning verbal chains are basically no different from those for operantly learned motor chains: (1) All S–R connections within the chain must have been previously established within the learner; (2) the presentation of the S–R links must be sequential and contiguous in time; (3) the performance of each link in the chain is contingent upon the completion of the previous link or combination of links; (4) the final link must be followed by reinforcement; and (5) with these conditions met, the verbal chain, like motor chains, is likely to be acquired on the initial trial, although the longer the verbal chain, the less probable that a one-trial chaining will occur. Thus, in verbal chaining, the learner builds a repertoire of words that at one time were learned individually through simple S–R ($S_s \longrightarrow R$) connections. Then, upon being required to emit some verbal chain that involves the association of several previously established words, the learner acquires a new set of relationships between these words.

The one special condition necessary for verbal-learning chains is what Gagné describes as *mediating connections* or *coding connections*. This factor serves the function of an intervening or bridging link which facilitates the combination of the verbal links in the chain. Such mediating links usually occur within the learner and involve no observable external behaviors. The more complex the verbal chain, the more important the role that the internal mediating or coding connection plays. In addition, some *external* factor will often account initially for the continuity of verbal links in the chain. Verbal cues or visual objects, for example, often serve as initial mediating connections for very simple verbal chains and may also be used effectively as aids to the internal coding when the verbal chain to be learned is illogical or particularly difficult.

When a child starts naming objects for the first time, a very simple two-link verbal chain develops. To illustrate, a child who receives a toy wagon learns to identify the toy as "wagon," as follows:

S_1	Object.	R_1	Perceiving the object.
S_2	"Wagon" (verbally cued).	R_2	Child says "wagon."

The child has the wagon before him, so he has a visual object (mediating connection) that aids him in associating the word "wagon" with the object. Someone verbally cues the child that the object is a wagon. The child in return says the word "wagon." He says and learns the word, then, with the aid of two cues—the visual object and the spoken word. Some type of verbal praise by the person who provided the stimulus would reinforce the child's behavior, thus increasing the likelihood of such behavior recurring upon subsequent elicitation.

More complex verbal chains consist of the connection of several units that are first individually learned as two-link chains. For example, a first grader is asked to recite the alphabet, a task that consists of a chain of 26 units or responses. If the child is to carry out this verbal-chaining task, we must assume that the following antecedent circumstances exist:

1. A chart of the alphabet (the visual object or mediating connection) is on a wall in the room.
2. The teacher has already instructed the child in pronouncing and writing the letters of the alphabet.
3. The child has had intermittent occasions to vocalize some letters in the alphabet during the pronunciation–writing exercises.

Thus, the child (1) has had the alphabet presented to him in a sequential, orderly manner; (2) has associated the verbal pronunciation (from the teacher) of each letter with writing the letters (his activity); and (3) has intermittently verbalized some parts of the chain he has been asked to recite. Therefore, upon being asked by the teacher to recite the alphabet, the child emits the following verbal chain:

S_1	Verbal cue: "Recite the alphabet."	R_1	Looking at alphabet chart.
S_2	Seeing letter "a."	R_2	Verbalizing "a."
S_3	Seeing "b." . . .	R_3	Verbalizing "b." . . .
S_{27}	Seeing "z."	R_{27}	Verbalizing "z."
S_{28}	Completing alphabet.	R_{28}	Looking at teacher.
S_{29}	Seeing teacher approval.	R_{29}	Satisfaction, knowledge of results (reinforcement).

In this example, the orderliness and fitness of the individually learned letters to one another make the lengthy chain easier than the numerous units would indicate. In addition, the visual aid of seeing the printed letters of the alphabet in proper sequential order serves as a mediating connection for guiding the emission of the chain of alphabetical responses.

As we noted, some external factor—usually a visual aid—is an effective supplement to the internal mediating or coding connection in facilitating the learning of a verbal chain that is not so logical or is particularly difficult. Consider the example of a student learning the clockwise placement of the Spanish terms for the eight points of the compass. Figure 5.3 illustrates the visual cues that would facilitate such learning.

When a person is to learn a verbal chain that is particularly long in terms of (1) the number of links in the chain or (2) the length of each link, he may encounter difficulty in establishing the chain. Gagné (1970a) interprets evidence from experiments (Miller, 1956; Jensen, 1962) to conclude that a verbal chain of about seven links, plus or minus two, represents the limit of what can be learned at one time. Gagné (1965) refers to this seven-link limit as the *immediate memory span,* noting that "chains longer than this must be broken up into parts in order for learning to occur most efficiently" (p. 101). Consider a particularly lengthy chain, such as the alphabet. Note that the traditional "alphabet song," by which generations of children have learned to recite their ABCs, breaks down the alphabet into segments of about seven links, thereby meeting the limits of the immediate memory span for learning chains efficiently.

Another example of this phenomenon of immediate memory span can be illustrated by the situation of a child learning the Twenty-third Psalm. Presumably, the most efficient way to learn scripture is one verse at a time. Based on this premise, the Twenty-third Psalm, having six verses, would become a six-link verbal chain in which the individual *links* would be relatively long and therefore difficult for a child to learn at one time. The learning is likely to be more efficient, then, if each verse-link is broken into smaller segments, as follows:

S_1	Verbal cue: "Repeat the Twenty-third Psalm."	R_1	"The Lord is my shepherd."
S_2	Having said it.	R_2	"I shall not want."
S_3	Having completed verse 1.	R_3	"He maketh me to lie down in green pastures."
S_4	Having said it.	R_4	"He leadeth me beside the still waters." . . .

The most important factor in the retention of verbal-chain learning seems to be frequency of repetition. Underwood (1964a) states that one of the best established laws of learning is that the more time spent in learning, the greater the probability that

FIGURE 5.3. Visual Cues for Learning the Eight Compass Points in Spanish

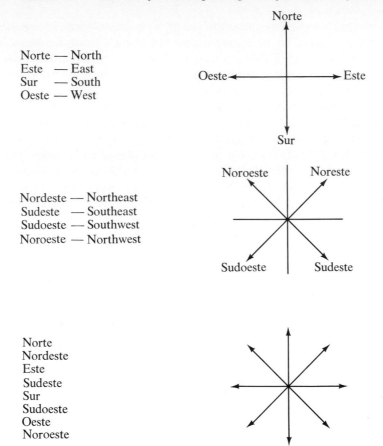

Norte — North
Este   — East
Sur   — South
Oeste — West

Nordeste — Northeast
Sudeste   — Southeast
Sudoeste — Southwest
Noroeste — Northwest

Norte
Nordeste
Este
Sudeste
Sur
Sudoeste
Oeste
Noroeste

what is learned will be retained. Underwood (1959) stresses that frequency is especially important in verbal learning because the verbal response that has been most frequently used in the past is the one most readily available when new stimuli are presented.

For example, there is continuous exposure in schools to the Pledge of Allegiance. It is not likely that a learner will successfully emit and retain this fairly lengthy verbal chain in one trial. However, as the stimuli for this chain are repeated each school day, the verbal chain becomes well-learned with minimal, if any, forgetting. Most students when they graduate from high school can recite without any hesitation or error the Pledge of Allegiance. On the other hand, the sixth grader who has learned the 50 states alphabetically is not likely to be able to "reel off" this less frequently repeated verbal chain, even during his next academic year, much less upon graduation from high school. Teachers usually assume that forgetting is inevitable. Their own experience indicates that, with the passage of time, some previously learned verbal skills and knowledge simply disappear. However, it should be kept in mind that the frequency with which a verbal chain is used will have a direct effect on how well it is maintained.

Retention of verbal chains also seems to be affected by the phenomenon of *interference*. McGeoch (1942) states that time has no bearing on forgetting of verbal associations; rather, a person forgets only when he learns something new that interferes in some way with the original learning. Underwood (1964a) also suggests that the linking of one verbal unit to another tends to reduce the retention of an earlier similar linking and also seems to reduce the likelihood that the new verbal chain will be retained.

Extinction in verbal chaining is somewhat more complex than in either stimulus–response learning or motor chaining because of this phenomenon of interference and because the inability to recall only one link in a verbal chain is presumed to mean extinction of the whole chain. Thus, if a student is asked to repeat a verbal chain which he has previously learned and finds that he has forgotten one link in the chain, then extinction is operating and the teacher will have to reteach the necessary link, emphasizing its place in the total chain.

The *meaningfulness* of what is being learned is yet another factor in the retention of verbal material. If the learner retains an idea by relating it to what he knows, and the material makes sense to him, then meaningful learning results. Underwood (1959) declares that the "higher the meaningfulness, the more readily are verbal units recalled" (p. 111). Underwood (1964b) also discusses three more factors that may affect the retention and the learning of verbal material:

1. *The ability of the learner.*   Since the learner brings this factor with him, the teacher has very little control over student entering abilities other than homogeneously grouping the students.
2. *The nature of the material being learned.*   The material must be within the range of the student's response capability. Then, if it is presented in an associative context,

it becomes meaningful and is not only more efficiently learned but better retained as well.

3. *Degree of or lack of similarity between the items being learned.*   Underwood (1964b) states, "the ultimate degree of learning is the critical factor in the rate of forgetting. If the degree of learning reaches a certain level, it makes no difference how long it took to reach that level" (p. 92). In other words, the teacher must allow sufficient time for good original learning in order to ensure a higher rate of retention.

MOTOR CHAINS AND VERBAL CHAINS—A SUMMARY

In the past two chapters, levels 1–4 of Gagné's learning hierarchy have been discussed, with the emphasis in this chapter on chaining (levels 3 and 4). Figure 5.4 illustrates the learning structure to this point in the text. In every chaining situation, the individual learner must meet a set of conditions that are important to the learning task at hand. Similarly, the teacher provides certain conditions that may have a profound effect of the learning activity. The discussion in this chapter leads to the following considerations of learning in both motor and verbal chains:

Learning Conditions

Motor Chains	*Verbal Chains*
1. Each S–R connection in the chain must have been previously learned for the chain to be acquired.	1. Each S–R connection in the chain must have been previously learned for the chain to be acquired.
	2. Internal, nonobservable mediating or coding connections serve to bridge the links of the chain.
	3. External mediating or coding connections between the verbal links should be available to the learner for long, difficult, or illogical chains.

Teacher Conditions

Motor Chains	*Verbal Chains*
1. A verbal cue is generally necessary to start the learner through the motor chain.	1. A verbal cue or visual aid is generally necessary to start the learner through the verbal chain.
2. Stimuli must be presented in an orderly sequence.	2. Stimuli must be presented in an orderly sequence.
3. Contiguity of each stimulus and response in the chain is essential to learning. Each link must be	3. Contiguity of each stimulus and response in the chain is essential to learning. Each link must be

FIGURE 5.4. *Gagné's Learning Hierarchy—Levels 1–4*

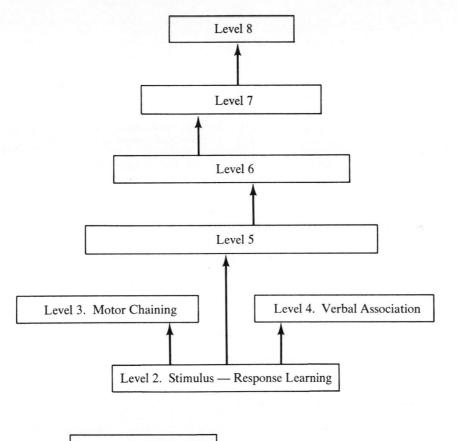

Since both motor and verbal chains represent the combination of two or more stimulus–response bonds, they are of equal importance in the learning and therefore assume coordinate positions.

presented and performed in close succession if the chain is to be learned.

4. The final link of the chain must be positively reinforced. The occurrence of this terminal satisfaction strengthens the whole motor chain. Immediacy of reinforcement is also essential to maximum learning.

5. With all of the above conditions met, many chains are learned in one performance. Others require repetition for learning efficiency.

presented and performed in close succession if the chain is to be learned.

4. Generally, knowledge of results is all that is necessary to reinforce the entire chain, although some method of giving the learner feedback as to his response is also important.

5. The materials to be learned at one time should be kept within the "immediate memory span" of about seven links or units.

6. Since verbal chains typically are longer than motor chains, some repetition is crucial.

In summary, then, the classroom teacher might keep in mind the following points when directing the student into a verbal chain:

1. Be certain that each S–R task involved in a verbal chain has already been learned before trying to teach the whole chain.
2. Strive for a highly orderly sequence of links in the chain, avoiding unnecessary links. Irrelevant S–R connections compound the learning difficulty and decrease learning efficiency.
3. If the total response chain exceeds the optimal seven-link chain described by Gagné, it might be better to break the information down into chain segments, making sure each segment is learned before they are combined to form the longer, desired chain.
4. Since contiguity is necessary for chaining to occur, make sure that all desired links in the chain are presented contiguously with each other.
5. Since a student learns by doing, arrange for the student to respond immediately (contiguity) to the presented stimulus.
6. Initially provide verbal cues and visual aids that will serve as external mediating connections for the learner and supplement the internal coding process.
7. After the final response of the chain is emitted, reinforce.
8. The frequency with which verbal chains are used will determine to some extent how well they are retained, although the demand for continuous practice of verbal chains is not as great as it is in the case of motor chaining.

APPLICATION OF CHAINING TO CLASSROOM LEARNING

The meaningfulness of theoretical concepts lies, of course, in their applicability to classroom situations. We have just discussed the learner and teacher conditions for chain learning. Now we can apply these conditions to a typical classroom verbal chain, as follows:

The Planets

> *Verbal cue:* "Students, we have discussed the planets and their relationship to the sun. Gerald, will you list the planets for us, beginning with the planet closest to the sun. You can refer to the diagram on the board [Figure 5.5]."

The following considerations are important to the emission and learning of this verbal chain:

Learner conditions. The learner needs to have an existing knowledge of each planet; and while the simple memorization of the planet names and their relationship to the sun would meet the demands of the task, a more complete and stronger understanding of the material would result if the student also has learned the size, revolution time, and atmospheric conditions of each planet. The more information the learner can bring into such a chaining situation, the greater the chances that *meaningfulness* will exist and that the chain will be learned and retained.

Teacher conditions. Presenting the nine-link verbal chain in a logical distance sequence aids the learner, as does the use of the visual aid (Figure 5.5).

Reinforcement. Verbal praise might be sufficient here, but whatever the form of reinforcement, the important thing is that the learner is aware of receiving a positive feedback for this relatively long verbal chain. Such reinforcement will, of course, increase the probability of learning and subsequent correct response.

Extinction. When a student is emitting a verbal chain as long as this one, the possibility of emitting each link in an improper sequence is increased. If a student makes a mistake, either (1) correct him before he proceeds, or (2) return him to the point of error after he has completed the chain, correct the error, and then have him complete the corrected chain. Always make sure that the student completes the chain correctly, then reinforce.

Retention. The strength of the chain is facilitated by the logical, sequential pattern that exists within the nature of the material being learned. In addition, the material is appropriate and meaningful to the entire unit of study, the planets. Thus, retention is enhanced.

The next two illustrations are comprehensive classroom applications that will be carried through Chapters 6, 7, and 8 to help you "walk through" Gagné's learning hierarchy.

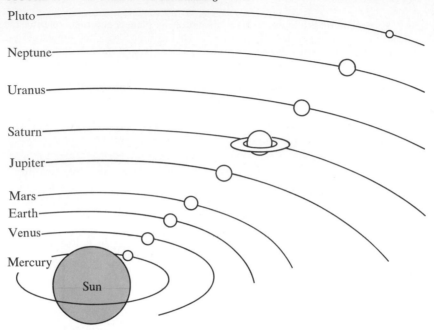

FIGURE 5.5.   The Planets—Verbal Chaining

The Chemical Plant Foods

Let us assume that a science class is going to learn the ten chemical foods required for plants to grow. The student must first learn the various chemical foods. The teacher might present the student with a very general stimulus—for example, "Name the ten plant foods"—but it would be better to tie each plant food to a specific stimulus, such as the atomic number (S_1), which would bring about the chemical (R_1). The eventual acquisition of the ten plant foods would occur when ten distinct $S_s \longrightarrow Rs$ had been learned.

It is important to remember that each $S_s \longrightarrow R$ when originally learned is an entity within itself; but to organize the ten level 2 responses more logically and therefore efficiently in the learner's repertoire, the teacher might build three subcategories that would encompass the already learned responses and could be learned as verbal chains. For example, the sources of chemical plant foods are of three categories: (1) air and water, (2) soil, and (3) fertilizers. Since the plant foods of carbon, hydrogen,

FIGURE 5.6.   The Chemical Plant Foods—Verbal Chaining

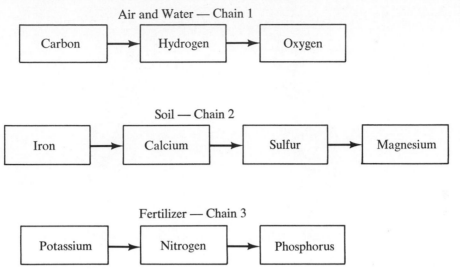

Air and Water — Chain 1

Carbon → Hydrogen → Oxygen

Soil — Chain 2

Iron → Calcium → Sulfur → Magnesium

Fertilizer — Chain 3

Potassium → Nitrogen → Phosphorus

and oxygen come from air and water, a verbal chain representative of this subcategory could be taught. It would appear as follows:

S_1 Verbal cue: "Name the plant foods which come from air and water." R_1 Carbon.

S_2 Having said carbon. R_2 Hydrogen.

S_3 Having said hydrogen. R_3 Oxygen.

The reinforcement for the chain would follow the final response. The teacher would then continue with a *soil* chain and a *fertilizer* chain (see Figure 5.6).

The Functions of Teeth

Since there are 32 teeth in the permanent arch, it is likely that the development of a verbal chain of responses would help the student's learning and retention of

FIGURE 5.7. The Upper-Arch Teeth—Verbal Chaining

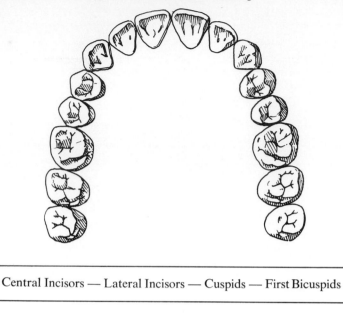

Central Incisors — Lateral Incisors — Cuspids — First Bicuspids

Second Bicuspids — First Molars — Second Molars —Third Molars

providing order to the subject. Thus, we can divide the teeth into two chains—the upper and the lower arch. In addition, starting with the teeth in the middle of each arch and moving to those teeth at the back of the arch will provide a logical sequence for the chains. The two verbal chains are, of course, identical, but they should be learned separately in order to make the student aware that while the names of the teeth in both arches are identical, they do not always have precisely the same physical appearance (see Figures 5.7 and 5.8). The identification and physical discrimination among the different teeth would be the subject of level 5 learning, which is explored in the next chapter. The *functions* of the teeth, which is the ultimate objective of this lesson, involves concept learning (level 6) and rule learning (level 7) and is discussed in Chapters 6 and 7.

FIGURE 5.8.   The Lower-Arch Teeth—Verbal Chaining

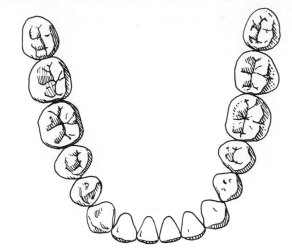

Central Incisors — Lateral Incisors — Cuspids — First Bicuspids

Second Bicuspids — First Molars — Second Molars —Third Molars

Copyright by the American Dental Association. Reprinted by permission.

SUGGESTED READINGS

Gagné, R. M.   Contributions of learning to human development. *Psychological Review,* 1968, **75,** 177–191. Reprinted in H. D. Thornburg (Ed.), *School learning and instruction: Readings.* Monterey, Calif.: Brooks/Cole, 1973, chap. 4.

Gagné, R. M., & Bolles, R. C.   A review of factors in learning efficiency. In E. H. Galanter (Ed.), *Automatic teaching: The state of the art.* New York: Wiley, 1959, pp. 13–53.

Green, R. B., & Rohwer, W. D., Jr.   SES differences on learning and ability tests in black children. *American Educational Research Journal,* 1971, **8,** 601–609.

Levin, J. R., Rohwer, W. D., Jr., & Cleary, T. A.   Individual differences in the learning of verbally and pictorially presented paired associates. *American Educational Research Journal,* 1971, **8,** 11–26.

Mathis, C.   Implications of modern learning theory for the secondary school. *High School Journal,* 1965, **48,** 411–418.

Rock, I.   The role of repetition in associative learning. *American Journal of Psychology,* 1957, **70,** 186–193.

Wike, S. S.   The effects of feedback, guessing and anticipation rate upon verbal discrimination learning. *Psychological Record,* 1970, **20,** 171–178.

Williams, J. P.   A test of the all-or-none hypothesis for verbal learning. *Journal of Experimental Psychology,* 1962, **64,** 158–165.

6

Multiple Discrimination and Concept Learning

This chapter is concerned with *multiple discrimination learning* and *concept learning,* levels 5 and 6 of Gagné's hierarchy of learning. Both have as their basis the phenomenon of *single discrimination learning* (level 2 of the hierarchy), which is the specific establishment within the learner of single S–R connections or chains $(S_s \longrightarrow R)$ that distinguish one class of things from another. Multiple discrimination is the learner's ability to discriminate among stimuli (objects, symbols, activities, or persons) that are all representative of a single *class* or *system.* In other words, this type of learning involves (1) the establishment of a number of different *single discriminates that are highly similar in their physical appearance and/or their characteristics,* and (2) a recognition of the differences among two or more of these similar single discriminates. Because the several similar but distinct single connections or chains (single discriminates) may interfere with one another's retention (Postman, 1961; Underwood, 1964a), multiple discrimination learning is considerably more complex than the single discrimination learning on which it is based.

Concept learning is the learner's ability "to identify (by class name or otherwise) a specific member of a class of objects, object properties, actions, or events, when that specific member is new to him" (Gagné, 1970b). Thus, the learner attains the capability to classify stimuli (to assign them into a class), to understand and respond to these stimuli as a single concept, and to extend this knowledge, or concept, to new and unfamiliar stimuli of that class. In Gagné's structure, concept learning is built on multiple discrimination learning. As we shall learn later, some theorists differ somewhat from Gagné on this latter point:

117

Consider the example of learning the color blue. When the student is asked to sort out the class "blue" by cards of various shades of blue (representative members of the class) from dark to light, multiple discrimination abilities are required. The learner must recognize that one card, named "navy blue," has discriminatory properties from (is distinct from) another, similar appearing card, named "sky blue." The basis of discrimination might be twofold: (1) recognition of the variation in shades in the cards from dark toward light, and (2) recognition of the differences in the cards by name, "navy blue" and "sky blue."

When the learner is asked the differences between the two cards, he must function at the concept learning level. It is no longer sufficient for him to recognize that the names or the shades of the cards are different. Now the learner must understand the *concept* of the class "blue" and have some knowledge of abstract properties of color and shade, such as hue, tint, brilliance, and saturation. This knowledge would then allow the learner to make an identifying response to an untitled card representing a third shade of blue—that is, to identify the unfamiliar shade as a member of the class "blue."

MULTIPLE DISCRIMINATION LEARNING

From early childhood through adulthood, an individual moves rapidly from knowing one object well to knowing two similar objects well while also understanding the differences between the two—that is, from learning not only two single discriminates but also one multiple discriminate. The ability to discriminate between similar, simultaneous stimuli makes multiple discrimination distinct from single discrimination learning. A three-year-old learns the difference between several stuffed animals he plays with; a second grader distinguishes between the different but similarly appearing words that he studies; a seventh grader learns the difference between geometric figures; a college football player acquires different offensive formations, and a vacationer uses different road maps while traveling. Each of these examples describes multiple discrimination learning.

Remember that multiple discrimination learning is the ability to make *different* responses to *similar* stimuli of the *same class* or *system* (Gagné refers to the latter as "sets of associates"). Single discrimination learning, in contrast, refers to the acquisition of simple S–R connections for the discrimination of stimuli from different classes. Level 5 learning (multiple discrimination) is a higher, more complex response than level 2 (single discrimination) because (1) the learner has learned discriminatory properties among several similar things, and (2) these discriminatory properties have more associative strength (level 4 learning) than they had when originally acquired as single level 2 connections.

The classroom teacher uses multiple discrimination quite often in his teaching. Within school, the learner acquires multiple discriminates among the members of a *class* of people, objects, subjects, and activities. This discrimination is expressed in terms of *characteristics*—the distinct sizes, shapes, dimensions, angles, colors, volumes, densities, actions, functions, symbols, or numbers, and so on, of the members of a class. Take, for example, the student of Spanish who is learning the first ten ordinal numbers in that language. The initial learning phase is the establishment of single $S_s \longrightarrow R$ connections (single discriminates) for each of the numbers:

$$
\begin{array}{lll}
S_1 & \text{primero} \longrightarrow R_1 & \text{first} \\
S_2 & \text{segundo} \longrightarrow R_2 & \text{second} \\
S_3 & \text{tercero} \longrightarrow R_3 & \text{third} \\
S_4 & \text{cuarto} \longrightarrow R_4 & \text{fourth} \\
S_5 & \text{quinto} \longrightarrow R_5 & \text{fifth} \\
S_6 & \text{sexto} \longrightarrow R_6 & \text{sixth} \\
S_7 & \text{séptimo} \longrightarrow R_7 & \text{seventh} \\
S_8 & \text{octavo} \longrightarrow R_8 & \text{eighth} \\
S_9 & \text{noveno} \longrightarrow R_9 & \text{ninth} \\
S_{10} & \text{décimo} \longrightarrow R_{10} & \text{tenth}
\end{array}
$$

Once the ten ordinal numbers have been learned separately, the basis is set for learning their discriminatory properties as a whole. These may be acquired in two ways: (1) by learning their differences in pronunciation and writing, and (2) by recognizing their usage in sentences. For example, the learner may be asked to translate the following phrases into Spanish:

the second time	la segunda vez
the seventh hour	el septimo hora
the third lesson	el leccion tercera
the fifth day	el quinto dia
the first month	el primer mes
the sixth exercise	el ejercicco sexto

Or he may be asked to respond, as follows:

Teacher: Is he *dos* (two) years old today?
Student: Yes, this is his *segundo* (second) birthday.

Teacher: Are you on lesson *seis* (six)?
Student: Yes, I am on the *sexto* (sixth) lesson.

The requirements for this learning are the following:

1. *Having the prerequisite knowledge.*   The teacher must be sure that the student has acquired all the basic information necessary to learn the multiple discriminatory material. Such prerequisite information would include the following, in order:
   a. The cardinal and ordinal numbers in English.
   b. The characteristics of ordinal numbers in English (if the learner knows the use of ordinal numbers as adjectives, it will be easier for him to distinguish between cardinal and ordinal numbers).
   c. The cardinal numbers in Spanish (if the learner knows the proper use of these numbers, his knowledge will facilitate his understanding and learning of the Spanish ordinal numbers).
   d. The ordinal numbers in Spanish (learned individually as single discriminates).
   e. The characteristics of ordinal numbers in Spanish (the learner must understand their use as modifiers, as in English, and he must also know their basic properties—that the Spanish ordinal numbers must agree in number and gender with the nouns they modify).
2. *Avoiding interference.*   Within a class of things, it is not uncommon for the learning of one single discriminate to interfere with the learning of another. The most efficient way to counteract interference is to repeat the learning process. Thus, in the situation

Teacher: Are you on lesson *seis* (six)?
Student: Yes, I am on the *septimo* (seventh) lesson.

The teacher could correct the failure of the student to make this multiple discriminate by expanding the use of *sexto* and *septimo* and reinforcing the distinction between the two terms until distinct discriminatory properties were expressed by the learner (see p. 122 on reinforcement and extinction with multiple discriminates).

Regarding the second point—the problem of *interference*—numerous studies have confirmed that multiple discrimination learning is seriously subject to this inhibition of one association by another similar association. All of these experimental studies have focused on paired verbal associates, ranging from paired nonsense syllables to paired synonyms. Deliberate interference conditions invoked in these experimental studies assess (1) how much interference may occur in the learning of two tasks at varying degrees of similarity, and (2) the retention rates of materials learned on a paired-associate basis. As a result of his studies, Gagné states that

> the most prominent phenomenon in multiple discrimination learning is interference. Whenever recall is attempted, whether during the course of learning the entire set or afterward, evidence is obtained of confusion among the links of the chains that make up the set. A response link that has been initially acquired as a part of one chain turns up in recall as part of a second chain, and vice versa. The chains GEX–JOYFUL, DAX–ANGRY, as members of a large set, have a tendency to be recalled as GEX –ANGRY, DAX–JOYFUL (p. 124).

The following studies have confirmed this finding:

1. Gibson (1940, 1941) presented subjects with two tasks of thirteen verbal chains. Task 1 involved highly similar nonsense figures, while task 2 involved dissimilar nonsense figures. Because of the high level of similarity in task 1, the multiple discrimination requirements were more difficult than in the dissimilar figures. Gibson found that task 1 required 19.8 trials to learn while task 2 took only 8.9 trials. Theoretically, task 1 was more difficult to learn because of the interference that occurred among the highly similar figures.
2. Underwood has studied interference and verbal association continuously since 1950 (1951a, 1951b, 1952a, 1952b, 1953, 1954, 1957; Underwood & Hughes, 1950; Underwood & Goad, 1951) has found that the greater the similarity of learned material, the greater the interference (errors) in recalling that material. An analysis of the errors also indicated that the more similar the errors were to the correct response, the more frequently they were likely to occur.
3. Coleman (1963) presented subjects with lists of paired noun–adjective associates. Upon learning, the subjects were asked to recall the lists, and Coleman found significantly fewer recall errors on the lists designed to have low-interference effects.
4. In a study designed to test the effects of learning facts in context or in isolation, Gagné (1969) found that facts presented in isolation were remembered better than facts presented in context, a phenomenon he attributes to the lack of interference in the former. A cautionary note should be made here. One might be mistakenly impressed that there can be little advantage to teaching material in a meaningful associative context. Quite the contrary has been shown; for when learning takes place, it occurs initially at level 2, which is the *association* of stimuli with responses, followed by reinforcement. The higher the meaningfulness in this type of learning, the more rapid the learning (Underwood, 1964b). The difficulty arises only with learning discriminatory properties among the members of a class—that is, among similar things. The concept of interference should not discourage the teacher from instructing at a meaningful level; rather, it should merely make one aware that the learner commonly has difficulty in sorting out multiple discrimination properties and, especially, in recalling such discriminates over time. Gagné (1969) stresses that

the real effects of interference show up most in the retrieval (recall) stage. They are not likely to be noticed in the learner at the acquisition stage.

While most learning in school requires verbal usage and involves facts, things, objects, or places, multiple discrimination is not always verbal, of course. Other things must be discriminated, and the phenomenon of interference must be dealt with in these kinds of learning too. Gagné (1965) makes this point well:

> The sender of Morse code learns a set of key-tapping patterns to differentiate the individual letters of the message he wants to transmit. The student of the clarinet learns to distinguish a set of printed notes by means of a set of fingering responses, each of which bears a specific relationship to a particular note. The operator of a panel controlling industrial or other machinery may have to learn a large number of different key-pressing responses that distinguish the various signals he receives. In all these instances, multiple discrimination is required of a set of chains that may have been (and preferably are) previously learned as individual entities. And in all these instances there are strong tendencies toward interference among the chains, interference that is overcome by the use of repetition [p. 124].

MULTIPLE DISCRIMINATION LEARNING IN THE CLASSROOM

The classroom teacher would do well to remember three basic principles regarding the building of multiple discrimination abilities in the learner: (1) Be sure that all material to be taught has previously been established as single discriminates—that is, at the stimulus–response level (level 2) of learning. (2) Be sure that the student has been presented with the material in such a way that he will recognize the basic physical distinctions among the discriminates. (3) Provide a *variety* of teaching–learning situations *(repetition)* for the material so that the student can confirm his understanding and acquisition of the discriminatory differences in the material.

As in all learning, *reinforcement* is an important factor in teaching multiple discriminates. If the student is reinforced for recognizing and acquiring the discriminatory properties of members of the same class of things, the chances of the same responses recurring on subsequent presentations are increased. *Extinction* may occur within multiple discrimination learning if the learner is not reinforced by the teacher, either purposely or inadvertently. However, the process of purposeful extinction (withholding of reinforcement) may not always be effective for level 5 learning. Unlike the earlier levels in Gagné's hierarchy, multiple discrimination learning is more effective if it is *intermittently* rather than continuously reinforced; and research has shown that intermittently reinforced learning is more resistant to extinction than learning with continuous reinforcement (Ferster & Skinner, 1957). To eliminate an inappropriate multiple discriminate response, then, it may be more appropriate to the learner—that is, to teach a desirable alternative response and continuously reinforce it so that it becomes stronger on subsequent stimulus presentations than the inappropriate response. For instance, if the teacher has imparted a unit on the difference between pronouns in the nominative and objective cases, using intermittent reinforcement, and a student continues to respond with an incorrect pronoun, the teacher should direct the student into the appropriate response and immediately reinforce it then and upon all subsequent emissions. The alternative process of attempting extinction of the incorrect response by simply failing to reinforce it is not likely to be as effective or fast in eliminating the undesirable response.

The following illustrations (Figures 6.1–6.5) show five different examples of multiple discrimination learning. You will immediately recognize that the level of complexity is different in all five tasks. It is important to remember, however, that the variable of complexity and difficulty does not necessarily mean that more complex material is at a higher level of learning. None of these five tasks go beyond the point of multiple discrimination to the level of conceptualization, or concept learning. On the other hand, since learning to recognize the differences among similar things is a prerequisite to conceptual learning, the exercises may be used to show the teacher that the students are capable of knowing the distinctive properties of different things of the same class and, therefore, that they are ready to conceptualize the class.

FIGURE 6.1. Multiple Discrimination Task I

The learner, when given a picture of an object or animal, will discriminate that object in a picture of a series of other objects of the same class.

The task for the learner is to see the similarity between the picture of the single object at the extreme left and the identical object pictured within the group of objects of the same class. This simple task demonstrates that the student can discriminate among objects of the same class—for example, apples and other objects that approximate roundness. In the case of the group of "B" words and "PI" words, the *terms* for the pictured objects are the focus of the multiple discrimination tasks, with the pictorial representations serving as aids for the task.

FIGURE 6.2.   *Multiple Discrimination Task II*

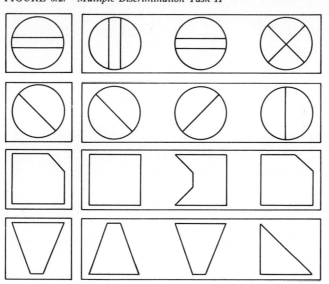

The student is asked to mark those geometric designs that are alike.

This task is not unlike the first. The primary difference is in the dimension of the task—that is, distinguishing among similar but distinct geometric designs is more subtle and difficult multiple discrimination task.

FIGURE 6.3.   Multiple Discrimination Task III

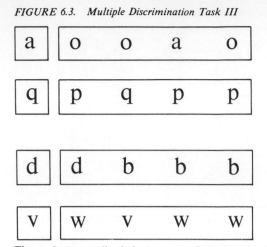

The student must discriminate among similarly appearing letters in the alphabet.

One of the common discriminatory tasks required in the primary grades is learning to distinguish between similarly appearing letters in the alphabet. This illustration shows how a teacher might teach such multiple discriminatory learning.

FIGURE 6.4. Multiple Discrimination Task IV

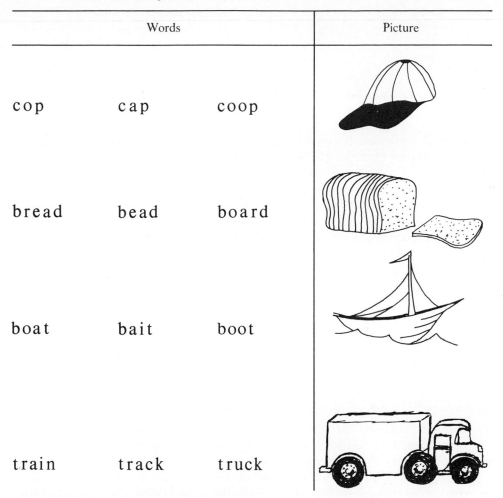

Words			Picture
cop	cap	coop	
bread	bead	board	
boat	bait	boot	
train	track	truck	

The learner is able to associate the name of the object with a picture of the object.

This is a more complex multiple discrimination task. The student must have previously acquired a recognition of each object and of the correct word associated with each object and must now distinguish among the similar appearing words. Thus, the words "cap," "cop," and "coop" are similar in appearance, and the picture of the cap provides a test of the student's ability to discriminate among these words.

FIGURE 6.5.   Multiple Discrimination Task V

Syllables	Phonetic Key
hom	ohm
ham	ahm
neu	nweh
qua	kwah
jue	way
bue	b'way

The student must pronounce the phonetically distinct Spanish syllables.

Upon cursory inspection, it would appear that the material in this task involves stimulus–response rather than multiple discrimination learning. If entirely dissimilar Spanish syllables were to be presented with their phonetic pronunciations, then, indeed, this would be the case. However, with several similar sounding syllable–phonetic combinations presented, the task requires discrimination. For instance, the distinction between pronunciation of "hom" and "ham" is subtle but very important. "Hom" is the first syllable in *hombre,* which means "man." "Ham" is the first syllable in *hambre,* which means "hungry." The same problems of pronunciation arise with the similar sounding syllables "neu," "qua," "jue," and "bue."

CONCEPT LEARNING

As was stated earlier, Gagné's hierarchy suggests that concept learning (level 6) is based on the learning of a number of multiple discriminates (level 5). Thus, when given a group of objects previously identified in single S–R connections, the learner can differentiate among them (single discrimination) and sort them out into categories of similar but distinguishable objects (multiple discrimination). Then when given a new object, the learner can identify it and place it into the appropriate category of objects and/or subcategory of discriminated similar objects (concept learning).

The basic difference between multiple discrimination and concept learning is the versatility of response that the latter affords the learner. When an individual learns distinguishable differences among a number of similar single S–R connections (members of the same class), multiple discrimination exists, and the learner is able to differentiate among things he has *already learned.* In contrast, when an individual learns to recognize a number of multiple discriminates as a class and is able to identify and respond to new and unfamiliar stimuli as members of that same class, a concept (the class) has been learned, and the learner is able to identify and differentiate among things that are new and not previously learned.

The simplest type of concept learning involves what Gagné (1970a) refers to as *concrete concepts*. These are any class of objects that can be *observed*. In contrast, there are *relational concepts* that are purely abstract and, thus, representative of a more advanced conceptual level. This level of concept learning is discussed in the next chapter under *rule learning* (level 7).

Concrete concepts are learned *initially* through the association of a term or action with an object—that is, through the learning of single discriminates (level 2 learning). For example, assume a teacher wishes his student to learn the concept "round." He then might place a set of three objects ○□□ in front of the learner. He tells the learner that a surprise is under one of the objects but does not reveal which object has the surprise. Unknown to the learner, he places the surprise under the round object and will continue to do so throughout the learning process. On the first trial, the student lifts the objects until he finds the surprise under the round one. The object is then identified as "round." The learner has, at this point, associated the stimulus (round object and word "round") with the response (lifting) and has been reinforced (surprise). To establish this single discriminate ($S_s \longrightarrow R$), the teacher presents the problem to the student again, varying the position of the round object—□□○, □○□—so that the learner comes to respond to the round object and the word "round" rather than to the placement of the objects. However, so long as the learner depends on the placement of the round object among these now-familiar other objects (□□), even without the continuous reinforcement of the surprise, he is exhibiting multiple discrimination learning. Only when the student is always able to identify *any* round objects as a member of the category "round" can we infer that concept learning has occurred.

Thus, to move toward concept learning, the teacher must now present the learner with various arrangements of different and *unfamiliar* sets of objects, including △○□, □○□, ○□△. The teacher will discover with successive trials and varying positions of the objects (with infrequent reinforcement) that the child learns always to select the round object on demand, regardless of its position or the shape of the accompanying objects. In other words, the learner comes to operate at a conceptual level—to discriminate among a variety of *new* sets of objects in order to identify and respond to the "new" round objects. He is responding, then, to the concept "round"; he understands the class of "round objects" and is able to identify and respond to an object of that class even though it is presented in an unfamiliar context.

Further confirmation of the conceptualization of "round" can be demonstrated by providing the learner with a variety of round objects that vary in size and context—for example, a quarter, a saucer, a volleyball, an automobile tire, a washtub, a clock, and a propeller. If the student recognizes that each object is round, although they are all different in some respects, he has learned the concept being taught.

More specifically, to point up the *prerequisite* learning that must take place in order to facilitate concept learning, we can examine another simple situation, the learning of the functions of eating utensils. The following concrete concepts are to be taught in this lesson: (1) when to use a knife, (2) when to use a fork, and (3) when to use a spoon.

Level 2 learning.   The learner must *know* (have established single discriminates for) the objects knife, fork, and spoon and the further subcategories of dinner knife and steak knife, salad fork and dinner fork, and teaspoon, soup spoon, and tablespoon.

Level 4 learning.   The learner may find it advantageous to develop verbal chains based on the subcategories of knives, forks, and spoons learned at level 2. This is not a compulsory prerequisite condition for concept learning, but verbal chains are helpful in efficiently organizing and handling a learning situation with numerous responses. The learner makes verbal associations between the responses that are common or that logically fit together. This process may facilitate the learning of the concepts of when to use the utensils since the student will have already logically organized the multiple discriminates among the similar subcategories.

Level 5 learning.   The learner is able to sort out numerous eating utensils (the class) according to known categories (multiple discriminates). In particular he is able to distinguish between the similarly appearing subcategories and the general categories, such as the salad fork and the dinner fork. The learner does not, as yet, acquire knowledge of the functions of the utensils.

Level 6 learning.   While the ultimate objective of this lesson is to have the learner acquire the appropriate *uses* of the utensils, the learner must also know that a salad fork and a regular fork, though serving different functions, are both members of the category "forks," just as the teaspoon, soup spoon, and tablespoon are all spoons. It would be best, then, to teach the concept or function of one utensil at a time. By so doing, the learner is able to recognize members of a class, such as forks, while also learning the different concepts (functions) of the two kinds of forks. The function of a dinner fork might be taught first. The learner would be presented with several foods only one of which would be appropriate for a fork. For instance, the learner might be presented with a bowl of soup, a serving of corn, and a hot roll. Upon subsequent similar presentations, the learner eventually emerges with the concept "fork"—that is, its appropriate use with certain categories of foods.

The learner might then be presented with a salad and the salad fork. When the connection was established, he would be presented with both forks and a serving of salad and corn and could be expected to distinguish the functions of the two kinds of forks. Eventually, upon acquisition of all the utensil concepts, the learner might be presented with a meal in which each utensil is to be appropriately used.

One further point should be made about this illustration. The learner has acquired some multiple discriminates regarding these eating utensils through everyday practice, although he may not have had specific teaching such as has been described. But, without question, the previous practical use of silverware does provide the learner with some preexisting knowledge about the names and uses of the utensils.

As we have seen, Gagné describes concept learning as a cumulative effect, after previously acquired knowledge is clearly evidenced at the lower levels of his hierarchy. Some theorists, such as Ausubel, Piaget, and Klausmeier differ slightly from the Gagné position. These men are cognitivists, writing within the traditions of *Gestalt psychology*. In the 1920s, when Gestalt psychology was popularized, proponents of that theory maintained that *insight*—discovering the relationships in a whole concept—was the fundamental basis of concept learning, not the gradual building of S–R connections for the component elements of a whole concept, as the stimulus–response theorists contended. Gestaltists indicated that through stressing the whole instead of the parts, the parts and relationships would follow intuitively. Contemporary Gestaltists have moved closer to the behavioral theorists' position on concept learning, although there are still notable differences in terminology and emphasis.

For example, Ausubel (1968) contends that we acquire concepts through two processes: *concept formation* and *concept assimilation*. In speaking of concept formation, Ausubel states:

> Concept formation is characteristic of the preschool child's inductive and spontaneous (untutored) acquisition of generic ideas (for instance, "house," "dog") from concrete–empirical experience. It is a type of discovery learning involving, at least in primitive form, such underlying psychological processes as discriminative analysis, abstraction, differentiation, hypothesis generation and testing, and generalization [p. 510].

Thus, in concept formation, the learner discovers relationships—the similarities within a class of objects—and gradually obtains a working concept through experience within the classroom or in real-life situations.

Ausubel's concept assimilation is a type of concept learning more characteristic of older children and adults. They learn "new conceptual meanings by being presented with the critical attributes of concepts and by relating these attributes to relevant established ideas in their cognitive structures" (Ausubel, 1968, p. 511). Thus, as the learner becomes aware of the various criteria that are the basis of all concepts, and as he applies these criteria to the ideas and information he has already acquired, new concepts and conceptual meanings are assimilated.

It is clear that the cognitivist view of concept learning is a much less ordered process than that put forward by the stimulus–response psychologists, who hold that the presentation and learning of cumulative sets of appropriate S–R connections are necessary for the acquisition of a concept. But aside from the more prescriptive and structured description of concept learning by behaviorists like Gagné, the cognitivist and behaviorist views really speak to the same point, which is that concept learning cannot be described as a new phenomenon within the learner. The writings of Ausubel (1968), Piaget (1952), Klausmeier & Ripple (1971), and Gagné (1970a) all attest that concept learning cannot take place without some kind of previously established learning. Ausubel speaks of "concrete-empirical experience," "underlying psychological processes," and "established ideas." Gagné refers to a hierarchy of learning levels and prerequisite knowledge. Both are acknowledging a cumulative effect in concept learning. Moreover, Gagné, like the cognitivists, wishes to acknowledge a clear-cut break between the more mechanical learning processes of his lower learning levels and the versatility and cognitive freedom and creativity of concept learning. If we look again at the learning processes described up to this point in the book, it is clearly evident that learning at level 2, levels 3 and 4, and level 5 is a result of the acquisition of specific responses to specific stimuli. However, with level 6, concept learning, Gagné (1970a) contends that the "effect . . . is to free the individual from control by specific stimuli" (p. 182). Therefore, Gagné introduces at level 6 a nonmechanized learning function—a mediational thinking process that has as its background relevant stimulus–response bonds and discriminates but does not require a specific stimulus for each conceptual response.

Finally, it should also be noted that Gagné's definition of concept learning requires concrete referents or concepts, a condition similar to the "concrete-empirical experience" described by Ausubel for his concept formation. Thus, in Gagné's hierarchy, concept learning cannot generalize to abstract relational concepts, which he sees as a higher learning function and describes at level 7. As we shall see, this latter learning is comparable to Ausubel's definition of concept assimilation.

CONCEPT LEARNING IN THE CLASSROOM

When a student operates at this level, the responses he has learned realize greater meanings and gain internal associative relationships and strengths with both previous and present learning materials. The teacher can best assist the learner by (1) establishing the prerequisite knowledge required for the concept learning, and (2) specifically teaching abstract properties or characteristics for classes of objects so that the learner acquires some basis for classification other than simply physical characteristics.

Once a student has learned a concept, he is no longer required to be under the strict stimulus control needed with lower-level learning. The student's dependency on the teacher for appropriate stimuli is reduced, and simple spoken or written verbal

---

The students in a geometry class have difficulty distinguishing different geometric shapes. Although they all know a triangle, they do not always correctly identify quadrilaterals, pentagons, hexagons, octagons, and decagons. *What type of learning is involved here, and how can the material be more effectively taught?*

This problem gives us an excellent opportunity to review briefly the distinction Gagné made between multiple discrimination learning and concept learning. At first glance, the above learning task appears to fit the multiple discrimination category. But in actuality, it requires that the student operate at the concept learning level. Why?

Multiple discrimination learning means that an individual is able to distinguish among several similar things on the basis of their physical differences. A triangle is distinctly different from an octagon, and so on. Therefore, the student must first learn the physical properties and the name of each distinct shape. Then when all of the above mentioned shapes are presented as a group to the student in a learning trial, he should be able to correctly identify them (to discriminate among them).

But what happens when the student encounters new and differently composed triangles or octagons? He is no longer able to simply distinguish between the shapes he has learned, because these new figures are shaped somewhat differently. He must now have learned the conceptual properties that go into making a triangle "three-sided," a hexagon "six-sided," or an octagon "eight-sided." Learning what makes a shape a particular geometric figure implies an understanding of the concepts of figures. The multiple discrimination tasks are prerequisite to the concept learning task, but the former is restricted to observable physical properties alone, while conceptualization infers some understanding of nonphysical, or abstract, properties. Therefore, such material can be most effectively taught by stressing the nonphysical identifiable properties that make one figure three-sided and another eight-sided—that is, the abstract properties of figures, such as space, area, proportion, and geometric design.

instructions become sufficient. He becomes capable of generating responses internally and environmentally without direct stimulus presentations, and he is free to apply his concepts to a multiplicity of events or situations. The environmental concepts will help the student apply his learning to the things he encounters and thus add relevance to the world around him. The internal academic concepts will help the student meet, acquire, and extend the varied stimuli subsequently presented to him within the classroom.

The requirements for reinforcement are not as demanding with concept learning as at the lower hierarchical levels. This is so because (1) to maintain a response up through level 6 means that the student has had, over a period of time, sufficient acquaintance with the response, (2) the increased associative strength within the learner may itself be reinforcing, and (3) the student may begin supplying his own internal reinforcers to the learning situations.

Since responses take on more meaning, become associated with one another, and may be internally reinforced at the concept learning level, the extinction process becomes so confused that it is not safe to conclusively say that extinction can take place at this level. As with multiple discrimination, the teacher will find it more advantageous to present alternative responses and reinforce them so that a strong substitute conceptual response may be made for an incorrectly learned concept.

MULTIPLE DISCRIMINATION AND CONCEPT LEARNING—A SUMMARY

The following comparison of classroom examples will help the reader to better distinguish between multiple discrimination (level 5) and concept learning (level 6).

1. *Level 5.* The learner is presented with both Arabic numbers and Roman numerals and is able to discriminate between samples of the two types of numerical systems.
   Level 6. The learner is capable of equating Arabic numbers and Roman numerals.
2. *Level 5.* The learner is able to differentiate the numbers 1 through 10. He knows their names and can correctly assign the name to the number.
   Level 6. The learner is able to order the numbers as to position on the numerical scale because he understands their relationships.
3. *Level 5.* The learner is able to discriminate among different colors and associate a color to its name.
   Level 6. The learner is able to make three secondary colors from three basic colors.

4. *Level 5.* The learner is able to distinguish the fly, bee, cricket, and grasshopper from one another.

   Level 6. The learner is able to classify the insects arthropods according to their appendages and body parts.

5. *Level 5.* The learner is able to distinguish different types of domestic and wild cats by their color, fur, size, names, and so on.

   Level 6. The learner is able to classify a group of cats according to the subcategories of domestic and wild.

The government instructor finds that his students remember why our nation enacted certain legislation but cannot remember when, or who introduced the bills. *Could the problem be that the student responses required here are on two distinct operational levels?*

This problem raises the question of what the teacher really wants his students to learn. Remembering reasons for enacting legislation is conceptual, whereas recalling dates and names is simple stimulus–response learning. However, since concept learning is a higher learning level and, thus, more representative of intellectual functioning than S–R learning, it would seem that the students are successfully learning the really crucial aspects of the material. Still, if dates and names are equally important to the teacher, simple practice and repetition will be the most effective technique for helping the students to retain them. It would be well for the teacher to remember, though, that teaching, learning, and retention is most effective when the students are focused on the central learning issues.

Figure 6.6 shows Gagné's hierarchy and the positions and relationships of multiple discrimination and concept learning. You will notice the heavy line between levels 5 and 6, which indicates the point on the hierarchy where nonconceptual learning is succeeded by conceptual learning. In other words, the first five levels on the hierarchy are thought to be learning that is acquired through specific stimulus–response patterns and without the necessity of conceptualization. Level 6, the first level of conceptualization, is based on but independent of specific S–R connections. It is therefore a mediating level that facilitates the acquisition of abstract, higher level responses.

FIGURE 6.6.   *Gagné's Hierarchy of Learning—Levels 5 and 6*

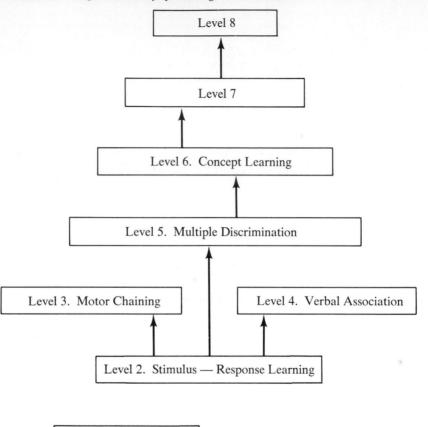

Multiple discrimination provides the physical discriminatory basis that allows the learner to formulate concepts based on nonphysical properties.

THE APPLICATION OF MULTIPLE DISCRIMINATION AND CONCEPT LEARNING TO CLASSROOM LEARNING

The Chemical Plant Foods

In the previous chapter, the learner acquired his level 2 responses for this lesson through verbal chaining. It is now possible for him to learn multiple discrimina-

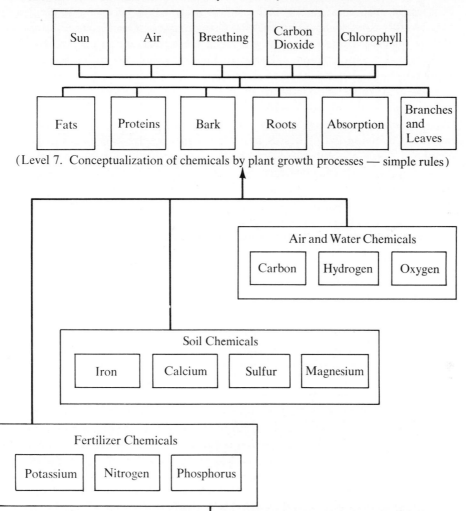

FIGURE 6.7. *Discrimination and Conceptualization of Chemical Plant Foods*

| Sun | Air | Breathing | Carbon Dioxide | Chlorophyll |

| Fats | Proteins | Bark | Roots | Absorption | Branches and Leaves |

(Level 7. Conceptualization of chemicals by plant growth processes — simple rules)

Air and Water Chemicals

| Carbon | Hydrogen | Oxygen |

Soil Chemicals

| Iron | Calcium | Sulfur | Magnesium |

Fertilizer Chemicals

| Potassium | Nitrogen | Phosphorus |

(Levels 5 and 6. Discrimination of chemicals and conceptualization by source and function)

Chemical Elements

tory responses. The requirement here is to be able to make distinctions, on the basis of physical properties, among each of the ten chemicals necessary to plant growth.

It is possible, however, that the distinctiveness of each chemical only becomes clearly relevant to the learner as a level of conceptualization occurs. The chemical element carbon, for example, takes on real meaning only when the learner knows the source from which it is derived and the function it performs as a plant food. Two levels of conceptualization are central to an understanding of the way plants get energy and grow. First, there are ten identifiable concrete concepts; namely, the ten chemical elements carbon, iron, potassium, and so on. Second, there are the more abstract concepts involving the processes by which plants receive energy from the chemical elements. These concepts are hierarchically advanced beyond the concrete concepts, since a level of abstract learning is required. Gagné (1970a) calls such advanced concepts *defined concepts* and states that they are more characteristic of simple rules (level 7), since the relationship between two or more concrete concepts is involved. This second conceptual level, then, will be explored in the next chapter. The first level—the ten concrete chemicals—is represented in Figure 6.7.

The Functions of Teeth

As we have learned, multiple discrimination learning is the ability to recognize the distinctive features among several similar things. The teeth provide a good example of how such discrimination can be learned. Two different discriminatory responses are shown in the example in Figure 6.8: The upper part of the illustration shows the differences in appearance of the first permanent molar and the central incisor and of the cuspid and the first bicuspid—all in the upper arch. The bottom part of the illustration shows the difference between the central incisors of the upper and lower arch. For complete multiple discrimination to occur in this lesson, the learner must be able to distinguish each of the teeth in the mouth in either arch (see Figure 6.9).

No understanding of function is expected at this point; but once the learner is able to identify all the teeth by appearance, he must then learn to identify them by growth and function—the beginning of concept learning. Now the learner must know that the central incisors are not just the middle teeth in the arch but also the first permanent teeth to erupt and the teeth that function to cut food. Therefore, the concept "cutting teeth" is learned, and the teeth that represent this function (the central and lateral incisors) are identified. Similar concepts are learned for the tearing teeth, tearing-grinding teeth, and grinding teeth (see Figures 6.10 and 6.11). The knowledge of these concrete concepts then makes it possible for the learner to acquire *rules* regarding the function of teeth—which involves rule learning, level 7 of Gagné's hierarchy.

FIGURE 6.8. *Discriminating Classes of Teeth*

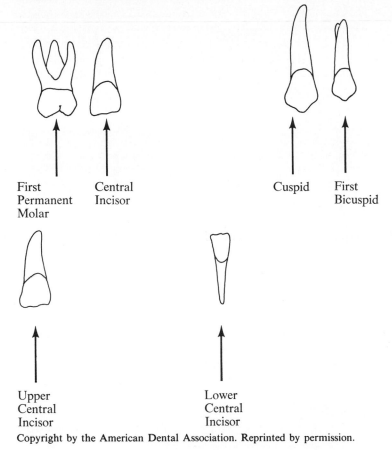

First
Permanent
Molar

Central
Incisor

Cuspid

First
Bicuspid

Upper
Central
Incisor

Lower
Central
Incisor

Copyright by the American Dental Association. Reprinted by permission.

The Varieties of Triangles

Multiple discrimination means that the learner can correctly distinguish triangles from other geometric figures and one triangle from another by name (see Figure 6.12). It does *not* mean that the learner knows *why* the triangles are different shapes. When the teacher and student begin to explore this latter question—what makes up

FIGURE 6.9. *Discriminating Teeth of Permanent Arch*

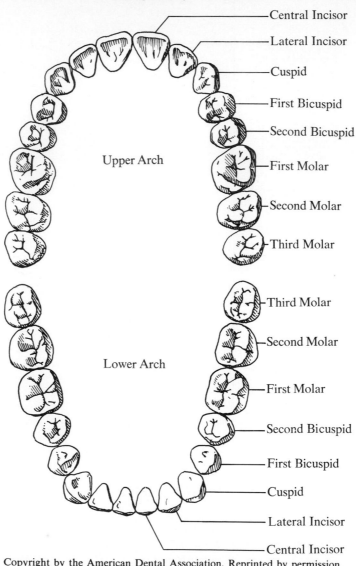

Central Incisor
Lateral Incisor
Cuspid
First Bicuspid
Second Bicuspid
First Molar
Second Molar
Third Molar

Upper Arch

Third Molar
Second Molar
First Molar
Second Bicuspid
First Bicuspid
Cuspid
Lateral Incisor
Central Incisor

Lower Arch

FIGURE 6.10. Conceptualizing Teeth by Growth and Function

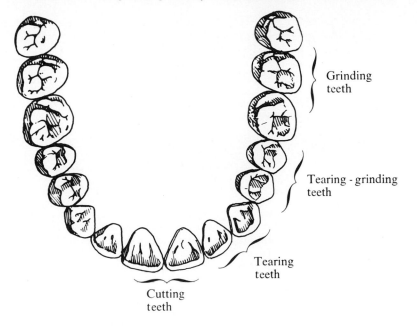

Grinding teeth

Tearing - grinding teeth

Tearing teeth

Cutting teeth

a triangle and why one triangle varies in shape from another—the concept level of learning is operating. The following sequence of background information would be necessary for the student to learn concepts about triangles:

A point . is a location in space. Once it has been located, it never moves. *Geometric figures* are sets of points connected by *lines,* and a *line* is a continuous movement from a point in space.

point

line

A *line segment* is the specific part of a line connecting two designated points.

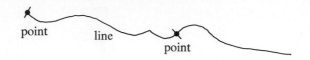

point   line   point

A *straight line segment* will always be the shortest pathway between two designated points in space. In most geometric figures, we must use straight line segments.

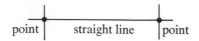

point   straight line   point

To form the geometric figure called a *triangle,* we must join *three* straight line segments in some way other than a straight line. The connection between the point of one of the straight line segments with the point of another of the straight line segments is called a *vertex (vertices).* We have now formed a *triangular region,* which is the three points and straight line segments of the figure, plus all the points (the *plane surface*) inside the figure. Now, we have a triangle.

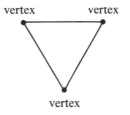

vertex   vertex

vertex

The following concepts have been learned in regard to the formation of triangles:

point
line
line segment
straight line segment
vertex
triangle
triangular region
plane surface

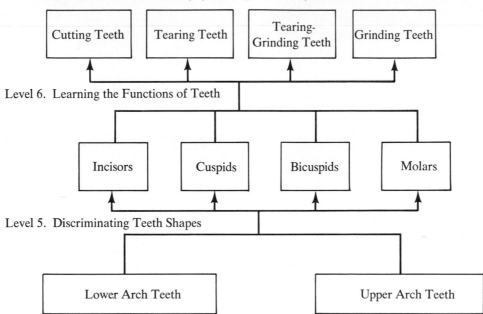

FIGURE 6.11.   *The Hierarchy of Learning Functions of Teeth*

Now, how is the learner to conceptualize the differences among the six varieties of triangular figures? This is dependent upon the student's learning the concept of *angle*. Thus, when a student sees a scalene triangle, he not only recognizes its difference in shape from the other triangles (multiple discrimination) but he knows that a scalene triangle has three unequal sides and straight line segments which form three unequal interior angles. The concept of angle would be learned, as follows:

An *angle* is a figure formed by two straight lines diverging from the same point. An *angle degree* is the measurement of the size of an angle. The measurement is based on the number of straight lines encompassed by the two lines of the angle if 360 straight lines were joined at a common point and placed side by side, and if the vertex of the angle were also joined to this common point. Each one of the 360 lines, then, represents *one* angle degree, and the number of angle degrees between the two lines of an angle determines the size and the classification or identity of that angle. Angles are classified as follows:

FIGURE 6.12.   Discriminating Triangles

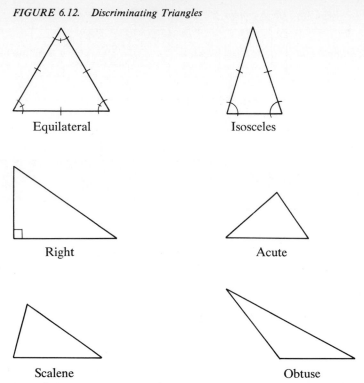

Equilateral   Isosceles

Right   Acute

Scalene   Obtuse

FIGURE 6.13. *Conceptualizing Triangles by Lengths of Sides and by Interior Angles*

Equilateral Triangle is a triangle that has three equal sides. An equilateral triangle is also *equiangular*. That is, the triangle's three interior angles are equal. In plane geometry, each interior angle in an equilateral triangle equals 60°.

Isosceles triangle is a triangle that has two equal sides. The third, unequal, side is called the *base*. The interior angle opposite the base is called the *vertex*. The two interior angles opposite the vertex are always equal.

Right triangle is a triangle one of whose interior angles is a right angle. That is, one interior angle equals 90°. The side opposite the right angle is called the *hypotenuse*. The other two sides are called *legs*.

Acute triangle is a triangle whose interior angles are all *acute*, or sharp. That is, each interior angle is less than 90°.

Scalene triangle is a triangle in which the lengths of none of the sides are equal. None of the angles of a scalene triangle are equal.

Obtuse triangle is a triangle one of whose interior angles is *obtuse*, or blunt. That is, one of its interior angles is greater than 90° and less than 180°.

From *The World Book Encyclopedia.* © 1971 Field Enterprises Educational Corporation.

Acute angle.   An angle that contains more than 0 and less than 90 angle degrees.

Right angle.   An angle that contains exactly 90 angle degrees. The lines, or *rays,* of such an angle are said to be *perpendicular* at the vertex.

Obtuse angle.   An angle that contains more than 90 but less than 180 angle degrees.

Reflex angle.   An angle that contains more than 180 but less than 360 angle degrees.

Straight angle.   An angle that contains exactly 180 angle degrees.

Once the learner conceptualizes what makes each triangle different (angle degrees), he then can identify the triangles by angle classifications rather than simply by multiple discriminatory differences (see Figure 6.13). This allows the student to consider other relevant aspects of angles and increase his knowledge of what makes a triangle what it is.

The following concepts have been learned about angles in order for the student to know the conceptual differences among the six triangular figures:

angle
interior angle
angle degree
acute angle
right angle
obtuse angle
reflex angle
straight angle

If the ultimate learning task of this lesson is either to find the area of a specific triangle or to draw a triangle, all of the concepts listed above are crucial to learning

FIGURE 6.14. *Discriminating and Conceptualizing Right-Angle Triangles*

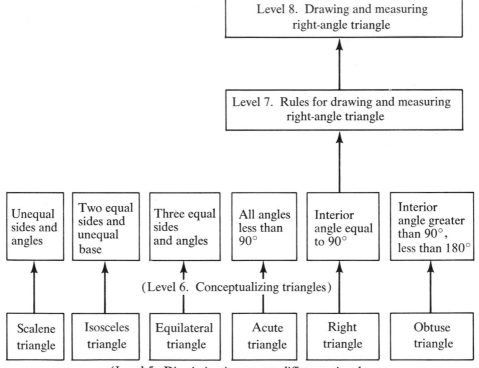

rules for dealing with triangles, the learning represented at level 7 of Gagné's hierarchy. We will single out the right triangle in the next chapter to show how rules emerge out of concepts (see Figure 6.14).

Possessive Nouns

For multiple discrimination to occur in this lesson, the student must be able to identify the singular possessives and plural possessives in a list of possessive nouns (see Figure 6.15). In addition, the student should be able to identify singular or plural possessives when they are presented out of the context of a list of possessives. The acquisition of this level 5 knowledge makes it much easier for the student to move on to the concept of possessive nouns—*why* a noun is possessive or nominative and why a possessive noun is singular or plural. This level 6, conceptual knowledge will, in turn, provide the learner with the necessary understanding to form *rules* (level 7) that demonstrate the contextual use of possessives. The learning of these rules is discussed at the conclusion of Chapter 8.

Finding the Circumference of Circles

Before the student can learn how to find the circumference of a circle, which involves rule learning and problem solving abilities (shown in Chapter 7), he must be able to distinguish a circle from all the other geometric figures (multiple discrimination) and to understand the meaning of circle and circumference (concept learning). Several other prerequisite concepts are necessary if the student is to be able to apply the mathematical formula (rule) for finding the circumference of a circle. First, the student must understand the difference between *rational* and *irrational numbers,* as illustrated:

$$
\text{Rational numbers}
\begin{cases}
.25 & \text{terminating decimal} \\
.333 & \text{repeating decimal} \\
.272727 & \text{periodic decimal}
\end{cases}
$$

*Irrational
number*   .314159

Upon learning what an irrational number is, the student can then see that *pi* (π), approximating the number 3.14, is an irrational number.

$$\pi = 3.14$$

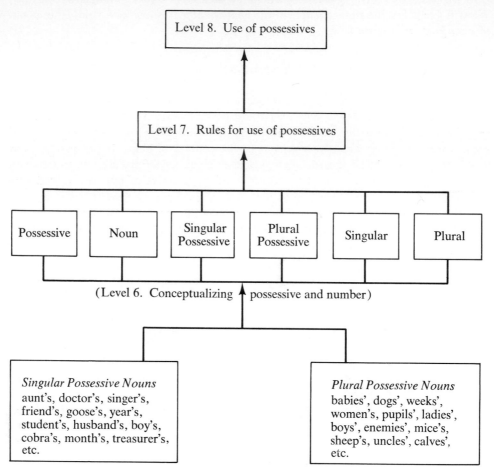

FIGURE 6.15. *Discriminating Singular and Plural Possessives*

Level 8. Use of possessives

Level 7. Rules for use of possessives

| Possessive | Noun | Singular Possessive | Plural Possessive | Singular | Plural |

(Level 6. Conceptualizing possessive and number)

Singular Possessive Nouns
aunt's, doctor's, singer's,
friend's, goose's, year's,
student's, husband's, boy's,
cobra's, month's, treasurer's,
etc.

Plural Possessive Nouns
babies', dogs', weeks',
women's, pupils', ladies',
boys', enemies', mice's,
sheep's, uncles', calves',
etc.

(Level 5. Discriminating singular and plural possessives)

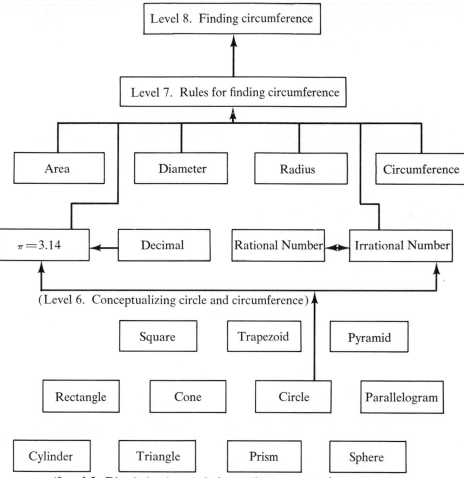

FIGURE 6.16. *Discriminating and Conceptualizing the Circle, Conceptualizing Circumference*

Level 8. Finding circumference

Level 7. Rules for finding circumference

Area   Diameter   Radius   Circumference

$\pi = 3.14$ Decimal   Rational Number   Irrational Number

(Level 6. Conceptualizing circle and circumference)

Square   Trapezoid   Pyramid

Rectangle   Cone   Circle   Parallelogram

Cylinder   Triangle   Prism   Sphere

(Level 5. Discriminating circle from other geometric figures)

Thus, other relevant concepts in finding the circumference of a circle are *pi, fraction,* and *decimal,* as well as *area, diameter,* and *radius.* Some of these concepts would, of course, also apply to the rules for finding the area of many other geometric shapes. See Figure 6.16 for a diagram of the relationship of these concepts in the hierarchy of learning to find circumference.

Finding Mathematical Unknowns

The terminal behavioral objective for the student in this illustration is the ability to apply two equations (level 7, rule learning) to problem solving situations (level 8 learning). The first equation involves finding the product when two factors are given; the second involves finding the unknown factor when one factor and the product are given. The basic mathematical concepts required are *multiplication* and *division.*

For this portion of the illustration, we will focus on the important prerequisite concepts (level 6 learning) necessary for the two rules to be learned. First, the learner must understand the basic terminology and units of measurement involved, including the concepts of *addition, sets, plus, equals, union, disjoint sets,* and *joint sets.* In addition, multiplication must be understood as an efficient way of addition. Consider the following illustration involving the union of sets, each of which consists of discrete (disjoint) elements:

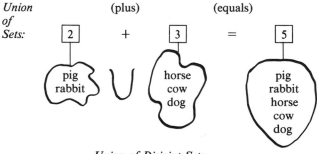

Union of Disjoint Sets

These basic concepts then provide the basis for learning the concept of *equal subsets:*

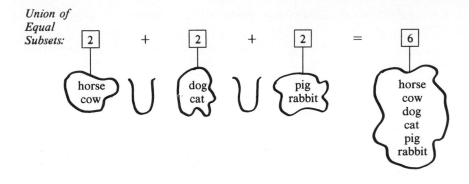

Union of Disjoint Subsets

Because the three subsets are equal and disjointed, the learner can now see that three subsets of two members each can be computed by the *multiplication equation* 3 × 2 = 6. In addition, knowing that there is a total of six objects and three equal subsets, the learner can determine how many members are in each subset by the *division equation* 6 ÷ 2 = 3.

All the basic processes (concepts) relevant to the two equations (rules) for this lesson are learned. Figure 6.17 shows the hierarchical arrangement of the concepts necessary for the acquisition of these rules. With the student understanding the basic concepts that go into set theory, such as the union and the intersection of sets, the basic mathematical operations illustrated here can be more easily understood and applied. This illustration is continued in Chapter 7 to demonstrate the relationship between concepts and rules. In addition, the rules and concepts may be seen operationally in their application to problem solving.

Three Types of Erosion in Streams

This illustration is confined to concept learning. For simplicity, only three types of erosion in streams are considered: *deepening, widening,* and *lengthening.* The goal of this lesson is the student's ability to observe a stream and tell which of the three erosion categories are represented by the stream's action. These conceptual responses are taught within a classroom situation through photographs, films, and field trips showing the student how to recognize one type of erosion from another (multiple

FIGURE 6.17. *Conceptualizing Multiplication and Division*

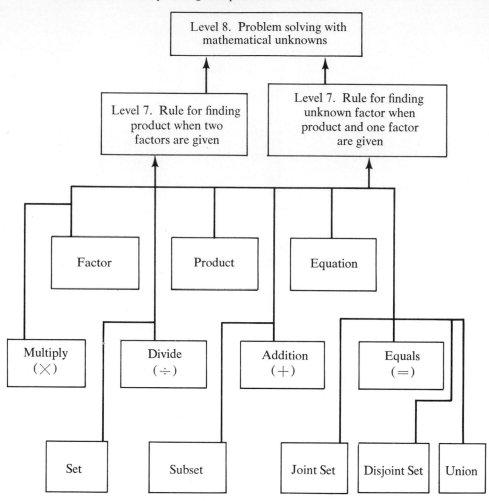

(Level 6. Conceptualizing terminology and units of measurement)

FIGURE 6.18.   *Conceptualizing Stream Erosion*

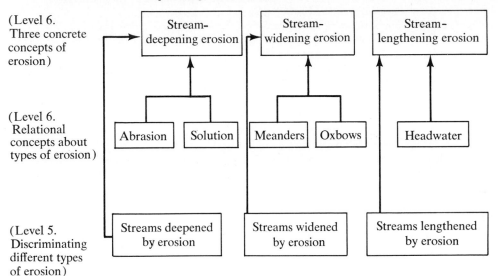

(Level 6. Three concrete concepts of erosion)

(Level 6. Relational concepts about types of erosion)

(Level 5. Discriminating different types of erosion)

discrimination) and the relationship of five different *causes* of erosion to these types of erosion (concept learning).

Thus, if a student recognizes *stream deepening* (multiple discrimination), he should also be able to extend this recognition by stating the two primary causes of such erosion: *abrasion* (wearing down by friction of pebbles, and so forth) and *solution* (dissolved material). In other words, two concepts are formed in the student's mind, abrasion and solution, and they provide the student with an understanding of how they contribute to stream deepening.

In a similar manner, the student should understand that *meanders* (back and forth cuts) and *oxbows* (meanders that are isolated from stream) contribute to *stream widening* and that *headwaters* contribute to *stream lengthening* by deepening gullies leading to the main stream bed. Figure 6.18 shows the hierarchical arrangement of this learning.

SUGGESTED READINGS

Carroll, J. B.   Words, meanings and concepts. *Harvard Educational Review,* 1964, **34,** 178–202.
Ellis, H. C.   *Human learning and cognition.* Dubuque, Iowa: Wm. C. Brown, 1972, chap. 5, pp. 136–155.

Eustace, B. W. Learning a complex concept at differing hierarchical levels. *Journal of Educational Psychology,* 1969, **60,** 449–452.

Gagné, R. M. The learning of concepts. *School Review,* 1965, **73,** 187–196.

Kendler, H. H. The concept of the concept. In A. W. Melton (Ed.), *Categories of human learning.* New York: Academic Press, 1964.

Klausmeier, H. J. Cognitive operations in concept learning. *Educational Psychologist,* 1971, **9** (1), 1–8. Reprinted in H. D. Thornburg (Ed.), *School learning and instruction: Readings.* Monterey, Calif.: Brooks/Cole, 1973, chap. 5.

Markle, S. M., & Tiemann, P. W. Behavioral analysis of cognitive content. *Educational Technology,* 1970, **10** (1), 41–45. Reprinted in H. D. Thornburg (Ed.), *School learning and instruction: Readings.* Monterey, Calif.: Brooks/Cole, 1973, chap. 5.

Spence, J. T. Verbal reinforcement combinations and concept-identification learning: The role of nonreinforcement. *Journal of Experimental Psychology,* 1970, **85,** 321–329.

7

Rule Learning and Problem Solving

This chapter discusses the two highest levels in Gagné's learning hierarchy, *rule learning* (level 7) and *problem solving* (level 8). Actually, both levels involve rule learning processes, with level 8 encompassing more complex rules. The rules infer the ability of the learner to function—that is, to use the knowledge he has acquired by learning both the rules and the cumulative prerequisite knowledge of the lower hierarchy levels.

The rules of both levels 7 and 8 are considered to be *relational concepts,* concepts that characteristically give meaning and strength to the simpler, concrete concepts of level 6. The following comparison of the conceptualization involved in these three levels will clarify this point:

> *Concrete concepts (level 6).* When a concept is learned through direct observation of physical objects or through an understanding of words that characterize the qualities or properties of objects, it is concrete (Gagné, 1970a). In this type of learning, a common identifying response may be made to several objects representative of the same class.
>
> *Relational concepts (level 7).* The concepts at this level are formed by two or more concrete concepts. Essentially, at this level, the learner is able to identify the functional relationship of two or more concrete concepts and to distinguish this relationship from other such relationships. "When the individual possesses the rule as a capability, he is able to identify the component concepts and to demonstrate that they relate to one another in the particular manner of the rule" (Gagné, 1970a, p. 192).
>
> *Higher-order relational concepts (level 8).* When new problematic situations occur, the learner combines two or more relational concepts to form a *new rule* that, when applied, will lead to the solution. In other words, "problem solving may be viewed as

a process by which the learner discovers a combination of previously learned rules that he can apply to achieve a solution for a novel problem situation" (Gagné, 1970a, p. 214).

Thus, the three levels of conceptual learning move from concrete to abstract understandings and result in the emergence of complex abstract thought. These three levels further imply a capability of intellectual functioning that is not found in levels 2 through 5. The learner's response repertoire becomes more flexible and less dependent on the immediate stimulus situation he encounters.

RULE LEARNING

If one understands what something is (a concept) and is able to relate it in a meaningful and functional way to another concept, we may assume a rule has been learned. Thus, in rule learning (level 7), it is not the complexity of the prerequisite concepts that is accentuated but rather their relationship, which allows the rule to emerge. As an individual learns more and more concepts, he gradually comes to use them in a variety of ways, so that, eventually, more complex rules are formed. The learning of rules thus ranges from simple to complex and operates in the learning of both very young children and adolescents and adults.

Of necessity, the rules that are learned are usually *verbal statements.* However, there are characteristic differences in these two elements of higher level learning. A rule is an "inferred capability" and a verbal statement is a "representation of a rule" (Gagné, 1970a, p. 193). Therefore, the learner's ability to verbalize a rule does not mean that he has also *learned* (*understood*) that rule. Verbal statements are built on verbal associations (level 4 learning), in which the learner combines several learned responses to make a logical statement. The statement does not, however, indicate any level of rule understanding or capability to act. Rules are built on concrete concepts, and the understanding of and implicit capability to act on these concepts determine whether the rule is learned. For example, the rule "Water is a compound of H_2O" is a verbal statement, but it is also characterized by certain concepts—"chemical," "elements," "hydrogen," "oxygen," "parts," and "compounds"—which must be learned if the rule is to be understood. On the other hand, while "knowing the verbal statement" does not necessarily mean "understanding the rule," it is, nevertheless, important to recognize that verbal statements usually enter in a crucial way into the process of *learning* a new rule.

Some pertinent comments from Gagné's *The Conditions of Learning* (1970a) seem most appropriate here for further clarification of this point:

> When a student is able to state the proposition that represents the rule, one does not usually assume from this evidence that he has, in fact, learned the rule. For example, a student may be able to state the verbal proposition "A millimeter is four hundredths of an inch," but his statement of this rule is unlikely to be taken as convincing evidence that he "knows the rule." Obviously, he may have learned the proposition as a verbal chain. To determine whether the rule, rather than merely its verbal statement, has been learned, one must find out whether the student can (1) identify the component concepts, namely, *inch* and *four hundredths,* and (2) show the relation between these concepts that constitutes a millimeter. There are various ways of doing this, but all of them appear to reduce to the act of *demonstrating* what a millimeter is. The student might be shown a scale of inches divided into hundredths and asked the question, "If each of these major divisions is an inch, show me how to determine how many millimeters an inch contains." The expected performance would be for the student to identify the "four hundredths" and by counting, obtain the number 25 [p. 194].

Simple rules

The theoretical framework for simple and complex rule learning is the same; the difference between the two rests in the substance of the material that is being learned. Since a young child has neither the prerequisite knowledge nor the intellectual maturity to learn algebraic equations or chemical formulas, such information is not taught until the necessary background knowledge and skills have been acquired. However, children do learn concepts and relations between concepts (rules) of a simple nature.

For example, a teacher can tell a young child that "Square objects can be stacked." This statement (a simple rule) requires prior learning of the concepts "stack" and "square objects." Two questions arise. First, if the student is presented with the task of stacking square objects, will he do it? Second, how does the teacher know that the prerequisite concepts for this task have been learned?

Let's answer the second question first. The child must understand square things. To do this, he must encounter a variety of objects that fit the general category "square." This may be accomplished by presenting the child with some objects that are round, others that are square, and still others that are highly similar to square (for example, rectangular). The name and appearance of the square objects are then taught with appropriate reinforcement (multiple discrimination). Then, when the child is presented with a new or novel square stimulus and he either identifies it or selects it rather than the round object, the teacher may assume that the concept "square" has been learned.

The child must learn the concept "stack," as opposed to "roll," in the same way. While this concept may be more difficult than "square" to teach, it can be done effectively if the square objects the learner already knows are used in the presentation of the stacking process. Also, it may be that the learner already knows the concepts "round" and "roll." If so, this knowledge will facilitate the learning of "square" and "stack." Eventually, the concept "stack" emerges, confirmed by the student's ability to apply it to new or novel square stimuli.

Now the first question can be answered. Once the two complementary concepts of "square" and "stack" have been learned, the child can be presented with a series of new objects that represent the two general categories "square" and "round." The teacher may then simply ask the question, "Which objects can you stack?", and the child should be able to apply the concepts he has learned and thereby acquire and act on the rule that "Square objects can be stacked."

Suppose a student, after having learned this rule, encounters hexagonal objects and discovers that they too will stack. Does this suggest that the hierarchical nature of Gagné's learning theory is naïve, that concept learning is based on discovery rather than on the prerequisite knowledge of lower levels of learning. Not at all. Two things have happened: (1) the concept "stack" is still operating, and (2) the concept "square" has simply been generalized by the student to flat-surfaced objects. This would give the teacher an opportunity to confirm the more sophisticated rule, "Flat-sided objects stack." The teacher would teach the concept "flat-sided object" in the same manner as "square" was taught; and if a high degree of discrimination among flat-sided objects is considered desirable by the teacher, then the learning must begin back with level 2, in which the learner acquires names for such objects as hexagon, octagon, triangle, and so forth. The learning of these objects at levels 5 and 6 would then follow.

Complex rules

Complex rules are based on (1) more difficult or sophisticated concrete and relational concepts, or (2) a greater number of concepts. The latter can be illustrated with the following rule:

To change an improper fraction into a mixed number, you must divide the numerator by the denominator and carry the remainder.

A relatively large number of concrete and relational concepts are prerequisite to the understanding and use of this rule:

> Fraction
> Improper fraction
> Whole number
> Mixed number
> Numerator
> Denominator
> Divide
> Change
> Carry
> Remainder

The other condition of rule complexity—more difficult or sophisticated concrete and relational concepts—can be illustrated with the following rule:

To write with unity in a paragraph, the student must present interrelated, coherent ideas that develop the intent of the paragraph.

This general rule is based on numerous concepts as well as the following *coordinate rules:*

(a) A unified paragraph has a clear intent: Its topic is either summed up in one of its sentences or definitely implied by its subject matter.
(b) The sentences in a unified paragraph develop a single central idea.
(c) The sentences in a coherent paragraph are arranged in a logical order.
(d) The sentences in a coherent paragraph are carefully related and connected to one another.
(e) A paragraph should develop its topic sentence adequately.
(f) The subject matter of the paragraph and the intent of the writer determine the way in which a paragraph is developed.

Each of these six coordinate rules states specific principles that the learner must know in order to understand and act on the more generally stated rule. They are called *coordinate rules* because they are equal in strength with one another and with the general rule in contributing to the learning and use of the general rule. Each of these coordinate rules is built, of course, on a number of *concepts,* among them:

1. Topic sentence (a)
2. Implied topic sentence (a)
3. Placement of topic sentence (a)
4. Intent (b)
5. Clarity (b, e)
6. Consistency (b, d)
7. Restriction (b)
8. Unity (b)
9. Logical order (c)
10. Chronological listing of events (c, f)
11. Coherence (c, d)
12. Repetition of grammatical structure (d)
13. Transitional words or phrases (d)
14. Repetition of key words (d)
15. Supportive reasons (e)
16. Use of examples (e)
17. Spatial order (f)
18. Logical order (f)
19. Expository writing (all)
20. Argumentative writing (all)
21. Deductive development (all, especially a)
22. Inductive development (all, especially a)
23. Narrative style (all)
24. Descriptive style (all)
25. Person (all)
26. Tense (all)
27. Number (all)
28. Parallel form (all, especially d)

All these concepts must be conceptualized and interrelated by the student writer as he formulates and organizes his ideas into sentence and paragraph form. They give the learner a working knowledge of the coordinate components that make up the principal rule for paragraph unity and coherence.

In short, the learner must acquire numerous complementary concepts and several coordinate rules in order to understand and apply an important rule regarding the writing of an effective paragraph. Therefore, a teacher wishing to instill such a complex and difficult rule must analyze all the components that go into the rule and make sure that these prerequisite concepts and coordinate rules have been learned. Nor should the teacher lose sight of the fact that concepts also have prerequisites and that several earlier learned stimulus–response bonds, verbal associations, and multiple discriminations are vital to the emerging concepts and rules. For example, let us trace just one of the 28 prerequisite concepts for paragraph development through its preconceptual levels:

13. Transitional words or phrases

In this concept, the student learns that sentences may be connected coherently by the use of transitional words or phrases. This knowledge is based on the recognition (conceptualization) of different categories of transitional words and the words that are representative of the categories:

a. *To indicate addition:*

again, also, and, and then, besides, equally important, first, finally, further, furthermore, in addition, last, lastly, likewise, moreover, next, second, secondly, third, thirdly, too.

b. *To indicate contrast:*

at the same time, although, true, but, for all that, however, in contrast, nevertheless, notwithstanding, on the contrary, on the other hand, still, yet, in spite of.

c. *To indicate comparison:*

likewise, in a like manner, similarly

d. *To indicate summary:*

in brief, in short, on the whole, to sum up, to summarize, in conclusion, to conclude.

e. *To indicate special features or examples:*

for example, for instance, indeed, incidentally, in fact, in other words, that is, specifically, in particular.

f. *To indicate result:*

accordingly, consequently, hence, therefore, thus, truly, as a result, then, in short.

g. *To indicate the passage of time:*

afterward, at length, immediately, in the meantime, meanwhile, soon, at last, after a short time, which, thereupon, thereafter, temporarily, until presently, shortly, lately, then, of late, since.

h. *To indicate concession:*

after all, of course, naturally, I admit, although.*

The learner must acquire enough familiarity with the words represented in each category to be able to discriminate among them and between them and other kinds of words when they are presented in a variety of situations (level 5). Thus, when the learner encounters the word "however," he recognizes it as a transitional word indicating contrast, as opposed to another transitional word, such as "similarly" (indicating comparison), or another type of word, such as "how," which is an adverb functioning to modify a verb. In addition, the words in each multiple discriminate category must have gained prerequisite associative strength (level 4) based on their function, because the words and their functions were originally learned as stimulus–response bonds (level 2). Of course, the ultimate task of learning rules for paragraph development is probably indicative of a high school level function, whereas most of the S–R bonds, associative

* Adapted from Leggett, G., Mead, C. D., & Charvat, W. *Prentice-Hall Handbook for Writers, Second Edition.* Prentice-Hall, Inc., © 1954, pp. 133–134. Used by permission of the publisher.

FIGURE 7.1.   *Learning Use of Transitional Words in Paragraph Development*

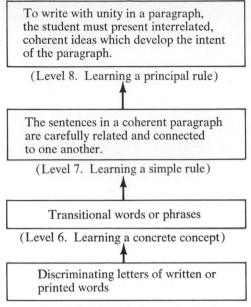

To write with unity in a paragraph, the student must present interrelated, coherent ideas which develop the intent of the paragraph.

(Level 8. Learning a principal rule)

The sentences in a coherent paragraph are carefully related and connected to one another.

(Level 7. Learning a simple rule)

Transitional words or phrases

(Level 6. Learning a concrete concept)

Discriminating letters of written or printed words

(Level 5. Multiple discrimination)

chains, and multiple discriminates have been learned at an earlier school level. It is even likely that many of the concepts were previously learned. Thus, this illustration shows the theoretical nature of the process of learning the task, but it does not really describe the task operationally. In operational terms, the teacher would be synthesizing these previously learned materials with the current learning of concepts and coordinate rules, so that the principal rule may emerge which gives the learner the basis for problem solving. This learning hierarchy is illustrated in Figure 7.1.

RULE LEARNING IN THE CLASSROOM

The accurateness and adequacy of rules depend on the level of concept attainment at the time the rule is learned. Thus, the first step to be undertaken by the teacher is to specify and analyze the rule he wishes the learner to acquire and, then, to make sure that the learner has previously acquired the concepts that are essential to the understanding and application of that rule. The rule will usually take the form of a verbal statement, and if it does, the teacher must be certain that what the learner ultimately acquires is not merely this verbal utterance but, rather, a true conceptualization of the rule. As we have noted, this level of learning is most easily and surely accomplished by reviewing for the student the concrete concepts that are the components of the rule to be learned. If the teacher finds that the student has not acquired one of the components, then, of course, it must be taught prior to the rule.

Once the teacher has (1) brought the relevant concepts to the learner's attention, and (2) indicated the rule that is being learned, it is also generally important to give the student an opportunity to demonstrate the functionality of the rule by both applying the rule and stating what has happened. If the rule infers capability, as most rules do, the learner can, of course, benefit by seeing the rule in operation. In addition, the recognition of successful performance both from the teacher and by the student himself has reinforcing value.

As in all learning, reinforcement at appropriate moments can be important in the retention of rules. The other important mechanism in retention—*contiguity*—is operant in rule learning when the component concepts of a rule are presented simultaneously. Indeed, this has proved to be the most functional way to learn a rule. It is also conjectured by some theorists that another mechanism—*meaningfulness*—may contribute to retention of rules more so than either contiguity or reinforcement. Let us consider the following points:

1. Response patterns that are prominent at the rule learning level have gained increased associative strength and meaning through contiguity and reinforcement as they have moved up the hierarchy from level 2 to level 7.
2. As the component concepts that form a rule become relevant for the learner acquiring that rule, the concepts gain a greater level of meaningfulness.
3. Rules are not simply responses to stimuli. A rule is a *conceptualized* thing; by its emergence from two or more concepts, it holds a meaning independent of lower level responses.
4. A rule is also a *productive* thing; that is, rule learning requires application, which may infer more meaningfulness than at lower levels of the hierarchy.
5. There is a greater resistance to forgetting at level 7 than at lower points in the hierarchy. Therefore, repetition does not seem to be a necessary condition for learning rules.

Research to substantiate these conjectures is very limited. Numerous studies have given evidence to the correlation between acquisition and meaningfulness (Ausubel, 1960, 1968), and a similar study by Rothkepf and Bisbicos (1967) indicates increases in retention by experimental groups who were presented with questions within a meaningful context. However, none of these studies considered meaningfulness within the dynamics of Gagné's hierarchy. It could be that the combined effects of (1) the movement of cumulative responses up through the hierarchy and (2) the increasing meaningfulness accompanying such movement make rule learning more resistant to forgetting than the lower levels of learning.

PROBLEM SOLVING

When an individual is confronted with a problem, it is not enough to say that he will intuitively come up with the solution. The simple fact is that every day people encounter problems that are new and very difficult and, often, insoluble. The individual does not always have the necessary "resources"—the prerequisite knowledge and thinking abilities—to solve problems. *Problem solving,* as level 8, is the highest type of learning within Gagné's hierarchy. Based on the combination of two or more rules, problem solving is the ability to encounter a novel situation and resolve it with a new rule. It provides the resources for encountering, for thinking, and for summoning up relevant materials previously learned.

In its simplest terms, problem solving means that an individual has learned the prerequisite skills and information necessary to the solution of a problem. More formally, we say that through the combination of two or more rules (level 7), the learner acquires new rules or new learning (level 8) that facilitates the solution of problems. Problem solving is often referred to as *complex rule learning* since two coordinate rules (level 7) are combined to form a more complex, *superordinate* rule that provides the capability of problem solving. Emerging from the new, higher-order rule, and from the problem solving behavior itself, is a new level of learning and capability that may be applied to subsequent problem situations either alone or in combination with other higher-order rules. Thus, a complex rule may be said to be prerequisite to actual problem solving behavior, while new learning and capability results from the behavior.

Two problem situations may serve to illustrate the processes at this level of learning:

Problem 1.   The following example is representative of a unit of instruction that would be taught in a third-grade English class. The teacher wishes the students to learn proper verb construction and to find several different ways to express an idea without changing the verb tense. At the moment, the past-perfect tense of the verb "to see" is being taught. The students are presented with the following information:

The teacher is discouraged. Regardless of the number of efforts he has made to teach his class the difference between a coordinating conjunction and a subordinating conjunction, the students do not do well in their work exercises. *Do we know enough today about how students learn, to help the teacher solve his problem?*

To help this teacher, we must first consider what student performances the teacher desires and what important prerequisite English skills the students must have in order to learn at the designated level. Materials to be learned should always be presented sequentially, on the basis of increasing complexity. For example, the student would undoubtedly be expected to learn simple sentences before he is taught compound or complex sentences. Similarly, one does not try to teach coordinating and subordinating conjunctions out of the context of sentences, clauses, and, particularly, compound and complex sentences. Thus, concepts and abilities should already have been learned for this lesson, including the following:

> Simple sentences
> Compound sentences
> Coordinating conjunction
> Complex sentences
> Independent clause
> Dependent clause
> Subordinating conjunction

Thus, the teacher would facilitate the student's learning of coordinating and subordinating conjunctions by presenting them in their roles as integral parts of compound and complex sentences. In other words, once the student has learned the concept, rules, and use of simple sentences, he would be introduced to the compound sentence and, at the same time, to the coordinating conjunction, with an explanation of the crucial role the conjunction plays in the concept and formation of the compound sentence. In this way, these two concepts would be related and made more meaningful. Once these factors have been learned, the teacher would move on to complex sentences, which, of course, provides the opportunity to discuss subordinating conjunctions. Then, having this information, the student would have acquired the prerequisite knowledge for learning rules governing the use of coordinating and subordinating conjunctions. The rules might be explicated as follows:

1. A coordinating conjunction is used to combine two independent clauses, thus forming a compound sentence.
2. A subordinating conjunction is used to combine an independent clause and a dependent clause, thus forming a complex sentence.

Once these basic concepts and rules are established, the student can then be given the opportunity to use both types of conjunction in a variety of situations.

Teachers often teach relevant concepts but never really formulate an operational rule for the students to learn and apply. If the teacher distinctly teaches the two aforementioned rules, then the continued practice of the rules in different learning contexts can confirm learning and enhance the possibility of the student's remembering and using the rules beyond the immediate teaching–learning situation.

> Marty and Tim live near the city zoo. Yesterday, they took their cousin Marcia there. Marcia saw many animals she had never seen before.

The teacher then has the students express themselves in the following ways:

> Marcia saw an elephant.
> Had Marcia ever seen an elephant before?
> Marcia had never seen an elephant before.
> Marty and Tim had seen an elephant before.

With the past-perfect participle "had seen" presented, the teacher might also teach its contracted forms:

> Had Marcia ever seen an elephant before? No, she'd never seen an elephant before.
> Had Marty and Tim ever seen an elephant before? Yes, they'd seen an elephant before.

The teacher can also show that "never" is used in a statement, whereas in a question, "ever" is used. The examples would be restated to illustrate this rule:

> Had Marcia ever seen an elephant before?
> Marcia had never seen an elephant before.

Finally, the teacher would show the students the correct construction of a tagging question in the past-perfect tense:

> Marcia had never seen an elephant before, had she?
> Marty and Tim had seen an elephant before, hadn't they?

The teacher might now want to move the students from the past-perfect form "had seen" to another form, such as "had been," before testing them on their learning.

> Had Marcia ever been to a zoo before?
> Marcia had never been to a zoo before.
> Marty and Tim had never been to the zoo together before.

By then giving the students several more illustrations and several work problems, the teacher can affirm the students' acquisition of the rules and their ability to apply these rules to solve and create sentences using correct construction and form of past-perfect verbs. If the problems may be solved by the direct application of the rules, then we would say that the student is using a *complex rule* to solve a problem. If the student is able to generate his own problem solving information, using the combination of coordinate complex rules to solve the problems, then we would say that a higher-order principle (rule) has emerged and is in use.

Problem 2. A student is given the problem of (1) selecting the most appropriate form of discourse for developing each of the following topic sentences into a paragraph, and (2) choosing one of the topics and developing a paragraph from it.

1. Attending a large university has disadvantages as well as advantages.
2. The idea that women are poor drivers is not supported by evidence.
3. Television has replaced motion pictures as the primary form of popular entertainment.
4. Farming is the backbone of the American economy.
5. Most adolescents have difficulty gaining emotional independence from their parents.

In the earlier illustration (p. 159) on effective paragraph writing, you will recall that a complex rule for paragraph development emerged from six coordinate rules. Thus, the student must do three things in fulfilling this task: (1) He must recall and apply the complex rule (level 7) that states the prerequisite conditions for the problem solving behavior required in this task. (2) He must recall and apply coordinate rules (level 7) that facilitate his understanding of the complex rule and his performance of the problem solving behavior. (3) In the case of part (1) of this task, he must also go back to the *concept* learning level (level 6) to recall and apply the different categories of discourse and paragraph development, such as exposition, argument, deductive and inductive development, and narrative. In short, by combining and using the relevant concepts and simple and complex rules previously learned, the student can meet and resolve the problem with new and *functional* rules for judging and acting on the *intent* of topic sentences and for writing an effective paragraph. And from the actual experience of evaluating and developing a topic sentence into a paragraph, the student acquires new learning (level 8) that he may use in writing whole essays and in judging the writing of others. (Figure 7.2 illustrates the hierarchy of conceptual learning involved in this problem.)

The theoretical learning model advanced by Gagné (1968) for the problem solving level of learning is shown in Figure 7.3. The primary factors within this hierarchical model are the problem solving *behavior* to be emitted by the learner and the prerequisite concepts and rules that are combined and conceptualized by the learner

FIGURE 7.2. *Conceptualizing and Writing Effective Paragraphs*

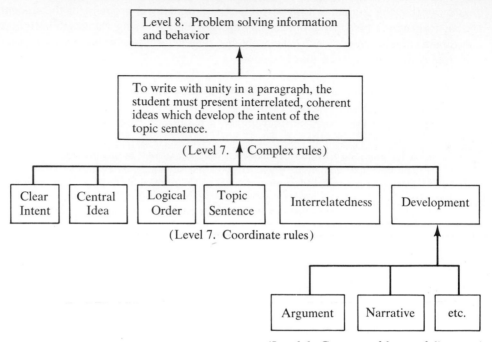

in acquiring the problem solving capabilities. The model clearly shows how several concepts are instrumental in rule emergence and how a combination of many rules, in turn, assist problem solving. Of course, the complexity of each rule determines the necessary prerequisite concepts for that rule and for the problem solving behavior. Similarly, the complexity of the superordinate problem solving rule determines the prerequisite rules for the behavior. Regarding the latter, let us refer to Gagné (1968), who carefully explains how each rule in his model serves as a prerequisite condition to the problem solving behavior.

The first subordinate learning that the child needs to have learned is the rule that volume of a liquid (in rectangular containers) is determined by length, width, and

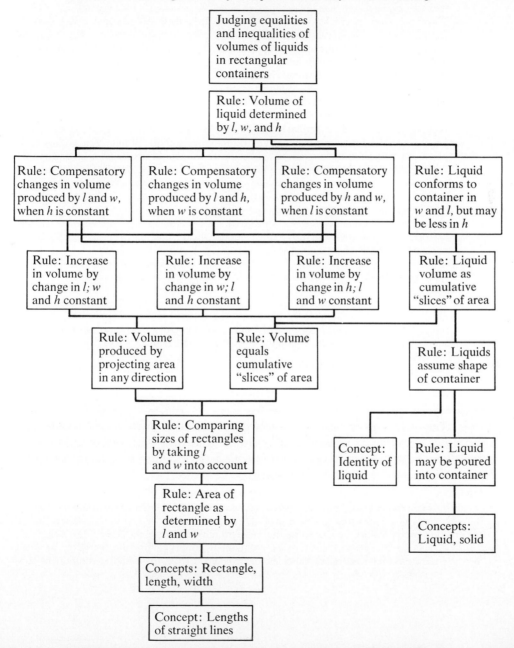

FIGURE 7.3. The Gagné Model of Prerequisite Conditions for Problem Solving

Gagné, R. M. Contributions of learning to human development, *Psychological Review,* 1968, **75,** 177–191. Copyright 1968 by the American Psychological Association and reprinted by permission.

height. A change in any of these will change volume. This means that the child knows that any perceived change in any of these dimensions means a different volume. Going down one step in the learnings required, we find three rules about compensatory changes in two dimensions when another dimension remains constant. That is, if the height of a liquid remains the same in two different containers, one can have the same volume if a change in width is compensated by a change in length. Similarly for the other instances of compensatory change.

Now, in order for a child to learn these compensatory rules, . . . he must have previously learned three other rules, relating to change in only one dimension at a time. For example, if length is increased while width and height remain constant, volume increases. Again, similarly for the other single dimensions. These rules in turn presuppose the learning of still other rules. One is that volume of a container is produced by accumulating "slices" of the same shape and area; and a second is that volume can be projected from area in any direction, particularly, up, to the front or back, and to the right or left. Finally, one can work down to considerably simpler rules, such as those of comparing areas of rectangles by compensatory action of length and width; and the dependence of area upon the dimensions of length and width. If one traces the development sequence still farther, he comes to the even simpler learned entities, concepts including rectangle, length, width, and an even simpler one, the concept of length of a straight line.

Just to complete the picture, the model includes another branch which has to do with liquids in containers, rather than with the containers themselves, and which deals on simpler levels with rules about liquids and the concept of a liquid itself. This branch is necessary because at the level of more complex rules, the child must distinguish between the volume of the liquid and the volume of the container. Of particular interest also is the concept of liquid identity, the recognition by the child that a given liquid poured into another container is still the same liquid [p. 185].

PROBLEM SOLVING IN THE CLASSROOM

The conditions for acquiring problem solving capabilities and behavior (level 8 learning) are similar to those for rule learning. In fact, there is probably more similarity in the prerequisite conditions for these two types of learning than at any other point in the hierarchy. Consider the following:

1. The learner must know the verbal statement of the rule before he learns it. Similarly, he must know the problem and the general nature of the performance that is expected before he can solve the problem and complete the level 8 learning.
2. Just as the learner must recall component concepts for rule learning, he must summon relevant relational rules for problem solving. Essentially, component con-

cepts in rule learning and relational rules in problem solving involve the same process; for rules are formed from a chain of concepts, and when these rules are associated with a problem, they become a chain of rules which must be learned before solving a problem.

3. Contiguity is present in problem solving in that there must be contiguity of the rules that bring about this learning, just as the concepts that form the rules must be contiguous.

4. Gagné makes no specific statement regarding reinforcement as a condition for problem solving, although it appears that reinforcement would have value in establishing the superordinate rules prerequisite to problem solving behavior.

5. As with rule learning, there is a greater resistance to forgetting at level 8 than at lower points in the hierarchy.

A model presented by Briggs (1970) specifies the upper levels of Gagné's learning hierarchy in the useful terms of behavioral objectives and clearly demonstrates the value of seeing learning as a cumulative process leading ultimately to problem solving behavior (the behavioral objective of the lesson in Briggs' model).

At the top of the hierarchy (see Figure 7.4), Briggs has specified the behavior desired. After we analyze this specification it becomes apparent that several prerequisite learning conditions are required. Briggs thus considers the sequence of learning in order to gain the concepts, principles, and complex rules necessary to a higher-order rule that infers problem solving capability. Note in Figure 7.4 that sequence ① "student can define natural resources" is a *concept* necessary to learning sequence ② "student will be able to read a standard geographic map" as a *rule*. Sequence ① is not required, however, to learning sequence ⑦ "having heard the history of an individual, student can discuss ways in which the individual influenced change in Florida." Rather, Briggs' model shows how the concepts are oriented toward specific rules. Note, however, that sequence ② and ⑦ are comparable in difficulty and both lead through different routes to the same complex rules (⑨ and ⑩).

This model also shows how relational concepts ③, ⑤, and ⑧ are all prerequisite to the emergence of the complex, problem solving rules ⑨ and ⑩. In turn, sequences ⑨ and ⑩ become prerequisite for sequence ⑪ which, in turn, makes it possible for the specified problem solving objective to be realized.

For the teacher, such a sequence has important instructional implications: (1) The teacher can see that students can move effectively toward a specified objective through a planned instructional sequence, and (2) the teacher can, at any point within the sequence, readily ascertain what learning is prerequisite to teaching the next higher step. Now, in Figure 7.5, we can view Gagné's full hierarchical model of learning.

FIGURE 7.4. The Gagné Hierarchy Stated as Behavioral Objectives

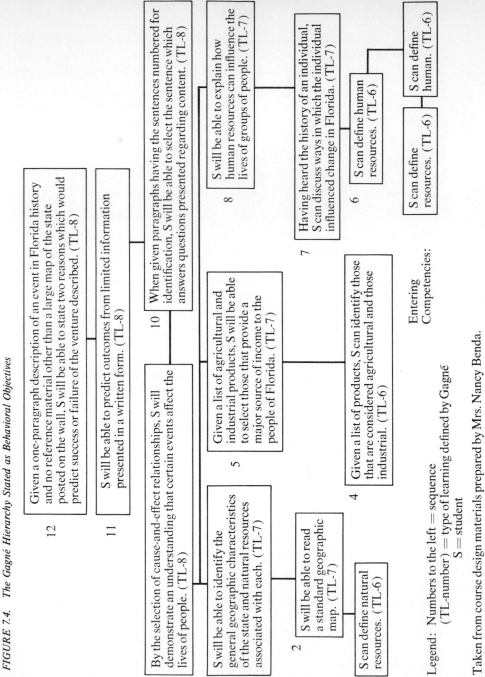

12 — Given a one-paragraph description of an event in Florida history and no reference material other than a large map of the state posted on the wall, S will be able to state two reasons which would predict success or failure of the venture described. (TL-8)

11 — S will be able to predict outcomes from limited information presented in a written form. (TL-8)

10 — When given paragraphs having the sentences numbered for identification, S will be able to select the sentence which answers questions presented regarding content. (TL-8)

9 — By the selection of cause-and-effect relationships, S will demonstrate an understanding that certain events affect the lives of people. (TL-8)

8 — S will be able to explain how human resources can influence the lives of groups of people. (TL-7)

7 — Having heard the history of an individual, S can discuss ways in which the individual influenced change in Florida. (TL-7)

6 — S can define human resources. (TL-6)

5 — Given a list of agricultural and industrial products, S will be able to select those that provide a major source of income to the people of Florida. (TL-7)

4 — Given a list of products, S can identify those that are considered agricultural and those industrial. (TL-6)

3 — S will be able to identify the general geographic characteristics of the state and natural resources associated with each. (TL-7)

2 — S will be able to read a standard geographic map. (TL-7)

1 — S can define natural resources. (TL-6)

S can define resources. (TL-6)

S can define human. (TL-6)

Entering Competencies:

Legend: Numbers to the left = sequence
(TL-number) = type of learning defined by Gagné
S = student

Taken from course design materials prepared by Mrs. Nancy Benda.

Reprinted from Briggs, L. J. *Handbook of procedures for the design of instruction.* Pittsburgh: American Institutes of Research, 1970, p. 89. Used with permission of the publisher.

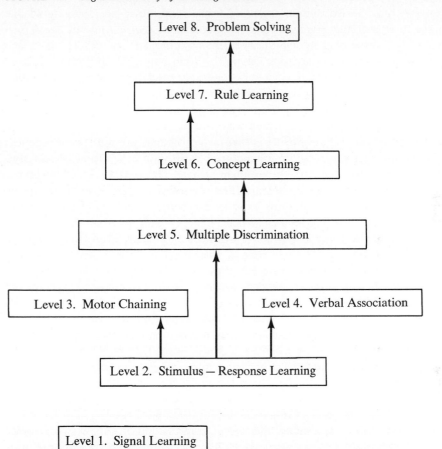

FIGURE 7.5.   Gagné's Hierarchy of Learning—Levels 1–8

Based on concepts, rules are learned which give the student a capability of functioning when confronted with problem solving situations.

THE COGNITIVIST VIEWS ON PROBLEM SOLVING

Problem solving behavior is conceived somewhat differently by the cognitivist theorists. Ausubel (1968) refers to an *insight* as the key to this type of learning, while Bruner (1961, 1966) advances the idea of *discovery learning*. For Ausubel, the meaningfulness of a problem situation underlies a learner's solution to a problem. The problem solving may be the simple cognitive transfer of intact previous knowledge to new situations, or it may involve a basic restructuring of previous knowledge and experience in order to meet and resolve the problem situation; but, in either case, ultimately the meaningfulness of the situation allows the learner to intuit and then apply a solution.

In other words, in Ausubel's cognitivist model, problem solving is an extension of cognitive functioning beyond the information given within the problem situation. In order for this to occur, the learner must relate the confronting situation to his existing cognitive structure, which was attained through previously related and meaningful situations. The net effect is that most problems are not solved independently of the learner's existing cognitive structure but through integration or reorganization of the structure to cope with the problem at hand (Bruner, 1957). If the learner is able to see the means–end relationship, then the solution may be more easily discovered. Where no meaningful patterns exist in a problem situation, Ausubel contends that trial-and-error learning inevitably occurs.

Discovery learning, which is advanced by Bruner, occurs as a result of meaningful relationships in the environment. Bruner's contentions are not unlike those of Ausubel, although the role of student exploration is quite important within his theoretical model. Bruner is uncertain as to whether learning is a natural outcome of behavior or whether discovery learning occurs through the imitation of persons within one's environment (1961). Bruner does feel, however, that the learner discovers through continuously experiencing. In the same sense that Harlow suggested that we learn through learning, so Bruner contends that we learn how to discover through discovering. The retentive strengths of such learning are seen by Bruner as a product of the complexity of problem encounters; the more complex the problem, the greater the retention rate.

Thus, problem solving behavior for the cognitivists is somewhat different from the view of stimulus–response theorists, as represented by Gagné's hierarchical system —although both positions attest to the learner's ability to go beyond previous acquisitions and the immediate problem situation and both represent this particular learning to be the highest form of behavior within man. The cognitivists cannot conclusively state whether the solutions to problematic encounters are facilitated by the learner's existing cognitive structures or by his past experiences—a situation that makes teacher planning difficult. In contrast, Gagné describes all necessary prerequisite conditions which build the theoretical basis for a learner's problem solving behavior. While, in Gagné's system, the learner goes beyond that which is apparent in the problem situation and must recall additional knowledge to solve the problem, all of this knowledge must have been previously established within the learner, and we can safely conclude that solutions will occur. Without the prerequisite concepts and rules, solutions to many problems would not be readily available and may often be completely undiscoverable.

Regarding the validity of Gagné's hierarchical view of problem solving as a type of learning, Wiegand (1969*) set up experimental conditions to see whether prerequisite capabilities were necessary to performance at the problem solving level. Working with sixth-grade students, Wiegand began by identifying the necessary prerequisite conditions for student capability in the task of deriving and demonstrating the relationship of variables in an inclined plane. Her identifications were formulated into the hierarchical arrangement shown in Figure 7.6.

Wiegand hypothesized that if all the prerequisite skills were learned and present, the students should be able to solve the problem. She began testing at the problem level (level 8) and found that 31 of the students (70 percent of the group) were unable to accomplish this problem solving task. Wiegand then worked in reverse until she found the point at which all the students exhibited common prerequisite learning capabilities. She then again reversed her teaching operation and built all of the prerequisite skills identified in Figure 7.6 up to the problem. The results of this research indicated that 90 percent of the 31 students who had previously been unable to solve the problem were now able to, after having attained the identified prerequisites. As Gagné (1970b) points out, this research evidence confirms and clarifies the importance of prerequisite learning to successively complex stages in the learning hierarchy.

THE APPLICATION OF RULE LEARNING AND PROBLEM SOLVING TO CLASSROOM LEARNING

The Chemical Plant Foods

In Chapter 6, the relevant concrete and abstract *concepts* (level 6) about chemicals and growth processes in plants were introduced. You will recall that the ten chemicals involved in plant nutrition and growth processes are derived from three different sources: Air and water supply the chemicals of carbon, hydrogen, and oxygen; the soil supplies iron, calcium, sulfur, and magnesium; and potassium, nitrogen, and phosphorus are derived from fertilizers. Upon conceptualizing the functions of these

---

* Also cited at length in Gagné, R. M., Some new views on learning and instruction. *Phi Delta Kappan*, 1970b, **51** (9), 468–472.

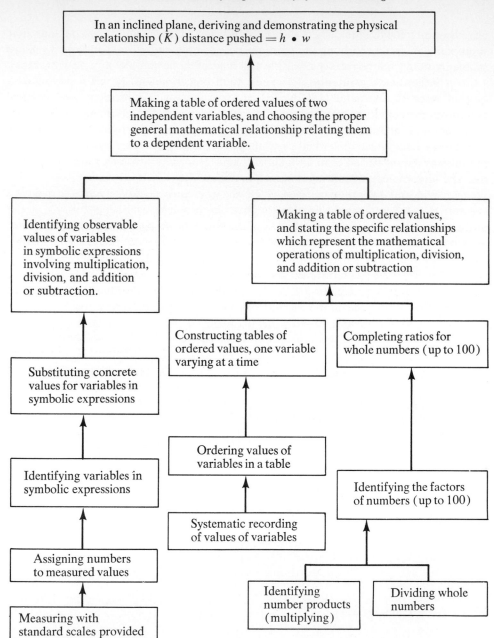

FIGURE 7.6.   *A Research Model of Gagné's Theory of Problem Solving*

In an inclined plane, deriving and demonstrating the physical relationship (K) distance pushed $= h \bullet w$

Making a table of ordered values of two independent variables, and choosing the proper general mathematical relationship relating them to a dependent variable.

Identifying observable values of variables in symbolic expressions involving multiplication, division, and addition or subtraction.

Making a table of ordered values, and stating the specific relationships which represent the mathematical operations of multiplication, division, and addition or subtraction

Substituting concrete values for variables in symbolic expressions

Constructing tables of ordered values, one variable varying at a time

Completing ratios for whole numbers (up to 100)

Identifying variables in symbolic expressions

Ordering values of variables in a table

Identifying the factors of numbers (up to 100)

Assigning numbers to measured values

Systematic recording of values of variables

Measuring with standard scales provided

Identifying number products (multiplying)

Dividing whole numbers

Used with permission of the author and the publisher from R. M. Gagné, Some new views on learning and instruction. *Phi Delta Kappan,* 1970, **51,** 468–472.

ten chemicals, the student will find it possible to formulate rules (level 7) governing their use. Four examples of such rules and a related problem solving situation are listed in Figure 7.7.

Assume you are presenting the student with this problem of counteracting a lack of calcium in soil due to high amounts of acid. The first learning to be applied is the rule that soil chemicals enter the plant through water. This rule is formed from concrete concepts regarding the soil chemicals necessary to plant life and from abstract concepts regarding growth processes in plants. On the basis of this rule, the learner might meet the problem situation by suggesting that some way must be found to enrich the soil with necessary calcium in solution (mixed with water). This suggestion calls into play another rule—that a missing chemical element in soil may be artificially supplied through fertilizers—which is based on the previously mentioned concrete and abstract concepts as well as on concrete concepts regarding the properties of fertilizers. This rule will require the student to learn additional concepts about special fertilizers, such as dolomite, limestone, and hydrated lime, which contain the nutrients that will provide calcium to the soil. In other words, it is not enough for the learner simply to select a commercially prepared fertilizer containing all the soil chemicals; instead, he must consider the question of whether a particular fertilizer will supply the calcium deficiency and then select the fertilizer most likely to solve the problem.

Essentially, then, the learner has acquired the following types of learning:

Level 8: The problem solving behavior of selecting an effective fertilizer for calcium deficient soil.

Level 8: The higher-order rule that acid soils must be treated with certain calcium rich fertilizers, such as dolomite, limestone, or hydrated lime.

Level 7: The relational rule that calcium is lacking in acid soils.

Level 7: The rules that soil chemicals enter the plant through water and that a missing chemical element in soil may be artificially supplied through fertilizers.

Level 6: Additional concrete concepts specifically relevant to the problem situation— that is, concepts regarding special fertilizers (dolomite, limestone, hydrated lime) that provide calcium soil.

The Functions of Teeth

This illustration has been developed sequentially from stimulus–response bonds through chaining, discrimination, and concept learning. Now, knowing the names, shapes, positions, and distinct functions of the teeth, we can consider rules governing their use. These rules are possible, of course, because the students can relate the various concepts regarding teeth functions.

FIGURE 7.7. The Chemical Plant Foods—Rule Learning and Problem Solving

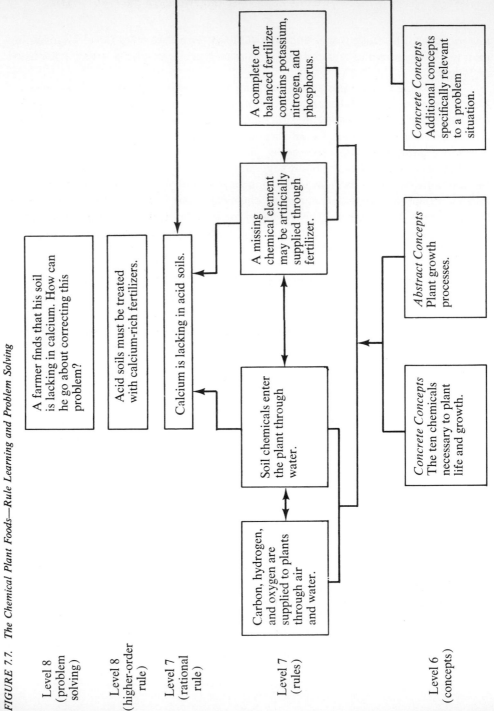

Level 8
(problem
solving)

A farmer finds that his soil
is lacking in calcium. How can
he go about correcting this
problem?

Level 8
(higher-order
rule)

Acid soils must be treated
with calcium-rich fertilizers.

Level 7
(rational
rule)

Calcium is lacking in acid soils.

A missing
chemical element
may be artificially
supplied through
fertilizer.

A complete or
balanced fertilizer
contains potassium,
nitrogen, and
phosphorus.

Concrete Concepts
Additional concepts
specifically relevant
to a problem
situation.

Level 7
(rules)

Soil chemicals enter
the plant through
water.

Abstract Concepts
Plant growth
processes.

Carbon, hydrogen,
and oxygen are
supplied to plants
through air
and water.

Level 6
(concepts)

Concrete Concepts
The ten chemicals
necessary to plant
life and growth.

FIGURE 7.8. *The Functions of Teeth—Rule Learning and Problem Solving*

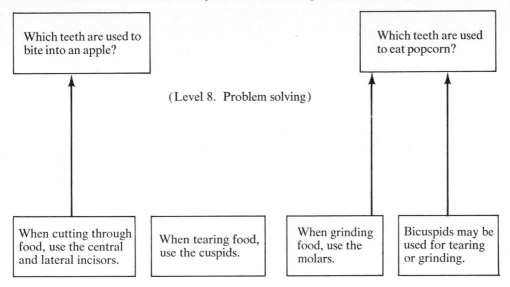

Four rules that relate the functions of teeth are formulated in Figure 7.8, and two uses of teeth are presented in a question form describing hypothetical situations. These questions represent problem solving learning (level 8) in that the answers involve higher-order rules that infer capability. By applying relevant rules and concepts to these and other comparable problem situations, the student will understand that certain teeth are used to perform certain functions.

The Varieties of Triangles

Having learned the six types of triangles on the basis of physical appearance (level 5) and conceptual differences (level 6), we can proceed to formulate rules (level 7) for finding the areas of these triangles (level 8). We shall single out the right triangle for our illustration. The rule for finding the area of a right triangle must be based on the learner's understanding of the relevant prerequisite concepts of area, rectangle, height, base, and the various concepts of arithmetic and measurement (all advanced in Chapter 6). On the basis of these concepts, the rule "Area equals base times height divided by two" may be learned. And this rule allows the student to compute the area of any right triangle, regardless of the length of its straight line segments (see Figure 7.9). Once the rule has been learned, it may be subsequently applied to several different types of problems for which it is appropriate.

Possessive Nouns

Two rules make it possible for the student to encounter and solve learning problems involving possessive nouns. The first deals with singular possessives: "To form the possessive singular of a noun, add '*s*." The second rule applies to plural possessives: "To form the possessive plural, add '*s* to words not ending in *s* and merely an apostrophe to words ending in *s*." If you recall the concepts learned in this lesson in Chapter 6, you will see how it was possible to formulate these rules. And if you look at the problems posed in Figure 7.10, you can see how one or the other of the two rules will be instrumental in helping the student solve the problems.

Finding the Circumference of Circles

In Chapter 6, the circle was discriminated from all other geometric shapes, and the concepts relevant to finding the circumference of a circle were identified and hierarchially arranged. In this illustration, the rules relevant to this problem-solving behavior will be developed. The prerequisite concepts are also restated here.

There is one basic rule for finding the circumference of a circle:

$$\frac{c}{d} = \pi.$$

The concepts directly involved in this rule are circumference *(c)*, diameter *(d)*, and *pi* (π). From this basic rule come two rule variations that are applicable depending on the known values available for the circle to be measured. If the student has acquired all the concepts that make up the basic rule, then he can apply these same concepts to each of the rule variations. For example, suppose the radius *(r)* of a circle is given. The rule variation in use under these circumstances would be:

$$c = 2 \pi r.$$

"2 πr" indicates that you must multiply the radius times 2 times *pi* (3.14). The result of this computation is the circumference. The other rule variation for finding circumference is shown in Figure 7.11.

FIGURE 7.9.   *Finding the Area of a Right Triangle—Rule Learning and Problem Solving*

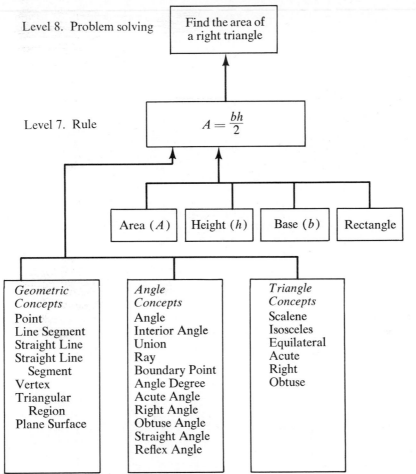

Level 8. Problem solving

Find the area of a right triangle

Level 7. Rule

$$A = \frac{bh}{2}$$

Area (*A*)   Height (*h*)   Base (*b*)   Rectangle

Geometric Concepts
Point
Line Segment
Straight Line
Straight Line
   Segment
Vertex
Triangular
   Region
Plane Surface

Angle Concepts
Angle
Interior Angle
Union
Ray
Boundary Point
Angle Degree
Acute Angle
Right Angle
Obtuse Angle
Straight Angle
Reflex Angle

Triangle Concepts
Scalene
Isosceles
Equilateral
Acute
Right
Obtuse

Level 6. Conceptualizing

Finding Mathematical Unknowns

This lesson, which began in Chapter 6, is continued here to demonstrate the necessity of formulating rules from concepts in order to successfully work out problems —in this case, mathematical unknowns. The hierarchical relationship between the

FIGURE 7.10.   *Use of Possessives—Rule Learning and Problem Solving*

Write as a possessive "magazine of last month."

Write the singular possessive for "raven" and "Patricia."

Correct this sentence: "Mother rosebushes survived the cold winter months."

Write the possessive for: "Have you seen my mother coat?"

Correct this sentence: "Tourist love Hawaii palm tree, beautiful beach, and brilliant flower."

Correct this sentence: "Is the yellow sweater Chris or Harvey?"

(Level 8. Problem solving)

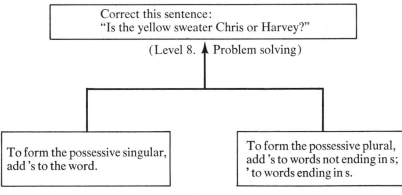

To form the possessive singular, add 's to the word.

To form the possessive plural, add 's to words not ending in s; ' to words ending in s.

(Level 7. Rules)

FIGURE 7.11.   *Finding Circumference—Rule Learning and Problem Solving*

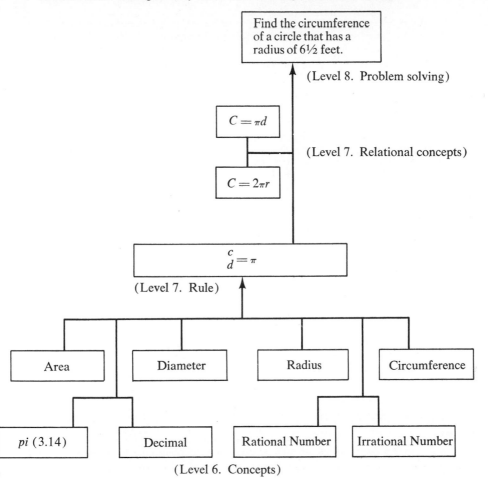

concepts, rules, and problem solving is shown in Figure 7.12, and the problems based on these concepts and rules are reprinted in Figure 7.13 from a well-known sixth-grade mathematics textbook.

As you read through the problems in Figure 7.13, it becomes clear that two rules must emerge if the problems are to be solved. In equation form, they are:

FIGURE 7.12.   *Finding Unknowns in Measuring Lengths of Animals Drawn to Scale—Rule Learning and Problem Solving*

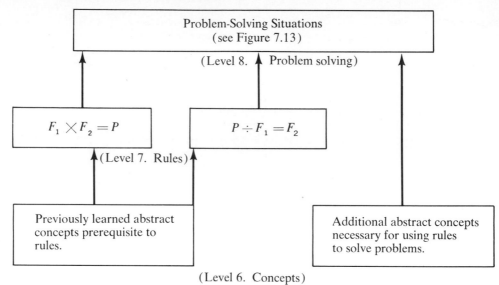

Rule 1: $F_1 \times F_2 = P$

Rule 2: $P \div F_1 = F_2$ *or* $P \div F_2 = F_1$

Rule 1 states that when two factors are known and the product is to be found, one must *multiply* the two factors. Rule 2 states that if one factor and the product are known, one must *divide* the product by the given factor in order to find the missing factor.

As we have noted, all of the concepts necessary to these rules were given in the previous chapter. However, some additional concepts are needed to solve the problems here, because they involve measurements (in feet, inches, and fractions of inches) of the lengths of certain animals. Note that these additional concepts are necessary not for the two mathematical equations for finding unknowns but for the specific type of problems presented. These additional prerequisite concepts are:

Whole number
Mixed number

Fraction
Proper fraction
Length
Measurement
Inches
Feet

The animals shown on page 186 are drawn to scale. You can use division to find the actual size of each animal. For example, the 1⅛-inch blue crab is ¹⁄₁₂ its actual width. You can write the multiplication equation

F　　F　　P
¹⁄₁₂ × W = 1⅛ and find the actual width by dividing to find the missing factor.

¹⁄₁₂ × actual width

1. [A] Find the actual length of a termite.
   [B] Find the actual length of a flea.
   [C] Which is longer? How much longer?
2. Find the length of an armadillo:
   [A] in inches　　[B] in feet
3. Find the length of an antelope's horns:
   [A] in inches　　[B] in feet
4. One of the longest elephant tusks is about 4⅗ times as long as the antelope's horn. How long is the tusk?
5. How tall is a penguin:
   [A] in inches　　[B] in feet
6. [A] How long is a frog's body?
   [B] If a frog can jump 17½ times as far as the length of his body, how many feet can he jump?
7. If a toad is ¾ the length of a frog, how long is a toad?
8. How many inches longer than a house fly is a scorpion?
9. [A] How long is a lizard?
   [B] How long is a sea horse?
   [C] How much longer is the lizard than the sea horse?
10. What is the actual height of the blue jay:
    [A] in inches　　[B] in feet
11. [A] What is the length of a sword-fish in inches and in feet?
    [B] The length of the "sword" on the swordfish is half the length of the body of the swordfish. Find the length of the swordfish's sword in inches and in feet.

FIGURE 7.13. *Problem Solving Situations: Animal Lengths Drawn to Scale*

Animal lengths

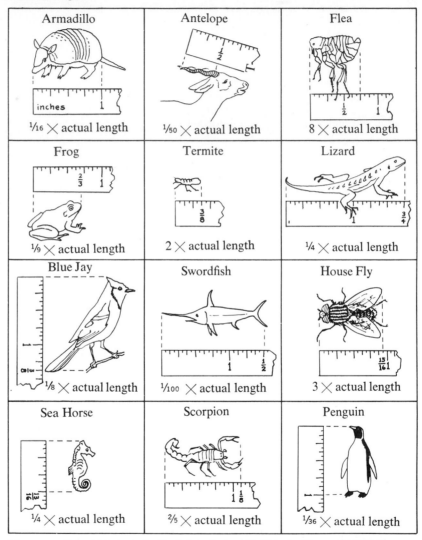

SUGGESTED READINGS

Bloom, B. S. Learning for mastery. *UCLA Evaluation Comment,* 1968, **1** (2), entire issue.

Buser, R. L., & Rooze, G. E. Learning: The role of facts and generalizations. *Elementary School Journal,* 1970, **71,** 129–133.

Gagné, R. M., & Wiegand, V. K. Some factors in children's learning and retention of concrete rules. *Journal of Educational Psychology,* 1968, **59,** 355–361. Reprinted in H. D. Thornburg (Ed.), *School learning and instruction: Readings.* Monterey, Calif.: Brooks/Cole, 1973, chap. 4.

Guthrie, J. T. Relationships of teaching method, socioeconomic status, and intelligence in concept formation. *Journal of Educational Psychology,* 1971, **62,** 345–351.

Jacobson, L. I. The effects of awareness, problem solving ability, and task difficulty on the acquisition and extinction of verbal behavior. *Journal of Experimental Research in Personality,* 1969, **3,** 206–213.

Keislar, E. R. Teaching children to solve problems: A research goal. *Journal of Research and Development in Education,* 1969, **3,** 3–14.

Kieren, T. E. Activity learning. *Review of Educational Research,* 1969, **39,** 509–522.

Millham, I., Jacobson, L. I., & Berger, S. E. Effects of intelligence, information processing, and mediation conditions on conceptual learning. *Journal of Educational Psychology,* 1971, **62,** 293–299.

Scandura, J. M., & Voorhies, D. J. Effect of irrelevant attributes and irrelevant operations on rule learning. *Journal of Educational Psychology,* 1971, **62,** 352–356.

Simon, H. A., & Newell, A. Human problem solving: The state of the theory in 1970. *American Psychologist,* 1971, **26,** 145–159.

8

Learning and Instruction: Practical Applications

The intent of this book is to provide the reader with more than the basic learning theories and principles. By advancing an instructional theory model (Chapter 2) complementary to Gagné's hierarchy model (Chapters 4–7), the author has tried to bridge the gap between theory and practice, so that prospective teachers will have some encounter with the practical applications of learning theory before stepping into the classroom for the first time. It is the author's opinion that no learning theory exists today that is more operationally defined than that of Robert Gagné, and this chapter will show how it and the author's instructional theory can work together in dealing with several typical classroom learning situations. Before we discuss these situations, let us review the main points of the two models:

Gagné's Learning Hierarchy Model

Level 2: Stimulus–response learning.   The learner acquires a specific motor or verbal response (single discriminate) to a specific, identifiable stimulus ($S_s \longrightarrow R$). A type of learning used when the learning task to be accomplished is the simple acquisition of basic information requiring no prerequisite knowledge.

Level 3: Motor chaining.   The learner combines two or more motor stimulus–response connections to acquire a chain of motor behavior involving either academic or social information. A type of learning used when the learning task to be accomplished requires a series of previously learned motor $S_s \longrightarrow R$ connections. Thus, level 2 learning serves as the prerequisite knowledge for this level.

FIGURE 8.1.   *Gagné's Learning Hierarchy Model*

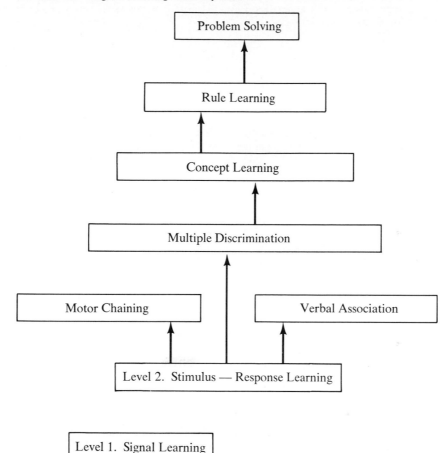

Level 4: Verbal association.   The learner combines two or more verbal stimulus–response connections to acquire a chain of verbal information. A type of learning used when the learning task requires a logical, sequential chain of $S_s \longrightarrow R$ connections. Level 2 learning serves as the prerequisite knowledge for verbal associations.

Level 5: Multiple discrimination.   The differentiation among several *similar* S–R connections (all of a class). A type of learning used when the learner must make distinct identifying responses (multiple discriminates) to many different stimuli with similar appearance or characteristics. Level 2 learning serves as the prerequisite knowledge for multiple discriminates.

Level 6: Concept learning.   The learner is capable of categorizing and making a single identifying response to a whole class of stimuli that may differ in appearance. A type of learning used when a learner begins to conceptualize (understand the abstract meaning of) different responses and is able to extend his understanding to new, previously unlearned stimuli. Multiple discrimination (level 5) serves as the prerequisite knowledge for the concrete concepts of level 6.

Level 7: Rule learning.   The learner relates two or more concrete concepts to form a chain of abstract understanding stated as a simple rule or relational concept. A type of learning used when the learning task is the formulation and acquisition of a rule that infers a functional capability. The prerequisite knowledge is conceptualization (level 6).

Level 8: Problem solving.   The learner combines two or more rules or relational concepts to formulate a chain of cognitive strategies for meeting and resolving problem situations. A type of learning to produce a new, higher-order complex rule and a new, complex level of thinking and problem solving capability. The prerequisite knowledge is the rules and relational concepts of level 7.

Thornburg's Instructional Model

Identifying student needs.   The preliminary behavior of the teacher in determining the student's readiness for the tasks to be taught. This step, which is often facilitated by diagnostic testing, may serve as the basis for the next step, stating student behavioral objectives, or it may be planned in coordination with that step.

Stating student behavioral objectives.   The teacher's formal statement of the learned behaviors expected of the student upon completion of a particular unit in the teaching–learning process.

Developing a teaching strategy.   The actual teaching procedure used by the teacher to facilitate student learning. The following principles of learning must form the core of an effective teaching strategy:

1. *Student preparation.* Focusing student attention toward the learning task at hand (the principle of readiness).
2. *Stimulus presentation.* Deciding on the most effective way of presenting stimuli to the learner (the principle of sequential, discriminated stimuli).
3. *Student response.* Planning the time and opportunity for students to respond to presented stimuli (the principle of contiguity).
4. *Reinforcement.* Selecting the most effective way to reinforce learner responses (the principles of continuous and intermittent reinforcement).

5. *Evaluation.* Measuring the student learning rate according to behavioral objectives and providing feedback regarding the effectiveness of the teaching strategy and theory.

6. *Spaced review.* Evaluating and ensuring student retention by the periodic presentation of both previously learned materials and new but related information and problems.

Assessing student behavioral change. The evaluation, through teacher observation and student examination, of the appropriateness of the student behavioral objectives, the effectiveness of the teaching strategy, and the rate of student learning. This step also may serve as a basis for grading.

CLASSROOM SITUATION 1

Upon diagnosing student needs, a teacher of mathematics finds that his class has the necessary prerequisite knowledge for learning the rules for *multiplication* and *division.* (1) State the student behavioral objectives you would write for this task. (2) What teaching strategy would you use to accomplish such objectives? (3) List the most immediately relevant prerequisite knowledge necessary for learning these rules.

Sample Answer*

1. The following *behavioral objectives* should be met upon completion of the teaching unit:

   a. The student will understand and demonstrate the definition of multiplication as "the addition of groups or sets of numbers."

   b. The student will understand and demonstrate the definition of division as "the counting of subsets in a universal set."

   c. The student will know the operations signs for "multiply" and "divide."

   d. The student will learn the rules governing multiplication and division.

2a. *Teaching strategy: multiplication*

   a. *Student preparation.* The teacher places the problem "7 + 7 + 7 + 7 + 7 + 7 + 7 = " on the board. After the students have added the

---

* The reader is cautioned to remember that with this classroom situation and those that follow, the various instructional and learning principles that are emphasized are merely illustrative. The methodology for such learning is and should be variable from one teacher to the next.

numbers to get the sum, he points out that there is an easier way, called *multiplication,* to obtain the answer and that multiplication is a shorter way to add certain groups of numbers.

b. *Stimulus presentation.*   The teacher uses several examples, such as:

$$3 + 3 = 6 \qquad\qquad 3 + 3 + 3 = 9 \qquad\qquad 3 + 3 + 3 + 3 = 12$$
$$3 \times 2 = 6 \qquad\qquad 3 \times 3 = 9 \qquad\qquad 3 \times 4 = 12$$

to show the students that a number added to itself is a set which is complete within itself as well as being a factor in the addition or multiplication of several sets. Thus, the sum in addition and the product in multiplication are the same. This reinforces the rule that multiplication is a shorter form of addition of numerical sets. Once these examples have been learned, more complex stimuli should be presented. Finally, the ability to "multiply" should be confirmed through the presentation of entirely new problems of multiplication.

c. *Student response.*   There are three response levels required here. To be assured that learning is occurring, the teacher must provide the students with opportunities to make the responses and to have them acknowledged in some way. The first response desired in the student is in reaction to the teacher's instructional examples. Once the student sees what the teacher is working through, he may have the basic information necessary for the introduction of new problems. The second desired student response is to the more complex stimuli that the teacher presents. For example, rather than simply presenting all multiplication processes at one- or two-digit levels, the teacher may present a variety of such processes, so that the rule is applied to a wider stimuli range. Finally, the teacher must provide the opportunity for the student to respond to the entirely new problems he presents. If the teacher gives the student time to think through his responses and continually associates the responses with the stimuli, the learning rate for the new problems will be increased.

d. *Reinforcement.*   Since this is a new learning task, it would be helpful to immediately reinforce each response by providing knowledge of results. Then, as the students confirm this learning and become more confident of the multiplication process, intermittent reinforcement should maintain the learning rate.

e. *Evaluation.* The rate of student progress with multiplication can be determined by teacher observation of student participation in class and by checking daily assignments and evaluating periodic examinations.

f. *Spaced review.* The later presentation of increasingly complex multiplication problems would require student recall of previously learned facts and concepts and would increase the probability of retention.

2b. *Teaching strategy: division*

The teacher's basic instructional procedures would be the same as with multiplication. Of course, the teacher must be sure to establish the basic difference between multiplication and division by using examples showing that division is the inverse of multiplication. Having clearly established the differences, the teacher would use reinforcement, evaluation, and spaced review as before.

3. *Prerequisite knowledge*

Within Gagné's hierarchy, concept learning (level 6) is immediately prerequisite to rule learning. Thus, the following concepts would have to be previously acquired if the student is to learn the rules for multiplication and division:

a. Recognizing multiplication and division symbols.
b. Capability of writing the correct symbols for multiplying and dividing.
c. Recognizing the need to multiply or divide, depending on the problem and the information given.

CLASSROOM SITUATION 2

An English teacher wishes the class to learn the rule "The first letter of the first word in a sentence must be capitalized." (1) State the teaching strategy you would use in teaching this rule. (2) What concepts go into the development of such a rule?

Sample Answer

1. The first task in the *teaching strategy* is to prepare the student for learning. The teacher might write several sentences on the board, some of which are

not properly capitalized. Upon student recognition of the difference between capitalized and noncapitalized sentences, a verbal statement of the rule will serve to guide the learner in the ensuing task. Students should then be presented with stimuli that will pull the relevant concepts into a *functional* rule. This would include a review of upper- and lower-case letter forms and the sentence, and the learning of some of the conditions under which to capitalize words and the functional uses and purposes of capitalization. The teacher would then present additional sentence stimuli to which the student must respond by capitalization in order to correct the sentences. The teacher can determine through this student behavior whether the desired learning has taken place.

Since rule learning is relatively high on the hierarchy and requires much prerequisite learning, it presupposes that sufficient reinforcement has already taken place at the lower learning levels. Therefore, in learning this rule on capitalization, the student may merely be intermittently reinforced when the teacher deems it necessary. It is possible that teacher evaluation of the student's written responses will provide sufficient feedback to the student as to the appropriateness of his response. This evaluation will also provide the teacher with an indication of student progress, of course. Use of the rule in subsequent learning situations keeps the rule in use and assures its retention.

2. Figure 8.2 indicates the prerequisite concepts to the learning of this rule.

FIGURE 8.2.   Relevant Concepts for the Rule on Sentence Capitalization

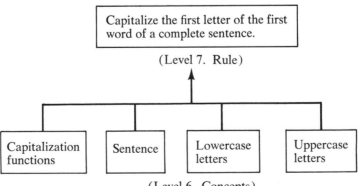

CLASSROOM SITUATION 3

A teacher is assigned to an English class for native speakers of Spanish. Thus, he is teaching a *new* task for which none of the students have prerequisite knowledge. The final behavioral objective involves the correct use of the *past tense* of the verb *"to be"* in *declarative* sentences, *negative* sentences, and *interrogative* sentences. (1) What would you do to prepare your students for learning the task? (2) State the behavioral objectives for the task? (3) What principles would you use in your teaching strategy? (4) How might you evaluate yourself on the task? (5) How would you assess student behavioral change?

Sample Answer

1. The teacher determines that the Spanish-speaking students lack the following prerequisite capabilities:
   a. Saying the words "was" and "were."
   b. Saying each of the English subject pronouns with the appropriate past-tense form of "to be" ("I was," "you were," "he was," and so on). Therefore, before proceeding with instruction directly related to the specific behavioral objective of this unit, the teacher would provide the instruction to establish these necessary capabilities.

2. *Behavioral objectives*
   a. The student will be able to use the past tense of the verb "to be" in declarative sentences.
      (1) The student will be able to use the present tense of the verb "to be" ("am," "is," "are") in statements.
      (2) The student will be able to change statements, such as "We are in the same class," from present to past tense.
      (3) The student will be able to translate into English several statements containing any of the four past-tense Spanish equivalents of "was" and "were" (example: "Yo *era* buen estudiante."—"I was a good student." "Yo *estaba* enfermo."—"I was sick.").
      (4) The student will be able to supply the correct English past-tense form when given sentences, such as "He *(was/were)* late yesterday."

    b. The student will be able to use the past tense of the verb "to be" in negative statements.

       (1) The student will be able to discriminate between declarative statements and negative statements.

       (2) The student will be able to use the present tense of the verb "to be" in negative statements.

       (3) The student will be able to form the negative of the past tense of the verb "to be" by placing the word "not" before the verb.

       (4) The student will be able to translate into English several statements containing the Spanish equivalents of the negative "to be."

       (5) The student will be able to change statements in the past tense to a negative form (example: "We were absent."—"We were not absent.").

    c. The student will be able to use the past tense of the verb "to be" in questions.

       (1) The student will be able to discriminate between declarative sentences and questions.

       (2) The student will be able to use the present tense of the verb "to be" in questions.

       (3) The student will be able to form questions by placing the verb in front of the subject.

       (4) The student will be able to translate into English several questions using the Spanish equivalents of "to be."

       (5) The student will be able to change past-tense statements to questions (example: "John was sick all week."—"Was John sick all week?").

3. *Teaching strategy*

    a. *Student preparation.*

       (1) *Restatement of general behavioral objectives.*   The teacher will remind the students that their objective is to communicate effectively in English and that the verb "to be" is one of the important English verbs.

       (2) *Warm-up.*   The teacher will provide a review (a) of the prerequisite capabilities learned immediately prior to this teaching unit and (b) of the use of the present tense of the verb "to be."

(3) *Readiness.*   The teacher has determined that all students are able to use the present tense of the verb "to be" and that they are able to distinguish among declarative, negative, and interrogative sentences.

b. *Presentation of stimuli.*   The teacher must devote particular attention to the presentation of discriminated stimuli; for he must be sure not only that the stimuli are strongly associated and clearly differentiated but also that they are presented in such a way that they can be understood by students with a minimal knowledge of English.

c. *Student response and reinforcement.*   Since the group involved is more deficient than an average class, and since a great deal of the work is oral, immediate reinforcement should be provided more often than in the usual classroom situation. Each student should have the opportunity to make several responses, and the teacher must immediately reinforce the correct responses.

d. *Evaluation.* Evaluation should occur at each point that the teacher believes that a behavioral objective has been accomplished. For example, the performance of the behavior of translating the four past-tense Spanish equivalents of "was" and "were" should be evaluated before instruction on the next objective is begun. The evaluation will provide feedback (and reinforcement) to the student concerning the adequacy of his performance and will also enable the teacher to determine the effectiveness of his teaching strategy.

Final evaluation of each of the three specific behavioral objectives will require the student to demonstrate the newly learned capability by constructing and using original sentences which employ the past tense of the verb "to be" in different situations.

e. *Spaced review.* Review is planned in conjunction with periodic evaluations. At each evaluation, the review will involve all prior learning to that point.

4. *Assessment of student behavioral change*

An effective way of measuring behavioral change in this situation is to observe whether a student is able to use the past tense of the verb "to be" in his daily speaking and writing. If simple observation seems insufficient, a teacher-made test could be devised to measure the following:

a. The student's ability to make an original statement using the past tense of the verb "to be."
b. The student's ability to answer a question with a negative answer using the past tense of the verb "to be."
c. The student's ability to ask an original question using the past tense of the verb "to be."

CLASSROOM SITUATION 4

In a mathematics class, the learning task is to recognize and learn the differences between the shapes of a circle, square, and triangle. (1) State the behavioral objectives. (2) What instructional materials might you use in teaching this discriminatory task? (3) How would you test the students to determine if the differences had been learned?

Sample Answer

1. Upon completion of the teaching unit, the student should be able to

   a. Recognize the shapes of a circle, square, and triangle in objects presented by the teacher.
   b. Recognize the shapes of a circle, square, and triangle when presented with other objects.
   c. Name the three shapes.
   d. Classify new and unfamiliar objects by their shapes as circles, squares, and triangles.

2. Since the learning task is at both the multiple discrimination (a and b) and concept learning (c and d) levels and is dependent on concrete objects, the teacher would naturally find it advantageous to use instructional materials illustrating circular, square, and triangular objects as the stimuli. The teacher may select large assorted shapes (properly labeled) to work with as well as sets of familiar objects, such as

   Circles: ball, coin, clock, wheel, cookie, ring, plate.
   Squares: box, blocks, stamp, photograph.
   Triangles: slice of pie, musical instrument, wedge.

In addition, the teacher might hand out special materials which present the various shapes; for example, a puzzle made up of the different shapes, worksheets with shapes to be colored differently, worksheets with incomplete shapes for the student to complete and flash cards with the shape on one side and its name on the other.

3. To determine how much learning had taken place, the teacher could

   a. Test the first behavioral object by saying, "On the bulletin board is a picture of a circle. Find the object in your box of shapes that is like that picture." Similar activities would be carried out with objects representing the square and triangle.
   b. Test the second behavioral objective by stating, "Tell me something that is in this classroom which has the shape of the circle (square, triangle) placed on the bulletin board."
   c. Test the third behavioral objective by tracing the outline of a circle (square, triangle) in the air with his finger and asking, "What is the name of this shape?"
   d. Test the fourth behavioral objective by giving the student an assortment of objects he has not seen before and telling him to group all of the objects that are shaped like a circle, all shaped like a square, and all shaped like a triangle.

CLASSROOM SITUATION 5

It is the beginning of the school year, and a seventh-grade science teacher faces students from several different elementary schools. The teacher suspects that the students differ in their science achievement level. While a standardized diagnostic test could be used to determine the achievement level of the incoming students, the teacher prefers to make his own diagnostic test because it will help him evaluate the science achievement level in relationship to the behavioral goals he has in mind for the class. (1) Develop some sample questions that would be diagnostic. (2) What particular goals or objectives would this preassessment help you reach? (3) What student mastery level do you expect on the diagnostic test?

Sample Answer

1. Sample items on the diagnostic test.

   a. An "empty" bottle open to the air is (1) empty (2) not empty.
   b. Air is mostly (1) nitrogen gas (2) oxygen gas.

    c. When air is bubbled into a bottle of water, the air (1) displaces the water (2) dissolves the water.

    d. A medicine dropper is squeezed into water, then released. Water goes up into the medicine dropper because the water is (1) sucked up (2) pushed up.

    e. When iron rusts, it combines with (1) oxygen (2) nitrogen.

    f. All substances are made up of (1) other substances (2) molecules.

2. The specific learning outcomes assisted by such diagnostic testing are

    a. Substances have properties which distinguish one from another.

    b. Molecules move around.

    c. Molecules of substances interact with one another.

3. Since the learning represented in the diagnostic test is quite elementary and necessary to the subsequent teaching–learning tasks, a 100 percent mastery level would be desired. In the event that students did not know the facts indicated within the questions, the teacher would, of course, teach the relevant prerequisite skills before embarking on the new learning tasks.

CLASSROOM SITUATION 6

    A reading teacher wishes to assess the reading ability of a group of children entering the fourth grade. She plans to give an informal reading inventory, which is an instrument designed to provide diagnostic information about reading. The inventory is not normed in the customary way, although there are certain parts, such as word calling and speed, which can yield percentages for norm reference. What types of information and what value would such an assessment yield?

Sample Answer

The following are the different tests of a typical information reading inventory:

1. *Word calling, or vocabulary.* Graded words (those words generally taught in a particular grade) are presented according to increasing difficulty, and the student must name the words. Such a test would be norm referenced to require a 90 percent mastery at the midyear third-grade order for the

student to proceed successfully to a fourth-grade reader. This high proficiency level is chosen by the teacher because there usually is a relatively large increase in reading-skill expectations from third to fourth grade.

2. *Reading comprehension.*   This test requires a student to silently read a page-long passage from a reader graded at the beginning third-grade level. To demonstrate readiness for fourth-grade reading, the student must then be able to state coherently (as judged by the teacher) the main idea or concepts derived from his reading. The reason the teacher places mastery at the third-grade level is that the student is reading silently (no auditory feedback), and it is assumed that he knows practically all the words in the passage.

3. *Listening comprehension.*   Stories ranked by teacher evelation at the fifth-grade level are read to the student, and he must coherently (as judged by the teacher) summarize the content of the story. These stories are approximately two pages in length. The rationale for this test is that in order to read meaningfully, a person usually has to bring some of his own ideas or concepts to the material on the printed page. The mastery level is established at one grade above the student's instructional level because the subject does not have to read in this test.

4. *Speed and fluency.*   The student must orally read a graded one-page passage at approximately normal talking rate for the student. The "normal talking rate" is subjectively evaluated by the teacher, as is the proficiency of the student in reading smoothly and with expression. The student first reads the passage silently and is given assistance with words he does not know. The norm-referenced mastery level is placed at the midyear third-grade level because the student is allowed a silent practice trial with assistance.

5. *Phonetic generalization.*   The student is given unfamiliar words that can be analyzed phonetically and is asked to pronounce them. The criterion for mastery is that he is able to apply (not state) four phonetic rules, such as the "silent *e*" rule (mat—mate).

6. *Mathematical reading.*   Every student has his own vocabulary. Some children who can handle readers at this grade level cannot read efficiently in other subject areas at that level, particularly mathematics books. In this test, the student is required to read a page of story problems from a third-grade math book and is asked to describe in his own words what the

question is about. He need not know how to do the problem. The mastery level is placed at the third grade because the student must be able to adequately read third-grade mathematics material in order to be able to begin fourth-grade mathematics.

Because the requirements for these tests would be difficult for some students to master totally, the teacher would allow the student to fall short of meeting one requirement by one grade level. For example, if the student's listening comprehension is at the third-grade level instead of the fourth-grade level, the teacher might assume that he is still able to be instructed in reading at the fourth-grade level. The teacher must, of course, help the child in his weak area. In the instance of vocabulary, on the other hand, being one grade level low probably precludes functioning at the higher grade level. In this case, the teacher's task becomes one of remediation. Special attention must be given to build the skills that the student lacks, so that he will have an adequate basis for learning.

A person trained to give an informal reading inventory is able to administer it in approximately 20 minutes. Thus, even with a class of 30 students, the trained teacher should be able to administer and place his students by the end of the first week of school and, at the same time, carry on with normal instruction.

CLASSROOM SITUATION 7

A teacher is planning a unit on animals, selecting the major animals of the world and grouping them according to their environments—the mountains, woodlands, tropical forests, grasslands, oceans, deserts, and polar regions. (1) Briefly state the desired student behavior objectives. (2) At what level in Gagné's hierarchy is this teaching–learning situation? (3) List the immediate prerequisite learning the student should bring to this task in order to learn efficiently.

Sample Answer

It's your turn. Using your learning up to this point, work through this situation as if you were the teacher.

CLASSROOM SITUATION 8

When the student is learning at the rule-learning level in Gagné's hierarchy, he is learning to formulate rules applicable to problem-solving situations. The following example of rule learning (Figure 8.3) demonstrates various ways in which the teacher can present stimuli to his students to confirm their learning level. After reading through the example, why not work out a similar strategy for yourself?

CLASSROOM SITUATION 9

After discussing *area* in a math class, the teacher gives students the following problem:

June's mother plans to lay new carpet in the family room. The room is 14 feet long and 8 feet wide. How many square yards of carpet must be purchased?

This problem requires the conversion of the dominant numbers into yards and a knowledge of the concept of area. The following rules are prerequisite to this problem solving:

1. To find area, multiply length (l) times width (w).
2. To convert feet into yards, take the divisor (constant 3) into the dividend (total feet) to find the quotient (yards).
3. To express the remainder in rule 2 as a fraction of a yard, make the remainder the numerator and the divisor (constant 3) the denominator.

Plan the teaching of this problem, (1) identifying the concepts necessary to these rules and (2) stating the teaching strategy you will use.

FIGURE 8.3   *Confirming the Learning of Boyle's Law (Level 7)*

1a. Given the verbatim statement of the principle, the student can supply its name.

1a. The volume of a gas varies inversely as the absolute pressure, while the density varies directly as the absolute pressure, providing that the temperature is constant.

1b. Given the verbatim statement of the principle, the student can select its name.

1b. The volume of a gas varies inversely as the absolute pressure, while the density varies directly as the absolute pressure, providing that the temperature is constant. This principle is called:
   (a) Charles' law
   (b) Boyle's law
   (c) Dalton's law

2a. Given the name of the principle, the student can supply a verbatim statement of the principle.

2a. State Boyle's law.

2b. Given the name of the principle, the student can select the verbatim statement of the principle.

2b. Which of the following is Boyle's law:
   (a) The volume of a gas varies directly as its absolute temperature, if the pressure remains constant.
   (b) The volume of a gas varies inversely as the absolute pressure, while the density varies directly as the absolute pressure, providing that the temperature is constant.
   (c) The partial pressure of each gas in a mixture is proportional to the relative amount of that gas in the mixture.

3a. Given an example, the student can supply a statement of the principle.

3a. A balloon containing 10 pints of air at sea level is taken 33 feet below the seawater. Its volume is compressed to 5 pints while its density is doubled. This demonstrates, in technical terms, _____.

3b. Given a familiar example, the student can select the statement of the principle.

3b. A balloon containing 10 pints of air at sea level is taken 33 feet below the seawater. Its volume is compressed to 5 pints while its density is doubled. Which of the following is the best explanation of what has happened?

FIGURE 8.3 (continued)

(a) The volume of air in the balloon decreased inversely as the water pressure, so long as the temperature remained constant.

(b) The volume of the gas decreased directly as the temperature, since the pressure remained constant.

4a. Given a new example, the student can supply a statement of the principle.

4a. A diver at 66 feet below the sea will use up his air twice as fast as he would at 33 feet if all else remains equal. Explain why this happens.

4b. Given a new example, the student can select the statement of the principle.

4b. A diver at 66 feet below the sea will use up his air twice as fast as he would at 33 feet if all else remains equal. Which of the following is the best explanation of why this happens?

(a) The volume of gas varies inversely as the absolute pressure, while the density varies directly as the absolute pressure, provided that the temperature remains constant.

(b) The volume of the air will be varying inversely with the temperature, since the pressure is remaining constant.

5a. Given the statement of the principle, the student can supply an example included in the reading for the unit.

5a. The volume of air will vary inversely as the absolute pressure, while the density varies directly as the absolute pressure, provided that the temperature is constant. Give a concrete example of this which appeared in your reading.

5b. Given the statement of the principle, the student can select an example included in the reading for the unit.

5b. The volume of air will vary inversely as the absolute pressure, while the density varies directly as the absolute pressure, provided that the temperature is constant. Which of the following best illustrates this principle?

(a) A balloon contains 10 pints of air at sea level, but the volume decreases to only 5 pints under 33 feet of seawater while its density is doubled.

FIGURE 8.3 (continued)

(b) A high pressure cylinder placed on the beach in the hot sun will blow its safety valve.

6a. Given the statement of the principle, the student can supply a new example.

6a. The volume of a gas will vary inversely as the absolute pressure, while the density varies directly as the absolute pressure, so long as the temperature remains constant. Explain this principle in a concrete example which was not included in your reading.

6b. Given the statement of the principle, the student can select a new example.

6b. The volume of a gas will vary inversely with the absolute pressure, while the density varies directly with the absolute pressure, provided that the temperature remains constant. Which of the following best illustrates this principle?
(a) A deep-sea diver ascending without exhaling risks an air embolism.
(b) A deep-sea diver has to go through decompression when he exceeds the depth time given in the U.S. Navy's diving-limits table because of his body's absorption of nitrogen at below–sea-level pressures.

The communications teacher wants his students to have an understanding of the forms of speech. *Can he maximize learning by moving sequentially from a relatively unstructured internal "speech" to such highly structured forms as debate, oratory, or choral reading?*

The forms of speech are most certainly sequential; that is, if the student learns a simple speech form, that learning is transferable to increasingly more difficult and sophisticated speech forms. Thus, the teacher can use *transfer* here quite effectively.

The typical way to begin the study of speech is through an analysis of its forms. The teacher should convey the idea that no communication is formless, because communication infers meaning and meaning emerges only through form. In addition, the student should learn that form in speech varies from the simple internal induction of meaning by the encoding of feelings into thoughts and inner conversations to the most complex outer forms of speech that have been formalized through the conventions and rules evolved from the experiences of public speakers and critics over a period of time. In teaching these ideas, the teacher is instilling in students the prerequisite concepts for an understanding of the sequential nature of speech forms. In short, the following concepts are prerequisite to a learning of the forms of speech and the rules relevant to the more highly stylized outer forms:

1. All communication has form.
2. Meaning in speech is created through form.
3. The simplest speech form is the internalization of meaning through encoding our feelings.
4. The more complex, highly stylized forms of outer speech have emerged out of tried conventions and rules.
5. The forms of speech are sequentially built, with inner conversations setting the basis for outer conversation forms in an interaction between the internal state and the environment.

Having learned these basic concepts about speech, the student is ready to view and acquire the various outer speech forms in a hierarchy based on complexity and formality of structure and circumstances. Public speaking is the most common conventionalized form of outer speech. As the speaker becomes more self-conscious and begins adding more conventions and rules to his speech, the forms become more stylized. One more complex form of public speaking is extemporaneous speaking, characterized by the ability to think on one's feet. Even more structured speech forms are represented by round-table discussions, symposiums, and forums. Another highly conventionalized speech form is debate. This speech form follows very rigidly prescribed rules, has defined topics, and involves the interaction of presentation and rebuttal among its participants. Even more sophisticated speech forms, such as oratory, oral interpretation of literature, and dramatic reading, involve a speaker–audience format and interaction and, while technically speech forms, are more characteristic of acting.

Implicit in teaching such a wide spectrum of speech forms is the building of concepts and rules and the presentation of problematic situations in which the student can exercise his abilities. The learning of one speech form effectively sets the stage for the teaching and learning of a second. A hierarchical arrangement of this learning process is as follows:

Level 8: A variety of simple and complex problem-solving encounters designed to give the student the opportunity to use each of the forms as he learns the related rules and concepts.

↑

Level 7: The learning of rules governing form of presentation, preparation for presentation, and evaluation of presentation.

↑

Level 6: Specific concepts governing each speech form.

↑

Level 5: General concepts which affect all speech forms and give the students an operational understanding of speech and the forms that it can take.

2

The Teaching-Learning Situation

The woodworking teacher is puzzled that some students have a real knack for making things, while others, no matter how hard they try, are invariably unsuccessful. *What should this teacher realize about individual differences in students?* (See page 234.)

In social studies class, one student persists in his antisocial behavior, upsetting the class and affecting the classroom learning environment. *How can the teacher modify this student's behavior?* (See page 280.)

A physical education teacher notices that increased abilities occurred when his boys found out that their grade was determined by the amount of self-improvement they made with physical fitness exercises. *How does the research on motivation explain this behavioral change?* (See page 255.)

A heated discussion occurs in a health education class over the pros and cons of smoking marijuana. *What learning domains are operational here?* (See page 289.)

The science teacher is troubled by the selection of the most appropriate way to assign marks and final grades. *Is there one way of grading that is distinctly preferable?* (See page 352.)

A group of teachers have a lengthy discussion on the purposes of intelligence tests and achievement tests in school. The consensus opinion is that an achievement test tells them more about their students than intelligence testing. *Why might they draw that conclusion?* (See page 223.)

The philosophy of one school district is to have each teacher write his teaching units in behavioral terms. Some of the teachers complain because they find the stating of behavioral objectives to be cumbersome and not that advantageous to teaching. *Is there a simple, nonambiguous way to write behavioral objectives?* (See page 312.)

The art teacher strives to instill in her students a strong sense of creative expression. *What type of learning is this?* (See page 293.)

All of these questions are concerned in some way with the factor of individual differences and its effect on teaching and learning theory and methods. This is the subject of Part 2 in this book. Chapters 9 through 13 and both Appendix A and B provide information which will broaden the prospective teacher's understanding of the total teaching–learning situation.

Chapters 9 and 10 discuss intelligence and motivation, two individual variables that every learner brings into the learning environment. The chapter on intelligence discusses intelligence tests and theories, the developmental nature of intelligence, and shows how this variable affects learning.

Chapter 10 discusses several classroom indications of motivation and deals with a variety of teacher concerns, such as the source of motivation, the ability of a teacher to motivate a student, and the types of motivation most central to classroom learning.

Behavior modification is a topic of increasing concern and relevance to the teacher. This is a relatively new and controversial procedure in which the learning principles of operant conditioning are used systematically in modifying or changing a student's undesirable social or academic behavior. The effectiveness and limitations of behavioral modification and its function in and relationship to the teaching-learning environment are the subjects of Chapter 11.

Chapter 12 discusses affective learning, which is the emergence of attitudinal and value systems within students. Attitude structures and personality traits are the dominant part of this chapter. In addition, because teachers often instruct with attitudinal or social goals in mind, a discussion of attitude teaching and attitudinal behavioral objectives will demonstrate how affective and cognitive learning may occur within the same teaching-learning context and strategies.

Chapter 13, the final chapter in the book, is not the traditional summary; rather, it reviews some of the most current research and innovations in teaching and learning. In addition, computer technology and the movement toward computer-assisted instruction as a teaching alternative are discussed. Measurement and statistics are discussed in Appendix A to help the teacher in the formulation of ideas and methods for systematically evaluating student learning. Appendix B is a reprint of an article which will serve, in combination with Chapters 2 and 12, in understanding behavioral objectives.

In short, the reader can expect the following learning outcomes from a study of Part 2 of this text:

1. An awareness of the basic theories of intelligence, as well as the concept of measuring intelligence.
2. An understanding of the relationship between intelligence and learning, especially in regard to mental growth and complexity.
3. An understanding of basic motivational forces within the learner and within the classroom.
4. The learning of the theory and usefulness of behavior modification procedures within a classroom setting.
5. A recognition of the difference between using behavior modification as a method of eliciting desirable alternative behaviors and using it as an alternative to punishment.
6. An understanding of the controversy over the use of behavioral objectives in the classroom.
7. An operational understanding of affective behavioral domains.
8. An awareness of the current trends in educational psychology.
9. An introductory acquaintance with different statistics which might be used in classroom measurement.
10. An understanding of the basic distinction between norm-referenced and criterion-referenced measurement and the implications for classroom evaluation.

9

Human Intelligence

"How to Raise Your Child's IQ"; "You and Your Child's IQ"—these typical titles from articles appearing in popular magazines reflect the public's concern and curiosity about one of the more controversial issues in education. What is intelligence? Are there relationships between intelligence, environment, and race? Are intelligence tests fair? How much does intelligence affect classroom learning?

Essentially, intelligence is a measure of how an individual behaves. The intelligence of the preschool child is frequently judged on the basis of his alertness, attentiveness, motor ability, language ability, and "cleverness." During the educational years, estimations of intelligence are very often tied primarily to the child's school achievement, although other factors, such as those mentioned for the preschool child, may enter into the estimation. The post-education period usually brings a largely different kind of estimation, which is most frequently derived from occupational status, language ability, and interests and conversational topics.

Clearly, this type of definition of intelligence is operational in nature; that is, intelligence is being measured by the individual's behaviors and achievements. It is a useful but somewhat imprecise measure. A parent of a cerebral-palsied child who has just been told her child's intelligence quotient and asks, "But what is his real IQ?", is intimating that there is a more basic intelligence, a capacity which cannot be actualized because of the nature of the child's impairment. Those psychologists who criticize current, largely "operational" intelligence tests on the basis of their being culturally biased against certain minority or socioeconomic groups are making the same point— that existing tests do not measure "real" intelligence. This viewpoint of intelligence as a *potential capacity,* based, most likely, on heredity and genetic factors, may very well be theoretically correct, but at the present time, we have no reliable measuring instruments to determine this capacity.

Thus, for the time being, intelligence must be considered to be what intelligence tests measure. And, therefore, we must continually keep in mind that the test itself is determining our concept of intelligence and that we must be cautious in extending this measurement to areas other than those for which it was intended—which, in the case of most tests, is "how is the student functioning now" and "what are the possibilities of his functioning at a higher level if learning conditions are modified."

THEORIES AND MEASUREMENT OF INTELLIGENCE

The number and variety of concepts and definitions of intelligence are reflected in the plethora of intelligence tests which are available. Buros' *Tests in Print* (1961) lists 263 standardized tests of intelligence or scholastic ability. Not each of these has an individualized definition of intelligence, of course, but, still, such a large number of different tests indicates the often bewildering array of conceptual possibilities for measuring intellectual capability and achievement.

Single-factor tests

Historically, the *single-factor theory* of intelligence was the first concept to be applied to intellectual measurement. This theory is exemplified in the testing scales developed in France by Alfred Binet in 1904. Brought to the United States, these scales were further developed and revised by Lewis Terman in 1916 and have, since, been revised several times, with the latest revision in 1960. Terman defined intelligence as the ability to think in abstract terms, and this ability (the single factor) is the primary emphasis in the test items of what is now called the *Stanford–Binet Intelligence Scale.* Examples of questions from the Stanford–Binet are illustrated in Figure 9.1. The number of questions that the examinee is able to answer correctly represents his *mental age* (MA), which serves as the measure of intellectual status. The score is reported in terms of years and months of *mental growth;* that is, a child who scores X-3 has correctly answered the same number of questions as the *average* child with a chronolog-

FIGURE 9.1.   *Sample Questions from Stanford–Binet Scale, Form L–M*

Year II-6   *Identifying Parts of the Body*

The child is shown a large paper doll and is asked to point to the hair, mouth, feet, ear, nose, hands, and eyes.

Year VI: *Differences*

What is the difference between a bird and a dog?

Year VIII   *Verbal Absurdities*

A man had flu (influenza) twice. The first time it killed him, but the second time he got well quickly. What is foolish about that?

Year XIV   *Vocabulary*

Examinee must define 17 words correctly.

Reprinted from the Stanford–Binet Intelligence Scale, Form L–M, by permission of Houghton Mifflin Company.

ical age of 10 years, 3 months. Then, with the child's chronological age (CA), the MA can be converted to an intelligence quotient (IQ) which represents a rate of mental growth. Thus, the quotient reflects a *relative* degree of "brightness," or intellectual growth. A child who is 8 years, 4 months of age and demonstrates a mental age of 10 years, 5 months would have an IQ of 125, which indicates that he is growing mentally at the rate of 1¼ years for each year of chronological growth.

Until the 1960 revision of the Stanford–Binet scales, the intelligence quotient was computed by the formula IQ = MA/CA × 100. The 1960 revision reports *deviation intelligence scores,* which are scores that are statistically more accurate than those based on the earlier formula. However, the IQ is still interpreted in the same manner, representing a ratio of mental age to chronological age.

The Binet tests were first developed in France to screen out those children who could not benefit from regular academic school experiences. In America, they were revised to assist the schools in predicting and preparing for the capabilities of individual children in classroom learning. Since schools were then and still are highly oriented toward verbal and abstract learning, and since the test questions on the Stanford–Binet are highly verbal in content, the single-factor intelligence score of the Stanford–Binet serves adequately for predicting a child's success in school.

However, we cannot assume that the single-factor intelligence measure of the Stanford–Binet will be reflected in the whole range of activities or learning behaviors which the child will perform within and outside of the classroom. If the child is "average" in intelligence according to the Stanford–Binet, he is not necessarily capable of showing an average performance in arithmetic or mechanics or any other less verbal school activity. This test predicts quite well for performances on tasks that are verbally oriented, but it will not serve as well in predicting achievement in tasks that are not highly related to verbal ability.

Another commonly used group intelligence test which provides a single-factor score and reflects the same verbal orientation is the *Otis–Lennon Mental Ability Test,* which measures and predicts at six levels ranging from kindergarten through twelfth grade.

Two-factor tests

The most popular approach in two-factor testing is reflected by the three *Wechsler Scales:* (1) Wechsler Pre-school and Primary Scales of Intelligence (WPPSI), (2) Wechsler Intelligence Scale for Children (WISC), and (3) Wechsler Adult Intelligence Scale (WAIS). David Wechsler (1944) defines intelligence as "the aggregate or global capacity of the individual to act purposefully, to think rationally, and to deal effectively with his environment" (p. 3). Wechsler cites the concept of an *aggregate* or *global intelligence,* which refers to the idea that there are several components of the mind which, as a whole, make up an individual's intellectual capacity. His tests, then, were designed to yield three measures of intelligence; the *verbal IQ,* the *performance IQ,* and the *total IQ,* which is a combination of the other two scales.

The verbal score within the WISC and WAIS tests is measured in sub-tests that are termed *General Information, General Comprehension, Arithmetic, Similarities,* and *Vocabulary,* with *Digit Span* as an alternate test. The performance scale in these tests is found through sub-tests called *Picture Completion, Picture Arrangement, Block Design,* and *Object Assembly,* with *Coding with a Maze Test* as an alternate. The WPPSI taps the same abilities, but the names and subject matter of the sub-tests are slightly different. Each sub-test of the various Wechslers yields a standard score which is then combined with other sub-test scores to produce the verbal IQ or performance IQ. The total IQ is then computed from the combination of these two measures. Sample questions paraphrased from selected sub-tests of the Wechslers are shown in Figure 9.2.

The verbal and total IQs of the Wechslers relate highly with the results of a Stanford–Binet test. The correlation of the performance scale of the Wechslers with Stanford–Binet results is somewhat lower, of course. One advantage of the Wechsler two-factor testing is that significant differences between sub-test scores and between

FIGURE 9.2.   *Paraphrased Wechsler-type Questions*

Verbal IQ Sub-tests

General Information

1. How many wings does a bird have?
2. How many nickels make a dime?
3. What is steam made of?
4. Who wrote "Paradise Lost"?
5. What is pepper?

General Comprehension

1. What should you do if you see someone forget his book when he leaves his seat in a restaurant?
2. What is the advantage of keeping money in a bank?
3. Why is copper often used in electrical wires?

Arithmetic

1. Sam had three pieces of candy and Joe gave him four more. How many pieces of candy did Sam have altogether?
2. Three men divided eighteen golf balls equally among themselves. How many golf balls did each man receive?
3. If two apples cost 15¢, what will be the cost of a dozen apples?

Similarities

1. In what way are a lion and a tiger alike?
2. In what way are a saw and a hammer alike?
3. In what way are an hour and a week alike?
4. In what way are a circle and a triangle alike?

Vocabulary

This test consists simply of asking questions like "What is a _____?" or "What does_____ mean?" The words cover a wide range of difficulty and familiarity.

Performance IQ Sub-tests

The various performance tasks in these sub-tests involve the use of blocks, cut-out figures, paper and pencil puzzles, etc.

These paraphrased Wechsler-type test items were prepared by The Psychological Corporation and are reprinted with their permission.

verbal and performance IQs may assist the teacher in recognizing certain intellectual strengths or weaknesses within a student.

Other group intelligence tests representative of the two-factor approach are the *Lorge–Thorndike Intelligence Tests,* the *Kuhlmann–Anderson Intelligence Tests, seventh edition,* and the *Henmon–Nelson Tests of Mental Ability, revised edition.* The

Lorge–Thorndike test reflects a concept of intelligence much like that of the Wechslers. Two different kinds of abilities are measured: (1) *verbal*—knowledge and ability to work with symbols, and (2) *nonverbal*—ability to work with figural and spatial relations. The Kuhlmann–Anderson and Henmon–Nelson scores are called *verbal* and *quantitative.* Their tests for verbal ability are similar in nature to the Lorge–Thorndike and appear to tap basically the same abilities. However, the quantitative score represents a somewhat different orientation—the examinee's ability to work with, manipulate, and see relations between numbers. The Kuhlmann–Anderson tests are designed for kindergarten through twelfth grade, while the Lorge–Thorndike tests begin at grade three and extend through the college freshman year. The Henmon–Nelson tests also begin at grade three and extend through the college sophomore year.

Multi-factor tests

The Thurstone test of Primary Mental Abilities is perhaps the most representative of several multi-factor tests which expand the global IQ concept of the two-factor tests. Through a statistical procedure called *factor analysis,* L. L. Thurstone (1938) analyzed 60 IQ sub-tests and was able to isolate seven abilities which in his opinion comprise a person's intelligence: *number, word fluency, verbal meaning, associative-memory, reasoning, space,* and *perceptual speed.* The *Thurstone Primary Mental Abilities Test,* with sub-tests representing each of these seven factors, was derived from this research. In order to make his test marketable, Thurstone shortened it by eliminating the entire Memory sub-test and by reducing the number of questions in the other sub-tests. Unfortunately, as a result of the fewer questions, the reliability of the sub-tests decreased, and prediction on the basis of the differential scores on the separate sub-tests is extremely risky. However, the total test score for the Thurstone sub-tests gives an adequate prediction of future academic achievement.

Theories of individual intelligences

With the advent of statistical analysis, and especially factor analysis, the concept of a global intelligence quotient was weakened. Statistical-analysis techniques were used to show that a global IQ concept was useful in predicting the achievement of an individual in certain learning activities, but it was less effective in accounting for the variances in an individual's abilities in a wide range of activities. Consequently, psychologists interested in intelligence and IQ testing have developed a number of theories which attempt to better explain the differences of abilities both within individuals and between groups of individuals. These theorists speak of individual intelligences rather than intelligence.

Spearman's "g" factor.   Charles Spearman, a British psychologist, came to the conclusion through a factor analysis (1927) that intelligence is composed of a *g* (general) factor and a large number of *s* (specific) factors. In a later formulation (Spearman & Jones, 1950), he amended his original thinking to reflect an overlapping of s factors into certain group factors. Spearman proposed that there is a controlling capability (the g factor) in all intellectual functioning and that this is the predominant factor called upon and measured on most intelligence tests. A person who is high in this g factor tends to do well in a variety of tasks, and a person low in g tends to do poorly. He also suggested, however, that there are *specific* abilities (the s factors) which are fairly insignificant in terms of the total functioning of the individual but which overlap and form certain group factors—verbal ability, numerical ability, mechanical ability, attention, and imagination, or creative ability—that are not always highly correlated with the individual's general capability, or g factor. For example, a student with below-average general achievement (g factor) might be exceptional in the area of mathematics or in creative ability. Thus, with this formulation, Spearman was able to explain the observed differences in an individual's overall achievement and his achievement in specific learning areas.

Guilford's structure of the intellect.   A more extensive factor analysis of intelligence is that of J. P. Guilford (1956,1967). Guilford conceptualizes the intellect as consisting of three major dimensions: (1) the *contents of thought,* (2) the *operations of thought,* and (3) the *products of thought.* Each of these dimensions is subdivided into a number of factors which, when combined in various interactions of thought, give a possible 120 different factors of intelligence. Approximately 80 of these factors have been delineated thus far. Guilford's concept of intelligence is represented figurally as the three dimensions of a cube, as shown in Figure 9.3. Guilford's system is a complex one; and for the purposes of this chapter, we need examine only one dimension of his concept of the intellect—that of the *contents of thought.*

The contents of thought are described by Guilford as the materials involved in thinking. Guilford proposes four kinds of content: *Figural content* represents concrete objects, the things that we perceive through the senses. Much of the young child's

FIGURE 9.3 *Guilford's Structure of the Intellect*

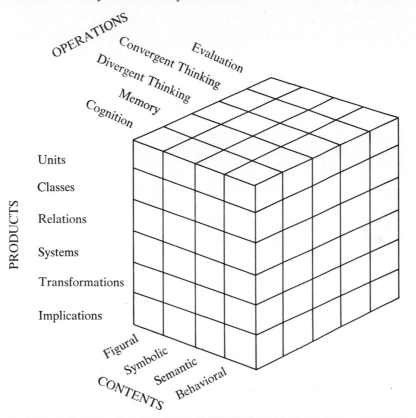

Guilford, J. P. Three faces of intellect, *American Psychologist,* 1959, **14,** 469–479.
Copyright 1959 by the American Psychological Association and reprinted by permission.

thinking is figural in nature, and some of adult thinking is also figural. The second type of content is *symbolic,* which includes letters, symbols, digits, or signs that have no real significance in themselves but have meanings attached to them. The symbol A, for example, has different meanings attached to it in the following situations:

He built an A-frame house.

$A = l \times w.$

He was playing A-sharp instead of A.

She received an A on her paper.

The meaning of each use of the symbol A is derived from the context and/or the figural referent which the symbol represents.

The third kind of content, *semantic,* is used in verbal thinking and verbal communication. For example, the word "apple" has meanings attached to it which make it possible for a person to visualize the figural referent, just as the abstract word "faith" has meanings which allow two people to converse about the concept. The fourth kind of content is *behavioral* or *empathic,* which refers to essentially nonverbal thoughts that are used in social interactions. Behavioral content can be illustrated by the *actions* that would cause a child to say, "The teacher says she likes me, but I know she doesn't." Guilford has described this content as being a "social intelligence."

Cattell's g_c and g_f factors.   Cattell (1940, 1963, 1968), a colleague of both Spearman and Thurstone, theorizes that the g (general) factor of intelligence measured by intelligence tests is actually made up of two factors. One g factor is the *crystallized general ability,* g_c, which reflects the effect of culture upon the person's mental functioning. The g_c factor stretches across the whole range of cultural acquisitions and involves such materials as vocabulary, analogies, numerical skills, and habits of logical reasoning.

Cattell's second factor is the *fluid general ability,* g_f, which has little to do with the learned or experiential aspects of the culture but, instead, reflects the inherent intellectual ability of the individual. This type of intellectual ability is thought to be measured by *culture-fair tests,* which, in essence, attempt to measure some general intellectual trait that is not culture-bound, such as numerical reasoning or exercises of judgment. A person with high g_f possesses the ability to perceive certain problem situations that are not culturally related, to reorganize these perceptions, and to arrive at a solution more quickly than a person with low g_f. For example, excellent chess players usually possess a high g_f which allows them to "see" whole patterns of strategic moves before they are made. A man with little formal education can operate quite well in such a situation if he possesses a high fluid general ability.

The individual with a high level of crystallized general ability has different capacities. He is able to readily *learn* many astute and "proper" responses to diverse problem situations, but his high g_c may be fairly useless in an unexpected turn of affairs or a situation that doesn't fit the culturally acquired response pattern. On the other hand, skills connected with high crystallized ability often would not be acquired if the person does not possess the high fluid ability to perceive the problems to which the skills might be applied.

Cattell hypothesizes that the two different abilities, g_c and g_f, show a different pattern, or curve, of growth rate. Fluid ability growth follows other biological maturational developments, reaching its peak in the individual at about 14 years of age, and declining somewhat after about 22 years of age. Crystallized intelligence, however, continues to grow into adulthood, and maintains its level for as long as adequate learning input continues.

Jensen's mental ability levels.   Arthur Jensen (1969) also hypothesizes that there are two different levels of intellectual functioning. Jensen's research began in an examination of the reasons for the rather limited effects of compensatory educational programs, such as Head Start and Higher Horizons, which were aimed at improving the educational success of lower socioeconomic class (culturally different) children. The primary purpose of these compensatory programs, as determined from evaluation studies, was the improvement of the IQ of these children; but the studies showed little average gain, and follow-up studies have shown that most of the gains that *were* made were not maintained through the first year of schooling (U.S. Commission on Civil Rights, 1967).

The basic premise upon which these compensatory programs were based was that the lower IQ of the culturally different child is due to a lack of preschool environmental stimulation and that a change in the environment to one more like the middle-class environment would increase the IQ. Thus, most of these programs were aimed at broadening the experimental backgrounds of these children by bringing them into direct contact with those experiences which were "normal" for the preschool child in the middle-class home. Jensen rejects this environmental-deprivation hypothesis as the cause of different intellectual ability levels between the various socioeconomic and racial groups and proposes, instead, that the level of intellectual ability is primarily a function of *heredity.* He acknowledges environment as a factor but terms it a *threshold variable,* in the belief that if the environment is not *severely* restricted, changes in the environment will not make an appreciable difference in IQ. If the environment is severely restricted, as, for example, in cases where children have been maltreated by being shut in a room with no environmental stimulation, then changes in the environment will make a significant difference in the level of intellectual functioning.

Thus, according to Jensen, the primary variance factor in different mental abilities is heredity. He hypothesizes (1969) that there are two levels of learning ability. *Level I, associative ability,* involves the registration of stimulus inputs in the neural mechanism, the consolidation of these inputs, and the formation of associations, with very little internal transformation of these inputs as they are emitted in the form of the responses. Digit memory, serial rote learning, and paired-associate learning would be included at this level of intellectual ability. *Level II, conceptual ability,* involves the *self-initiated* substantial transformation and elaboration of the stimulus input before a response is emitted. Concept learning and problem solving would be examples of this kind of ability, which is most truly measured by tests that are relatively "culture free" and high in the g factor of overall intellectual functioning.

On tests which measure level I abilities and which, by definition, are relatively "culture free," Jensen and his co-workers (1969) found that lower-class children, regardless of ethnic and racial origins, did no more poorly than environmentally "privileged" middle-class children. But on less culture-free tests measuring level II abilities, the lower-status children did not score as highly as the middle-class children. Jensen concludes from this research that two kinds of abilities, associative and conceptual, are indeed components of intellectual functioning; and through further research, he has developed the hypothesis that level I associative ability is necessary but not a sufficient requisite for the conceptual ability of level II. That is, he believes that high performance on level II tasks depends upon better than average ability in level I but that the reverse does not hold true. This hypothesis and the test results in his research also suggest to Jensen that level I ability is distributed about the same in all socioeconomic classes but that level II conceptual ability is distributed differently in lower and middle socioeconomic classes as a result of hereditary factors.

Jensen avers that the reason lower-status children do more poorly in school is that the schools tend to emphasize those skills connected with conceptual activities (his level II abilities). His plea is that the schools recognize different types of learning abilities among different groups and provide different methods of instruction that will capitalize on the *existing* abilities of each learner. He believes that we can provide equal education for all children only when we have recognized these differences and modified our instructional procedures to account for them.

DISTRIBUTION OF INTELLIGENCE

Although there is some evidence to the contrary, as we have seen in the research of Jensen (1969), the distribution of measured intelligence, like many other measured human traits and characteristics, tends to fall in a normal distribution pat-

A group of teachers have a lengthy discussion on the purposes of intelligence tests and achievement tests in school. The consensus opinion is that an achievement test tells them more about their students than intelligence testing. *Why might they draw that conclusion?*

Remember, intelligence tests attempt to measure a general capacity or potential for functioning. The common type of intelligence test given in a school is a *group* test which yields an intelligence quotient and maybe a grade equivalent. However, it is based heavily on verbal ability and may not be representative of the wide range of cultural backgrounds within any one classroom. In addition, it gives a single index of potentiality, the IQ, and may not yield information as to the strengths or weaknesses of a student within any specific academic subject.

Most teachers are more interested in how a student is actually doing than in his potential for learning, and achievement tests are more useful than intelligence tests in this regard. Consider the following achievement-test profile:

Name: Karen Southern   *Grade:* 5.1   *Test Date:* 10–1–72

Area test	Grade Equivalent	Average Grade Equivalent	National Percentile
Reading Vocabulary	6.4	5.7	67
Reading Comprehension	6.0	5.6	58
Language Mechanics	5.3	5.2	51
Arithmetic Concepts	6.8	5.5	85
Arithmetic Application	5.5	5.5	55
Science Concepts	4.8	5.1	45
Social Science Skills	5.4	4.9	53

From reading this profile, teachers get a good idea of how well Karen is doing in each subject area represented within the achievement-test battery. For instance, her reading teacher will recognize that Karen has a very good reading vocabulary and comprehension, much better than most of Karen's classmates and better than the national averages. Perhaps the teacher could give Karen accelerated work in reading. The science teacher, on the other hand, can see that although Karen is not too low in science, she is nevertheless slightly below her classmates and the national averages and will need attention if she is to handle beginning fifth grade science units.

Similarly, in math, the teacher could determine that under regular instructional procedures Karen can learn the relevant concepts being taught. However, there is considerable discrepancy between Karen's ability to formulate concepts and to work math problems. This information tells the teacher that somewhere between understanding and application, Karen has difficulty in learning, and appropriate instructional procedures should be used to help Karen bridge this difficulty gap. The teacher may find it necessary to give many different math problems to Karen, making sure that she is reinforced and given appropriate feedback information as to the accuracy of her performance. In short, data such as these allow the teachers to consider the range of individual differences within each classroom and to plan instruction accordingly.

While this is just a brief analysis of a hypothetical profile, it does point out why the teacher's consensus was that achievement tests were more worthwhile in the classroom than intelligence tests. The former are clearly more valuable to the classroom teacher because they reflect actual performance as compared to potentiality.

---

tern, or *curve,* among the population. The *mean* (middle point between the extremes) of this distribution curve is an IQ score of 100, and the *standard deviation* from the mean is usually 15 or 16 score points (see Figure 9.4), although in certain IQ tests, the distribution of scores may vary somewhat from these standard deviations.

In order to interpret a test score, then, a teacher must know, first of all, which test has been administered. The importance of this knowledge is that (1) as we have seen, the test maker defines his concept of intelligence by the kinds of questions he asks, and (2) a test for which the standard deviation differs from the usual 15 or 16 percent will produce a markedly different IQ figure than a test that complies to this "normal" standard deviation. As an example, assume that we have IQ scores for one student from three different tests on which he performed equally well. Assume also that the means are all 100 (although if this is *not* true, then the IQ scores on the different tests are apt to vary even more). However, the standard deviations of tests X, Y, and Z vary at 15, 16, and 20 points respectively. The differences in recorded IQs for the student are illustrated in Table 9.1.

Such differences between IQ scores on tests with different standard deviations have been the main reason that many teachers have lost faith in intelligence scores. If a student has taken two IQ tests, X and Z, and the teacher sees only that one test scores the student 115, while the other gives him an IQ rank of 120, the teacher is naturally confused and concerned about the differing results. And as a student scores farther from the mean, the differences in the two test results become greater and even more bewildering. The obvious answer is for teachers to be aware of the differences in standard deviations (as well as mean figures) in the distribution curves of different IQ tests. It is also useful for teachers to note the *percentile scores* of students on the

FIGURE 9.4. *Normal Curve of Measured IQs among the Population*

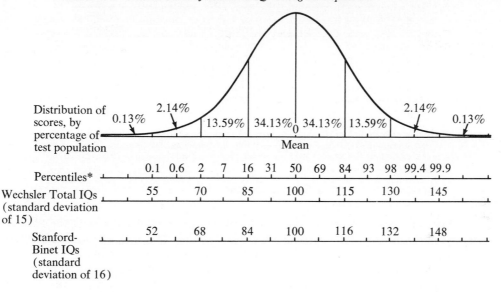

different tests—if these figures are available. For example, the percentile figures for the student taking tests X and Z would reveal that the student ranked at the 84th percentile for both tests, which would show (1) that the IQ scores of 115 and 120 are comparable on the two tests, and (2) that the student's performance—his adeptness and concentration—was apparently comparable for the tests.

Another important consideration for a teacher in his interpretation of student scores on intelligence tests is the *error factor*. In any testing situation, there are uncontrolled factors which tend to detract from the student's true score. These factors are represented as the error factor, which is normally standardized and published in the

TABLE 9.1 *Equivalent IQ Scores for Tests with Different Standard Deviations*

Percentile Scores*	0.1	2	16	50	84	98	99.9
Test X (stand. deviation of 15)	55	70	85	100	115	130	145
Test Y (stand. deviation of 16)	52	68	84	100	116	132	148
Test Z (stand. deviation of 20)	40	60	80	100	120	140	160

* The *percentile* score measures the percent of the test population that an examinee surpasses.

TABLE 9.2   Intelligence Classifications

IQ Score Range	Classification	Percent of Population
130 and above	Very Superior	2.2
120–129	Superior	6.7
110–119	Bright Normal	16.1
90–109	Average	50.0
80–89	Dull Normal	16.1
70–79	Borderline	6.7
69 and below*	Mental Defectives	2.2

* For educational purposes regarding the mentally retarded, the lower end of the distribution has been further subdivided into the following classifications: 50–75, Educable Mentally Retarded; 25–49, Trainable Mentally Retarded; and 0–25, Institutionalized.

Reprinted from the *Wechsler Intelligence Scale for Children,* 1949, p. 16. Used by permission of The Psychological Corporation.

technical manual which accompanies each test. For most intelligence tests, the standard error of measurement is approximately 5 IQ points. The meaning and use of this standard error of measurement are illustrated in the following example:

Suppose a teacher has 30 children in her class who have been administered an intelligence test, and she wishes to take the error factor into consideration in studying their scores. Using the test's published standard error of measurement of 5 IQ points, and following the mean and standard deviations of the normal curve (see Figure 9.3), the teacher could compute that if the test were to be administered a second time 20 of the students (68 percent) would probably score within 5 points of their IQ score on the first test. Eight students (27 percent) might vary as much as 10 points from their first score, and two (5 percent) could vary as much as 15 IQ points. Thus, if the teacher takes one student's test score, say 103, and adds and subtracts 5 IQ points (98–108), she could assume at a 68 percent probability that this range of 98–108 includes the student's *true* IQ rank. By adding and subtracting 10 IQ points to the test score (93–113), the teacher could assume a 95 percent probability that this range includes the student's true IQ; and by adding and subtracting three standard errors of measurement, or 15 IQ points, to the student's test score of 103, she could be virtually certain—a 99.8 percent probability—that the range of 88–118 includes the student's true IQ score.

The important point here is that if IQ scores are reported as *ranges* instead of specific points, then the inevitable variations in scores from one test to another and from subsequent presentations of the same test will not be so alarming to a teacher. It is also likely that the use of IQ ranges would eliminate such invidious comparisons as the too-common conclusion that a child with an IQ of 102 is "brighter" than a child with an IQ score of 100. (Table 9.2 presents one of many different classifications of IQ score ranges according to comparative "brightness" or capability among the general population.)

THE DEVELOPMENT OF INTELLIGENCE—JEAN PIAGET

Jean Piaget's writings (1950, 1952, 1958, 1960; Piaget & Szeminska, 1952) reflect an interest in intelligence different from that of the preceding theoretical approaches. Instead of focusing on the measurement of intelligence or the components necessary to intellectual functioning, Piaget's primary interest is in *cognitive growth,* the course of development of intellectual functioning. His earliest methodology for studying intelligence has been judged inadequate by more statistically oriented critics, and much of his writing is in such a general tone that his conclusions are untestable. In addition, the translation of his writings from French to English undoubtedly suffers from the difficulties inherent in all translations. Nevertheless, even with these limitations, Piaget's theory of cognitive growth has probably spawned more research in the past 15 years than any other single education theory.

Piaget offers several definitions of intelligence, all couched in somewhat general terms. For example, "intelligence is a particular instance of biological adaptation" (1952) reflects his training as a biologist. In another source (1950), he defines intelligence as a "form of equilibrium toward which all the structures . . . tend." Still another definition states that intelligence is a "system of living and acting operations" (1950). Thus, in these three definitions, Piaget suggests his concept of intelligence as a biological adaptation, involving mental activity, in which the person seeks equilibrium with his environment.

Piaget's framework hypothesizes that all species inherit two "invariate functions"—*adaptation* and *organization*—which determine the manner in which any organism behaves and develops intellectually. Organization is a hereditary property which allows the organism to come to terms with his environment through either physical or psychological mechanisms. Physically, organization involves the coordination of certain organs and systems in the body as it responds to the environment. Psychologically, organization involves the integration of the organism's sensory and cerebral structures in responses to the environment.

The "invariate function" of adaptation is the inherent tendency of all organisms to modify behavior in response to the environment. The ways in which adaptation occurs vary from species to species, from individual to individual within a species, or from one developmental stage to the next within an individual. Regarding the latter, an example would be the newborn infant, uncomfortable in wet diapers, who seeks to adapt (to relieve the discomfort) by crying. At a later stage, he may use non-verbal gestures, and, still later, words may be involved in his adaptation to the environment.

Adaptation consists of two complementary processes: *assimilation* and *accommodation*. Assimilation refers to the organism's incorporation of external reality into already existing psychological structures. Accommodation is the process by which the organism's psychological structures are modified to specific aspects of the environment. The two processes occur simultaneously and are essential to the adaptation function.

As man *organizes* his behavior and thought and *adapts* to his environment, he creates in the process certain new psychological structures which Piaget terms *schemata*. The schemata represent a kind of conceptual framework into which incoming environmental stimuli (inputs) must fit if the individual is to perceive and act on these stimuli. Though the processes of adaptation and organization are invariant, these schemata, or conceptual structures, are variant; that is, they change as a result of experience. In other words, through his experience with his environment, a child constantly creates new schemata in order to continue the innate processes of organization and adaptation to the environment.

The first schemata are necessarily exemplified in the reflexes of the newborn infant. As the infant interacts with his environment, certain *ready-made* schemata that already exist (reflexes) begin to vary with circumstances and experience. For example, the "sucking schema" of the newborn may be evidenced with any kind of object that is placed near the infant's mouth. However, as he experiences nursing, the child begins to differentiate objects, and some will bring on the sucking response while others will not. Thus, a new, more discriminatory schema replaces the original ready-made schema of sucking. This process can be termed *intellectual development*.

Piaget hypothesizes that man develops in this way through a series of defined maturational *periods* and sub-periods, or *phases*. The periods and phases of interest here consist of (1) the *sensorimotor period* (0–2 years); (2) the *pre-operational period*, with phases of (a) *pre-conceptual thought* (2–4 years) and (b) *intuitive thought* (4–7 years); (3) the *concrete operations period* (7–11 years); and (4) the *formal operations period* (11–15 years). Though Piaget has attached ages to each period, experiments by him and by others have made the age boundaries less rigid. However, the developmental progression remains invariant (see Table 9.3).

TABLE 9.3.   *Piaget's Stages of Intellectual Development*

I. Sensorimotor period	0–2
II. Pre-operational period	2–7
A. Pre-conceptual thought	2–4
B. Intuitive thought	4–7
III. Concrete operations period	7–11
IV. Formal operations period	11–15

Period of sensorimotor development (0–2 years)

At birth and through the first month of life, the infant is unable to distinguish himself from the world around him and depends mainly upon his reflexes for interactions with the environment. The infant makes orienting responses to light and sound, he sucks when his lips are touched, and he grasps an object placed in his hand. However, contrary to the concept of the newborn being a passive organism, totally dependent upon stimulation from the environment, Piaget also records incidents that reflect some voluntary activity on the part of the infant.

The second stage of this period (1–4 months) is characterized by changes in the ready-made reflexive schemata into higher-order schemata involving coordination. Piaget notes that the first coordination of schema very often is accidental in nature. For example, by chance, an object in the visual range of the infant is touched by the child and then is grasped, so that the "looking schema" is coordinated with the "reaching schema," which is then coordinated with the "grasping schema." When this has occurred once, it may be repeated upon future stimulation, and these schemata become integrated into one. During this stage, a primitive differentiation of objects also begins as the infant responds differently to different objects in his environment. The infant may also begin to repeat actions, such as smiling, when an adult responds by imitating that action.

During the third stage of the sensorimotor period (4–8 months), the infant firmly establishes the distinction between himself and the world beyond himself. In his actions upon objects, the child shows the first sign of intention and a rudimentary means-end relationship. For example, he performs motor acts that produce effects on the environment, such as kicking while lying in the crib to make toys move. Primitive concepts of object permanence, of space, and of time are also formed during this period, as evidenced by the child's momentary search for objects that are absent.

The first evidence of symbolic meaning is manifested during the fourth state of this period (8–12 months). The child anticipates events from signs that predict their imminence, such as a reaction to the mother's putting on her coat to leave. True imitation also begins during this period, and the child begins to react to novel objects in his environment in an exploratory manner.

During stage five of this period of development (12–18 months), the child begins real experimentation leading to a concept of causality. His actions seem to represent a "What would happen if?" attitude, and means-ends relationships take on new meaning with a focus upon the creation of new means.

In the final stage of this period (18–24 months) the child's experimentation becomes more covert. Before this stage, the child tried to gain ends by actively manipulating objects in his environment overtly—that is, observably. During this final stage, the means for reaching ends seem to be manipulated mentally, or covertly. Thus, schemata appear to be assimilated internally, as opposed to the motoric kinds of assimilation in previous stages (Lovell, 1968). The child, at this stage, imitates complex types of presented behaviors as well as behaviors that he remembers from an earlier time. Both anticipation and memory become firmly established, which indicates a strengthened concept of time.

Period of pre-operational development (2–7 years)

Just as the child developed schemata to represent his *interactions* with things and people in his environment during the sensorimotor period, the pre-operational period is typified by the development and assimilation of internal schemata which represent the actual objects and people in his environment. For example, the development of language—internalized symbols that represent the objects and people—takes place during this period. Thus, during the *pre-conceptual phase* of this period (2–4 years), the child achieves the capacity to form and articulate mental symbols which stand for absent things, people, or events. This ability frees the child from his previous intellectual ties to the here and now. Internal imitation, which the child developed during the sensorimotor period, provides the basis for this formation of mental symbols, and meaning is attached to the symbols by their assimilation into existing schemata. This phase is termed "pre-conceptual" because these early concepts of language and symbols are primitive in nature and may be highly specific or too general. For example, the child's concept of "up" may be related only to "being picked up" and therefore serves primarily as a signal for desired action rather than as a concept.

The first rudimentary reasoning, based on past occurrences, is also exhibited by the child during this phase. Piaget (1951) describes his daughter's remark, "Daddy's getting hot water, so he's going to shave" as reasoning from having seen the two events occur consecutively in the past. Such *transductive reasoning*—reasoning that because two things are alike in one way, they must be alike in all ways—is typical in this period of development. Because the child's concepts are not yet clear, in adult terms, there are many "errors" from the adult's point of view, and these "errors" constitute much of the exchange of cute stories that parents relate to each other about their children.

During the *intuitive thought phase* of this pre-conceptual period (4–7 years), the child moves toward socialized behavior. This change is evidenced as the four-year-old child who basically communicates with himself begins moving toward communication which is largely with other people (Hunt, 1961). As a result, the child's concepts of objects and experiences become more precise; for he must be able to communicate these concepts to other people. This phase is termed "intuitive thought" because the process of arriving at answers concerning causality and rightness or wrongness is based on incomplete thinking. Children of this age make decisions on the basis of intuition rather than on the basis of logical reasoning.

Period of concrete operations development (7–11 years)

The age span included in this period is roughly equivalent to the time that the child is in elementary school. The most obvious change during this period is the child's ability to use written words and numbers. During the preceding stages, the spoken word came to symbolize people, experiences, and concrete objects. Now, the written word or number possesses the same signification.

During this operations period, the child also develops relational and combinational procedures whereby he is able to classify, order, and group. He is able to perform, for example, additive, subtractive, repetitive, and equalitive functions. These abilities are in contrast to the preceding stages, when the child's attempts to systematize were incomplete and characterized by irreversibility of thought, transductive reasoning, and egocentric thinking.

To illustrate the movement from the pre-operational to the operational period, consider the example of a child presented with identical beakers A and B, both filled to the same height with a liquid. Asked if the quantities of liquid are equal, the child agrees that they are. The liquid from one of the beakers is then poured into a differently shaped beaker C (see Figure 9.5). Asked the question of equality again, the pre-

FIGURE 9.5   Conservation of Continuous Quantities

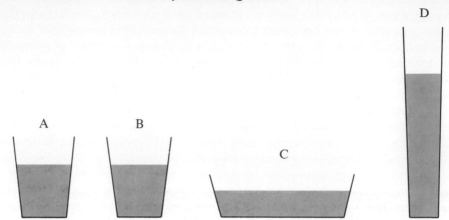

From Ginsburg, H., & Opper, S. *Piaget's theory of intellectual development.* Used with permission. Englewood Cliffs, N.J.: Prentice-Hall, Inc. © 1969, p. 162.

operational child will answer "no." The child at this pre-operational stage can focus on only *one* aspect of the situation, either the height or the breadth of the liquid in container C in relation to the height or breadth of the liquid in container A. If he centers on the height, he will signify that A has more liquid; if he centers on the breadth, then C will have more liquid. If the procedure is reversed by pouring the liquid from C back into B, the child will then judge the two amounts of liquid as being equal. And if a fourth beaker, D, of still another shape is introduced, and the liquid from B is poured into it, the child will again judge an inequality.

The child at the *operational* level has the ability to *decenter;* that is, to focus not on either height or breadth but on both properties. Thus, he would be able to judge equality between any combinations, A and B, A and C, or A and D. The child recognizes that transforming the shape of the liquid does nothing to the quantity.

Period of formal operations development (11–15 years)

This period is typified by the development from thoughts about reality to thoughts about the possible. Before acting on a problem which confronts him, the adolescent analyzes the situation and suggests hypotheses as to the possible outcomes. And as he hypothesizes the possible outcomes, he is also able to devise experiments to test these hypotheses, so that he can reach a conclusion on the basis of these experiments. The child at the previous, concrete operations, stage can reason and hypothesize about current and concrete experience, but it is only at this formal operations period that the individual becomes capable of understanding and directly manipulating relations between abstractions. The adolescent no longer needs concrete or current experiences on which to base his reasoning. The thoughts of the adolescent involve second-order constructs, abstract ideas and understandings based on previously established verbal abstractions. Reality becomes secondary to possibility, and the form of the argument becomes as evident as the content.

During this adolescent, and final, stage of intellectual growth, the individual also goes through a phase of development known as *egocentrism.* Simply stated, egocentrism is the inability to differentiate between the real and the ideal. It is characterized by the development of two mental configurations, one, an *imaginary audience,* and the other, a *personal fable* (Elkind, 1967). Both represent the typical adolescent mental preoccupation that others are as obsessed with his behavior and appearance as he is himself. Within this mental construct, the imaginary audience is either approving or critical of his looks and behavior, and the attitude of this "audience" is inevitably directly related to his own self-perception. The personal fable usually provides the adolescent with a personal view of his uniqueness among all others, even to the point of immortality. This is not an emotional delusion but, rather, a normal function of mental growth.

Usually, adolescent egocentrism passes at about age 15 or 16, as the individual's intellectual growth is fully realized. Through a series of experiences, the adolescent eventually comes to sort out the real from the unreal and move from preoccupations solely with himself to the consideration of others. This development indicates that the cognitive structure during the formal operations period has become firmly established.

The significance of cognitive growth for classroom learning

Having just read a summary of Piaget's theory of cognitive growth, it is logical to search for the relationship between this view of intellectual growth and the learning

The woodworking teacher is puzzled that some students have a real knack for making things, while others, no matter how hard they try, are invariably unsuccessful. *What should this teacher realize about individual differences in students?*

Some students have an aptitude for working with things that others do not have. This ability is part of an individual's intelligence. David Wechsler has been one of the strongest proponents of a performance capacity in the intellect. He holds that this aspect of intelligence may be greater than, less than, or comparable to one's verbal ability.

It is likely that this teacher is working with some students who have high verbal ability but less performance ability. This would be evidenced by the ability of the "unsuccessful" students to conceptualize woodworking functions and projects but their inability to realize these projects effectively. It is not unusual to find these individual differences in a woodworking class or any other performance class. Perhaps the teacher will find it necessary to specifically direct some students through their work projects so that they are able to make the transition between conceptualizing what should be done and actually performing the behaviors. There is also a possibility that the teacher may want to get the learner directly involved in the performance task, minimizing the verbal component of such a task until the task in completed. Once the final product has been realized, the student then has his own work to reflect upon and to relate to verbal concepts and rules.

that occurs in the classroom. It is notable, first of all, that Piaget's theory places the importance of human functioning within the intellectual structure of each individual rather than within the learning environment. This is not to say that the environment is unimportant to learning but, rather, that learning is a result of intellectual development instead of intellectual development being a result of learning. These two differing theoretical positions will be briefly reviewed before discussing their implications for the classroom.

You will recall that intelligence is a matter of cognitive adaptation to the environment within Piaget's theory and, therefore, in his view, learning is but one adaptive factor in intellectual development. Developmentally, the child gains increasing capacities to function with increasing age. Initially, the primary intellectual activity is *sensorimotor,* which is the reaction to things within the child's environment through motor action. As the child matures, objects in his environment begin taking on some meaning, known as *symbolic activity,* and intelligence increases through the child's *assimilation* of new environmental experiences into his existing intellectual structure or through his acquisition of new intellectual structures to *accommodate* demands imposed by the environment.

Throughout this childhood period (2–11), concrete objects serve as reference points for increasing intellectual capacity, since the mind has not yet matured to the point of abstract functioning. Not until early adolescence does *symbolic representation* become the characteristic thought process as the mind moves toward full adult maturity. Thus, while the child is at the concrete operational stage or below, "telling" does not affect the schemata in the same way that actual interaction with people and objects in the environment does. Of course, the teacher "telling" a student can bring about changes, in that the child can verbalize what the teacher was "telling." However, Piaget's conception of intellectual development requires that the child also be able to handle, manipulate, and experiment with reality, with concrete things, if "real" learning is to occur. In other words, for a *child* to develop a cognition, there first must be motoric understanding, which is followed by intellectual understanding and, finally, the level of verbal understanding. In Piaget's view, educational programs that attempt to start at the upper level tend to leave the student with "empty verbalizations"—a child may be able to repeat that "A hexagon is a closed figure with six sides" and still not be able to recognize a hexagon.

In contrast, the learning theorist is likely to consider intelligence as the outcome of environmental opportunities to function. Within Gagné's system, for example, learning is viewed as the major factor in intellectual development; his learning hierarchy suggests that "learning contribute[s] to the intellectual development of the human being because it is cumulative in its effects" (1968, p. 181). At the stimulus–response learning level, basic information is learned by simple connections in the mind of stimuli and responses. An individual then moves hierarchically from this basic learning level toward conceptualization (level 6), a thought process generally essential to most intellectual skills. Implicit in this position is the fact that an individual cannot learn concepts or rules unless he has previously learned discriminations, chains, and simple S–R connections.

In short, intellectual functioning within Piaget's system is developmental; that is, one type of intellectual activity must necessarily precede another, from simple to complex thinking abilities. But within Gagné's hierarchy, the levels of learning are not restricted by these developmental stages. Whatever the learning task, if the learner has the necessary prerequisites, he is ready to learn the immediate task and, theoretically, can do so. Despite these fundamental differences, it is possible to consider these two theories in conjunction, and a comparative analysis of Piaget's developmental periods and Gagné's hierarchical levels is depicted in Table 9.4. In combination, the two theories give the teacher a basic understanding of intellectual capacity within a certain age range (or grade level). In addition, these theories clearly show that the learning level, or complexity, of academic tasks must be commensurate to the child's ability to respond. Fortunately, the gradation of most instructional materials makes this judgment possible for teachers.

It is possible, of course, to tie Gagné's hierarchy to age development in the manner of Piaget's system. For example, we could say that levels 2 through 5 within Gagné's hierarchy are the only types of learning possible within the first two years of life, because there is no conceptualization with Piaget's sensorimotor stage. Then, at around two years of age, the upper levels (6–8) of Gagné's hierarchy might be realized, since the child is now beginning to conceptualize and could, presumably, learn concepts, rules, and problem solving behaviors. This does not infer, of course, that learning at levels 2 through 5 ceases to exist or that when a person reaches the abstract thought stage, the primary characteristic of Piaget's mature formal operations period, the individual will think only in conceptual or problem solving terms. The lower levels of learning continue throughout a lifetime, and the attainment of the age of formal operations merely means that the individual can carry on more complex problem solving functions.

In review, the two theories are not conflicting, nor are they directly equatable. However, as the teacher plans instructional strategies based on the student's existing learning level and his approximate range of intellectual functioning, the two theories prove their value in combination.

TABLE 9.4.   Summary of Positions of Piaget and Gagné

Piaget's Developmental Stages	*Major Intellectual Abilities*
Sensorimotor (0–2)	Motor, mainly reflexive responses
Pre-operational (2–7)	Increasing symbolic activity
Concrete Operations (7–11)	Developing rules of logic
Formal Operations (11–16)	Abstract thinking, critical analysis
Gagné's Learning Hierarchy	*Major Intellectual Activities*
Levels 2 to 5	S–R connections, chains, and multiple discriminations
Levels 6 to 8	Concept learning, rule learning, and problem solving

THE IMPLICATIONS OF INTELLIGENCE THEORIES FOR CLASSROOM TEACHING

Though psychologists are clearly not in agreement on what intelligence is or on all of the variables that affect intellectual functioning, the various theories do hold certain implications for the teacher. For the outstanding teacher always takes account of individual differences in the classroom, and one of the prominent ways in which individuals do differ is in intellectual functioning.

First of all, the teacher must understand that the global intelligence quotient measured in most current IQ tests predicts future school achievement of a student with some degree of accuracy, so long as the teacher is aware of the theoretical base, the error factor, and other variables in the different tests. In addition, by considering past school achievement and certain motivational factors described in Chapter 10, the teacher may supplement and increase the predictive accuracy of the tests.

The concept of intelligences, rather than an intelligence, also holds implications for teachers. If individuals do possess different figural and semantic operational abilities or different degrees of g_c and g_f or level I and level II abilities, then the teacher must take account of these differences in her *modus operandi.*

If, for example, a child operates better figurally than symbolically, there are obvious procedures that the teacher can initiate to help the student learn the material through figural operations. Or, as Meeker (1969) has suggested, there may be strategies that the teacher can use to increase the child's ability to operate with symbols. Similarly, if, as Jensen hypothesizes, there are two levels of mental ability, the teacher can assume that those students possessing a high level I ability but low level II ability should do well on learning tasks representing the first five levels of Gagné's hierarchy but would not be expected to do as well on the last three. The teacher must then continually vary the instructional methodology in an attempt to provide successful educational experiences for all.

In relating Piaget's intellectual stages to Gagné's learning levels, the following two points may help clarify the issues:

1. Intellectual development theory does not deny the importance of learning. In fact, it asserts that learning is crucial to the realization of intellectual potential.
2. Learning theory's central stress is on increasing the individual's system of responses, but it also recognizes that to present intellectual tasks advanced to the learner's intellectual development is illogical and will not result in learning.

Since man realizes himself through the processes of environmental stimulation and hereditary potential, the interaction of the two results in human development. The ability of the classroom teacher to recognize these factors and capitalize upon them in instruction will be a strong factor in determining the quality of the intellectual growth which takes place.

SUGGESTED READINGS

Deese, J.   Behavior and fact. *American Psychologist,* 1969, **24,** 515–522.

Ebel, R. L.   Cognitive development of personal potential. *NASSP Bulletin,* 1966, **50,** 115–130.

Elkind, D.   Conceptual orientation shifts in children and adolescents. *Child Development,* 1966, **37,** 493–498.

Elkind, D.   Giant in the nursery—Jean Piaget. *New York Times Magazine,* May 26, 1968.

Feldman, D. H.   Map understanding as a possible crystallizer of cognitive structures. *American Educational Research Journal,* 1971, **8,** 485–502.

Herenstein, R.   I.Q. *Atlantic Monthly,* 1971, **228** (3), 43–64.

Holtzman, W. H.   The changing world of mental measurement and its social significance. *American Psychologist,* 1971, **26.**

Jensen, A. R.   How much can we boost IQ and scholastic achievement? *Harvard Educational Review,* 1969, **39,** 1–123.

Lovell, K.   Developmental processes in thought. *Journal of Experimental Education,* 1968, **37,** 14–21.

Piaget, J.   The attainment of invariants and reversible operations in the development of thinking. *Social Research,* 1963. Reprinted in H. D. Thornburg (Ed.), *School learning and instruction: Readings.* Monterey, Calif.: Brooks/Cole, 1973, chap. 3.

Shockley, W.   A debate challenge: Geneticity is 80% for white identical twins' I.Q.'s; Jensen, A. R. The causes of twin differences in I.Q.: A reply to Gage; Gage, N. L. The causes of race differences in I.Q.: Replies to Shockley, Page, and Jensen (three articles). *Phi Delta Kappan,* 1972, **53** (7), 415–427.

Tisdall, W. J., Blackhurst, A. E., & Marks, C. H.   Divergent thinking in blind children. *Journal of Educational Psychology,* 1971, **62,** 468–473.

Wechsler, D.   Concept of collective intelligence. *American Psychologist,* 1971, **26,** 904–907.

10

School Motivation

Formally stated, motivational factors "refer to states of the organism that are relatively temporary and reversible and which tend to energize or activate the behavior of organisms" (Logan, 1970, p. 149). The classroom teacher most likely thinks of motivation in more practical terms as those factors within a teaching–learning situation which trigger and affect the intensity and direction of student learning behavior. This chapter is designed primarily to explore the practical aspects of motivation, so that the classroom teacher will be able to recognize and plan classroom situations which may provide motivation for learning. However, a brief consideration of motivation research will be given first in order to provide a theoretical framework for the more practical aspects of the subject.

THEORIES OF MOTIVATION

Hedonism

The early works of most stimulus–response psychologists were built around the concept of learning as a process in which physiological needs of an organism were reduced by a new (learned) behavior. Theoretically, the deprived physiological state of the organism compelled the organism to act, and this state was termed the *motivation* for the behavior. This organismic process of changing the physiological status from deprivation to satiation with new behavior was termed *hedonism*—the tendency of an organism to seek pleasure while avoiding pain.

While such a theory of motivation and behavior was actually suggested several hundred years ago in classical Greece, it became quite formalized within Thorndike's learning laws. You will recall that Thorndike's *law of effect* stated that every act is followed by either a satisfying or an annoying state of affairs. Presumably, the actor would perform behavior that would produce a satisfying state of affairs; that is, he was *motivated* to behave in a way that would bring about a pleasurable state. However, in some cases, despite the actor's intentions, an annoying (painful) state of affairs followed his behavior—an occurrence that would have a diminishing effect on the actor's motivational level when he re-encountered the same situation.

Drive theory

Directly resultant from Thorndike's work came the *drive reduction theory* of Hull. Hull concluded that all motives were related to basic physiological needs and that these physiological needs gave rise to certain psychological or social drives which were learned by the organism. Hull termed the physiological needs *primary drives,* which he defined as an aroused state of the organism (motivation) produced by basic physiological needs (food, water, elimination, breath, or sex) that compelled the organism to act to reduce the drive and restore equilibrium. The psychological or social drives were termed *secondary drives,* and Hull postulated that these secondary drives are learned by the organism as they accompany a primary drive and are associated by the organism with the physiological drive reduction. For example, as an individual goes about trying to reduce the physiological drive of hunger, he may be exposed to social rules for eating behavior. These rules are then associated with the drive reduction of eating and are learned as a secondary drive. Upon subsequent occasions, then, the individual's newly learned social behavior may determine the way in which he reduces his hunger drive. Thus, the individual is not only motivated by hunger to eat (primary drive) but also to eat the food in a socially accepted way (secondary drive).

Since Hull's work in 1943, there have been many questions raised about the effectiveness of drive reduction theory as a satisfactory explanation for motivation. Several writers (Butler, 1957; McKeachie & Doyle, 1970; White, 1959) have intimated that, at best, drive reduction is only a partial explanation of motivation, and many new theories have been proposed to account for psychological and social motivations that may *not* be directly tied to primary physiological needs.

Needs theories

Needs theory obviates the Hullian condition of a physiological basis for all motivation. In contrast to drive theory, needs theory suggests that most of man's needs are learned, thus psychological in nature. In other words, as an individual interacts with his environment, he acquires certain needs which allow him to respond to the experiences he encounters. Thus, when a person is motivated by a need, he is responding to a psychological condition which he has acquired through learning. When a person is motivated by a drive, he is responding to a physiological condition.

Among several needs theories that have been devised, one of the most elaborate is by H. A. Murray, who published his work in 1938, even before the definitive explanation of Hull's drive theory. Murray listed 12 physiological needs (viscerogenic) and 28 independently based psychological (psychogenic) needs. The 28 psychogenic needs were presented in five broad categories:

1. *Needs associated with acquiring and retaining inanimate objects.* This classification refers to those psychological motivations involving (a) acquisition, (b) conservation, or (c) retention of personal possessions, property, and other inanimate things. Someone with a strong conservation need might collect, restore, and preserve things. In contrast, a strong retention need may be reflected by people who are quite frugal or miserly.
2. *Needs associated with achievement and striving.* This refers to motivations to exercise power and to organize objects, people, or ideas in a way that masters them. A person with a strong superiority need seeks to excel others and gain recognition, and other achievement-striving needs may be exhibited in self-exploration and curiosity. This particular need classification has probably been researched and advanced more than any other part of Murray's system.
3. *Needs associated with prestige and esteem.* Recognition is one of the strongest motivations within this class, which is characterized by the individual who seeks praise, commendation, and respect from others. Also, this need may be expressed as attention-seeking in exciting, amusing, or shocking others; or it may be expressed in defensive behaviors designed to avoid shame, failure, or ridicule.
4. *Needs associated with power relationships to others.* Murray lists (a) dominance, (b) deference, (c) similance, (d) autonomy, and (e) contrariness as the major motivational factors within this classification. Dominance is manifested in the influence or control of others. Deference motivates an individual to gain admiration and support of a superior. Similance is shown in imitating or identifying with others. Autonomy is the striving for independence. Contrariness is the need to be different, unconventional, or arbitrary.

5. *Needs associated with emotional and social relationships to others.* Affiliation—forming friendships or gaining the affection of associates—is one of the strongest motivations here. Aggression is also a strong need in this class, as is rejection in a contrary social relationship.

A considerably more popular categorization of individual psychological needs was established by A. H. Maslow in 1943 and is still advanced as the most satisfactory explanation of motivation by many contemporary writers. Although Maslow recognized physiological needs as strong motivators, he felt that motivation had a broader basis than basic drives. Maslow refers to the physiological needs as deficiencies and contends that as long as such deficiencies exist the individual is not free to seek out other needs. In this way, the physiological needs serve as the basis for the other social needs. Yet, it is these other needs that enlarge the scope of human functioning and understanding. The social or psychological needs which motivate an individual to behave were defined by Maslow in a hierarchy (see Figure 10.1).

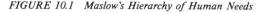

FIGURE 10.1   Maslow's Hierarchy of Human Needs

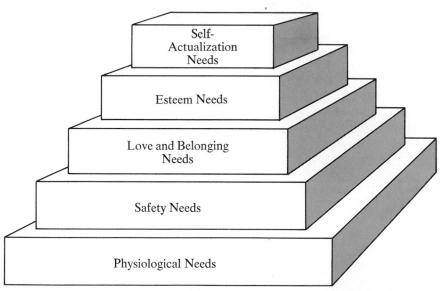

Maslow, A. H. Hierarchy and prepotency of needs. *Psychological Review,* 1943, **50,** 370–396. Copyright 1943 by the American Psychological Association and reprinted by permission.

Within Maslow's system, once physiological needs are satisfied, the individual first seeks to satisfy *safety needs,* which refer to the desire for good health and for security from harm and danger. Maslow contends that the major outcome of attaining safety needs is the desire to seek and give love to others, the third needs category on his hierarchy *(love and belonging needs).* The individual seeks to share with his immediate circle—family, sweetheart, wife, children, friends—so that he may (1) assure himself of being loved as well as (2) know that he is accepted by others. An inability to love and belong may motivate a person to act in many different ways to gain such acceptance. For example, a failure to accomplish this need often becomes apparent in an individual's attempts to use achievement as a substitute for love.

Achievement needs fall within the category Maslow describes as *esteem needs.* It is not enough to be loved by others; one must also be respected by others, and one gains some measure of self-respect through achievement. Thus, in looking for signs of being respected by others, one goes about accomplishing those things which he feels will give him such respect. Many children achieve within classroom situations in order to gain the respect of their teacher.

Maslow assumes that if an individual has been able to satisfy all of these lower needs on the hierarchy, then he becomes motivated by a strong desire to be himself, to be *self-actualized.* This need has to do with developing one's potential or becoming what one is capable of becoming. It is the attempt to make one's behavior consistent with what one is. Furthermore, Maslow contends that if an individual has satisfactorily meet the other four needs, then the need for self-actualization is potent enough to serve as the primary motivation for *all* of an individual's behavior.

While only limited empirical research exists on Maslow's categories of motivation, they are logical constructs and serve as a plausible theory of why individuals behave as they do. His theory is also widely admired and accepted because it goes beyond a strict physiological explanation for behavior and assumes certain independent psychological and social needs as motivational sources and causes for behavior.

MOTIVATION IN THE CLASSROOM

Do students in the classroom have basic physiological drives that affect their learning behavior? Is Murray's psychogenic-needs system useful in explaining classroom motivation? Can we attribute Maslow's need for self-actualization to basic classroom learning behavior? The answer to all of these questions is "yes." All educators would undoubtedly agree that motivation is a very important variable in classroom learning. To increase our understanding of classroom motivation is to increase the probability of student learning as well as to gain more insight as to effective instructional procedures. The following overview lists the major factors in classroom motivation, which are the subject of discussion in the remainder of this chapter:

1. *Achievement motivation.*   An extension of Murray's achievement-striving needs by contemporary psychologists (McClelland et al., 1953; Atkinson, 1958, 1964) to objectively identify and assess the variables in student motivation for successful learning within the classroom.
2. *Task motivation.*   The motivational factors involved in student encounters with and mastery of specific classroom tasks and skills.
3. *Aspirational motivation.*   Behaviors related to the student's long-range goals and/or expectancies, which are categorized on an ideal-real continuum (Shaw, 1967).
4. *Competition motivation.*   The factors of (a) a self-imposed standard of excellence, or (b) competition with others in student learning behaviors (Talbert, 1968).
5. *Affiliative motivation.*   Behaviors which exhibit the need for (a) adult approval and acceptance, and (b) peer approval and acceptance (Talbert, 1968).
6. *Anxiety.*   A common factor that may facilitate learning (minimal anxiety levels) or inhibit it (high anxiety levels).
7. *Avoidance motivation.*   Behaviors related to the avoidance of punishment, reprimand, unpleasantness, or guilt within the classroom. The preferred and more effective alternative to such motivational factors is always the motive for behaviors that bring teacher approval (Jones, 1967; Loree, 1970).
8. *Reinforcing motivation.*   Teacher approval and grades are often the primary reasons for students doing things. Peer competition and acceptance may also be reinforcing motivations (Marx and Tombaugh, 1967; Kuethe, 1968).
9. *Individual guided motivation.*   A behavioral scheme developed by Klausmeier et al. (1971) that categorizes self-directed behaviors in a classroom setting and suggests ways for the teacher to utilize these motivational factors internalized within each student.

Achievement motivation

The basic human need for achievement and striving was first discussed by Murray (1938), although he did not view this motivational factor strictly within a school setting. It has since been interpreted mostly in terms of the classroom, particularly in an approach developed by McClelland et al. (1953) and his associates (Atkinson, 1958). In their studies adapted from the Thematic Apperception Test (TAT), which consists of four picture cards which are presented to subjects who must then describe what they see, McClelland and his associates proposed that the subjects who developed themes that were high in achievement–relatedness could be considered to be high in need for achievement *(nAch)*. The researchers then found that subjects with high nAch performed better on arithmetic problems, obtained better grades in school, and also had high aspirational levels. Lowell (1952) also found actual achievement to be greater among high nAch male college students than among the low nAch students. Such findings have been supported in other studies as well (Gough, 1964; Rosen & d'Andrade, 1959).

Since McClelland's original work, several similarly based studies have been conducted to determine the relationship between achievement motivation (nAch) and other individual student variables:

1. Winterbottom (1958) investigated parental variables. She found that boys with high nAch had mothers who expected self-reliance, independent behaviors, content mastery, and accomplishment from their sons. Such mothers were relatively more demanding than mothers who had sons with low nAch.
2. Feather (1966) examined the effects of initial success or failure on overt achievement and found that failure experiences had the effect of producing a lower achievement rate among students than they did in the case of those students who experienced success.
3. Crootof (1963) found greater nAch scores among bright normal-achievers than among bright under-achievers.

While each of these studies have given evidence of a correlation between actual achievement and high nAch scores, the following cautions should be observed in considering all such research: (1) Different administrations of the McClelland nAch test (based on the TAT picture test) have not shown consistent results (Birney, 1959). (2) The McClelland approach tends not to assess the achievement motives of women as consistently as it does men (McClelland et al., 1953). (3) The nAch test has shown some limitations since the test has not consistently measured all the different motives that it has attempted to define (Talbert, 1968).

Despite these limitations, most critics feel that McClelland's work on achievement motivation can be considered successful and quite valuable (Christie & Lindauer, 1963). Above all, his nAch test has proven to be a good indicator of academic achievement (Maehr & Sjogren, 1971), and it also seems to have implications for the area of personality development. However, it is likely that a score on McClelland's nAch scale reflects a much broader type of achievement motivation than is specifically operant or necessary for the accomplishment of classroom tasks. What is seen in the classroom is more likely to be *task-oriented motivation,* the term used to designate motivational factors involved in specific classroom behaviors.

Task motivation

When a student accomplishes a difficult task, achieves success when encountering a learning situation, or uses his own initiative to explore learning beyond the limits defined by his teacher, task motivation seems to exist. There is some controversy as to the nature of this type of motivation. Ausubel (1968) contends that successful accomplishment of a task is intrinsically rewarding and will motivate the learner toward additional tasks regardless of the strength or existence of affiliative (acceptance) and other social motives. In contrast, Veroff (1969) sees task motivation as varying at different stages of the child's development, with social and other motivational factors performing important functions in task achievement at the different stages.

For example, in early stages of development, Veroff suggests that *competence* —an intrinsic need to cope with the environment—is the basic motivational force. The competence drive is represented by such task-fulfilling behaviors as grasping, crawling, walking, language acquisition, thinking, manipulating objects, learning skills, etc. By middle childhood, Veroff sees *social motives*—particularly the needs for affiliation and acceptance from others—as the basic motivational source for much task-learning behavior. By adolescence, an *integrated* task-achievement pattern exists, built on the motivational forces of the earlier developmental stages (Veroff, 1969; Maehr & Sjogren, 1971).

Perhaps the most useful theory of task motivation in terms of the classroom situation is that offered by Atkinson (1965). From the original work undertaken by McClelland and his associates, Atkinson has theorized that task motivation is related to either (1) the need to achieve success, or (2) the need to avoid failure in learning tasks. When encountering a specific task in the classroom, one student may approach it enthusiastically and confidently by anticipating success. Another student may show great hesitancy, even to the point of not doing the task, if he is afraid of failure. The teacher can facilitate the first motivational situation by being aware of the existing relevant learning or lack of learning within the student and, thereby, preparing the student's capabilities and attitude for the successful completion of the task. Consider the following classroom example:

An eighth-grade math instructor is teaching pre-algebra to a group of above-average students. One unit of instruction includes learning the concepts and rules governing the use of commutative property, associative property, and distributive property. The attainment of these concepts and rules will be applied not only to addition, subtraction, and multiplication but also to eventual attainment of more complex mathematical behavior. Thus, the primary task involved in this teaching unit focuses on the following behavioral objectives:

1. The students will learn the concepts "commutative property," "associative property," and "distributive property."
2. The students will learn the rules governing the use of commutative property, associative property, and distributive property.
3. The students will learn applications of the rules for commutative property, associative property, and distributive property to the mathematical procedures of addition, subtraction, and multiplication.
4. The students will learn the significance of these intellectual tasks in regard to their subsequent use with the more complex learning of similar mathematical concepts and rules.

Clearly, a student's general desire to achieve provides him with the motivation to proceed with the intellectual tasks at hand. However, this type of learning specifically involves task motivation as well, because three distinct learning behaviors are required within the teaching unit, and each of these behaviors must be specifically motivated in some way if the unit task is to be successfully completed. The distinction being made here between achievement motivation and task motivation is a fine but important one. The essential difference is that task motivation is really the specific application of the more generalized achievement motivation to particular classroom tasks. Thus, achievement motivation refers to a general trait while task motivation relates to specific content—the successful accomplishment of student behavioral objectives.

In this example from a mathematics class, and in most academic situations, the following motives may be operant in the student or may be encouraged by the teacher for the accomplishment of specific tasks:

1. The student may be motivated by the intrinsic satisfaction of learning.
2. The student may see the importance of learning specific materials in terms of a larger learning context.
3. The student may see the importance of learning specific material in terms of his eventual academic and educational plans.

4. The student may relate knowledge of the material to its practical use in the world.
5. The student may be spurred by the competition of others to do well on the task.

Aspirational motivation

If given the opportunity within the classroom, many students will set for themselves goals or expectancies which they hope to reach during a specific period of time. While such aspirational goals may be long-range, they are more often immediate for most students and are likely to be operant even in daily academic tasks.

If a teacher desires to have students set their own goals, or levels of aspiration, it is very important that the students be able to realize them. Research has shown that success not only perpetuates goal setting but also leads to a rise in the level of aspiration. In contrast, failure tends to lower the aspiration level. (See the results of such research by Child and Whiting (1949) in Table 10.1). Significant studies by Sears (1940), Lewin et al. (1944), and Mursetin (1965) reach the same conclusion.

Of course, it is not always possible for a student to experience success or for a teacher to provide the student with experiences that will invariably lead to success. On the other hand, it is vitally important for the teacher to see that the student is not repeatedly experiencing failure. Successive or prolonged failures will inevitably cause the student to set unrealistic goals as well as to lose interest in the activity with which failure has occurred (Israel, 1960). Sears (1940) also found a more variable and unrealistic goal-setting pattern among students who experienced failure rather than success. Among successful students, goals tended to be slightly higher for the next succeeding task, whereas among unsuccessful students, goals tended to be either distinctly higher or lower for the next succeeding task.

A more recent investigation was conducted by the author (1971b) in which

TABLE 10.1   Shifts in Level of Aspiration Produced by Success and Failure

Type of Incident	N	Percentage Shift in Level of Aspiration		
		Lowering	None	Rise
Complete frustration	140	47%	26%	27%
Frustration followed by goal attainment	125	12%	12%	76%
Simple goal attainment	141	2%	12%	86%

Child, I. L., & Whiting, J. W. M. Determinants of level of aspiration; evidence from everyday life, *Journal of Abnormal and Social Psychology,* 1949, **44,** 303–314. Copyright 1949 by the American Psychological Association and reprinted by permission.

new instructional procedures were used with a group of 43 high school freshmen considered to be potential dropouts. They entered high school with (1) low IQs (mean of 85.3) as measured by the Lorge–Thorndike Intelligence Scale (Verbal), (2) low academic promise (median at 14th percentile) as measured by the Academic Promise Test, (3) low reading ability (median at 15th percentile) as measured by the Nelson–Denny Reading Test, (4) poor teacher ratings, (5) one or more grades repeated during elementary school, (6) excessive absenteeism, (7) negative attitudes toward school, and (8) poor self-concepts (mean of 13th percentile) as measured by the Tennessee Self-Concept Scale.

The students were given one year of special instruction in mathematical and English tasks that were relevant to them and within their ability range. In many cases, this meant figuring interest on automobile loans for the boys and doubling or tripling recipes for the girls. Classics Illustrated was used in preference to standard literature texts. The results were that the students learned, that they expressed the desire to accomplish additional tasks, and that they set goals they were capable of accomplishing. The students were also found to have a more positive attitude toward school and self, with a new self-concept median score at the 29th percentile, which represents a significant shift. This improvement most likely resulted from the fact that these students realized, perhaps for the first time, that school did not have to be frustrating and, most important, that they could learn.

In addition to the enhancement of their immediate learning experiences, an increased desire to be in school was reflected by a lower absentee rate and dropout rate than among the other ninth-grade students. The rate of absenteeism among the 43 students was 5 percent compared to the total ninth-grade rate of 12 percent, and only three of the 43 students (7 percent) dropped out of school, compared to 17 percent of the total ninth-grade student body. While the number of subjects under investigation was small, the study confirms that aspiration and interest levels (motivation) increase with successful experiences.

Competition motivation

A self-imposed standard of excellence, or self-imposed competition, can be a strong motivating factor. This factor is associated with the need to achieve mastery of one's environment. Self-imposed competition may be inferred by the "disposition to strive for the attainment of self-imposed standards of good performance or to strive for the attainment of personally accepted, long-term achievement goals, and by the capacity for satisfaction in the attainment of those goals" (Talbert, 1968, p. 5). It is probable that many classrooms are generally not conducive to student recognition of the availability of such a motivational source; for all too often, classroom environments are geared around a different motivational-competitive source—competition with others.

The motivational factor of competition with others is represented by the student who is motivated to learn or achieve in order to do as well as or better than his peers.

It is unlikely that classroom learning can go on without the influence of student competition. Yet, it would probably be to the advantage of most students if the stress is on cooperation rather than competition; for there is not a loser, and a sense of failure, in a cooperative structure. If the teacher thinks student competition is a useful motivational technique in some circumstances, caution should be exercised that students are not put into an unequal competitive situation. A recent investigation by Clifford (1971) indicates that *homogeneous* competition—that is, competition among the equally able—*with reward* is an effective motivational source. Heterogeneous competition, or competition among those poorly matched in ability, was found to have less value.

Affiliative motivation

Students are always motivated to gain approval from peers and adults within the classroom and home environment. The incentive is the intrinsic need to gain self-assurance that one is acceptable to others (Birch & Veroff, 1966). Most young school children express a strong need for adult affiliation, which is generally evidenced by the tendency to strive to establish, maintain, or restore a positive affective relationship with their teachers (Talbert, 1968). Typically, the child sees a classroom environment controlled by the teacher, who demands a degree of obedience and respect. In order to minimize conflict and to gain acceptance by the teacher, the student usually tries to conform to the teacher-established expectations.

As the child advances in grade level, there may be a growing conformity to teacher expectations for some years and then an emerging tendency to build stronger affiliations with classroom peers. It is not uncommon, eventually, for the student's affiliative needs to shift almost entirely to peer-approval and -acceptance motives.

Teachers should realize that these peer affiliations are important. The peer

TABLE 10.2.   *Characteristics Considered Most Important for Popularity*

	Percent Responding (N = 10.019)
Being in the leading crowd	64.3
Being an athletic star	18.7
Having a nice car	12.7
High grades, honor roll	4.2

TABLE 10.3   *Characteristics Considered Necessary for Membership in "Leading Crowd"*

	Percent Responding (N = 10.019)
Friendliness	51.3
Good looks	25.4
Money	13.8
Athletic ability	7.0
Academic excellence	2.5

Tables 10.2 and 10.3 are from Friesen, D. Academic-athletic-popularity syndrome in the Canadian high school society. *Adolescence*, 1968, **3**, 39–52. Reprinted by permission of the publisher.

groupings apparently form a kind of subculture; and, as a result, students are often motivated to do things acceptable to peer standards, even if the behavior is incongruous with teacher or other adult expectations. For example, students may not achieve beyond that which they know their peer group will accept. Research studies by Goldberg (1960) and Coleman (1961) have shown that high-intelligence students play down making good grades in order not to receive disapproval from peers. Coleman also found, as did Cawelti (1968) and Friesen (1968, see Tables 10.2 and 10.3), that when high school students were asked to rank peers in terms of (1) popularity and (2) "who would you like to be like most," they showed a strong preference for socially and athletically oriented students over academically oriented students.

Anxiety

One of the strongest intrinsic motivational variables in the classroom is anxiety. While there may be several reasons for classroom anxiety, such as personality conflict, deficit peer relations, or lack of orientation toward academic achievement, most research has focused on task and test anxiety. Scharf (1964) studied high-anxiety and low-anxiety subjects with problem-solving tasks involving anagrams. The subjects were divided into three test groups: high anxiety, low anxiety, and stress-neutral. No differences were found between high- and low-anxiety groups in solving easy anagrams, but low-anxiety students performed significantly better when the anagrams were difficult and when a time period was placed on the task. Another study by Sarason et al. (1960) indicated that students with low test-anxiety performed better in school than did students with high-test anxiety, and a comparable study in which anxiety level was considered in relation to the scholastic aptitude level (Spielberger, 1966) confirmed the high achievement of low-anxiety students.

The effects of achievement motivation and anxiety levels were checked by Raynor and Rubin (1971) on a three-step arithmetic task in which two different sets of instructions were given. One group was given *contingency* conditions; that is, they had to be successful on one test before they could go on to work on a successive test. The conditions for the second group were non-contingent; that is, success on one test was not necessary for work on the others. All subjects were led to believe that their chance of success on the task was 50–50. As Table 10.4 illustrates, subjects who were high in achievement motivation and low in test anxiety ("high-low motives" group) performed significantly better under the contingent than the non-contingent conditions. In addition, this high-low group performed significantly better under the contingent conditions than those students who were low in achievement motivation and high in test anxiety ("low-high motives" group). In contrast, the low-high subjects performed significantly worse under the contingent than the non-contingent conditions. This study clearly shows that low anxiety is a better motivational state than high anxiety for

TABLE 10.4.   *Mean Number of Problems Answered Correctly as a Function of Achievement Motivation and Test Anxiety*

Motive Group	Conditions			
	Noncontingent		Contingent	
	n	*M*	*n*	*M*
High-low	8	13.00	7	17.43
High-high	6	8.83	6	12.00
Low-low	10	12.70	6	11.33
Low-high	7	11.86	8	7.00

Raynor, J. O., & Rubin, I. S. Effects of achievement motivation and future orientation on level of performance, *Journal of Personality and Social Psychology,* 1971, **17**, 36–41. Copyright 1971 by the American Psychological Association and reprinted by permission.

classroom test conditions—and particularly for *stressful* test conditions (the contingency test).

Since anxiety is primarily intrinsic, it is usually beyond the control of the teacher. But it is important that the teacher at least attempt to become aware of the different anxiety states among the students, so that high-anxiety students can be given some special concern. For example, if a teacher knows that a student becomes very anxious at the prospect of having to give an oral report, perhaps the teacher can accept a written one as an alternative. In addition, teachers should strive to avoid creating tension-producing situations within the classroom; for, generally speaking, teacher-initiated anxiety does not tend to increase either motivation or learning, and learner-supportive instructional approaches have proven to be more effective (Flanders, 1951).

Avoidance motivation

Sometimes, classroom anxiety is severe enough that students will be motivated to *avoid* certain classroom learning and behavioral conditions. This is especially true under the threat of punishment or reprimand by the teacher. Such disciplinary techniques frequently produce anxiety, emotional upset, and guilt among the students. Even less open or severe forms of teacher disapproval, such as a student's knowledge that he has not achieved up to the teacher's expectations, may produce detrimental effects on classroom learning conditions. Lewin et al.(1944) found, for example, that knowledge of failure might cause the student to avoid setting an aspirational level for himself.

A great deal has been written about punishment in the classroom, typically in emotionally loaded terms. It is generally thought to bring about student dissatisfaction as well as some undesirable emotional repercussions. The theoretical, nonemotional view of punishment has best been stated by Klausmeier and Ripple (1971):

> A punishment by definition brings pain or dissatisfaction to the recipient. Punishment takes many forms, including the withholding or withdrawal of anything that serves as a reward; expressing disapproval, either verbally or in nonverbal ways; threatening, either verbally or in nonverbal ways; giving low grades or other indications of unsatisfactory work or conduct; removal from a desired situation; and depriving of basic needs. Punishments may be administered by groups as well as by individuals. Receiving a punishment immediately after a response may weaken the response; or it may lead to the recipient's temporarily suppressing the response or to his suppressing it only in the presence of the punisher; or it may result in evasion of or open aggression against the punisher. Being promised a punishment for not performing a task may lead

Photo courtesy of Herbert Klausmeier.

to performance of the task, but it may lead to avoidance of the task, the punishment, and the punisher. Being promised a punishment if a specified anti-social behavior is manifested may lead to nonmanifestation of it, but it may [also] lead to avoidance of the punishment and punisher while still expressing the anti-social behavior. In addition, punishment may result in undesirable anxiety in the child, negative feelings toward the punisher, and negative feelings toward school [pp. 336–337].

It is clear that the teacher should be cautious of the way punishment is used. Above all, a student should not be punished because of inability to accomplish an assignment. Nor should a misbehaving student be given additional assignments. Either action misuses the purposes and the content of the learning situation and affects the interest and motivational levels of the student.

When the teacher tells a student, "Either get your assignment finished or you will stay in from recess," what is being accomplished? Has the teacher sufficiently motivated the student to "get on the ball" and get the assignment done? Has the teacher inferred that his academic subject is more important to the student than physical activity? Will the student be motivated on subsequent assignments to complete the work on time? Isn't it more likely that the student is learning to dislike the particular academic subject because of the teacher's behavior toward him? These are the types of questions a teacher must consider prior to expressing punishment behavior. Most important, the teacher must assess the long-range learning effects of such action, even if he believes that the punishment may effectively motivate the student for the immediate task situation. Generally, if a student cannot apply a rule to a problem he should be given additional help in order to accomplish the task, not punished.

Reinforcing motivation

Three reinforcing techniques can be discussed as motivational sources: *knowledge of results, praise,* and *tests and grades.* Skinner (1938, 1953) has contended that knowledge of the correctness of a response is sufficient reinforcement for a learning task. It is most likely that knowledge of results also serves as a motivator because it tells the student the amount of success he is having. Since it is virtually impossible for the teacher to reinforce every student on every response, such awareness as to the accurateness of academic responses can motivate the student toward additional learning situations.

A physical education teacher notices that increased abilities occurred when his boys found out that their grade was determined by the amount of self-improvement they made with physical fitness exercises. *How does the research on motivation explain this behavioral change?*

In searching for strong school motivational sources, research has revealed that many students are sufficiently motivated by a self-imposed standard of excellence, or self-competition. The idea behind self-imposed standards of excellence as a motivational source is to provide goals or a record of continuing scores or rates by which the learner can measure his success. In such situations, the individual generates a need to increase his own performance and is not tied to normative comparisons against classmates.

Consider, for example, a physical-fitness test given once in each of four nine-week periods in high school. There are five tasks on the test which each individual must perform: (1) push-ups, (2) pull-ups, (3) sit-ups, (4) squat thrusts, and (5) the 300-yard run. Let us say that a sophomore boy, Otis Brown, performed the test in October and did 12 push-ups, 3 pull-ups, 83 sit-ups, 22 squat thrusts, and ran 300 yards in 60.5 seconds. The final score for Otis in the May testing was 26 push-ups, 6 pull-ups, 90 sit-ups, 23 squat thrusts, and a 58-second 300-yard run. The fact that he had self-comparative standards from test to test provided the necessary motivation for self-improvement.

Praise has been exalted by many learning theorists as a good motivational technique. Praise serves as a motivator because it generally acts to encourage achievement, increase aspiration levels, and facilitate learning. Three different studies that have shown the effects of teacher praise are reported here, although praise from peers is also highly motivational.

1. Page (1958) has studied the incentive effects of marking test papers in three different ways—test score only, test score with personal teacher comments, and test score with stereotyped teacher comments. The results of the study indicated that (1) students whose papers had personalized comments did better than the other two groups on subsequent testing; (2) students whose papers had stereotyped comments did better than the no-comment group on subsequent testing; and (3) students whose papers had only the test score showed no significant change in subsequent tests. The effects of praise as a motivational source were clearly demonstrated.

2. Zigler and Kanzer (1962) have investigated the effects of verbal "praise reinforcers" ("good" or "fine") and verbal "correct reinforcers" ("correct" or "right") upon subsequent academic behaviors of middle- and lower-class children. Working from the persuasion that there was a distinct difference between the two reinforcing classifications, the authors found that among middle-class children "correct" reinforcements improved performance better than "praise" reinforcements. The opposite finding occurred with lower-class children, who responded more notably to "praise" reinforcements than to "correct" reinforcements.

3. The investigation by Clifford (1971) compared the performance of students at four ability levels, with homogeneous competition and reward (praise) and non-reward conditions. She found the effect of praise to be much greater in the low-ability and high average-ability groups than in the low average-ability and high-ability groups.

4. Zigler, Butterfield, and Capobianco (1970) have investigated the motivational effects of praise among children who were mentally retarded and institutionalized. One research variable was the nature of the pre-institutional environment; that is, whether or not it was culturally deprived. Reporting evidence over an eight-year time period, the researchers found that the children from highly deprived pre-institutional environments were less motivated by praise reinforcement than their non-deprived counterparts. In addition, the researchers found that the effect of praise as a motivational source decreased among the children from relatively "good" homes as they became more socially deprived from institutionalization. The researchers concluded that social deprivation becomes an integral part of the individual's expectations and thus mediates his response to praise and achievement, even some ten years later (Zigler, 1963).

Tests and grades have always been considered a basic motivational source. Tests typically motivate students to study for the test and not "to learn," although this does not preclude learning taking place. Similarly, while grades may serve as good reinforcing motives for study, they often do not accomplish the ultimate learning that is desired by the teacher. For example, it is questionable that a semester grade can be clearly established as the motivator for an ongoing academic performance, and these types of grades certainly do not provide specific feedback for completed work. A daily or weekly grade or a test grade, however, may provide specific feedback and is likely to motivate the student on succeeding work.

The teacher should be cautious that grades do not become the primary source of motivation within a classroom. It is logical to use such reinforcing techniques for motivation; for, in fact, they are powerful conditions for learning. But they should be used as part of the total motivational system and not as "the motivational system" itself. Too often, grades are emphasized as motivators and become associated with classroom competition or with anxiety-producing parental pressures for "acceptable grades" or "going-to-college grades." Neither situation is conducive to learning.

Individually guided motivation

The work of Klausmeier et al. (1971) has focused on the categorization of self-directed motivational factors as behavioral objectives for classroom students. Table 10.5 presents a listing of those student behaviors that are indicative of individually guided motivation; that is, the activities that the self-motivated student is likely to do within the teaching–learning situation. The statements are an outcome of the coordinated research of the Wisconsin Research and Development Center for Cognitive Learning and a Wisconsin public elementary school.

Klausmeier et al. (1971) have also stated eight principles of motivation by which these behavioral objectives can be analyzed. These principles, summarized in Table 10.6, give the teacher an understanding of the basic psychological principles which research has shown to be instrumental in guiding motivation. Table 10.6 also suggests the instructional implications of each principle. Note that principles 1 through 4 are specifically related to learning subject matter, while principles 5 and 6 relate to conduct, focusing on the learning and maintenance of pro-social behaviors. The latter usually take two forms of expression: (1) those which indicate what the teacher expects the child to do (for example, listening, cleaning up after a project), and (2) those which indicate self-direction (for example, reading in spare time). Principles 7 and 8 may apply to either learning or pro-social behaviors.

The concept of individually guided motivations as advanced by Klausmeier

TABLE 10.5 Classroom Behaviors Indicative of Self-motivation

A. The pupil starts promptly and completes self-, teacher-, or group-assigned tasks that together comprise the minimum requirements related to various curriculum areas.
  1. Attends to the teacher and other situational elements when attention is required.
  2. Begins tasks promptly.
  3. Seeks feedback concerning performance on tasks.
  4. Returns to tasks voluntarily after interruption or initial lack of progress.
  5. Persists at tasks until completed.

B. The pupil assumes responsibility for learning more than the minimum requirements without teacher guidance during school hours and outside school hours. In addition to behaviors 1–5, the pupil
  6. Continues working when the teacher leaves the room.
  7. Does additional work during school hours.
  8. Works on school-related activities outside school hours.
  9. Identifies activities that are relevant for class projects.
  10. Seeks suggestions for going beyond minimum amount or quality of work.

C. The pupil becomes self-directive in connection with use of property, relations with other pupils, and relations with adults.
  11. Moves quietly within and about the school building during quiet periods and activities.
  12. Interacts harmoniously with other pupils.
  13. Interacts harmoniously with the teacher and other adults.
  14. Conserves own and others' property.
  15. Tells other pupils to behave in accordance with school policies.

D. The pupil verbalizes a value system consistent with the preceding behaviors.
  16. When asked, gives examples of his own actions illustrative of behaviors 1–15.
  17. When asked, gives reasons for manifesting behaviors 1–15.

Klausmeier, H. J., Sorenson, J. S., & Ghatala, E. S. Individually guided motivation, *Elementary School Journal,* 1971, **71,** p. 340. Copyright 1971 by The University of Chicago Press. Reprinted by permission.

provides the teacher not only with a way of capitalizing on self-motivational conditions within the learner but also with a way of assessing student motivation within the classroom setting. Certainly, by being aware of the student's potential motivational system, the teacher is better able to utilize student motivation within the teaching–learning situation.

The application of sources of motivation within the classroom

The following classroom illustration focuses on three ideas presented thus far in this book: (1) the level of learning involved is identified in terms of Gagné's hierarchy; (2) the instructional strategies presented in earlier chapters are in use throughout the illustration; and (3) four different sources of motivation are designated as operant in

TABLE 10.6. *Principles of Motivation and Corollary Instructional Implications*

Principle	*Instructional Implications*
1. Attending to a learning task is essential for initiating a learning sequence.	A. Focus pupil's attention on desired objectives.
2. Desiring to achieve control over elements of the environment and to experience success is essential to realistic goal-setting.	B. Use the individual's need to achieve and other positive motives.
3. Setting and attaining goals requires learning tasks at an appropriate level of difficulty; feelings of success on current learning tasks heighten motivation for subsequent tasks; feelings of failure lower motivation for subsequent tasks.	C. Help each pupil to set and attain goals related to the educational program of the school.
4. Acquiring information concerning correct or appropriate behaviors and correcting errors are associated with better performance on and more favorable attitudes toward the learning tasks.	D. Provide for informative feedback.
5. Observing and imitating a model facilitates the initial acquisition of prosocial behaviors such as self-control, self-reliance, and persistence.	E. Provide for real-life and symbolic models.
6. Verbalizing pro-social values and behaviors and reasoning about them provide a conceptual basis for the development of the behaviors.	F. Provide for verbalization and discussion of pro-social values.
7. Expecting to receive a reward for specified behavior or achievement directs and sustains attention and effort toward manifesting the behavior or achievement. Non-reinforcement after a response tends to extinguish the response. Expecting to receive punishment for manifesting undesired behavior may lead to suppression of the behavior, to avoidance or dislike of the situation, or to avoidance and dislike of the punisher.	G. Develop and use a system of rewards as necessary to secure sustained effort and desired conduct. Use punishment as necessary to suppress misconduct.
8. Experiencing high stress and anxiety is associated with low performance, erratic conduct, and personality disorders.	H. Avoid the use of procedures that create temporary high stress or chronic anxiety.

Klausmeier, H. J., Sorenson, J. S., & Ghatala, E. S. Individually guided motivation, *Elementary School Journal*, 1971, **71**, p. 342. Copyright 1971 by The University of Chicago Press. Reprinted by permission.

the learning situation. In addition to these four basic motivational sources, the teacher might specifically motivate students for the task in some of the following ways:

> Readiness for the task might be accomplished by giving relevant warm-up exercises. Then by reinforcing student responses during the warm-up period, the teacher might instill a motivational carry-over to the new task. The teacher might also behaviorally state the intellectual task and specify the desired ultimate learning—a simple behavior which often induces individually guided motivation. Similarly, the teacher might show the importance of the task by relating it to practical situations with which the students might want to get involved. Another motivational source could be a particular student's energy which the teacher might focus on with the hope that this energy would spread to the other students. Yet another technique is to show the relationship of the learning task with a larger task or area of knowledge.

Intellectual task: Using the multiplication algorithm

Academic level: Grades 8 or 9

Learning level: Concept learning, rule learning, and problem solving (levels 6–8)

Instructional strategy: Utilization of already known concepts for the immediate intellectual task through the presentation of sequential stimuli.

Motivations operating: 1. *Task motivation.* The student indicates an energy level toward achievement of the specific task. This is likely the primary motivational source.

2. *Achievement motivation.* The student may be using achievement needs to accomplish the task.

3. *Competition motivation.* The confrontation with peers in learning the task may spur academic success for the student.

4. *Reinforcing motivation.* Seeking reinforcement for his accomplishments, the student might be motivated by anticipation of teacher feedback.

Prerequisite learning: The following *concepts* would be necessary as prerequisite intellectual skills:

1. Expanded notation
2. Commutative property
3. Distributive property
4. Associative property

The following *rules* would be necessary as prerequisite intellectual skills:

1. Commutative property of addition
2. Associative property of addition
3. Commutative property of multiplication
4. Associative property of multiplication

The teacher might begin by restating the relevant concepts and rules and then presenting the students with a problem that would illustrate the efficiency of multiplication as opposed to addition. (The economy of multiplication might provide some motivation to the learner.) Consider the following strategy, which pulls together prerequisite skills and new learning:

We will take 6×24. In using the two factors to come up with the multiplied product, consider the following already known arithmetic concepts:

$6 \times 24 = 6 [(2 \times 10) + 4]$	Expanded notation
$= 6 [4 + (2 \times 10)]$	Commutative property of addition
$= (6 \times 4) + 6 \times (2 \times 10)$	Distributive property
$= (6 \times 4) + [(6 \times 2) \times 10]$	Associative property of multiplication
$= 24 + [12 \times 10]$	Basic multiplication facts
$= [(4 + (2 \times 10)] + (12 \times 10)$	Expanded notation
$= 4 + [(2 \times 10) + (12 \times 10)]$	Associative property of addition
$= 4 + [2 + 12) \times 10]$	Distributive property
$= 4 + (24 \times 10)$	Basic addition fact
$= 4 + [(2 \times 10) + 4] \times 10$	Expanded notation
$= 4 + [(2 \times 10) \times 10] + (4 \times 10)$	Distributive property
$= (2 \times 10^2) + (4 \times 10) + 4$	Commutative and associative properties of addition and multiplication
$6 \times 24 = 144$	Decimal numeration

The following steps illustrate why the algorithm works:

$$\begin{array}{r} 24 \\ \times\ 16 \\ \hline 144 \\ 24 \\ \hline 384 \end{array}$$

1. Multiply 24 and 6 and write the product.
2. Multiply 24 and 1 and write the product one place to the left.
3. Add the results of steps 1 and 2.

$$24 \times 16 = (20 + 4) \times 16 \qquad \text{Expanded notation}$$
$$= (4 \times 20) \times 16 \qquad \text{Commutative property of addition}$$
$$= (6 \times 16) + (20 \times 23) \quad \text{Distributive property}$$
$$= 144 + 240 \qquad \text{Products}$$
$$= 384 \qquad \text{Addition algorithm}$$

Do the following problems and make notations as to the principles involved in deriving the answers:

A. 12×43

B. 9×85

C. 17×149

D. 28×280

E. 152×312

Student motivation may be facilitated in working out the yet-unsolved problems by this combination of new knowledge with old knowledge and the application of the combined concepts and rules to the problems. The ultimate working out of such problems not only confirms learning but provides the students with achievement levels and reinforcing statements, both of which motivate the students to continue learning.

SUGGESTED READINGS

Clifford, M. M.   Motivational effects of competition and goal setting in reward and non-reward conditions. *Journal of Experimental Education,* 1971, **39,** 10–16.

Clifford, M. M.   Competition as a motivational technique in the classroom. *American Educational Research Journal,* 1972, **9,** 123–137.

deCharms, R., & Carpenter, V.   Measuring motivation in culturally disadvantaged school children. *Journal of Experimental Education,* 1968, **37** (1), 31–41.

Elkind, D., Deblinger, J., & Adler, D.   Motivation and creativity: The context effect. *American Educational Research Journal,* 1970, **7,** 351–357.

Hunt, J. McV.   Experience and the development of motivation: Some reinterpretations. *Child Development,* 1960, **31,** 489–504.

Klausmeier, H. J., Sorenson, J. S., & Ghatala, E. S.   Individually guided motivation: Developing self-direction and pro-social behaviors. *Elementary School Journal,* 1971, **71,** 339–350. Reprinted in H. D. Thornburg (Ed.), *School learning and instruction: Readings.* Monterey, Calif.: Brooks/Cole, 1973, chap. 4.

Maehr, M. L., & Sjogren, D. D.   Atkinson's theory of achievement motivation: First step toward a theory of academic motivation? *Review of Educational Research,* 1971, **41,** 143–161. Reprinted in H. D. Thornburg (Ed.), *School learning and instruction: Readings.* Monterey, Calif.: Brooks/Cole, 1973, chap. 4.

Raynor, J. O., & Rubin, I. S.   Effects of achievement motivation and future orientation on level of performance. *Journal of Personality and Social Psychology,* 1971, **17,** 36–41.

White, R. W.   Motivation reconsidered: The concept of competence. *Psychological Review,* 1959, **66,** 297–333.

11

Behavior Modification

Basically, *behavior modification* is an attempt to apply the general principles of learning in order to achieve desired changes in an individual's behavior. Although behavior modification procedures vary considerably according to the types of behavioral problems they deal with, all such techniques usually share the following characteristics: (1) They seek to change only those responses that are observable or measurable. (2) They require specification of the particular behavioral goal. (3) They require detailed specification of the probable conditions responsible for the response that is to be changed or introduced. (4) They involve the collection of objective data as to current strength of an unwanted behavior. (5) They require continual data collection to assess the effect (the success) of the modification. Within this chapter, the characteristics and application of classical conditioning, operant conditioning, and reinforcement principles are presented as procedures by which deviant classroom behaviors may be modified. The emphasis will be on a basic and general understanding of these principles. There is no attempt to provide an extensive review of the theoretical foundations underlying each principle; for although there exists an extensive literature of theoretical research studies in this area, the bulk of the studies involve the treatment of *exceptionally* deviant behaviors, which, for all practical purposes, lie outside the domain of applied educational psychology. For an in-depth discussion of the more technical aspects of behavior modification processes, and for literature on the modification of markedly deviant behaviors, the work of Bandura (1969), Wolpe (1969), and Wolpe and Lazarus (1966) will be helpful.

264

RESPONDENT CONDITIONING IN BEHAVIOR MODIFICATION

Behavior modification procedures utilizing classical conditioning principles are applied primarily in the elimination of inappropriate or deviant behaviors that appear to be respondent in nature. The skills needed by the change agent and the control necessary for the implementation of these procedures usually preclude their use by school personnel, and, in any case, respondent-type behavior problems are not typically encountered in school settings.

The most common applications of classical conditioning principles for behavior modification are found in the elimination of phobic reactions, severe anxiety, aberrant sexual behavior, alcoholism, and drug addiction. Several behavior therapies based upon classical conditioning principles have been developed, among them *counter-conditioning therapy, implosive therapy,* and *reciprocal inhibition therapy.* The two basic concepts underlying these therapies are *respondent extinction* and *counter-conditioning.* Respondent extinction is the process whereby a conditioned response (CR) will be weakened when the conditioned stimulus (CS, reinforcement) is repeatedly presented without any further pairing with the unconditioned stimulus (UCS). Counter-conditioning is basically the procedure whereby a competing response (a new CR) is conditioned to the eliciting stimulus (CS) for the unwanted conditioned response.

Counter-conditioning therapy

Counter-conditioning therapy for effecting behavioral change rests on the principle that if two responses are incompatible—that is, cannot occur at the same time—the increased occurrence of one of the responses must be accompanied by a decrease in the other. For example, you cannot be relaxed and anxious at the same time. Thus, if a person can be conditioned to relax in a situation that normally produces high anxiety, the anxiety response would be reduced or eliminated. A classic example of counter-conditioning was reported by Jones (1924). After a child had developed conditioned fear reactions (CR) to the sight of a white rat (CS), the fear reactions were reduced by pairing the sight of the white rat with the presentation of food. Since consuming food was incompatible with a fear response, the gradual introduction of the white rat during the feeding of the hungry child established a new conditioned response (eating) in the presence of the stimulus (CS) that originally elicited fear. Thus, the child was able to overcome his fear reaction to the sight of a white rat.

Implosive therapy

In implosive therapy (Stampfl & Lewis, 1967), the conditioned stimulus which is eliciting the undesired reaction (CR) is tentatively identified—it is often obsure in aberrant behavior problems—and then presented to the subject in the absence of the unconditioned stimulus. By continually presenting the CS and not allowing it to be paired with the UCS, the CS eventually undergoes extinction and loses its power to elicit the conditioned response.

The actual procedure is more complex than this account would indicate, since it is often nearly impossible to determine what stimuli were involved in the original conditioning situation. The therapist using the implosive procedure typically relies upon verbal reports by the subject and forms tentative hypotheses as to what the original negative learning conditions might have been. The accuracy of these hypotheses is not really as crucial as it might seem; for the purpose of the therapy is simply to remove the unwanted reaction in the presence of the particular conditioned stimulus. If, for example, a person experiences severe anxiety reactions when required to speak in a group setting, it is not essential to know exactly how such a fear developed. It is simply necessary to repeatedly expose the subject to potentially anxiety-producing situations (group settings) and ensure that no unconditioned stimuli for anxiety (fear of failure, rejection, authority, rebuttal, and so on) are present. Implosive therapy, then, is the attempt to systematically extinguish an undesirable conditioned response by presenting the presumed conditioned stimuli in a sequence of gradually increasing eliciting situations while ensuring that each particular conditioned stimulus has lost its eliciting potential before presenting the next threatening situation.

Reciprocal inhibition therapy

Reciprocal inhibition therapy, as developed by Wolpe (1958, 1969), refers to a group of related counter-conditioning therapeutic procedures designed to remove classically conditioned maladaptive behaviors. Basically, the procedures involve the establishment in the subject of a state of deep relaxation which inhibits or precludes anxiety or fear reactions. Although different authors have developed variations in techniques, the following procedure is typical: (1) Initially, the subject who desires to rid himself of some behavioral pattern is taught the skills necessary to achieve a state of deep muscle relaxation. Wolpe (1969) reports that most subjects learn the skills quickly and are able to self-induce deep relaxaton within a few minutes. (2) After relaxation has been achieved, the therapist attempts to determine the range and types of stimulus situations which elicit the unwanted behavior. Techniques for determining these stimuli vary but generally involve fear and anxiety tests, inspection of the subject's history, and interviews in which the subject is asked to recount the situations he finds fearful or anxiety-producing. (3) Once a list of fear-producing situations is constructed, the therapist attempts to arrange them hierarchically. (4) The subject is then directed to induce relaxation and is asked to imagine a situation involving mild fear-producing stimuli. If the subject indicates no fear reaction, he is asked to imagine the next most fear-producing situation. If the subject indicates that he is becoming fearful, he is told to stop thinking of that situation and relax. He would then be asked to re-imagine a less threatening situation for which the fear reaction had previously been extinguished. In this way, it is often possible to eliminate the unwanted response.

This type of procedure, which is often referred to as *systematic desensitization,* has been reported as effective in remedying fears and anxieties related to such things as height, illness, storms, sex, and examinations (Wolpe & Lazarus, 1966).

OPERANT CONDITIONING IN BEHAVIOR MODIFICATION

Although a significant number of human behaviors are undoubtedly acquired through respondent conditioning, they would seem to represent a small segment of a person's total behavior pattern. Most social behavior is controlled not by the stimuli that precede and thereby elicit it but by the effect of that behavior on the environment. Walking, talking, and book-writing behaviors are not directly elicited by stimuli but, rather, are emitted in hope of some favorable consequences. Such behavior is called operant behavior, as we have learned. It is behavior that is acquired, modified, or eliminated as a result of events that follow the behavior. Operant behavior is also commonly referred to as being voluntary, purposeful, goal-directed, and intentional.

In discussing operant behavior conditioning and behavior in terms of behavior modification, we must consider the concepts of *reinforcement* and *punishment,* which are the most important variables. Reinforcement is defined functionally as the stimulus event which, when presented immediately following a response, increases the probability of that response occurring again in the same or a similar situation. Punishment is the identical process which accounts for decreasing the probability of a response.

As we learned earlier in this book, reinforcement effects are divided into two classes: *positive reinforcement* and *negative reinforcement*. In positive reinforcement, the strength of a response is increased as a result of the behavior being followed by a stimulus presentation (the reinforcer), while negative reinforcement increased the probability of a response as a result of the behavior being followed by the removal, termination, or avoidance of a particular stimulus. Examples of positive reinforcement are giving a hungry rat a food pellet after it presses a bar or complimenting a student when he finishes his assignment. Remember that these examples are illustrative of positive reinforcement only if the reinforcing consequence results in an increased probability of the response occurring again. The presentation of a peanut-butter sandwich would not function as positive reinforcement for a child who doesn't like peanut butter.

Examples of negative reinforcement would be removing an infant's wet diaper when he cries or discontinuing the "evil eye" when a student gets started on his homework. In these examples, the effect of the removal of an unpleasant state of affairs would increase the likelihood that whatever response immediately preceded the removal of the unpleasant stimulus would be repeated in a similar situation.

Punishment can take two forms: (1) It may be the infliction of a painful experience, such as spanking, sarcasm, or ridicule. (2) It may be taking away something the student likes, such as a loss of privilege. In most cases, punishment tends to create aversive attitudes and personality-conflict problems between the teacher and the pupil being punished, and it is therefore rejected by most educators as a viable alternative for behavior modification. Punishment is also the least effective procedure—for the following reasons:

1. *Punishment does not last.*   If the threat of punishment or actual punishment is severe enough, the student's behavior will be controlled for a while. However, when the punishment effect wears off, the behavior will likely appear again.
2. *Punishment does not teach alternative responses.*   This is the most serious limitation of punishment. Children very often do not have the skills to behave appropriately in the classroom. Will punishment teach them the new skills? In contrast, reinforcing techniques are instrumental in learning new alternatives.
3. *Punishment is upsetting.*   Most teachers find punishment upsetting, not only to the child being punished but to the teacher and the rest of the class as well. It intensifies the emotional climate of the classroom, often engendering feelings of anger, frustra-

tion, dislike, and hostility. It puts extreme strain on the social relationship between the punished child and the teacher. In similar fashion, it often makes the child socially ill at ease with the rest of the class through embarrassment and loss of face.

4. *Punishment causes counter-aggression.*   It is not uncommon for students to "get even" with a teacher because of the way they have been handled by the teacher.

5. *Punishment demonstrates punishment.*   Students learn through imitation *(modeling)*, and they can therefore learn to be punitive by seeing and experiencing it in their classroom environment. We would be deluding ourselves if we believe that students imitate only the appropriate behaviors they see in their environment.

6. *Punishment causes withdrawal.*   Children often withdraw both mentally and physically from punishing persons or from places where punishment occurs. The student may avoid coming to school, or, if he physically attends, he may avoid academic and social interaction.

Types of reinforcers and reinforcement procedures

Primary and secondary reinforcers.   How is a teacher to know, without empirical testing, what stimulus events are reinforcing for any particular child? Although different people are reinforced by many different types of things, some reinforcers tend to be nearly universal. For example, food for the hungry, warmth for the cold, and water for the thirsty would presumably be reinforcing for almost any organism. Such reinforcers, which do not depend upon a person's prior experience, are called *primary reinforcers.* Obviously, primary reinforcers have limited use in modifying human behavior; food, water, or warmth are not generally made intentionally contingent upon specific behaviors. For most of us money, prestige, praise, recognition, signs of affection, grades in school, diplomas, and so forth exert a powerful influence on our behavior. Such stimuli, whose reinforcing power is acquired, are known as *secondary* (acquired or conditional) *reinforcers.* Certain acquired reinforcers, such as money, are also often called *transitional reinforcers* (DeCecco, 1968) because of their ability to reinforce a large number of different behaviors under a variety of conditions.

Although academic performance could probably be maintained for most school children by applying monetary reinforcement for specific academic performance, such a system would have obvious limitations. In addition, it is generally the hope of educators and parents that academic endeavors will acquire some more "natural" reinforcing properties—good grades, attention from teacher, parents, and peers, and knowledge of progress—which will allow the student to continue his pursuits without the need for elaborate and "alien" external reinforcements. However, what if, for a particular child or group of children, this is not the case? Must we then anticipate that an external reinforcement like money will be necessary for the duration of his or their education, or can a procedure be developed whereby these "natural" consequences of academic behavior acquire sufficient reinforcing power to maintain academic learning.

A study reported by McKenzie et al. (1968) illustrates an attempt to establish grades as reinforcers for a group of children, classified as "learning disabled," for whom grades apparently had no reinforcing function. The essential characteristics of the researchers' procedures involved the setting of specific academic tasks for which a specified amount of output was given the grade A, B, or C, depending on the quality of the work. No grades lower than C were given, since, in the typical school situation, Ds and Fs are not positive reinforcers. Arrangements were then made with the parents of the children to pay the children certain sums, depending on the particular grade.

A fairly high rate of appropriate academic performance was established by this procedure. But after a reasonably stable rate of academic production had been developed, a curious phenomenon occurred. Several of the children began to "forget" to take their grades home, even though they could not be paid for their work if they didn't present their grades to their parents. Ordinarily, if the maintaining reinforcer is not received, the behavior would be expected to undergo extinction. However, in this case, the level of academic work remained constant; in effect, the children had voluntarily removed their own terminal reinforcement. Apparently, the grades themselves had gradually acquired sufficient reinforcing power to maintain an adequate level of performance.

Discriminative stimuli. *Antecedent* stimuli—those occurring before the behavior—also play an important role in the development and maintenance of operant behaviors. As with respondent behavior, in which an antecedent stimulus invariably elicits a reflexive-type response, many operant responses also occur only in the presence of a particular stimulus. The difference between the preceding stimuli of respondent and operant behavior lies in the locus of control. For respondent behavior, the preceding stimulus has direct control over the occurrence of the response, whereas with operant behavior, preceding stimuli simply function as *discriminative (signal) stimuli* which indicate the probability of particular reinforcing conditions and, therefore, the likelihood of certain behaviors. For example, a person driving down the street will stop when the stop light turns red. The red light functions as a discriminative stimulus which, through the driver's experience, has assumed the function of indicating the presence of certain aversive reinforcement probabilities, such as a traffic ticket or a collision. In other words, the red light does not elicit a conditioned reflex for stopping, which would be respondent behavior, but rather signals the driver of potential consequences and promotes a particular behavior (stopping). Behavior that is developed in relation to a discriminative stimulus is called *discriminated operant behavior*. Much of our social behavior involves learning how to successfully interpret discriminative stimuli, and many so-called behavior problems exhibited by children in school result from an inability on the student's part to adequately differentiate the appropriate and inappropriate time for certain behaviors. For example, a first-grade teacher was having a great deal of trouble establishing a routine for her class at the beginning of the year. The children were quite capable academically but spent most of their time socializing. The teacher suspected that they simply had not learned to discriminate between situations requiring quiet seatwork and situations in which free discourse was acceptable. (Note how easy it would have been for the teacher to assume that the children were simply discipline problems and to have attempted to institute some form of punishment to establish order.) In order to aid her students in learning this discrimination, the teacher devised the following procedure: First, she constructed a small red flag which could be positioned on the teacher's desk in full view of the students. She then told the children that when the flag was down, talking was appropriate, but when the flag was raised, it indicated a time when quiet seatwork was appropriate. In no way was a threat of punishment suggested if the flag was ignored.

Three developments resulting from this procedure warrant mentioning. First, the procedure effectively controlled the verbal "misbehavior" of the students. They talked when the flag was down and remained quiet when the flag was raised. Second, the children soon began to anticipate when the flag should and should not be raised. This development was indicated by the fact that the children began reminding each other and the teacher when it was time to raise or lower the flag. Technically speaking, the children were recognizing "natural" discriminated stimuli for talking and non-talking, such as the teacher's expression, her instructions, whether an assignment had been given, and so. The third development was the gradual elimination of the flag itself. After approximately two weeks of using the flag, the teacher and the children began to forget to raise or lower the flag, and the talking continued to occur only at appropriate times. After the third week, the use of the flag was discontinued entirely with no adverse effect on the classroom behavior. Apparently, the children had learned to interpret the "natural" discriminative stimuli and no longer needed the flag as a cue.

Operant extinction.   Any response that has been established through reinforcement may be reduced and eventually eliminated by a procedure technically known as *operant extinction*. In this procedure, the reinforcement for the undesirable response is discontinued, with the effect of a gradual (or, in some cases, rapid) reduction in the strength of that behavior. For example, a child who continuously whines because in the past whining had been reinforced by attention from his mother will eventually stop the behavior if his mother never again attends to the whining. Similarly, a teacher who feels that his disapproving attention may be maintaining some disruptive behavior from one of his students might achieve extinction of that behavior by changing his response to one of neutral recognition. If, in fact, the student was being reinforced by the teacher's disapproving looks, the replacement of the disapproving look with a noncommittal one may be effective in reducing the undesirable behavior.

The problem in applying operant extinction procedures is that, in many cases, it is difficult to identify or isolate the reinforcer. Many human behaviors are simultaneously reinforced by a number of different reinforcing events, and it may be extremely difficult to identify and/or remove all the potential reinforcing events for any particular unwanted behavior. And even when the probable reinforcer is readily identifiable, as in the case of a child who cries when he is put to bed until his mother comes in and holds him, extinction is difficult to employ. In such cases, it might be more effective simply to substitute (counter-condition) a different type of response (such as turning on a bedside lamp) rather than to attempt to make no response at all.

Shaping.   In many cases in which a teacher wishes to instill a desired behavior by applying reinforcement procedures, the desired behavior will not exist in the child's repertoire. How can a behavior be reinforced if it does not occur? One possibility is to reinforce an existing behavior that most closely approximates the desired behavior. Then, as the strength of that response increases, only closer and closer approximations of the desired terminal behavior are reinforced. This procedure is known as *shaping* —the application of differential reinforcement to successive approximations of a desired terminal behavior.

Natural shaping no doubt plays a significant role in the development of much of our social behavior. For example, when an infant is first acquiring a rudimentary vocal repertoire, he is apt to be reinforced by attention from his parents for very crude approximations of real words. The adage that only a mother can believe that her infant's babblings mean "Mama" attests to the fact that parents initially reinforce rather remote approximations of words. As the child grows older, there is a tendency for parents to require gradually better and better productions. A three-year-old who babbles the way an infant does is not likely to be reinforced.

An illustration of shaping procedures in a classroom might be teaching a child to raise his hand and be recognized by the teacher before speaking. The first procedure that could be used is twofold. First, the teacher should avoid recognizing the student when he speaks in class without raising his hand (extinction). Second, the teacher should reinforce (reward) any student behavior that approximates the teacher's expectation. Therefore, if the child raises his hand and then blurts out an answer, the teacher should reinforce the idea of raising the hand but point out that the student still should have waited until he was called on. Thus, through ignoring (failing to reinforce) undesirable behaviors and reinforcing desired responses (differential reinforcement), the teacher may fairly quickly shape the student's behavior with an acceptable alternative. Shaping, by itself, can be a rather slow and laborious procedure. However, shaping procedures are often coupled with other procedures, such as verbal instructions.

Reinforcement of competing responses. *Competing responses* are responses that cannot occur at the same time. You cannot stand up and sit down at the same time. Since competing responses cannot coexist, if one of the competing responses is increased in strength, the other response must decrease. Therefore, if a response that competes with an unwanted behavior can be identified and increased by positive reinforcement, the unwanted response will decrease. In an educational setting, the behavior that most logically competes with undesired behavior is that of doing academic work. Classroom behavioral problems often disappear when a child's academic efforts are put under a successful positive reinforcement program. A practical application of the combination of operant extinction and reinforcing competing responses is reported by Brown and Elliott (1965). Physical and verbal aggressive behavior was dramatically reduced for 27 male nursery-school students by having the teacher ignore (whenever possible) any occurrence of physical aggression and, at the same time, provide positive reinforcement (attention, praise) for cooperative nonaggressive behavior.

DRO scheduling. Known technically as *differential reinforcement of other behavior,* a DRO schedule is a procedure for reducing an unwanted behavior. Essentially, this procedure involves the delivery of a reinforcer after a prescribed length of time, provided that a specified undesirable response has not occurred. Since, technically, one cannot contingently reinforce a nonbehavior, the word *other* in the name signifies that *any* behavior other than the designated response will be reinforced. Many of the unsophisticated behavioral modification procedures employed in the home are applications of DRO procedures—"If you do not break anything else until lunch time you may have extra dessert"; "If you do not wet your pants this morning you may go swimming after lunch."

In designing a DRO procedure, the teacher must give special consideration to the existing strength of the unwanted behavior. For example, if a child is currently emitting an unwanted behavior at the rate of ten times per hour, it is probably unrealistic to expect him suddenly to stop responding for any protracted time period. The reinforcer should be initially delivered after a brief period in which the child does not perform the unwanted behavior. Then, if such a procedure proves effective for short periods, the length of the periods can be gradually lengthened.

As with other positive reinforcement procedures, the more frequently and quickly the reinforcer is delivered the less powerful each reinforcer must be. For example, a procedure specifying a potentially very powerful reinforcer ($25, for example) for not emitting a particular response for a long period of time is probably less likely to be effective than a procedure employing a less powerful reinforcer, such as a special food treat, delivered after a short period of time. And if the time period to be used in a DRO procedure is of significant length, some provision should be made for periodically reminding the child of the contingencies involved. For example, "Remember, Johnny, if you do not hit anyone today you may stay after school and clean the gerbil cage."

Token economy systems.   Another type of reinforcing procedure especially effective for children who are unresponsive to "natural" school reinforcers (grades, approval, and so on), is called the *token economy system.* The basic procedure involves the use of reinforcers that are originally neutral (nonfunctional) but acquire reinforcing power when they are established as discriminative stimuli for responses leading to existing *back-up reinforcers,* such as privileges and tangible rewards. Initially, a token system involves selecting certain behaviors (academic tasks, appropriate social acts, and so on) and assigning them a value in tokens (such stimuli as poker chips, checkmarks, gold stars, play money). A procedure is then set up whereby the child may "cash in" accumulated tokens for the existing back-up reinforcers. The advantages of a token system are that it uses a reinforcer (the token) which (1) can be quickly and easily delivered following an appropriate response, (2) will not satiate so long as the back-up reinforcers are desirable for the child, (3) can be applied to a variety of appropriate behaviors, and (4) provides a way of reinforcing children for whom recognition and praise are not effective reinforcers.

A rather elaborate token system was used by Phillips (1968) in modifying social behavior with a group of predelinquent boys in a home-type environment. Score-card points, supported by back-up reinforcers (privileges, activities, tangible goods), were used to effect marked changes in a variety of behaviors, such as school work, personal habits, swearing, neatness. An interesting aspect of this program was that the boys did all their own record keeping, adding points for appropriate behaviors and subtracting points for rule infractions. Examples of successful token systems are also reported by Bienbrauer and Lawler (1964) and O'Leary and Becker (1967).

In analyzing a token system that did not function effectively, Kuypers et al. (1968) made the following suggestions for implementing a token system: (1) If the token system involves delays in giving tokens, differential *social* reinforcement should be continuous. (2) Tokens should be used for *shaping* desirable behavior rather than for reinforcing only completely correct responses.

Factors affecting the effectiveness of reinforcers and reinforcement procedures

Power of the reinforcing stimulus.   The effectiveness of secondary reinforcers in changing behavior depends, at least to some extent, on how desirable that reinforcer is for the particular person whose behavior is to be changed. Good grades may be an extremely powerful reinforcer for some students, neutral for others, and occasionally even aversive for others. The same is true for almost all reinforcing events; people are "turned on" by different things. In selecting a potential reinforcer for a particular child, the teacher must be sure that the reinforcer to be used is in fact an effective reinforcer for that child.

Deprivation and satiation.   *Deprivation* refers to the length of time since the organism last received the reinforcer. For example, in studies using subhuman organisms, the animals are usually deprived of food for some time prior to the training session in order to ensure that food will function as a powerful reinforcer. Deprivation is rarely manipulated in classroom settings, of course, but even so, some assessment of deprivation should normally be made when selecting potential reinforcers to be used in modifying behavior. Such assessment may be no more than keeping track of how often a student's behavior is reinforced. The crucial point here is, of course, that if a student is highly dependent on reinforcement and has experienced a time in which some reinforcement has been withheld, then he is more likely to adopt an alternative behavior that is followed by reinforcement.

Satiation describes the condition in which the organism has received so much of a given reinforcer that its effectiveness in changing a behavior is markedly reduced or eliminated all together. One of the most important factors in selecting a reinforcer is to ensure that the reinforcing power of the reinforcer will not be diminished if it is applied often. Satiation is most likely to occur with a behavior that is not meaningful.

If, for instance, a particular student behavior is representative of good manners, the teacher might continuously reinforce that behavior without its reaching the satiation point. In contrast, if the teacher reinforces the position in which a child stands in lunch line, such reinforcement may reach the satiation point rather quickly, since the position in line is likely to be of little consequence to the student.

Immediacy of reinforcement.　The more quickly a reinforcer follows a behavior, the greater its strengthening power. In studies involving subhuman animals, it has been found that even a split-second delay between response and reinforcer can greatly weaken the effect of the reinforcer. For humans with adequate language development, the effective length of time between response and reinforcer may be greatly lengthened by verbally establishing the contingencies of the desired behavior and the reinforcement. For example, "since you completed all of your math assignment this morning, you may now select whatever activity you desire for this afternoon." In this way, delayed reinforcement may still exert a powerful effect.

When verbally reminding the child of the reinforcement contingencies, the teacher must carefully specify the particular behavior that is being reinforced, the conditions under which it occurred, and the reinforcer that is being presented: "You were a good boy yesterday, so you may do whatever you want to today" would probably not function as an effective reinforcer, since the child will not know precisely what behaviors he had engaged in or avoided in order to receive the reward.

Related to how quickly the reinforcer follows the response is the issue of whether the reinforcer or something similar has been delivered previously. Especially in a situation in which the child has no prior experience with the reinforcer and/or the teacher who is manipulating the reinforcer, a promised reinforcer may have little effect on current behaviors. For example, if the parents of a child were to offer him a new bicycle if he completes all his homework for a month, the procedure would probably have little effect on current homework behavior unless the child had actually received similar reinforcers in the past. One of the more common errors in attempting to apply reinforcement procedures for behavior modification is that of using a potentially powerful reinforcer but one that can be obtained only with a great amount of effort. In most cases, it is more effective to select a reinforcer that can be delivered more frequently for smaller bits of behavior.

Schedule of reinforcement.　Another related factor affecting reinforcement is that of how often the reinforcer is delivered in relation to the number of responses. Technically, this is known as the *schedule of reinforcement.* If each and every target response is followed by the reinforcer, the procedure is known as *continuous reinforcement*. Continuous reinforcement has two distinct advantages for effecting behavioral change, especially during the initial stages of modificiation: (1) It ensures that if the subject ever makes the correct response, it will be reinforced; and (2) it allows for the delivery of the greatest number of reinforced responses. As a result, continuous reinforcement is the preferred schedule in many behavioral change procedures.

Continuous reinforcement also has three potential disadvantages, however. (1) It may be extremely time consuming for the teacher, in that he must carefully observe the child's behavior and be prepared to deliver the reinforcer any time the target behavior occurs. (2) Unless the reinforcer is carefully selected, reinforcing every response may (as the child rapidly accumulates reinforcers) reduce the effectiveness of the reinforcer (satiation). For example, the first few pats on the head during reading class may motivate the child to greater effort, but by the thirty-second or thirty-third pat, the child may find it less reinforcing. (3) If a behavior has been established through continuous reinforcement and the reinforcer is suddenly terminated, the behavior will undergo extinction more rapidly than if it had been maintained on an *intermittent* schedule of reinforcement. For example, if a child is given a candy bar every time he empties the garbage over a two-week period and, then, is no longer given the candy bar for his task, it is likely that the frequency of garbage-emptying would diminish rapidly.

Although this lack of resistance to extinction would seem to greatly limit the usefulness of continuous reinforcement, in actual cases of classroom application, extinction rarely occurs. Consider a case where a child is given continuous tangible reinforcement for academic behavior and, as a result, academic performance increases. If the tangible reinforcer is then withdrawn, will academic performance extinguish? In most cases, no; because once increased academic output is achieved, it will be reinforced by other, less tangible reinforcers. Quite likely the teacher, parents, and even the peer group will respond to the student's improved performance in a different and reinforcing way. Thus, in many cases, once the behavior has changed, other external reinforcers in the environment may serve to maintain the changed behavior.

Noncontinuous (intermittent) schedules of reinforcement offer several potential advantages. Since the response requirement for continuous schedules is greater than for intermittent reinforcement, responding can be maintained with a lesser amount of reinforcement, and there is less chance that the effectiveness of the reinforcer will be weakened by satiation. In addition, since fewer reinforcers are delivered under intermittent scheduling, it takes less time and effort for the teacher to apply the reinforcer and necessitates less imposition on the normal classroom situation. Another theoretical advantage is that behavior acquired with intermittent reinforcement is more resistant to extinction once the maintaining reinforcer is withdrawn.

The delivery of the reinforcer in intermittent reinforcement schedules may be made contingent upon the number of responses *(ratio schedule)* or upon the length of time between reinforcers *(interval schedule).* And within both ratio and interval schedules, the delivery of the reinforcer may be either *fixed* or *variable.* Thus, there are four general types of intermittent schedules: fixed ratio, variable ratio, fixed interval, and variable interval.

Selecting effective reinforcers for behavior modification

In light of the discussion thus far in this chapter, a desirable reinforcer for classroom use would be one that (1) will be effective for the particular child, (2) can be delivered quickly, (3) is economical for the teacher in cost and time, (4) will not satiate quickly, (5) is a natural part of the classroom environment. Since events that have reinforcing power vary considerably among people, a potential problem arises when the teacher attempts to select an appropriate reinforcer to modify a given child's behavior. Withholding the primary reinforcers of food or water from a child in school would not seem a very desirable procedure—certainly not politically—and the use of secondary, transitional reinforcers, such as money or tokens, raises the problem of a rather drastic departure from regular classroom routine as well as their costliness both in time and money.

Undoubtedly, the best possibility would be to select from those normally occurring activities and duties that seem, in general, to be desirable for children. Special duties, such as taking roll, leading the flag salute, taking messages to other rooms, being a crossing guard, and feeding the fish, or such preferred positions as committee chairman, lunch-line leader, and captain of recess games have all been used effectively as reinforcers in specific cases. In addition, perhaps the most useful source is the child himself—ask him what activity or privilege is most reinforcing. Oftentimes, appropriate and unsuspected reinforcers can be selected in this way. In one case where a potential reinforcer had been tried unsuccessfully, the child, when asked, indicated that for him a powerful reinforcer would be to pick up the trash from the playground (Moore, 1969). And when ten minutes of this activity was made contingent on the desired behavioral change, the strength of that new behavior increased rapidly.

Another interesting and useful procedure for selecting existent activities that can serve as reinforcers for changing behavior is discussed by Premack (1959). Briefly stated, Premack's principle is that a high-probability behavior may, if made contingent on a low-probability behavior, serve as a positive reinforcer for the low-probability behavior. High-probability behaviors may be identified by collecting data on the type and frequency of particular behaviors of the children during a free-choice period. For example, in an often-cited study (Homme et al., 1963), the highest probability behaviors for a group of nursery-school children were found to be running around the room, screaming, and pushing chairs. Although these activities would not seem to be appropriate reinforcing events, they did effectively increase contingent low-probability behaviors (for example, sitting quietly). A real advantage of using existing high-probability activities as reinforcers for low-probability desired behavior is that the only environmental manipulation necessary is a rearrangement of the order of classroom behaviors so that a low-probability behavior is followed by a high-probability behavior. For example, for a particular class (or child), simply reordering the curriculum presentation may result in increased academic performance in a weak area.

SELF-MANAGED MODIFICATION PROCEDURES

Although thus far the discussion has implied that a teacher is interested in modifying the behavior of other people, the principles and procedures of behavior modification are equally applicable when a teacher wants to alter his own behavior in certain ways. A basic understanding of behavior modification procedures should allow a teacher to arrange antecedent and consequent stimuli in such a way as to result in desirable behavioral changes. Types of problems that are of concern for self-management include studying behavior, elimination of unwanted habits or mannerisms (swearing, head scratching, nail chewing), personal problems (overweight, excessive smoking, reluctance to speak in groups), and skill acquisition (mastering specific content, learning to dance, report writing). An interesting study in which a group of adolescent students was able to modify problems selected by them after only a brief instruction in behavior modification procedures was reported by Duncan (1968).

In social studies class, one student persists in his antisocial behavior, upsetting the class and affecting the classroom learning environment. *How can the teacher modify this student's behavior?*

This is not an uncommon problem, and many teachers have difficulty coping with it. Some try to control anti-social behavior by such punishments as threats, detention, removal from the classroom. A more effective procedure is to engage some of the principles of behavior modification: First, the teacher should attempt to determine why the student is behaving in this manner. Second, the teacher must analyze why the student persists; perhaps the attention he gains from the disruptive behavior reinforces his behavior. If the reinforcer can be identified as such, there is then a basis for behavior modification procedures.

This teacher should try withholding reinforcement of the antisocial behavior and provide the student with alternative responses. Many students will behave differently if they know there are alternatives. Then, when the student has emitted alternative behaviors (presumably more acceptable), the teacher should positively reinforce the student. While such a process may be gradual, it is effective.

SUGGESTED READINGS

Bandura, A., & Barab, P. G.   Conditions governing nonreinforced imitation. *Developmental Psychology,* 1971, **5,** 244–255.

Brackmann, J. F., Jr.   Avoidance learning extinction, and latent extinction: A methodological note. *Psychological Record,* 1968, **18,** 71–73.

Curry, D. R.   Case studies in behavior modification. *Psychology in the Schools,* 1970, **7,** 330–335. Reprinted in H. D. Thornburg (Ed.), *School learning and instruction: Readings.* Monterey, Calif.: Brooks/Cole, 1973, Chap. 6.

Johnson, A. W.   Verbal conditioning and social learning. Paper read at the Southwestern Psychological Association Meeting, New Orleans, April 1968.

Palardy, J. M.   Classroom management—more than conditioning. *Elementary School Journal,* 1970, **71,** 162–165.

Pepitone, E. A.   Comparison behavior in elementary school children. *American Educational Research Journal,* 1972, **9,** 45–63.

Thelen, M. H.   Long-term retention of verbal imitation. *Developmental Psychology,* 1970, **3,** 29–31.

Whitman, M., & Whitman, J.   Behavior modification in the classroom. *Psychology in the Schools,* 1971, **8,** 177–186. Reprinted in H. D. Thornburg (Ed.), *School learning and instruction: Readings.* Monterey, Calif.: Brooks/Cole, 1973, chap. 6.

Wright, J., Clayton, J., & Edgar, C. E.   Behavior modification with low-level mental retardates. *Psychological Record,* 1970, **20,** 465–471.

12

Attitude Learning

An attitude is an emotional predisposition for a person to *act* in some way toward another person, object, or ideal. The importance of attitude learning within the classroom is becoming an increasing concern of many educators and psychologists. Students are increasingly acquiring attitudes and values within the classroom rather than in the home, and all too often, student learning of attitudes toward persons, objects, or ideals is either incidental or the result of unplanned exposure to classroom subject materials. Attitudes may be learned through stimulus presentations (Loree, 1970), and several studies have indicated that increasing stimulus exposures tends to strengthen attitudes (Litvak, 1969; Zajonc, 1968). Thus, the teaching of attitudes should be planned, just as a teacher plans academic material, with analysis of the intellectual domains involved and with careful statements of the behavioral objectives.

COMPONENTS OF ATTITUDE LEARNING

Generally, attitudes are considered to be one aspect of the more encompassing term *affective learning.* Affective learning indicates degrees of emotional involvement and is typically described within the framework of five levels of *expression: interests, appreciations, attitudes, values,* and *social-emotional adjustments.*

1. Interests are defined functionally as the behaviors that occur when an individual is free to choose. Raths et al. (1966) describe interests as "those things which excite us, which occupy our minds and hands, and which cause us to spend time, money, and energy on them" (p. 69). Interests may be considered, then, to involve strictly a "feeling" state.

2. Appreciations are behaviors that occur when an individual chooses an activity based on his feeling toward it and understanding of it. Thus, a person may attend the opera, not just because of interest in this type of music but because he has an understanding of the way a story may be developed both dramatically and musically. Appreciations may be considered to involve both a "feeling" and a "thinking" state.

3. Attitudes are the disposition to *behave* toward environmental objects in a positive or negative way. In other words, an attitude is more firmly developed than interests and appreciations because of this action tendency. If a student hates an academic subject, his behavior toward it will be negative, often to the point of not achieving well in it. It is also possible that a student will associate his dislike for the subject with the teacher and express a dislike for both. And attitudes therefore involve not only "feeling" and "thinking" states but also a "behavioral" state.

4. Values are best described as the consistent expression of attitudes to the point of internalization. In effect, values characterize an individual's behavior. Although values are comprised of the same three components as attitudes, they are more complex and lasting. For example, a person may have a positive attitude toward equal opportunity but express his true values by speaking against a fair-housing bill when he thinks that it could potentially devaluate his property.

5. Social-emotional adjustment, the most encompassing affective factor, describes an individual's ability to encounter, understand, and adjust to the social and emotional situations that arise within the culture in which he lives. The concept has strong implications for individual personality development and mental health, but it is too broad to be considered as a defined factor in the classroom attitude-learning situation. This social-emotional adjustment level is more akin to the complex of understandings, perceptions, and values found in the mature individual.

Although the focus of attitude-learning discussion is generally on these five levels within the affective domain, we must keep in mind that attitudes are learned and become a function of the mind; and, therefore, they may best be conceptualized as having all three components, or domains, of the mind within them—*affective, cognitive,* and *behavioral.* For example, when an affective attitudinal response is being made, the individual's nervous system becomes highly active, and there is a strong "feeling" component to the response. When a cognitive attitudinal response is made, it is more perceptual; the individual is expressing a belief that he has intellectually worked through. Therefore, while the expression of attitude is affective, it has a stronger "thinking" than "feeling" component. A behavioral attitudinal response is usually expressed through overt action or through statements indicative of such action. The predominant component of the response is behavior, with "thinking" and "feeling" playing a lesser role.

Travers (1965) contends that attitude learning depends primarily on the *affective thrust* and the *cognitive thrust.* As indicated in Figure 12.1, these thrusts should be related to behavioral objectives in trying to teach attitudes. That is, if the expected student attitude learning is chiefly affective, the teaching–learning situation should be focused on that element or level of the affective domain that is most appropriate to the specific behavioral objective. For example, if a specified student behavioral objective were to "select for listening, music that you enjoy," the teacher would be asking the student to use mainly the appreciation level of the affective thrust in meeting that objective. On the other hand, the teacher who expects the students to develop an attitude toward something on the basis of its cognitive components would state the objective and focus the teaching–learning situation according to the appropriate level within the cognitive thrust. Thus, the teacher might be asking the students to respond positively or negatively toward a situation on the basis of their *perception* of that situation. They would, then, be learning an attitude within the cognitive domain, or thrust.

Of course, almost all learning is both affective and cognitive in nature; and if an objective is written in the affective domain, it is likely to have a cognitive counterpart as well. Similarly, most cognitive objectives have affective counterparts. Thus, it should not be the teacher's role to try to develop strictly affective or cognitive objectives and learning situations so much as to understand which component is the more important one for the specific teaching–learning situation. Since this can be better

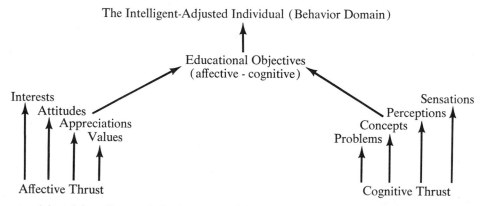

FIGURE 12.1   *Attitude Learning and the Affective and Cognitive Domains*

The Intelligent-Adjusted Individual (Behavior Domain)

Educational Objectives
(affective - cognitive)

Interests   Sensations
  Attitudes   Perceptions
    Appreciations   Concepts
      Values   Problems

Affective Thrust   Cognitive Thrust

Adapted from Travers, J. F., *Learning: Analysis and application.* New York: David McKay Company, Inc., 1965. Reprinted by permission of David McKay Company, Inc.

realized if the teacher has an understanding of the philosophy of affective and cognitive behavioral objectives for the classroom, we shall briefly review them, as they were advanced in Chapter 2 of this book, to show more directly their relationship to attitude learning.

Affective Behavioral Objectives (Krathwohl, 1964):

1.0 *Receiving.* The learner is sensitized to the existence of certain phenomena and stimuli so that he will be willing to receive or attend to them.
   1.1 *Awareness.* The learner is conscious of something in his environment.
   1.2 *Willingness to receive.* The person attends to something without avoiding it.
   1.3 *Controlled or selected attention.* The learner differentiates stimuli within his perceptual field.

2.0 *Responding.* The learner is going beyond the mere perception of phenomena and actively attends to and, to some extent, is committed to the phenomena involved.
   2.1 *Acquiescence in responding.* The learner complies with the expectation of another (the teacher).
   2.2 *Willingness to respond.* The learner voluntarily acts because of self-desire.
   2.3 *Satisfaction in response.* The learner feels positive emotional pleasure at his response.

3.0 *Valuing.* The abstract concept of worth becomes part of the individual's values or assessments regarding phenomena.
   3.1 *Acceptance of a value.* The learner ascribes worth to environmental behaviors.
   3.2 *Preference for a value.* The learner seeks out values important to him.
   3.3 *Commitment.* An increase in learner involvement; that is, internal commitment becomes consistent with external behavior.

4.0 *Organization.* The learner organizes values into a system, determining the relationships among them.
   4.1 *Conceptualization of a value.* The learner relates new values to existing values.
   4.2 *Organization of a value system.* The learner incorporates a complex of values in an internally meaningful way.

5.0 *Characterization by a value or value complex.* The learner establishes a value hierarchy that controls his behavior over an extended time period.
   5.1 *Generalized set.* The learner has an internal consistency to his system of values and beliefs.
   5.2 *Characterization.* The learner acts consistently with his internalized value system—his philosophy of life.

Although it is not possible to ascribe the defining elements of interests, appreciations, attitudes, values, or social-emotional adjustment to each distinct category of Krathwohl's taxonomy, Figure 12.2 depicts Travers' (1970) conceptualization of how these various affective levels encompass the five taxonomy classifications. Specific affective behavioral objectives for these five categories might be similar to the following suggestions:

1.0 *Receiving*
    1.1 The student is aware of the feelings of others, although their interests are quite diverse.
    1.2 The student will learn to listen well while others are talking.
    1.3 The student becomes sensitive to various social and political matters.

2.0 *Responding*
    2.1 The student will learn to observe classroom policies.
    2.2 The student looks in newspapers and magazines for information on environmental control.
    2.3 The student enjoys listening to good music.

3.0 *Valuing*
    3.1 The student will learn to participate in small-group interactions.
    3.2 The student will learn to exercise his role as a citizen in matters of public interest.
    3.3 The student learns to value the rights of all people to worship as they please.

4.0 *Organization*
    4.1 The student learns to form opinions as to his responsibility to his classmates within the school environment.
    4.2 The student will learn to channel his behavior into socially acceptable patterns.

5.0 *Characterization*
    5.1 The student learns to modify his attitudes when presented with new information which points to the need for modification.
    5.2 The student learns to align his values and behaviors into a consistent pattern.

As we have established, many attitude-learning situations also have strong cognitive components. Indeed, it is probable that to teach something from a strictly affective position, without considering basic cognitive components, is to distort the affective position and teach the student inadequately. A classroom situation will best illustrate attitude-learning within the cognitive domain:

The teacher is telling students how to attack a social problem and how to use resources in the solution of it. The following problem is presented to the class: "What might happen to the physical environment of the United States if industry were to

FIGURE 12.2 Taxonomy of Affective Behavioral Objectives and Levels of Affective Learning

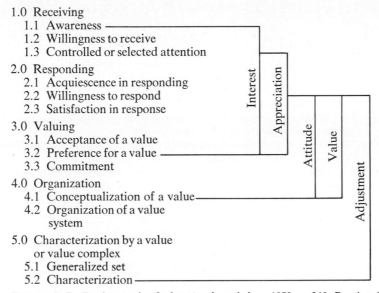

1.0 Receiving
 1.1 Awareness
 1.2 Willingness to receive
 1.3 Controlled or selected attention

2.0 Responding
 2.1 Acquiescence in responding
 2.2 Willingness to respond
 2.3 Satisfaction in response

3.0 Valuing
 3.1 Acceptance of a value
 3.2 Preference for a value
 3.3 Commitment

4.0 Organization
 4.1 Conceptualization of a value
 4.2 Organization of a value
  system

5.0 Characterization by a value
  or value complex
 5.1 Generalized set
 5.2 Characterization

Travers, J. F. *Fundamentals of educational psychology,* 1970, p. 268. Reprinted by permission of Intext Educational Publishers.

discharge waste products uncontrolled?" The class is then divided into small groups, each of which is to present its solution to the entire class. (1) What behavioral objectives should the teacher hope to accomplish? (2) How might the teacher measure the outcomes of this activity?

Sample answer

(1) *Terminal behavioral objectives*

A. The student will be able to select, gather, and organize appropriate reference material to solve a given problem and to present to the class as a whole.
 1. The student will be able to use reference guides as aids for selecting desired information.
 2. The student will be able to select information which is relevant to a topic and to reject information which is not.
 3. The student will be able to appraise and select sources from which reliable information may be obtained.

4. The student will be able to collect and organize data from reference reading in several sources.
5. The student will be able to arrange collected data in a logical form for presentation.

B. The student will be able to present attitudinal statements which represent his feelings about the topic.
1. The student will read materials which shape a positive attitude toward uncontrolled disposal of industrial waste products.
2. The student will read materials which shape a negative attitude toward uncontrolled disposal of industrial waste products.
3. The student will thoughtfully consider the opposite positions in the process of determining his own attitude toward the topic.
4. The student will consider the attitudes of other group members in formulating his attitude toward the topic.
5. The student will be able to clearly delineate his attitudinal position for classroom presentation.

(2) *Measuring outcomes*

Evaluation of objective A.1 would be accomplished by direct teacher observation during the period of research work. Should it be discovered that a student is lacking any of the desired capabilities, it would be necessary to provide instruction to overcome the deficiency before the student could proceed with the task. Some evaluation of the behaviors described in most of the other objectives could also be carried on during the research preparation. As the teacher supervises the students at work, he can make an effort to determine if they are correctly appraising information and selecting appropriate materials and can provide guidance where deficiencies are found.

Each group presentation could be evaluated according to a prepared checklist which would allow the teacher to note such problems as the irrelevant or unreliable use of material, difficulty in synthesizing materials, lack of consideration of other group member opinions, and logic in forming attitudes toward the issue. Providing a similar checklist to each student may assist the teacher in determining what learning has taken place. For example, if a student avoids unreliable information in his own presentation and recognizes it in the presentation of another student, the teacher has an even better basis for evaluating the student's ability to appraise the reliability of information. Asking each student to appraise his own performance in terms of stated objectives may also prove helpful to the teacher.

As a summary statement to this section on the components of attitude learning, we would do well to consider carefully the following brief analysis of the main differences between the cognitive and affective learning domains, as described by Kantor (1970):

A heated discussion occurs in a health education class over the pros and cons of smoking marijuana. *What learning domains are operational here?*

Attitude learning has cognitive, affective, and behavioral components. A "heated discussion" infers that the affective or emotional component is probably most dominant in this classroom situation. The nervous system of the students is highly activated, and they are "feeling" the pros and cons of the marijuana issue. To put the issue, and the discussion, on a sounder and more productive basis, the teacher must see that the cognitive and behavioral components of attitude learning are also operating. The cognitive component in an attitude toward marijuana is more perceptual; one's attitudes would be based on an intellectual understanding of the drug and its use as well as on feelings about the issue. The behavioral component involves the actual behavior that an individual might exhibit toward the drug, whether this behavior was one of participation or abstinence. The more all three components can be drawn into the discussion, the broader the perspective and the more balanced the outcomes.

1. *Goals.* For affective learnings of any kind, the goal is not mastery. There is no reachable endpoint on the way to which highly specific steps or objectives can be spelled out. Continuous growth is the goal.

2. *Nature of the learner.* The question of equality of learner capacities is not central to affective learning, since mastery is not the goal. What is of concern is a generalized affective ability that is indicative of the possibility of growth within oneself.

3. *Content analysis.* With the emphasis on the development and growth of affective powers, the analysis of what needs to be learned should be concerned with the nature of the process through which such powers develop rather than with the cognitive content itself.

4. *Materials.* The total learning environment in affective learning is of greater concern than any piece of material. The main emphasis in affective materials should be on richness and diversity rather than on precision.

5. *Methodology.* Affective powers are personal; their growth necessarily comes from individual use. The concern with an affective-learning methodology should be to provide many opportunities for the responsible exercise of affective abilities.

6. *Evaluation.* Since individual use and growth is the goal of affective learning, evaluation should be concerned with the individual rather than with the group and should probably be conceived in general, or global, rather than concrete terms.

7. *Organization.* While independent functioning needs to be planned for in affective learning, many personal affective powers require the presence of other people and

values for their proper development. Other significant people help a learner to discover affective meaning and also provide a reference point for his increasing affective development. Therefore, the presence and effects of other significant people should be accounted for in planning affective learning.

ATTITUDE LEARNING THROUGH MODELING

As we have seen, attitude learning may be related to definite stimulus situations or, indirectly, to objective learning situations that involve value questions. The latter situations may include concrete entities (union members, politicians, institutions), concepts or values (flag, equality), or social issues (civil rights, pollution). Attitudes are also learned through *modeling*, which involves the acquisition of attitudes through the observation and imitation of another person. Indeed, Gagné (1971b) has suggested that attitude learning, in contrast to intellectual skills and cognitive strategies, is best facilitated by modeling. As an individual interacts with admired sources in his environment, he is most likely to be persuaded attitudinally (Gagné, 1971d).

Modeling may be described as the tendency to imitate or perform responses similar to those of another significant person, or model. Although most of Bandura's work in the area of modeling (1965a, 1969) has centered on cognitive learning, it is most applicable to attitude learning as well. Bandura has found some of the following characteristics to be outcomes of the modeling process:

1. Social-behavior learning is not simply trial-and-error. By learning through imitation, we greatly increase our response repertoire (1965a). "Almost any learning outcome that results from direct experience can also come about on a vicarious basis through observation of other people's behavior and its consequences for them" (1967, p. 78).

2. While there is no recognized commonly accepted explanation for it, behavior that does not *exist* in a person's repertoire can be most efficiently acquired through modeling (1965b).

3. By observing and imitating a model, an individual can readily match the behavior of the model, for only the behavior being observed is desired from the learner (Bandura & Walters, 1963).

4. Modeling is effective in strengthening desirable and inhibiting undesirable social behaviors (1967).

5. It has been demonstrated through the use of film-mediated models that children exposed to aggressive models learn and demonstrate the same behaviors without

Photo courtesy of Albert Bandura.

reinforcement (Bandura, Ross, & Ross, 1963). The learning of verbal aggression has been similarly demonstrated (1965a).

6. No practice and, in many cases, no reinforcement is required in modeling, although Bandura (1969) does refer to the usefulness of vicarious reinforcement.

In short, teachers and other adults within the classroom can be extremely effective as models in student attitude learning and, particularly, in the socializing functions within a school. Real-life models are probably the strongest way to influence attitude learning, but representational models, such as films, may also be quite effective.

Granting the importance of the teacher as model in student attitude learning, we must give some consideration to the effects of *teacher attitudes* on classroom attitude learning and social behavior. Much investigation has established that teachers may create either positive or negative attitude teaching–learning situations in the classroom. As was suggested earlier, planning is all-important in every classroom situation. If certain attitudes are important enough to teach, they are important enough to be planned. This planning makes it possible for the teacher to positively approach an affective topic as well as to present an exemplary model for the students.

Of course, there is a great deal of student affective behavior that is both unexpected and undesired by the teacher. Usually, some kind of controlling response is made by the teacher, and the manner in which the teacher responds provides social reinforcement for the student, thus shaping his attitudes positively or negatively. Even in these situations, the teacher can, to some extent, plan for these undesirable affective behaviors by anticipating them to determine alternative appropriate behaviors and to teach the students the various situations in which the same affective behviors may be appropriate or inappropriate. This anticipation and planning make it easier for the teacher to maintain positive attitudes in the classroom.

Teacher attitudes toward individual students also have an important effect on student affective behavior and the attitude-learning environment of the classroom. Four distinct teacher attitudes toward students were found by Silberman (1969) upon interviewing 32 teachers:

1. *Attachment.*   This attitude is directed toward those students whom the teacher experiences as sources of pleasure in her work. The affectionate tie with such students is partially a result of the teacher's appreciation for, and perhaps a dependence on, the child's steadfast conformity to institutional and teacher expectations (Jackson et al., 1969). For example, one teacher reports, "He's one that I would be very happy to keep. He enjoys school and certainly is never any trouble or difficulty to me." Another teacher speaks of a girl on whom she is "rather dependent; she is kind of an interpreter of my wishes to the class because she responds to me in the way I want my whole class to." The student subject of the teacher's affection, then, is likely to be one who fulfills personal needs for the teacher and/or who makes few demands on the teacher's energies. Because students expect fairness from the teacher, it is likely that the teacher does not show distinct favoritism toward this favorite student.

2. *Concern.*   This attitude is directed toward those students who the teacher believes make extensive but appropriate demands on him. The teacher is willing to serve such children not only because of a sympathetic response to their needs but also because of a personal satisfaction that is derived from helping children who are receptive and appreciative. One teacher describes such a child as "my project of the year." Another teacher feels that such a child is "very gratifying to work with because she can see what you're trying to show her and really takes off on it." Thus, a candidate for the teacher's concern is a student who, in the teacher's eyes, is a worthy recipient of his or her professional attention.

3. *Indifference.*   This attitude is directed toward those students who neither excite nor dismay the teacher and therefore remain outside the scope of the teacher's involvement. For example, one teacher admits, "I really tend to forget he's in the room. I don't really have feelings toward him one way or the other." Another teacher says, "She doesn't strike me as either a goody-goody or a baddy-baddy." Since such students are in the periphery of the teacher's professional vision, whatever demands they make tend to go unnoticed.

4. *Rejection*.   This attitude is directed toward those students who are not worthy, in the teacher's estimation, of any professional energies. Such students make as many demands as do students who concern teachers, but their demands are perceived as illegitimate or overwhelming and are either ignored or attended to in a counter-productive way. As one teacher testifies, "She has problems that are beyond the scope of the classroom teacher; I've given up." Another teacher claims, "His arrogance makes him impossible to deal with."

The art teacher strives to instill in her students a strong sense of creative expression. *What type of learning is this?*

The teacher is promoting affective learning at the valuing level. In other words, once an appreciation of art is instilled in the students, the teacher is able to demonstrate the *value* of being able to express oneself through the various art forms. The appreciation of creative expression is more affective than cognitive in nature.

Generally, when teacher attitudes are formally assessed, rather elaborate questionnaires are employed, such as the Minnesota Multiphasic Personality Inventory (MMPI), the Edwards Personal Preference Schedule, the Guilford–Zimmerman Temperament Survey, the Sixteen Personality Factor Scale, or the Minnesota Teacher Attitude Inventory. From such tests, a tremendous amount of literature has accumulated on the personality characteristics of teachers, but most results tell more about the teacher's personal orientation than his effectiveness as a teacher. Still, certain teacher characteristics seem to be typical of instructional effectiveness.

Leeds (1954), in analyzing student likes and dislikes regarding teachers, found that they valued impartiality, patience, understanding, helpfulness, kindness, and consideration in their teachers. Similarly, research studies with the Sixteen Personality Factor Scale (Bulletin No. 9, 1963) found effective teachers to be (1) outgoing and warm-hearted, (2) sensitive, (3) quite intelligent, (4) conscientious, persevering, staid, and rule-bound, and (5) well-controlled, socially precise, self-disciplined, and compulsive.

Two of these traits—warmth and understanding, and imagination—seem to be especially effective in the classroom. Writing on the subject of teacher warmth, Ausubel (1968) states that teachers who exercise some warmth usually aid fulfillment of children's affiliative drives, especially for elementary-school children.

The warm teacher can be identified with ease by students. He provides emotional support, is sympathetically disposed toward pupils, and accepts them as persons. Characteristically, he distributes much praise and encouragement and tends to interpret pupil behavior as charitably as possible. He is relatively unauthoritarian and is sensitive to pupil's feelings and affective responses [p. 454].

LEARNING AND THE SELF-CONCEPT

As was indicated earlier, attitudes are often consistently expressed and internalized until they become part of an individual's value structure and are realized in a tendency to act "toward or against something in the environment" (Bogardus, 1931, p. 62). A very important variable in this process and in classroom achievement generally is the *self-concept*—the attitudes toward self. Self-concept is thought to emerge very early in life and to be influenced by three primary social-cultural forces: (1) peers within one's immediate social-cultural context, (2) peers representative of a larger societal context (schoolmates), and (3) adult figures who represent the larger community (teachers, parents, relatives).

Many writers (Combs & Snygg, 1959; Lipton, 1963; Maslow, 1962; and Rogers, 1961) consider an adequate self-concept to be the primary variable in learning and behavior. Bodwin (1957) found a positive correlation between immature self-concept and reading disability among third- and sixth-grade students. Similarly, Lumpkin (1959) found that the greater the self-concept, the greater the reading achievement level among fifth graders he studied. Research has found similar relationships between self-concept and achievement at the kindergarten level (Wattenberg & Clifford, 1964) through junior high school (Brookover et al., 1964). This research on self-concept and achievement may be best represented by Sears (1940), who commented that children's behavior in task situations was affected by success or failure and by the feeling the children had about themselves in such situations.

Among the mass of research recently conducted about minority-group children and adolescents, one special area of concern has been the self-concept that emerges in subcultures distinct from the parent culture in their values and social behaviors. Research has been rather conclusive that these minority children tend to develop negative self-concepts (Coleman et al., 1966; Havighurst & Moorefield, 1967; Healy, 1969; and Thornburg, 1971a, 1971c). One explanation has been that these children are reinforced for such behaviors within their own group. A related explanation suggests that since the general subcultural milieu is less aspirationally and motivationally oriented than the dominant culture, the expectancy level is typically not as high. Therefore, the children appear to function well within their own group, but when they are thrown into a more heterogeneous culture, their functioning is deficient and their negative self-concepts emerge.

Whatever the explanation, knowledge of ethnic differences seems to be solidified by age 7 (Clark & Clark, 1950), so it is reasonable to assert that minority children recognize the cultural and/or social-class differences throughout their elementary experiences and become more cognizant of these differences and, therefore, less sure about themselves as members of the parent culture as they progress through school. This causes many minority youth to enter high school with common and identifiable traits, such as (1) poor self-image, (2) frustration about academic programs, (3) limited ability to communicate, and (4) disillusionment that high school will be different from their elementary experiences (Cummings & Gillespie, 1971; Thornburg, 1971a).

One could most positively conclude from all the research that the poor self-image of minority children has strong implications for developing alternative curriculums and attitudes toward such children within the school structure. Attitude affects learning, and it is certain that if the learning of these children is to increase and become more meaningful, educators and psychologists must find more valid ways of approaching the needs and enhancing the self-concept of these children.

THE CHANGING OF ATTITUDES

Because of the recognized importance of attitudes, specific attempts to change student attitudes have been made, sometimes successfully, sometimes not. Kolesnik (1970) has summarized the results of numerous research studies that have yielded information pertinent to attitude formation and change. His analysis provides us with a broader understanding of attitudes and is reprinted here:

1. The effectiveness of a teacher's attempts to modify the attitudes of her students depends upon the nature and the intensity of the attitude. Matters about which the student has felt strongly for a long period of time are highly resistant to change, particularly when they are given continued support by parents or friends.

2. Schools can function most effectively in areas where attitudes have not already been formed. The learning of new attitudes is easier to arrange than the unlearning of those which have been long established and are firmly rooted. Ordinarily, one might expect the elementary school to be more effective in this regard than the high school, and the high school more so than the college.

3. Attempts to change attitudes by persuasion are affected by the prestige and credibility of the person proposing the change. One who is admired and respected and has been proved right in other instances is more likely to be believed and followed than one who is not.

4. Communication of factual data is more effective in changing attitudes when the information represents a position that is not at sharp variance with that which the individual has previously learned. Information consistent with existing attitudes is more readily received and assimilated than that which contradicts one's existing beliefs or perceptions.

5. Logical argumentation is likely to be more effective than emotional appeal when a person's existing attitude is not very intense, when he is favorably inclined toward the new position to begin with, or when he has no clearly defined attitude on the matter at all.

6. Emotional appeal is likely to be more effective than logical argumentation when the attitude is deeply grounded in the student's feelings rather than in his mind, when the new position is not anxiety-arousing or personally threatening, and when it does not deprive the individual of an ego-protective mechanism.

7. Active participation in the attitude-changing process is more likely to be effective than mere receptivity. The value of group discussion and role playing, for example, have been demonstrated time and again as producing greater changes than listening, watching, or reading.

8. The attitude to be developed must be clearly defined and understood by the person who wants to change another's predisposition. Such abstract concepts as "good citizenship," "brotherhood," and "respect for others," for example, must be translated into more concrete terms before others can be expected to accept and act on them.

9. Since a person's attitudes are often rooted in those of his associates and since one tends to modify his attitudes to conform to those of his group, particularly his group leaders, it is sometimes simpler to modify one's attitudes by changing his group memberships than it is to appeal to him as an individual.

10. Mere contact with a particular group does not necessarily change a person's attitudes toward that group. Such contacts, particularly if forced, might in fact have the opposite of the intended effect by reinforcing prejudice or fostering mistrust, for example, rather than bringing about the understanding and acceptance that was anticipated.

11. Reinforcement plays a major role in attitude formation, as it does in other forms of learning. Attitudes are often held—or, at least, publicly expressed—because of the approval they gain for the individual. Attempts at changing attitudes, therefore, must include some strategy for the provision of rewards as the learner gradually moves toward acceptance of the new position.

12. Since attitudes are often a means of satisfying some personal or social need, attitudes are sometimes changed most effectively by altering the individual's basic

motivational structure and his existing set of goals, or by satisfying in acceptable ways needs that are presently being met by behavior related to undesirable or unacceptable kinds of attitudes.

13. Changes in attitude are likely to occur when they promise to facilitate identification with another person or a group. A person is likely to assimilate and internalize the attitudes of another when their relationship is characterized by warmth, mutual trust, and esteem.

14. The individual should not be made to feel that his existing attitudes are basically unsound or all wrong. Rather, he should be led to believe that the proposed new position is but a relatively minor adjustment of his original one and that it is compatible with his own set of values. The approach, in other words, is likely to be most effective when it is as gradual and subtle as the situation permits.

15. Sincerity on the part of the teacher of the new attitude and a genuine respect for the humanity and individuality of the intended learner are even more critical in this sensitive, personal area than in the more academic disciplines. The learner must have no reason to suspect that he is being manipulated for the good of others.

16. The changing of attitudes is not a "one shot" affair to be accomplished some Tuesday morning between 10 and 10:30. The process, rather, requires the sustained effort and continuing cooperation of all teachers over an extended period of time.*

The operant conditioning behavior-modification techniques discussed in Chapter 11 have proved quite useful in changing student attitudes. As we have learned, the first step in these techniques is to define the behavior to be modified. Once this behavior has been determined, the teacher should be able to provide the student with an alternative stimulus situation that will bring about acceptable behavior. Then by failing to reinforce the inappropriate behavior and by sufficiently reinforcing the appropriate behavior, the teacher should be able to modify the student's attitudinal response pattern. Consider the following illustration:

Ralph is a disruptive ten-year-old boy in the fifth grade. He is the third of three boys who have gone through the same elementary school. Both of his older brothers are described as ideal students, although none of the three would be considered high achievers. Ralph finds many things annoying to him in the classroom. Because of the teacher's constant attempt to "keep him under her thumb," Ralph devises ways to do little things that are upsetting to the teacher. Thus, he has been successful in expressing an undesirable classroom attitude and in being reinforced for it by watching his teacher become upset.

---

* Reprinted from Kolesnik, W. B., *Educational psychology,* second edition. New York: McGraw-Hill Book Co., 1970, pp. 487–488. Used by permission of the publisher.

The teacher determines that some measure must be taken to correct the situation. She observes Ralph's behavior closely to identify his most frequent disruptive behaviors. After a sufficient time period, the teacher makes the following list of Ralph's inappropriate behaviors:

a. hits others
b. yells out in class
c. pushes children on the playground
d. meanders around the room during study time
e. crowds into lunch line

She then lists alternative behaviors for Ralph:

a. will keep his hands to himself
b. will raise his hand to talk in class
c. will be cooperative and agreeable on the playground
d. will stay at his seat during study time
e. will take his right place in lunch line

With the behavioral objectives listed, the teacher initiates the behavior modification techniques by ignoring, whenever possible, the undesired behaviors and giving continuous attention to the desired behaviors. The procedure is simple: (1) When Ralph is displaying any one of the five unacceptable behaviors, he should *not* be reprimanded for it or reinforced by even the slightest teacher attention to his behavior. (2) When Ralph displays one of the five desired behaviors, the teacher should reinforce it so that Ralph knows that the behavior he displayed is noted and appreciated by the teacher. The teacher may also facilitate the learning of acceptable behaviors by letting Ralph be first in the lunch line sometimes.

It may take several trials to shift Ralph from just one undesired to one desired behavior, and it may take weeks to shift all five behaviors. It may even be that some behavior will never be completely eliminated. But through the process of attending to desired behaviors and ignoring undesired ones, the teacher increases the chances of Ralph's learning those attitudinal and social skills that are most appropriate him within the classroom. This process does work, but teachers must not expect it to work instantaneously.

SUGGESTED READINGS

Ballif, B. L., & Egbert, R. L. Operant conditioning of attitudes toward school. Paper read at the Western Psychological Association, San Diego, 1968.

Bandura, A., & McDonald, F. J. Influence of social reinforcement and the behavior of models in shaping children's moral judgments. *Journal of Abnormal and Social Psychology,* 1963, **67,** 274–281.

Berk, L. E., Rose, M. H., & Stewart, D. Attitudes of English and American children toward their school experiences. *Journal of Educational Psychology,* 1970, **61,** 33–40. Reprinted in H. D. Thornburg (Ed.), *School learning and instruction: Readings.* Monterey, Calif.: Brooks/Cole, 1973, chap. 6.

Eisenman, R. Teaching about the authoritarian personality: Effects on moral judgment. *Psychological Record,* 1970, **20,** 33–40.

Hjelle, L. A., & Clouser, R. Susceptibility to attitude change as a function of internal–external control. *Psychological Record,* 1970, **20,** 305–310.

Kelley, H. H. Moral evaluation. *American Psychologist,* 1971, **26,** 293–300.

Thornburg, H. D. An investigation of attitudes among potential dropouts from minority groups during their freshman year in high school. In H. D. Thornburg (Ed.), *School learning and instruction: Readings.* Monterey, Calif.: Brooks/Cole, 1973, chap. 6.

Zirkel, P. A. Self-concept and the "disadvantage" of ethnic group membership and mixture. *Review of Educational Research,* 1971, **41,** 211–225.

13

Continuing Issues in Educational Psychology

It is hoped that at this point in the book, the reader has a better understanding of how an instructional theory and strategy makes learning theory clearer and more practical. It is, of course, impossible to discuss every aspect and viewpoint of the teaching–learning process within the confines of a single text, and there are many issues and theories of learning that stand in contrast to those presented in this book. There is also a surmounting body of additional research on the various learning and instructional issues that *are* available in this book. This final chapter is designed to provide a review of some of these additional materials in order to look at the issues that are of continuing concern to educational researchers and to consider ways in which we may expand our understanding of how man learns and behaves. Six areas are discussed: *learning, instruction, behavioral objectives, teacher self-evaluation,* and *educational technology.* Another important issue, *measurement and evaluation of student achievement,* is discussed in Appendix A.

LEARNING

Since Thorndike's (1898) animal experimentation, educational research has become increasingly concerned with human learning and behavior and has successfully identified many variables and conditions under which learning may occur. Yet, it has only been within the past two decades that serious consideration has been given to the various classroom conditions conducive to learning. In this area, two learning positions are of particular interest for contemporary educators and psychologists. The first is *learning domains,* as categorized by Gagné (1971a); the second is *mastery learning,* as suggested by Bloom (1968).

Learning domains

Gagné (1971a) lists five learning domains, or *outcomes,* which he contends encompass all learning operations in the classroom: (1) *motor skills,* (2) *verbal information,* (3) *intellectual skills,* (4) *cognitive strategies,* and (5) *attitudes.* Content material from any academic area is generalizable to these five domains. Table 13.1 summarizes the categories and their functions and measurement possibilities.

1. *Motor skills.*   Many of our learned capabilities are simple motor performances. To learn and maintain a motor skill, practice is required; as Gagné (1971a) states, "This requirement, in fact, is one of the main characteristics that distinguish motor skills from other domains of learning. It is not at all apparent that other kinds of learning do require practice, at least in the same sense" (p. 8).

TABLE 13.1.   Gagné's Learning Domains

Type	Example	Function	Measurement Possibilities
Motor skill	Printing letters.	Mediates motor performance.	Degree of precision or the attainment of a designated standard.
Verbal information	"The boiling point of water is 100°C."	(1) Directions for action, including further learning; (2) mediates transfer (?).	Estimation of amount of information by sampling within a learning domain.
Intellectual skill	Finding vectors of forces.	Component of further learning and thinking.	Mastery versus nonmastery of a defined class of tasks.
Cognitive strategy	Inferring a general rule.	Controls learner's behavior in attending, learning, remembering, thinking.	Degree of success in a variety of problem-solving tasks.
Attitude	Preference for music as an activity.	Determines individual's choices.	Strength of attitude, as indicated by choice of objects or activities within a defined range of situations.

Adapted from a table which accompanied a lecture by Robert Gagné to the Department of Educational Psychology, University of Arizona, 1971. Reprinted by permission of the author.

2. *Verbal information.*   Most academic content materials are learned as facts or generalizations that facilitate problem solving and further learning, and the learning domain of verbal information generally indicates the ability to recall such advantageous basic information. In other words, the learning of facts and generalizations provides the conditions for generalizing beyond the facts to new problem situations. Thus, verbal facts and generalizations represent cumulative learning that is also usable in basic life functions. In contrast to motor skills, verbal information does not require practice. Rather, as Gagné points out (1971a,c), verbal information requires an organized, meaningful context.

3. *Intellectual skills.*   Here, Gagné describes the type of learning that is characteristic of discriminations, concepts, and rules, as discussed in Chapters 6 and 7. Intellectual skills go beyond verbal information in that reference is made not to the recall of basic learning but to the *use* of it. However, the learning of verbal information is a prerequisite condition for learning and using intellectual skills. This prerequisite learning gives the learner the necessary capabilities to develop and apply conceptual meanings. Gagné contends that intellectual skills also do not need practice to be learned.

4. *Cognitive strategies.*   These are internally organized skills that govern the student's overall behavior in learning, remembering, and thinking. Cognitive strategies are not learned quickly or easily. Rather, they are continuing thinking processes that result from the accumulation of basic information and intellectual skills described in the two preceding points and, through use, become refined and increase the student's general problem-solving ability. Gagné (1971b) suggests that practice, the opportunity to use such strategies, is important in the development of thinking behavior. Therefore, it is likely that a teacher might best help the student develop cognitive strategies by providing him with instructional situations in which he may solve problems for himself.

5. *Attitudes.*   Perhaps the most effective way of learning attitudes is through direct involvement with a human model (Gagné, 1971a,c). Such learning is obviously different from either intellectual skills or cognitive strategies and, most likely, needs neither practice nor a meaningful context for success.

The usefulness of these five learning domains is related to their ability to encompass all types of learning and their applicability to classroom instruction. For within the confines of today's teaching–learning environment, it is likely that all learning and school curricula fall within these categories. Motor skills and verbal information may be more characteristic of early learning levels, although, to limited degrees, these categories of learning are a continuing process throughout the educational process and even throughout a lifetime. Intellectual skills and cognitive strategies are more characteristic of advanced learning stages, of course, and of life functions.

Mastery learning

Bloom (1968) contends that the existing educational system is too content to accept *degrees* of learning rather than mastery. He sees no reason why students cannot learn more and be expected to learn more, and he proposes mastery learning as the most desirable educational objective for all areas and levels of the educational system. This means moving away from the normal curve, which sorts out students and their achievements by percentages, and moving toward instructional strategies, which take individual differences into account.

Carroll (1963), who holds a similar contention, makes two points regarding mastery learning:

1. If students are distributed in the normal curve in their aptitudes for some academic subject, and if they are provided with the same instruction, the results of the instruction will be a normal distribution of achievements.

2. However, if students are normally distributed by aptitude for some academic subject but are provided instruction appropriate to the individual characteristics and needs of each student, the majority of the students may be expected to achieve mastery of the subject.

Mastery learning, then, requires analysis of and instruction adapted to the particular needs of each student. It requires more individual attention and a greater time commitment by the teacher. Research indicates that most students eventually accomplish mastery of a learning task (Atkinson, 1967), although the rate of acquisition is quite different. For example, recognition that not all fifth graders will be performing at the fifth-grade level is important for a teacher. It is not uncommon to find a range of four or more grade levels within a heterogeneous class. However, the important factor is the aptitude of each student at a given point in time. A student may not be able to acquire certain grade-level academic material as early or as rapidly as his classmates, but he may eventually master it with individualized instruction and attention.

One additional point made by Bloom (1968) is important to our discussion. In order to maximize learning to the point of mastery, the teacher must ensure that the student understands instruction. "The ability to understand instruction may be defined as the ability of the learner to understand the nature of the task he is to learn and the procedures he is to follow in the learning of the task" (p. 5). It is clear that the more understanding students have of what is being expected and how they may go about meeting these expectations, the greater are the chances that mastery learning will occur (Romberg, 1969). In short, the teacher must take much care to assure students of an appropriate sense of direction, which often means the modification of instruction in terms of individual student needs.

INSTRUCTION

The ideas of Gagné and Bloom point to the need for more adequate and systematized instruction and, particularly, for a closer look at teaching procedures in terms of their effectiveness for individual student learning. The individualization of instruction is encouraged by Bloom and other proponents of mastery learning as well as by Gagné; for they recognize that by personalizing and focusing on individual student needs, a teacher may ensure that greater learning takes place.

One of the first attempts at individualizing instruction was the use of programmed materials, which allow the student to function at a self-paced rate. Self-paced instruction is not restricted to programmed materials, however. For example, quite often, teachers organize content into graded segments and allow students to work through each segment at their own pace. Research has indicated that many students learn quite well this way, while others need a more structured teaching–learning situation (Congreve, 1965). Individualized instruction can also be provided within a structured situation, of course. If the teacher begins instruction at the point most appropriate to the past achievement of a learner, and if lectures are supplemented by specific, individual help for students, the teacher has, in effect, individualized his instructional procedures. Above all, the key to individualizing is recognition of student needs and the best instructional way to meet them.

Classroom instruction usually occurs in the cognitive domain, and this points out another factor of crucial importance in instructional procedures—the teaching of (1) verbal information, (2) intellectual skills, and (3) cognitive strategies. To teach verbal information and not go beyond it is to restrict learning, and to teach intellectual skills without having taught the verbal information germane to such skills will most likely result in unsuccessful instruction. The point being made here is that if true learning is to occur for students, the teacher must analyze the learning condition desired and the needs of individual students and then implement a teaching strategy complementary to these factors.

Gagné's emphasis on verbal information, intellectual skills, and cognitive strategies for instructional procedures assumes an understanding and application of his hierarchical levels, described in Chapters 4 through 8, to the development of more effective curricula. For example, on the basis of Gagné's learning hierarchy and his analysis of learning outcomes or domains, two new curricula, for elementary-school science and mathematics, have been recently developed. The extensive science curriculum guide was initiated during the 1971–72 school year by the American Association for the Advancement of Science (AAAS) and funded by the National Science Foundation. The program, which was used by some two million students, was designed to confront the children with learning processes that hierarchically build increasing intellectual skills and cognitive strategies (Two million, 1971). A brief overview of the program is provided here:

1. The curriculum guide suggests a guidance approach by the teacher to maximize student learning. The purpose of the curriculum is to present the child with an interesting array of educational experiences, with minimal direction from the teacher, in hopes that the child's own curiosity and initiative will lead him along.

2. The curriculum emphasizes *process*. Scientists, regardless of discipline, perform a common set of activities which can be generalized and which younger students can learn independent of the content of a particular scientific discipline. Such processes are observing, classifying, using numbers, measuring, using space–time relationships, communicating, predicting, inferring, defining operationally, formulating hypotheses, interpreting data, controlling variables, and experimenting.

3. The curriculum is designed so that each of these processes can be learned by a natural sequence in which each new skill builds upon an earlier one. A portion of this hierarchical arrangement of the science processes is found in Figure 13.1.

4. The curriculum has a built-in measurement and evaluation activity of two special exercises which test pupil achievement at the conclusion of each unit of instruction.

The math program was recently developed by the author for kindergarten through sixth grade. Three basic instructional components were used: (1) General and specific behavioral objectives were determined to specify the nature and scope of instructional strategies. (2) Mathematical materials were hierarchically delineated, from simple verbal information to problem-solving abilities. (3) Sequentially arranged *transfer problems* were included so that the learner might acquire social as well as academic uses from the materials. Figure 13.2 illustrates the organization of one of the mathematical units.

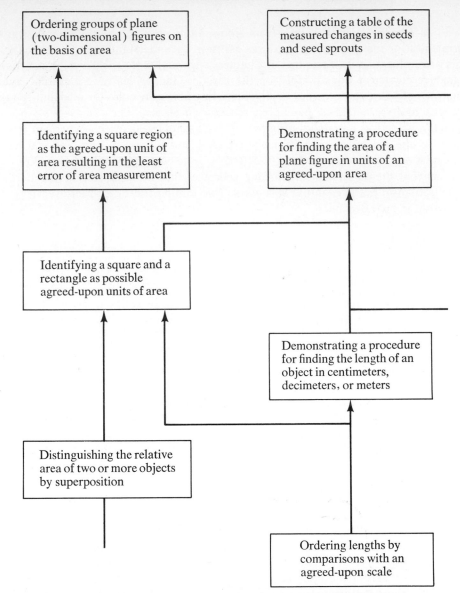

FIGURE 13.1. *A Portion of the AAAS Science Curriculum—A Process Approach*

| Ordering groups of plane (two-dimensional) figures on the basis of area | Constructing a table of the measured changes in seeds and seed sprouts |

| Identifying a square region as the agreed-upon unit of area resulting in the least error of area measurement | Demonstrating a procedure for finding the area of a plane figure in units of an agreed-upon area |

Identifying a square and a rectangle as possible agreed-upon units of area

Demonstrating a procedure for finding the length of an object in centimeters, decimeters, or meters

Distinguishing the relative area of two or more objects by superposition

Ordering lengths by comparisons with an agreed-upon scale

From the American Association for the Advancement of Science, "Two million youngsters in U.S. learn sciences with a new curriculum," *AAAS Bulletin*, June 1971, and *The basic processes hierarchy chart, Science—a process approach*, New York: Xerox Corporation, 1967. Reprinted with permission.

BEHAVIORAL OBJECTIVES

This book has taken the position that behavioral objectives are highly instrumental in the teaching–learning process. As we have learned, if the teacher specifies the expected student learning behaviors, such statements will (1) assist the teacher's instructional sequence, (2) serve as a reference point for students in understanding the instructional procedures, and (3) give both teacher and students a basis for evaluation upon completion of the teaching–learning tasks. In short, behavioral objectives can broaden student and teacher perception of the learning process and therefore result

FIGURE 13.2.   Mathematics Curriculum Guide

Behavioral Objectives: Sets

The student will

1. learn and use mathematical terms and symbols dealing with sets.
2. be able to describe a set accurately in terms of members or numbers.
3. demonstrate understanding of sets.
4. understand rules for set operations.
5. demonstrate ability to perform set operations.

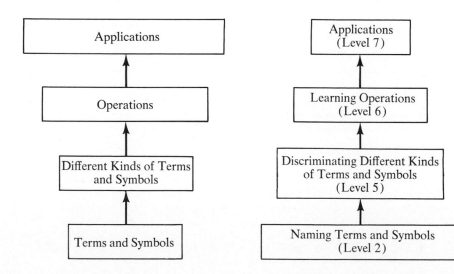

Teaching Sequence

Applications

Operations

Different Kinds of Terms
and Symbols

Terms and Symbols

Learning Sequence

Applications
(Level 7)

Learning Operations
(Level 6)

Discriminating Different Kinds
of Terms and Symbols
(Level 5)

Naming Terms and Symbols
(Level 2)

FIGURE 13.2 (continued)

Scope and Sequence

	K	1	2	3	4	5	6
Terms and Symbols	I	E	E	E	E	E	E
Kinds							
Empty	I	E	E	E	E	E	E
Subset	I	E	E	E	E	E	E
Disjoint		I	E	E	E	E	E
Proper			I	E	E	E	E
Universal					I	E	E
Super						I	E
Operations							
Comparison							
Equivalent	I	E	E	E	E	E	E
Nonequivalent	I	E	E	E	E	E	E
Equal			I	E	E	E	E
Intersect						I	E	E
Union and separation	I	E	E	E	E	E	E
Fractions			I	E	E	E	E	E
Multiplication					I	E	E	E
Division					I	E	E	E
Ordered pairs						I	E	E
Functions						I	E	E
Solution sets			I	E	E	E	E	E
Applications							
Problem solving					I	E	E	E
Social uses							I	E

I = Introduce material
E = Extend material

in more varied methods of teaching and evaluation and more effective learning (Montague & Butts, 1968).

It is difficult to know how widespread the use of educational objectives is. Many schools do not use them because they have no orientation toward them or because they consider them too inflexible and demanding (Eisner, 1967). Many educators also raise serious questions about behavioral objectives. For example, although Ebel (1970) offers some justifications for the use of objectives, he ultimately contends (1971) that command of knowledge should be the primary objective of education and that behavioral objectives are not imperative for the learning of knowledge and understanding, attitudes and values. Ebel (1970) states four problems with the use of behavioral objectives:

1. There is a continuing difficulty in knowing precisely what the concept "behavioral objectives" means. Some use it as if the behavior in which they are interested is that of the student while he is learning, or even that of the teacher. Others use it to refer to the student's behavior on special tasks designed to show whether or not he has learned something. Still others have in mind the student's use in life or on the job of what he has learned in school. One cannot speak or even think clearly about behavioral objectives without defining which type of behavior he has in mind.

2. The behavior specified in objectives is seldom the real objective of the instruction. When the stated behavior is that of the learner while learning, such behavior is clearly a means to an end, not the end itself. Nor can test behavior be the real objective, except in those cases where the test is a performance test in a natural setting. That is, only when the objectives are defined in terms of real-life or on-the-job performance can the behavior be the real objective.

3. It is difficult to specify the behavioral objective in sufficient detail. Any significant behavioral act in the teaching–learning situation—the construction of an achievement test for a course, for example—consists of a myriad of contributory acts. Very often, these acts are not easy to identify as separate elements in the total matrix of behavior.

4. To define a behavior as an educational objective requires us to say not only what the behavior is but also how well it is handled. But it is difficult to specify an appropriate level of skill or competence in most significant acts of behavior. Such behaviors cannot readily be said to be clearly either present or absent, available or unavailable; they simply occur more or less often at appropriate times and are handled more or less well.

Atkin (1968) has also questioned the use of behavioral objectives, expressing the fear that undue emphasis on objectives could result in the disappearance of worthwhile learning activities that cannot easily be identified with specific behaviors. He emphasizes the importance of unplanned, unanticipated learning, something strict behavioral objectives may not account for:

> Ideas are taught with the richest meaning only when they are emphasized repeatedly in appropriate and varied contexts. Many of these contexts arise in classroom situations that are unplanned, but that have powerful potential. It is detrimental to learning not to capitalize on the opportune moments for effectively teaching one idea or another. Riveting the teacher's attention to a few behavioral goals provides him with blinders that may limit his range [p. 29].

Does one have to assume that the use of behavioral objectives makes the user inflexible, vague in his intentions, and unable to capitalize on opportune moments? The author and many others think not. The ability of a teacher who uses behavioral objectives cannot be measured by his planning and development of the objectives. The behavioral objectives are no more than helpful reference points for his instructional procedures. If a teacher feels constrained by behavioral objectives, it is most likely a reflection of the teacher's personal instructional problems and not the use of objectives.

One can understand the problems suggested by Ebel and the fear expressed by Atkin. Others (Broudy, 1970; Macdonald & Wolfson, 1970; and Ojemann, 1971) have expressed the same concerns. Certainly, the area of behavioral objectives needs continued refinement and research; the failure of many teachers and school systems to use behavioral objectives undoubtedly is due in part to the ambiguity that easily creeps into the writing of the objectives as well as to the lack of understanding of the domains and levels of learning, which must be an integral element in any effective statement of objectives. Remember that the cognitive domain has six levels of operation; the affective domain five levels of operation. (There is no common agreement as to the appropriate components of a psychomotor domain.) Therefore, the teacher must first decide whether the behavior desired of the student is cognitive, affective, or psychomotor. If it is cognitive, then the teacher must decide if the behavior involves primarily knowledge, comprehension, application, analysis, synthesis, or evaluation. If the behavior is affective, a similar process must occur among the five levels of the affective domain. The instrumentation chart which is reprinted as Appendix B shows many available key words and infinitives that will help the teacher in such a categorization of objectives.

Admittedly, the chart in Appendix B and the process of planning objectives are somewhat complex, and some limited attempts have been made thus far to simplify the process. The most recent one was by Gagné, who, in a special tape made for the

American Educational Research Association, defined the behavioral objectives for six types or levels of learning with a single verb:

Learning type	*Major behavioral objective*
Chain	Reinstates
Discrimination	Discriminates
Concrete concept	Identifies
Defined concept	Classifies
Rule	Demonstrates
Higher-order rule	Generates

It is likely that this simple classification works well with the learning levels postulated by Gagné and elaborated on in this book. It is also likely that these six defining verbs are not applicable to all learning or instructional models. Nevertheless, this attempt to simplify the understanding and use of behavioral objectives should make it somewhat easier for the teacher (1) to know what behaviors to expect, (2) to know the level of learning occurring in a behavior, and (3) to remain general enough in the concept of a behavior that inflexibility will not occur in teaching and evaluating that behavior.

TEACHER SELF-EVALUATION

Many educational psychologists are particularly concerned about observing and analyzing teacher behavior in the belief that it is essential for teachers to have some objective awareness of their instructional procedures and some criteria by which to judge that teaching behavior. Ober (1967) contends that teacher-observation systems assist the teacher in performing six necessary operations for effective teaching:

1. They identify and categorize the contributing elements that constitute a given teaching–learning situation.
2. They allow the relationships between these interacting elements to be conceptualized into instructional theory.
3. They provide the basis for selection and planning of instructional strategies that will facilitate maximum student learning in a variety of teaching–learning situations.
4. They help the teacher to develop and sharpen the skills used in putting the selected instructional strategies into practice in the classroom.
5. They provide reliable and meaningful data that can be analyzed to provide feedback to the teacher concerning the quality of the teaching performance.
6. They improve future teaching performance by suggesting suitable modifications both in performance and in instructional theory.

The philosophy of one school district is to have each teacher write his teaching units in behavioral terms. Some of the teachers complain because they find the stating of behavioral objectives to be cumbersome and not that advantageous to teaching. *Is there a simple, nonambiguous way to write behavioral objectives?*

One of the reasons behavioral objectives have been under criticism is because they are ambiguous; it is hard for the teacher to know precisely what is meant. Three possible solutions to this problem are presently known. First, a teacher should identify the operational level involved in the expected learning behavior and select a word that best represents that level. Many educators use several words that have the same meaning, and, therefore, Appendix B is presented in this book to acquaint the teacher with these comparable behavioral terms. Second, on page 311, a specific verb is listed for each level in Gagné's learning hierarchy. This listing tremendously reduces the problem of ambiguity, although its usefulness is limited to the Gagné approach to the teaching–learning process. Third, a teacher can simply not state desired learning outcomes in behavioral terms. If a teacher feels strongly about using behavioral objectives but is troubled by the terminology, he should state objectives in his own factual/descriptive terms. Simply stating objectives in some way is, after all, the point of this procedure, which helps a teacher become more systematic, analytical, and effective and helps the student know what is expected of him. Behavioral objectives are intended to facilitate teaching and learning, not to make the process more burdensome.

Considerable efforts have been made to systematically evaluate the actual teaching behavior of the classroom teacher and to evaluate effectiveness in terms of predetermined criteria. Such teacher behavior research generally focuses on (1) *model systems,* which describes direct teacher–pupil interactions, (2) *instructional processes,* which is a more comprehensive system of interactions, and (3) *teacher behavioral characteristics,* which is a totally teacher-centered system of observation (Ornstein, 1971).

Model systems

Interaction analysis is one teacher-observation procedure that measures the verbal interchange between a teacher and his pupils, a model system that can be observed and coded (Flanders, 1965). Interaction analysis has been used (1) to study spontaneous teacher behavior and (2) to design research projects for helping teachers modify their behaviors. The work of Anderson (1939) began the thinking in this area, and many other researchers have continued his work in developing scales that are recognized as valid ways of assessing teacher behavior.

The most researched program for an interactional analysis of teacher behavior is the system developed by Flanders, which is based primarily on the verbal interchange between teacher and students. Table 13.2 sorts out teacher behaviors, both direct and indirect, into seven categories. Student behaviors comprise two more categories on the Flanders scale, and the tenth category records those periods of time where no formal teacher–pupil interchange is occurring. The premise of this system is that through self-observation and self-evaluation on the basis of this scale, the teacher gains better understanding and control over his teaching behavior, which in turn makes him a more effective teacher, which in turn allows the teacher to gain greater control over the amount of student learning that occurs. The selection of an observational system will be contingent, of course, on the equipment available within the school or district, but, generally, a video-tape recorder, a tape recorder, or simply another teacher are employed for this and similar evaluative processes.

Another systematic but simpler model system for the assessment of teacher–student interaction was devised by the author. Primarily, this system is concerned with teacher behavior; and while it is recognized that other teacher behaviors, such as facial expressions, are also instrumental in learning (Allen et al., 1970), for simplicity and practicality this system is confined to verbal statements.

1. *Direct teacher statements.* These are statements by the teacher which tell the student the course of action the teacher wants him to take. The evaluation of this verbal behavior is contingent upon the student's understanding, accepting, and pursuing the teacher's directions. Examples: "Follow the example on page 42 to work out the problems on the board." "The criteria for selection are outlined on the board."

2. *Problem-formation statement.* These are statements by the teacher which provide direction to the student's thoughts in an objective, nonthreatening manner. In contrast to direct teacher statements, which tell the student what to do or how to resolve a problem, these statements provide the student with less structured statements about the problem itself. Problem-formation statements should clarify a problem and facilitate the student's problem-solving activity. Examples: "Are some of our traditions really not as important as we think they are?" "In addition to federal regulations, what can our local government do about pollution?"

TABLE 13.2. Flanders' Interaction Analysis Categories

Teacher talk	Response	1.**Accepts feeling.* Accepts and clarifies an attitude or the feeling tone of a pupil in a nonthreatening manner. Feelings may be positive or negative. Predicting and recalling feelings are included.
		2. *Praises or encourages.* Praises or encourages pupil action or behavior. Jokes that release tension, but not at the expense of another individual; nodding head, or saying "Um hm?" or "go on" are included.
		3. *Accepts or uses ideas of pupils.* Clarifying, building, or developing ideas suggested by a pupil. Teacher extensions of pupil ideas are included but as the teacher brings more of his own ideas into play, shift to category five.
		4. *Asks questions.* Asking a question about content or procedure, based on teacher ideas, with the intent that a pupil will answer.
	Initiation	5. *Lecturing.* Giving facts or opinions about content or procedures; expressing *his own* ideas, giving *his own* explanation, or citing an authority other than a pupil.
		6. *Giving directions.* Directions, commands, or orders to which a pupil is expected to comply.
		7. *Criticizing or justifying authority.* Statements intended to change pupil behavior from nonacceptable to acceptable pattern; bawling someone out; stating why the teacher is doing what he is doing; extreme self-reference.
Pupil talk	Response	8. *Pupil-talk—response.* Talk by pupils in response to teacher. Teacher initiates the contact or solicits pupil statement or structures the situation. Freedom to express own ideas is limited.
	Initiation	9. *Pupil-talk—initiation.* Talk by pupils which they initiate. Expressing own ideas; initiating a new topic; freedom to develop opinions and a line of thought, like asking thoughtful questions; going beyond the existing structure.
Silence		10. *Silence or confusion.* Pauses, short periods of silence and periods of confusion in which communication cannot be understood by the observer.

* There is *no* scale implied by these numbers. To write these numbers down during observation is to enumerate, not to judge a position on a scale.

From Flanders, N. A., *Analyzing teaching behavior*, 1970, Addison-Wesley Publishing Company, Inc., Reading, Mass. Used with permission of the publisher.

3. *Reinforcement statements.* These statements give positive feedback to the student through praise or knowledge of results. Such statements should gain student interest and motivation in the learning at hand. Examples: "Very good," "right," "o.k.," "yes." "I'm glad to see you followed the example."

4. *Neutral (nonreinforcing) statements.* Many statements, such as administrative information or explanation of classroom procedure, are replies to student inquiry which receive classroom time but have no effect on learning. Examples: "In just one week, try-outs for the school play will be held." "Our senator will speak at a special assembly tomorrow." One other interaction which can be considered within this category is the event of *not* reinforcing a student when a response is made. This is called an *omission statement* and should be recorded as a failure to reinforce, unless it is a planned attempt at extinction of an undesirable response. In this latter case, it would be recorded as a *negative reinforcement statement.*

5. *Punitive (negative) statements.* These statements of disapproval give negative feedback (and perhaps even undesirable reinforcement to the student. Withall (1951) sees the intent of such statements as
   a. To represent to the learner societal values as the teacher sees them. Examples: "But if you become a welfare bum, most people will dislike you." "Sex is not something adolescents can play around with without serious consequences."
   b. To admonish the learner for unacceptable behavior and to deter him from repeating it in the future. Examples: "You haven't any interest in what we're doing, do you, Jerry?" "If you'd shut up and pay attention, you wouldn't have to ask such questions."
   c. To impress on the learner the fact that he has not met the teacher's criteria for successful achievement. Examples: "If you don't dig in and study, you're going to flunk the test." "I don't think it's relevant to the topic, do you?" Usually, such statements do not facilitate learning and may, in addition, create social-emotional conflicts within the teaching–learning situation.

6. *Teacher-centered statements.* These are statements in which the teacher defends or asserts his position (Withall, 1951). Most such statements reflect defensive or ego-attitudes of the teacher. Examples: "I don't think that legislative policy can be justified." "If someone can disprove my statement, he will have to base his answer on fact and not opinion."

Research indicates that reinforcing, learner-supportive statements produce more student-initiated behaviors and less teacher direction in the classroom (Anderson, 1946; Withall, 1949), which would indicate that more effective learning takes place when the student functions within a learner-supportive environment. Categories 2 and 3 of the above scale are learner-centered and highly supportive. Category 1 is teacher-centered, but such statements can be useful in helping the student learn. Categories 5 and 6 and the omission-statement element of category 4 are teacher-oriented and tend not to be conducive to learning.

Model systems have been repeatedly used to evaluate teacher effectiveness, and the results of some research in this type of teacher self-evaluation have been conclusive:

1. Amidon and Flanders (1961) found that teachers using student-initiated statements produced higher achievement and attitude development among students than those using direct teaching methods.
2. Nelson (1966), studying first-grade language arts, found student compositions to be both quantitatively and qualitatively superior in total verbal output and vocabulary with student-initiated learning situations.
3. Pankratz (1966) found that a group of biology teachers rated "more effective" on the basis of his subjective criteria used more indirect, or student-initiated, teaching procedures than those rated "less effective."
4. Soar (1967) studied students in grades three through six and found greater vocabulary growth among groups experiencing student-initiated learning situations. At grades three through five, greater reading growth was also a result of such indirect teaching methods.
5. Parakh (1965) found a low percentage of student verbal participation in situations with a high percentage of direct verbal teacher behaviors. A similar finding among physics teachers was reported by Snider (1965).

Instructional processes

Ornstein (1971) has developed a system of teacher observation and evaluation which he terms *instructional processes.* He considers two types of instructional-processes analysis and asserts that the first type, which "tends to be descriptive and based on nonsystematic observations" (p. 552), must necessarily be empirical in nature and will therefore tend to reflect the observer's preconceived notions of what should occur in the classroom. Ornstein had model systems of observation in mind when he voiced this criticism. He prefers the second instructional-processes approach, which attempts to describe and evaluate the teaching–learning process in terms of defined, abstract units of measurement. This second approach differs from model systems in that it goes beyond *verbal* teacher–student interaction and considers all types of classroom behaviors, such as teacher facial expressions, student talk and movements, teacher methods, and classroom events.

An example of such an observational approach has been advanced by Allen et al. (1970), who provide an elaborate system of coding and measurement for evaluating (1) verbal behaviors of students and teacher, (2) facial behaviors of the teacher, and (3) teacher methodology (see Table 13.3). The authors go beyond most observation

TABLE 13.3. An Instructional-Processes Approach to Teacher Observation

Teacher Code

	Categories	Tally	Total
VERBAL	1. Teacher Talks		
	2. Student Talks		
	3. Silence		
FACIAL	4. Teacher Smiles		
	5. Teacher Frowns		
	6. Neutral Expressions		
METHOD	7. Lectures		
	8. Questions		
	9. Directs		

From Allen, Paul, et al., *Teacher self-appraisal: A way of looking over your own shoulder*. Copyright 1970 and used by permission of Charles A. Jones Publishing Co., Worthington, Ohio.

systems when they consider teaching methods—how much the teacher lectures, directs, or questions within the classroom—and teacher facial expressions (smiles, frowns, and neutral expressions). Allen et al., like Galloway (1962), consider facial expression to be an important classroom variable of nonverbal communication with students. The verbal behaviors are accounted for by categorizing situations in which the teacher talks, the students talk, or there is silence. This system does not attempt to clarify the effects of teacher–student verbal interactions or the degrees of student acceptance as does the Flanders model system.

The weakness of instructional-processes approaches is that they attempt to cover every aspect of the total teaching–learning–methodology situation. It is certainly true that if one of the outcomes of teacher observation and evaluation is to produce more effective classroom teachers, then the broader our knowledge and understanding of teacher behaviors, the more likely teacher effectiveness will be increased. However, we must also recognize our limitations in identifying and systematizing these behaviors.

As will be seen in the next section, there is considerable difficulty in clearly and objectively assessing teacher behavioral characteristics—an assessment that would seem to be prerequisite to the kind of all-encompassing system being advocated by the instructional-processes proponents.

Teacher behavioral characteristics

There are numerous proposed systems and research studies designed to identify and assess teacher behavioral characteristics. The difficulty with all of them is that (1) they are totally teacher-centered, ignoring student–teacher interchanges, student acceptance, and instructional theory, and (2) they rely on the ability of researchers and observers to agree on the categorizations of teacher behaviors and the objective meanings of these distinct categories. Different individuals, both researchers and teachers themselves, naturally tend to classify the same teacher response differently. Ornstein (1971) gives an excellent example of this problem:

> Meux and Smith (1964), Ryans (1964), and Turner (1964) are of the opinion that linguistic usage, confusion over words, and/or interchangeability of words cause difficulties concerning agreement on operational or behavioral meanings of teacher behavior categories, or, according to Jenkins (1969) and Perkins (1964), in the way in which teacher behavior occurs, as well as the nature and scope of the behavior. For example, this investigator uses "welcomes and is respectful of views other than own" as a behavior phrase to help describe affective teacher behavior (Ornstein, 1970). A similar teacher behavior, "sincere sympathy with a pupil's viewpoint" (p. 88), is categorized by Ryans (1960) under *understanding behavior*. Dumas (1966) classified "sympathy with pupil viewpoint" (p. 24) with *empathy*. Medley and Mitzel (1963) identified "tried to see pupil point of view" (p. 276) with *teacher climate*. Remmers (1963), reviewing different rating scales, reported "accepted students' viewpoint with open mind" (p. 342) under *adequacy of relations with students*. Sontag (1968) itemized "shows interest in the viewpoint of pupils" (p. 395) with *concern for students*. Jersild (1940) linked "permitted expression of opinion" (p. 144) with *teacher performance*. This type of discrepancy, this inability to agree upon operational terms, causes a lack of generalizability in the findings; it often causes the research and related literature to be misleading too [p. 553].

It must be recognized, then, that there is no single, accepted criterion against which teacher behavioral characteristics can be validated and that such systems of teacher observation tend to be more confusing than helpful. The other teacher-observation systems all share this difficulty to some degree in their attempts to analyze and systematize the nature of the teaching–learning process. Observational systems in general have drawn some criticism from writers who feel that total variable control is impossible in a teaching–learning situation and, therefore, that research in this area is likely to be ineffective (Gage & Unruh, 1967). Other writers objecting to observational systems have agreed with Gage and Unruh:

1. Teaching has too many subtleties that are unidentifiable and uncontrollable (Atkin, 1968).

2. Teacher–pupil interchange is too complex to simplify into a model (Cronbach, 1967).

3. Teacher behavior is too spontaneous to categorize into a model (Jackson, 1968).

Clearly, the challenge ahead is to develop more refined, less subjective classification systems that will allow for greater agreement on the meaning of the expression "effective teacher–student interaction." However, for the time being, model systems, such as interaction analysis, can serve as simple and reasonably valuable procedures for observing and assessing the effectiveness of teacher behaviors and instructional strategies. In addition, as we shall see in the next section, these systems may result in greater teacher awareness of the requirements and difficulties of effective classroom instruction.

Self-evaluation among practice teachers

There is increasing evidence that (1) making education students aware of the concept "teacher self-evaluation" and (2) providing practice experiences in which the student can observe his own preteaching behaviors may be instrumental in placing more effective teachers in the classroom. Several research studies point to this, some of which will be cited here:

1. Kirk (1964) taught interaction analysis to an experimental group of education students, comparing them with other education students who had no interaction-analysis instruction. Results indicated that students in the experimental group talked less, had more pupil-initiated talk, and were more accepting of pupil ideas in their practice teaching than the control group.

2. McLeod's research (1967) indicated that during the first part of the practice-teaching experience, prospective teachers were more susceptible to change and that those students who were sensitized to examine and evaluate their classroom behaviors made more changes than those who were not.

3. Hough and Ober (1966) instructed one group of preteachers to observe their "teaching" behaviors through interaction analysis and a second group to analyze their behaviors without the help of a formalized system. Upon completion of a 20-minute simulated teaching situation, students who had been taught interaction analysis used significantly more verbal behaviors found to be associated with higher student achievement and with more positive student attitudes toward the teacher than did the other group.

4. Goldman (1969) studied the effect of classroom experience and video-tape self-observation on attitudes toward self and toward teaching among 63 sophomore elementary-education majors. The experimental group spent 30 minutes managing a third-grade class and then observed themselves on video tape, while the control group had neither experience. Goldman found that the experimental group developed a significantly better regard for themselves and were significantly more critical of teaching clichés and concepts than the control group.

EDUCATIONAL TECHNOLOGY

Educational psychologists have been interested in technology for years in their search for more effective ways of increasing the rates of student learning. Thus far, the contributions of educational technology have been mainly in two areas: (1) more effective research tools for better understanding learning theory and its application to education, and (2) instructional systems and devices which produce more effective learning as well as simpler and more efficient teaching procedures.

While the earliest teaching machine was advanced by Pressey in 1926, Skinner (1958) is appropriately credited with the modern teaching machine and the subsequent development of programmed and computer-aided instruction. Skinner's machine was a simple device, based on established learning principles, which could be used for a systematized instructional procedure. Essentially, the teacher directed a student or class through a series of instructional sequences (frames), and the student gradually learned the desired response, or terminal behavior. Although the machine lacked flexibility, it did bring about systematic learning by the student. Two additional outcomes of the teaching machine were similarly important: (1) it precluded aversive teacher comments, so that the student learned in a positively controlled environment, and (2) it proved to be a particularly effective and efficient technique for individualizing instruction.

Shortly after the teaching machine became well known, it fell under heavy criticism, usually on moral grounds. Fear was expressed that the teacher would be replaced, that teaching and learning would become dehumanized, and that children would become unsuspecting victims of manipulation through the "Skinner box." With greater knowledge, these fears generally dissipated, and the use of the machine proved programmed instruction to be a very useful teaching technique. Occasionally, someone still writes a moralistic plaint about educational technology, but most educators recognize and are quick to point out that technology itself is value free. It merely provides tools to better facilitate teaching and learning operations. It may be used to serve bad objectives as well as good ones, of course; but in neither case is the technology itself responsible.

Programmed instruction

As an instructional device, programmed instruction has proved quite effective. Much of its success can be attributed to the fact that it is built around established educational principles, as Hilgard (1961) has pointed out:

1. It recognizes individual differences by beginning where the learner is and by permitting him to proceed at his own pace.
2. It requires that the learner be active.
3. It provides immediate knowledge of results.
4. It emphasizes the organized nature of knowledge by requiring continuity between the easier (earlier) concepts and the harder (later) ones.
5. It provides spaced review in order to guarantee a high order of success.
6. It reduces anxiety, because the learner cannot be threatened by the task. He knows that he can learn and is learning at his own pace, and he gains the satisfaction that this knowledge brings.

Programmed textbooks are commonplace today, at every grade level and in every academic subject. Undoubtedly, most readers of this text will have been exposed to some type of programmed material by now. The Skinnerian-type program, called *linear programming,* is characterized by four features: (1) It uses small units of information, generally one or two sentences in length. (2) It forces student answers, which must be composed rather than selected. (3) It presents information and problems in a series of sequential, easily grasped steps (shaping). (4) It uses a linear format; that is, the student must proceed from step to step, without skipping or deviation for remedial work.

A second type of program, which uses multiple-choice–type questions, is called *branching*. This technique, advanced by Crowder (1960), typically presents a paragraph or two of information and then asks a series of questions about the information. If the learner selects the correct response to a question, he is allowed to go to the next question or source of information. If not, he is told, in a remedial section, or *loop*, why he was wrong and then he is referred back to the original question to select an alternative response. As with the linear technique, the student moves from step to step (reinforcement) as he selects the correct responses. Examples of programmed materials are included here as illustrations; the linear technique is Figure 13.3, the branching technique is Figure 13.4.

The success of programmed instruction has been responsible in part for the growth of an educational technology into an industry that now produces over $1 billion a year in *hardware* (equipment such as projectors, recorders, video-tape machines, and computers) (Stark, 1967) and millions of dollars worth of accompanying *software* (films, filmstrips, records, slides, video-tapes, and specially written computer programs). The huge popularity of technological materials, combined with advances in computer technology, has also paved the way for research and some use of computer-assisted programmed instruction. The following discussion of computer-assisted instruction will clarify some of the goals, benefits, and promises of this relatively new area of education.

Computer-assisted instruction (CAI)

It has been suggested that many of the technological techniques of instruction used in recent years have failed to meet the goals intended for them because of a lack of learning theory to undergird their use (Hall, 1971). This is one of the strongest reasons given by proponents of computer-assisted instruction (CAI) systems for use of the computer in educational settings. For CAI is not only based on good learning principles but also provides an instructional approach that is flexible enough to meet the academic needs of each student in a classroom.

FIGURE 13.3. Linear Programming

Stimulus and Response

Before we study the empirical definitions for "stimulus" and "response," let us consider their simplest dictionary definitions. These two words are words taken into English from Latin. "Goad" and "spur" are synonyms for the word "stimulus." "Answer" and "reply" are synonyms for the word (14) "_____."

When we say that "answer" and "reply" are synonyms for the word "response," we mean that "answer" and "reply" have the same or nearly the same meaning as (15) "_____."

Response means any change in an individual that is an (16) _____, or reply, to a stimulus.

In the quotation at the beginning of this lesson, Watson says that every (17) _____ _____ (*response* or *stimulus?*) is called out by some (18) _____ (*response* or *stimulus?*).

Most psychologists assume that every response, everything that an individual does, is dependent upon some stimulus. Thus, "stimulus" is a very basic term in the science of psychology. It is important to study its exact empirical meaning. In these lessons, you will learn definitions for *four* different usages of the term "stimulus." We shall study two of these definitions in this lesson.

When we refer to *more than one* stimulus we use the plural form, which is "stimuli." Thus we say "two (19) _____," not "two stimulus."

From Barlow, John A., *Stimulus and response*, pp. 6–7. Copyright © 1968 by John A. Barlow. Reprinted by permission of Harper & Row, Publishers, Inc.

In addition to the use of computers in record keeping and retrieval—a service that provides the classroom teacher with more time for instruction—the simplest use of computers in instructional settings is what Suppes (1968) calls the *individualized drill-and-practice system*. In this system, the learning of academic knowledge and concepts are taught in a conventional manner by the teacher. Then, the computer is employed to provide students with regular review and practice on important skills and concepts. The versatility of the computer in this role may be illustrated in the case of elementary mathematics:

FIGURE 13.4. Branching Programming

Frame 1.

When issued a driver's license, the driver is granted the privilege of using Wisconsin streets and highways as long as he obeys the traffic laws and drives in a safe manner.

Question 1.

Upon obtaining a Wisconsin driver's license, the driver
(a) is permitted to drive in any manner he chooses. (p. 5)
(b) should remember his responsibilities for safety. (p. 7)
(c) is obligated to renew his license periodically. (p. 6)

Student Answers

(p. 5) Upon obtaining a Wisconsin driver's license, the driver is permitted to drive in any manner he chooses.

Whoops! Obviously, this is wrong. Whether a driver has just received his license or is an experienced driver, he never has the right to drive as he pleases. One of the remaining two answers is better than this one. Go back to the question on page 1 and see if you can find it.

(p. 6) Upon obtaining a Wisconsin driver's license, the driver is obligated to renew his license periodically.

While this is true, it is not the answer for which you are looking. Return to page 1 and select a better answer.

(p. 7) Upon obtaining a Wisconsin driver's license, the driver should remember his responsibilities for safety.

Right you are! A driver must always assume responsibility when operating a motor vehicle. This means obeying the traffic laws and driving in a safe manner. Now you are ready to go to additional information in Frame 2 (page 2).

Frame 2.

Special attention must be given to traffic violaters, to drivers involved in accidents, and to those whose physical condition makes safe driving questionable. The Driver Improvement Bureau was created to deal with such people. If this cannot be achieved, the Bureau has no alternative than to suspend or cancel the driver's license.

FIGURE 13.4 (continued)

Question 2.

The agency created to deal with drivers whose physical condition is questionable is the
(a) Highway Patrol. (p. 8)
(b) Department of Public Safety. (p. 10)
(c) Driver Improvement Bureau. (p. 9)

Student Answers

(p. 8) The agency created to deal with drivers whose physical condition is questionable is the Highway Patrol.
No, not in this case. Of course, the Highway Patrol will apprehend a driver whose physical condition obviously is interfering with safe driving. But this agency was not created for the improvement of the individual's driving. With this clue you should return to page 2 and select another response.

(p. 9) The agency created to deal with drivers whose physical condition is questionable is the Driver Improvement Bureau.
Excellent! This is the correct answer. The Driver Improvement Bureau was specifically created to deal with traffic violaters, drivers involved in accidents, and with those whose physical condition is in question. The basic purpose of this agency is to create self-improvement in the licensed driver. Now that you have successfully answered this question, let's try Frame 3 (page 3).

(p. 10) The agency created to deal with drivers whose physical condition is questionable is the Department of Public Safety.
Incorrect! This answer is too general. The Department of Public Safety has many functions, but it was not specifically created to deal with drivers whose physical condition is questionable. Go back to page 2 and select a more appropriate answer.

Each student would receive daily a certain number of exercises, which would be automatically presented, evaluated, and scored by the computer program without any effort by the classroom teacher. Moreover, these exercises can be presented on an individualized basis, with the brighter students receiving exercises that are harder than average, and the slower students receiving easier problems [Suppes, 1968, p. 421].

A second type of computer instruction is the *laboratory computing device,* which has been used successfully in mathematics and science classes (Hall, 1971). With this device, the students are allowed to develop their own programs, via teletype or typewritten hook-ups with a computer, for the course work they are taking. The development procedure serves effectively as a learning event in which a great deal of academic material can be systematically handled and understood.

Tutorial systems are another computer program that is often used. Essentially, these systems assume teaching responsibility by presenting and developing concepts and skills for student application and understanding. This use of the computer differs from the drill-and-practice systems in that the latter are actually maintenance programs, whereas tutorial systems are actually teaching–learning events (Hall, 1971; Suppes, 1968).

Suppes (1968) mentions the future potential of *dialogue systems*, which permit the student to conduct a genuine dialogue with the computer. Such a system is, of course, a more complex level of computer functioning and represents a conceptual level of learning. Several mechanical problems must still be worked out within this system. Another promising area is the *simulation system*, which has already been used extensively in medical science to simulate pathological conditions (Abrahamson, 1969). This simulation use of a computer is a good learning device and could become quite functional in the classroom for appropriate academic materials. The simulation of reality by computer may someday provide learners with clear and vividly memorable applications of issues and problem solving.

Perhaps one of the greatest contributions that CAI will make to education is the individualization of instruction. The age-old problem in the conventional classroom is adjusting the rate and scope of the teaching–learning process to the various needs and abilities of each student. Since computers provide systematized and indefinitely repeatable educational programs, they are adaptable to whatever need or learning task is indicated by a student at a given time. It is simply impossible for a classroom teacher to do this as consistently, efficiently, and effectively.

Research with CAI has confirmed the benefits of this instructional process:

1. Studies indicate that students can learn as well by CAI as within the regular classroom and, in most cases, have a greater learning and retention rate (Bitzer, 1963; Hall, 1971; Suppes, 1966).
2. CAI makes logical decisions and adjustments to individual differences with regard to learning sequence, depth and mode of material, and rate of progress (Bundy, 1968; Atkinson & Hansen, 1966; Chapman & Carpenter, 1962).
3. The computer is capable of recording a variety of learning data about the student during instruction. This feedback can tell how well students are learning and what adjustments in the computer programming may be necessary.
4. Diverse academic materials can be incorporated into CAI programs. As in the case of programmed textbooks, there seems to be no area where CAI cannot eventually function (Suppes, 1966).

Continued research and instruction on computer-assisted instructional materials indicate great hope for highly functional uses of computers in the classroom (Gage, 1968; Suppes, 1966, 1968).

PLAN—a computer program

The Program for Learning in Accordance with Needs (PLAN) was developed by the American Institute of Research as a means of correcting deficiencies existing within our educational system. Built by Flanagan and his associates (1964, 1969), PLAN is a complete computer program which, when carefully followed, will correct learning problems. Deep (1970) in a recent issue of the *Elementary School Journal** gives the following account of PLAN in action:

> PLAN is an individualized educational system designed to provide each pupil with a program of studies geared to his needs, abilities, and interests. Mathematics, language arts, social studies, and science are presently being individualized in Grades 1, 2, 3, 5, 6, 7, 9, 10, and 11. In September, 1970 Grades 4, 8, and 12 will be added to complete the range from 1 through 12. In the near future, other subject areas such as art, music, and industrial arts will be added to the system.
>
> PLAN has six goals:
>
> 1. Pupil's personal formulation of goals.   PLAN assists the pupil in developing to his full potential, in making decisions relative to his educational and occupational future, and in providing information about his interests and possible leisure-time activities.
>
> 2. Pupil's personal development.   PLAN helps the pupil adjust to difficult situations, gives him responsibility in carrying out tasks, and encourages him to be creative and to show initiative when confronted with a special need.
>
> 3. Pupil's social development, which includes social adjustment, sensitivity to others, group orientation, and adaptability to rules and conventions.
>
> 4. Pupil's development of basic skills and abilities, which includes reading with comprehension, expression of oneself, and logical thinking on conflicting issues.
>
> 5. Pupil's acquisition of knowledge, concepts, and principles and ability to transfer these to new problems.

* From Deep, D., The computer can help individualize instruction, *The Elementary School Journal,* 1970, **7**, 351–358. Copyright 1970 by The University of Chicago Press. Reprinted by permission.

6. Pupil's management of his educational behavior.

PLAN encourages pupils to be self-directed learners and to be responsible for their education and personal development.

PLAN has five major components that assist the pupil in attaining these goals. These components are:

1. Comprehensive set of educational behavioral objectives. These objectives are observable and are to be achieved by the pupil under certain conditions by meeting an acceptable performance score.
2. Teaching–learning units. These are designed to teach the objectives and to take into account the different learning styles and interests of pupils.
3. Tests. The purpose of all tests in PLAN is to provide information for correct decision-making.
4. Guidance and individual planning system for each pupil. This system is designed to aid the pupil in learning about adult activities and roles with respect to both avocations and occupations. The system is designed also to help the pupil to learn the significance of his developed abilities and interests.
5. Evaluation system. An IBM 350 Model 50 computer is programmed to score tests used in monitoring the development of each pupil, to keep files on the experience and progress of each pupil, and to evaluate the effectiveness of teaching–learning units and guidance and planning procedures for each pupil.

How does PLAN work? In September each PLAN pupil receives his program of studies for each subject area. A program of studies is a list of modules in a subject area which is to be completed by the pupil in a year's time. The program of studies is individualized for each pupil and is based on the pupil's past achievement, his academic goals, his vocational goals, his interests, his style of learning in an individualized setting, and state or local school district requirements. Of course, not all six factors are applicable to the program of studies of pupils in elementary schools.

During the first week of school PLAN pupils are busily meeting with their teachers to discuss their program of studies and possible modifications. Actually, the program of studies can be altered at any time during the year. Also, during the first week the pupils complete their orientation, which consists of diagnostic tests and information pertinent to their role in PLAN.

After a pupil has completed his orientation program, he begins work in the first module in his program of studies. A module is a set of instructional objectives that the pupil is expected to achieve. The manner in which he achieves these objectives depends on the teaching–learning unit the computer suggests or the pupil chooses. Teaching–learning units are designed to accommodate learning differences among pupils. The units provide alternate paths for the pupil to take to achieve the objectives. The module objectives never change; the way a pupil achieves these objectives depends on his teaching–learning unit. One teaching–learning unit may be designed for a pupil who is an excellent reader; another for a pupil who, judging from his past performance, does well with manipulative devices; another for a pupil who needs to be directed step by step in his achievement of objectives; and another for a pupil who is independent and resourceful and likes to find his own resources and make his own decisions about what he needs to do to attain the objectives.

Once a pupil has worked through a teaching–learning unit (usually about two weeks) he takes the module test. If the test results indicate mastery, the pupil can proceed to the next module in his program of studies. If he fails one objective or more, the pupil and the teacher meet to decide on the next action. This could be the assignment of a different teaching–learning unit, a review of the same teaching–learning unit, peer assistance, or tutoring by the teacher.

Little, if anything, is kept secret from the PLAN pupil. He is well aware of what is expected of him and how much time is allotted for completion of his assignments, for he participated in the planning. He is also aware of the flexibility provided under teaching–learning units and other instructional resources.

Someone entering a PLAN classroom would see pupils in a variety of activities. Some pupils might be engaged in discussions in large groups or small groups. Some pupils might be engaged in independent study. Some might be taking module tests. Some pupils might be working with a tutor or might be in a counseling session with the teacher. Some pupils might be listening to a tape or a record. Others might be viewing a filmstrip or a film, or conducting experiments. Room arrangements and organization of materials are important to the success of a PLAN classroom and are stressed in the teacher training conference. Pupils know what they can and cannot do in the individualized setting. They are responsible for retrieving their study materials or equipment and returning them after use.

PLAN teachers have devised their own way of helping pupils signal their need for assistance. Some have pupils raise their hands. Some have pupils raise a distress signal on the desk. Some may have pupils write their names on the chalkboard. You seldom see PLAN pupils standing in line waiting for teacher assistance because of the flexibility built into the program. In the majority of PLAN classrooms pupils are allowed to seek out peer assistance any time the need arises. Although the teacher is available to all pupils, she will not instruct each pupil each day. She plans her day to work with certain pupils at certain times and to check the progress of the other pupils.

In a self-contained fifth-grade classroom, pupils may be working on any one of the four subject areas and may switch at any desirable time. Many of these pupils plan their own weekly and daily schedule. A pupil may spend the whole morning on mathematics and the whole afternoon on science. He may spend the next day on language arts and social studies. The important thing is that the pupil is involved in his schedule and goal assignment.

It is certain that CAI and other developments of educational technology will have a strong impact on education in the future. The fact that computer programs contain all the principles that help students learn, have the ability to individualize instruction, and can serve any type of academic material would seem to make their applicability and value virtually unlimited. In addition, as Ohanian (1971) has stated regarding educational technology,

> if these projects do no more than move American education in many schools from its deathbed of undifferentiated, teacher-dominated, verbal and print-oriented instruction toward differentiated, teacher–child administered, and multi-sensory and multi-media instructions, then the experiments will indeed have produced a revolution of historic proportions [p.196].

SUGGESTED READINGS

Anderson, G. J.   Effects of classroom social climate on individual learning. *American Educational Research Journal,* 1970, **7**, 135–152.

Deep, D.   The computer can help individualize instruction. *Elementary School Journal,* 1970, **70**, 351–358.

Feldman, D. H., & Sears, P. S.   Effects of computer-assisted instruction on children's behavior. *Educational Technology,* 1970, **10**, 11–14.

Flanders, N. A.   Interaction analysis and inservice training. *Journal of Experimental Education,* 1968, **37** (1), 126–133.

Gage, N. L.   An analytical approach to research on instructional methods. *Phi Delta Kappan,* 1968, **49**, 601–606. Reprinted in H. D. Thornburg (Ed.), *School learning and instruction: Readings.* Monterey, Calif.: Brooks/Cole, 1973, chap. 7.

Gagné, R. M.   Instruction based on research in learning. *Engineering Education,* 1971, **61**, 519–523. Reprinted in H. D. Thornburg (Ed.), *School learning and instruction: Readings.* Monterey, Calif.: Brooks/Cole, 1973, chap. 7.

Heimer, R. T.   Conditions of learning in mathematics: Sequence theory development. *Review of Educational Research,* 1969, **39**, 493–508.

Koran, M. L., Snow, R. E., & McDonald, F. J.   Teacher aptitude and observational learning of a teaching skill. *Journal of Educational Psychology,* 1971, **62**, 219–228.

Ober, R. L.   The nature of interaction analysis. *High School Journal,* 1967, **51**, 7–16.

Ohanian, V.   Educational technology: A critique. *Elementary School Journal,* 1971, **71**, 183–197. Reprinted in H. D. Thornburg (Ed.), *School learning and instruction: Readings.* Monterey, Calif.: Brooks/Cole, 1973, chap. 7.

Popham, W. J., & Husek, T. R.   Implications of criterion-referenced measurement. *Journal of Educational Measurement,* 1969, **6**, 1–9.

Seltzer, R. A. Computer-assisted instruction—What it can and cannot do. *American Psychologist,* 1971, **26,** 373–377.

Stolurow, L. M. SOCRATES, A computer-based instructional system in theory and research. *Journal of Experimental Education,* 1968, **37** (1), 102–117.

APPENDIX A

Measurement and Evaluation of Pupil Achievement in the Classroom

"Let me not mince words. Almost all educators feel that testing is a necessary part of education. I wholly disagree." This rather bold statement was made by John Holt in his latest book, *The Underachieving School* (1969), in which he argues against testing, grading, fixed curricula, compulsory school attendance, and other such policies that tend to separate learning from life. Few educators will deny that many teachers and principals in our schools encourage and, in some instances, thrive on the propagation of meaningless routines and rituals that are traditionally thought to be sacred adjuncts to learning. Lesson plans that are apparently successful are used repeatedly, dog-eared true-false tests are rationalized as good enough for another class, and scoring methods and interpretations are frequently borrowed from one of the teacher's former teachers without too much thought or understanding of what effect they might have on the present learning situation and students. In many respects, education has become a routine and almost mechanical process, depersonalized and detached from life.

Today, we have too many children crammed into a single classroom, where

The original draft of this appendix was prepared by Robert A. Karabinus, Northern Illinois University.

one teacher is expected to be an inspiration and guide to all children and at all times. To personalize instruction under such conditions is difficult without many accompanying changes in the learning environment. New teaching methods and learning environments must be developed and used for the mass education era of today, and the main portion of this book directs its attention to these matters. This section of appendix materials is concerned with a specific aspect of the new thinking in education today— that of the so-called measurement process. Specifically, testing and evaluating in the classroom must be viewed differently; these processes must be conceived and constructed with learning, reinforcement, and motivation as the primary considerations and, thereby, integrated so closely to the teaching–learning process that there is no need to use stereotyped and time-worn testing and evaluative devices.

The learning process is a complex array of forces, acting on and interacting with the child, with the end result of a change in his behavior (intellectual, emotional, and/or physical) in the direction of the educational objectives established by the instructor. Measurement is simply an attempt to describe quantitatively the behavior or, more specifically, the change of behavior. Many critics believe it impossible to quantify human behavior and argue that paper–pencil tests are artificial, removed from learning, psychologically damaging (because of student fear and misuse of test results), and noninterpretable. But some level of either qualitative or quantitative assessment of behavioral change (or progress) is necessary for the individual and society; for both positive and negative feedback (compliments and redirection) are necessary to learning. Each person needs to know or feel how well he is doing compared to his own or others' expectations, so that he may be reinforced and motivated (and may, therefore, learn) when these expectations are met or surpassed. It cannot be overemphasized that measurement expressed as reinforcement and motivation is an essential part of the learning process.

By definition, the term *measurement* is restricted to quantitative assessment in which ordinal numbers* are applied to data. Usually, qualitative assessment is closely tied to *evaluation,* which is a more comprehensive term than "measurement." In other words, evaluation is measurement plus a value judgment; decisions about the degree of "goodness" or "importance" of certain behavioral changes are made as a result of careful study of all the data available to the teacher. Most of these evaluative data are also quantitative in nature—even feelings about a student are often quantified

---

* *Ordinal numbers* are numbers that indicate rank order only, as opposed to numbers that indicate categories or numbers that assume equal-interval units as found on rulers. The item or person that is rated highest is given the rank of one, second highest, the rank of two, and so on.

by the teacher in an attempt to make that data compatible with and comparable to the preponderance of other measurement and evaluative information. The grading and marking systems of our society are simply translations of these often complex evaluations into meaningful symbols.

Many problems arise in the total process of evaluation, from testing and quantification of student behavior all the way to the interpretation of that data for grade decisions. Some of these and their solutions will be explored in the following pages.

MEASUREMENT PRACTICES AND PROBLEMS

At all levels of education, the determination and the meaning of marks have become serious issues. The problem is not new, but a decade ago there was little pressure on school administrations for study and improvement of the situation. Today, there is agitation coming from both students and teachers who are attempting to create real and meaningful learning situations that are evaluated in real and meaningful ways. In this section, we shall examine some of the practices, problems, and needs in measurement and evaluation at the three main educational levels—elementary, secondary, and college.

Elementary schools

In addition to teaching basic reading, writing, and arithmetic skills, the elementary school teacher is directly involved with the social development of the child in the classroom. Activities are planned to encourage group interaction in games as well as in work projects, and these activities are changed frequently to keep the children interested and alert. Academic training is often subtly cloaked within a game setting; and since attention spans are relatively short, there are no lectures of any length. There is constant oral communication between teacher and child and among the children, and the teacher faces the problem of trying to react constructively to several very active, boisterous, and inquisitive youngsters at the same time. When these children are neglected, or when proper individual attention is temporarily or permanently denied, behavioral problems of various kinds result. What about the resulting measurement problems? How can the teacher quantify accurately all the behaviors observed, measure the academic and social changes, and then make the required evaluations?

Because of the nature of the elementary-school curricula, few if any written tests are prepared by the teacher. Instead, the tests are printed and standardized by test companies or come from the ubiquitous workbook. Scoring is done by the test company for the former and by simple totals or percentages for the latter. Exact translation of these scores into letter grades is seldom expected or requested in most elementary schools today. Some schools still use a marking system of H, S, and U and send home the traditional report card, but many more employ periodic oral or written progress reports that provide with general aptitude and readiness test scores, grade-level achievement scores, averages from worksheets in various areas (word skills, fractions, social studies, and so on), analyses of sociograms,* and miscellaneous comments related to behavioral patterns. Therefore, the major problem of trying to reduce a complex array of observations and data to a single meaningful mark is eliminated. These progress reports have proven to be a very time-consuming procedure for the teacher, but they are also very rewarding, in that parents have an opportunity to learn much more about their children's school activities and learning progress than a single series of marks could possibly convey. Likewise, the teachers have a chance to listen to the parents' concerns and reports of specific home experiences, which, in turn, help the teacher better understand each child's total learning environment. (Of course, these parent–teacher conferences are also found, on a somewhat more limited scale, in those schools that retain the traditional, more formal marking and report-card system.)

It would seem, then, that with this increasingly popular progress-report system, the needs for communication of results of student learning to parents and for simpler and more flexible evaluative procedures for grade-school teachers are being successfully met, at least to some degree. There will always be the continuing debate about whether aptitude (IQ) scores should be given the parents, and how precise the teachers should be in reporting test scores or percentiles. Nevertheless, the children quickly learn how they are doing in the various subjects; they know who is best, second best, and worst in arithmetic, spelling, and baseball. Competition is keen and even exploited in the classroom and through the parents to motivate the children. A child also senses within himself and through the reactions of his peers, teachers, and parents when he is learning more quickly or more thoroughly than others.

The need to communicate evaluations to the school itself for official records

---

* A *sociogram* is a sociometric device that attempts to discover the patterns of choice and rejection among the individuals making up a group—that is, the ones who are chosen most often as friends or leaders, those who are rejected by others, how the group subdivides into clusters or cliques, and so on.

is met by summaries of the teacher–parent progress reports. These reports may be somewhat bulky, but they are informative and useful for future references by parents, teachers, and counselors.

Secondary schools

In the secondary school, a different set of problems and needs must be met in the evaluation procedures. First of all, the curriculum is more subject-oriented than at the elementary level, and the measurement and evaluation procedures must be more precise. In addition, students are taught and evaluated by many different people instead of the one teacher, and although the school system may try to encourage some form of consistency in measuring and evaluating student progress, there is inevitably a considerable divergence of thought and approaches among the various teachers. Finally, the use of teacher-made tests is much higher in secondary schools, though there is also much use of publisher-prepared achievement tests and workbook drills. In some high schools, there is also an attempt to measure such behaviors as pleasantness, cooperativeness, promptness, interest, and attendance—usually summarized in a separate mark for "citizenship." A single mark that represents this composite of academic work and social behavior is always rather difficult to measure and interpret, and, generally, the better procedure is to give separate marks for the two main areas of academic and social deportment.

Since testing is more frequent in high school and quarterly grade reports to students and parents are generally part of the evaluative procedure, high-school students frequently become preoccupied with grades and begin to value them above learning. And because of the pressures to evaluate achievement in a rather precise way, teachers contribute to this preoccupation. Grades are especially emphasized for those students following the college preparatory programs, since competition for college entrance and scholarship is keen. The fact that high-school grades (or rank in class, which is based directly on those grades) correlate with college grades only about 25 percent of the time suggests that there are other important aspects of high-school achievement that are either not being measured or are being measured inadequately.

The making of effective testing instruments is one of the most important skills for high-school teachers to acquire. Because of the time-consuming nature of test preparation, it is often given much less attention than is required. Teachers all too often think of their tests as necessary evils and prepare and give them without sufficient thought to their contribution to the total learning experiences of the students. The general result is that students acquire negative feelings about the abstractness and artificiality of tests and grading procedures, and teachers often make refined judgments from tests that do not really measure the educational objectives established for the courses.

Colleges

At the college level, courses and evaluative procedures and standards are as individually different as the professors who teach them. The majority of classroom tests are teacher-made and tend to be as sophisticated and effective as the professor's understanding of the subject matter and the learning process. Indeed, professors are characteristically known by their tests rather than by their teaching.

Grades themselves are often given more emphasis at the college level because survival at this optional education level is at stake. Doing poorly or flunking out has very significant social implications. Many college teachers and administrators who are concerned about the inequities and negative effects of this emphasis are attending workshops and seminars devoted to the improvement of assessment techniques at the college level. In addition, some colleges are experimenting with alternative grading systems that range from the very simple pass–fail to a complex system of 25 grade points. Others are attempting to do without grades entirely by merely certifying completion of academic programs. The problems that arise from these different systems are mostly in the articulation of student achievement to other schools. Colleges that institute new and often esoteric approaches to evaluation must all deal with the question of their responsibility in giving qualitative evaluations to other colleges, graduate schools, and employers.

TEST INSTRUMENTS

Standardized tests

Standardized aptitude and achievement tests are commonly used by both teachers and counselors in the public schools. The word *standardized* refers here to a professional test developed by an educational publisher and usually accompanied by a set of norms that helps the teacher interpret student scores by comparing them with the scores of many other similar students. The primary advantage of using standardized tests is that they are developed by experts to measure common educational objectives. Teachers usually feel that they can rely more on the completeness and fairness of the score results of such tests than they could on their own test-making efforts. The test publishers also tell how reliable and valid their tests are—that is, how accurately and consistently the tests measure the stated objectives. Two other advantages of standardized tests are the fact that comparative scores are available to aid in the interpretation of students' scores and that most test publishers offer scoring services, which relieve teachers of the burden of correcting papers and transforming scores into meaningful charts or percentiles.

There are also some disadvantages to using standardized tests: (1) The objectives that teachers want to measure may not be included in any standardized test, or (2) the tests may cover areas that were not included in the course. It is rather difficult to tailor a standardized test to fit a particular learning situation. A teacher who wants to approach certain subject areas differently from the standardized test has little choice but to devise his own testing instrument. There is always the temptation for the teacher to give professionally made tests, regardless of the particular classroom situation, because these tests remove the burden of item writing and scoring for the teacher. However, standardized tests that do not relate directly to a classroom's educational objectives are more likely to be invalid measures of the student learning that is occurring. For this reason, score results from standardized achievement tests should not be used to determine student grades. Teachers and counselors should use the results primarily for diagnostic purposes and academic counseling. This is true for aptitude, personality, and intelligence tests as well.

Despite these limitations and problems, the standardized achievement test does have an important role to play in education. It is helpful to teachers at the end of each year for evaluating the general progress of students, and it is useful to both the teacher and the school administrator in evaluating the effectiveness of the school's curricula. Comparing ability or IQ scores with achievement scores will also help teachers and counselors diagnose learning difficulties of children.

Teachers should acquaint themselves thoroughly with reliability, validity, normative data in test manuals. In addition, school systems should consider the preparation of their own local norms from year to year for comparison with the national norms found in the test manuals. Local norms are often preferred over national norms because they have more direct interpretive value for a particular school.

Teacher-made tests

For measurement of specific academic achievement in the classroom, the teacher has little choice but to devise his own testing instrument. Teacher-made tests are of all kinds and lengths and are used not only for measurement of learning but also for motivation and reinforcement. The main purpose of these tests is, of course, the determination of student grades.

There are many problems directly related to this purpose, and not the least of these is preparing the test items. Before writing items, teachers need to know what behaviors to measure. In other words, they need to know not only what they are trying to teach but also the nature of the learning situation. If a statement of the objectives and conditions of the learning is made before any instruction takes place, writing tests becomes a relatively easy task. The statement of behavioral objectives also ensures that subsequent tests measure not only areas of content but also the levels or domains of thinking involved in the learning situations. The latter are difficult to include in a test, but they are every bit as important as the usual content areas in the measurement and evaluation of learning.

The most common types of test items are true–false, multiple-choice, completion, short-answer supply, and essay. Although the first of these is still used on a small scale in elementary grades, it is being replaced by the more sophisticated multiple-choice variety at all other levels. All too frequently, the true–false test is comprised of statements lifted verbatim from textbooks, and when they are used out of context, they often have ambiguous meanings. The true–false test also restricts measurement to the knowledge level of thinking—rote memory of facts. The well-constructed multiple-choice test is easy to mark and can cover a large number of thinking levels, but it is limited to measurement of recognition abilities. This test type should be replaced by the completion or short-answer supply type if recall of information is desired. If analysis, synthesis, and evaluation objectives are desired, then the essay-type question is best. It gives the student freedom in which to think about and develop his answer. One problem with short-answer supply and essay tests is the care with which a teacher must prepare each item. It really takes serious thought to express precisely the response that is expected from the student. Words can so easily be misunderstood, and students frequently answer a question to their satisfaction only to find out later that the instructor's intention or interpretation of the question was quite different.

Another problem with essay tests is the grading. It is difficult for a teacher to be objective and not be influenced by extraneous factors, such as neatness, modes of expression, knowledge of student's previous work. Having a clearly outlined key and reading the answers *seriatim** will help to ensure consistent evaluations. Other techniques can be useful in essay grading, but the main thing to realize is that it will take no longer to do a good job of grading essay papers than it would have taken to prepare an equally long multiple-choice test. In the latter case, the preparation time is long and the scoring time short, which allows for quick return of tests to students. In the former, the preparation time is relatively short and the scoring time long.

There is no one test type that is ideal for all occasions, and a teacher should offer a variety for two reasons: (1) The level and kind of behavioral objective should dictate the test type, and, in most courses, there is a wide variety of levels and types of desired behavioral objectives. (2) Students may have special skills with certain types of tests—for example, skill in writing (essay) or skill in logically figuring out the correct given answer by careful elimination of poor distractors (multiple-choice)—and, therefore, the use of only one type of test throughout a course can work to the advantage or disadvantage of individual students as a result of factors other than those directly related to real academic achievement.

Most basic educational-measurement books give guidelines to help the teacher write test items that are clear and carefully constructed to have content validity. The simplified variations of item-analysis** techniques found in Gronlund (1965) and Diederich (1963) are highly recommended. A teacher can also learn much about the effectiveness of test items from the students themselves. If given the opportunity, students will freely offer information about the items they found misleading, vague, or otherwise faulty. In fact, they will fight for every extra score point they can obtain.

TEST SCORING AND INTERPRETATION

Once tests have been prepared and given, scoring the results and interpreting those scores to students, parents, and other institutions become primary concerns. On an objective test, the number of correct items is usually the score. Such data is termed a *raw score.**** A raw score is not very meaningful unless it is accompanied by

---

* *Seriatim* means in a series, or one following another. In other words, a teacher reads all student responses to question one before going on to all of the responses to question two, and so on.

** *Item analysis* usually involves determining the difficulty value and the discriminating power of each test item, as well as its correlation with some objective criterion.

*** A *raw score* is the initial quantitative data obtained in marking a test; that is, the number of correct responses, or the number of correct responses minus some fraction of wrong answers if correction for guessing is deemed necessary.

additional information about the test, such as the rank of the test score in the class, which, in turn, could be translated into percentiles. For example, if Johnny tells his mother that he earned a 41 on a test that day, the mother may be disappointed; for in her mind 60 or 70 would be a passing grade. If Johnny explains that there were only 45 items on the test and that he was fourth highest in the class of 25, it would make quite a difference to the mother. Moreover, if the score is stated as the 84th percentile (4/25ths = .16), which means that 84 percent of the scores fell below Johnny's score, Johnny's mother would probably be delighted.

Another way to put meaning into raw scores is to state the *range** of scores. If the lowest score in Johnny's class was 28 and the highest 43, the range is 15 points, which is simply the difference between the high and the low scores. Still another approach to indicating relative positions of raw scores is to determine how far a particular score deviates from the arithmetical average, or *mean,* of the set of scores. If the mean of Johnny's class was 36, then his score of 41 would be recognized immediately as being better than the average, although he and his mother would not know how much better, other than that it was 5 score points higher. The most sophisticated measure of dispersion using the mean as reference point is the *standard deviation,* which is calculated by taking the square root of the average of the squared deviations. The standard deviation is described as a score interval above and below the mean that encompasses about 68 percent of all the scores, or 34 percent on each side of the mean. For example, given a mean of 36 and a standard deviation of 5, about 68 percent of all the scores in Johnny's class fall between 31 and 41 (5 score units below and above the mean), and Johnny's score of 41 is one standard deviation above the mean, which could be translated as being the 84th percentile (34 percent above the mean, which is the 50th percentile).

A most useful tool for the teacher in recording and evaluating test scores is the transformation of all raw scores into *standard scores,*** which allow the teacher

---

* *Range* is a measure of the dispersion or spread of scores, specifically the difference between the highest and lowest scores obtained by a group of persons on a given test. The *10–90 interpercentile range* would include only the middle 80 percent of the scores and is used to eliminate some extremely high and low scores in order to give a more representative measure. The *IQR (interquartile range)* would include only the middle 50 percent of the scores, and the *SIQR (semi-interquartile range)* would be half this value.

** *Standard score* refers to raw scores which are converted in a variety of ways to a common or universal form for convenience, comparability, and ease of interpretation. The simplest type of standard score is that which expresses the relation of the deviation of an individual's raw score from the average score of his group to the standard deviation of the scores of the group. For example, a standard score (z), found by subtracting the raw score from the mean and dividing it by the standard deviation, would indicate the number of deviation units a given score is from the mean. Thus, a raw score of 37, with a group mean of 35 and a standard deviation of 2, would be converted to a z score of 1. The score of 37 is one standard

to perceive immediately the positions of all scores relative to the classroom mean. For example, if we use the standard-score model of a mean of 50 and a standard deviation of 10, Johnny's raw score of 41, which was one standard deviation above the mean, can be described as a standard score of 60 (10 points above the mean of 50, or a total of 60). By converting the raw scores of all tests and quizzes given during a semester into standard scores, a teacher can easily trace the relative achievement of her students; for each standard score, in itself, would tell the teacher whether the score earned was above or below the class as well as how far above or below. Standardization of test scores also automatically equates the weights of all tests given, so that the teacher can adjust the importance of the tests by simple multiplication of scores. For example, if the second test given during the semester was twice as important as all the others, the teacher merely doubles the standard scores of that test to automatically give it twice the weight of any other test. Most basic educational-measurement and statistics books contain tables that can be used for quick translation of percentiles to standard scores or of standard deviation units (z units) to percentiles.

A popular but rather coarse version of standard scoring used by many of the school systems today is the *stanine scale* (short for "standard nine"). A set of raw scores arranged in rank order (high to low) are divided into nine levels—the ninth containing the top 4 percent of the scores; the eighth, the next 7 percent; the third, 12 percent; the second, 7 percent; and the first, 4 percent. The mean stanine is the fifth, and the standard deviation unit is 2 stanines. Johnny's score would fall in stanine 7, one standard deviation unit (2 stanines) above the mean. Notice that the distribution of stanines is symmetrical, which may or may not be characteristic of the original data. However, the fact that the symmetry is forced with stanines, while with most other kinds of standard scores the distribution remains essentially the same as that of the raw data, need not concern the practicing teacher.

Unfortunately, all our attempts to make raw scores more meaningful by some kind of transformation do not make the original scores more accurate. Johnny's score of 41 is most likely not an accurate measure of his achievement. He might well have guessed at some of the answers, just as he might have been confused by ambiguities in some items. Moreover, there are countless other factors that might have been influencing Johnny's thinking when he took the test, such as other worries or disturbances in the classroom. In other words, we would like to believe that the score of 41

---

deviation unit above the mean. In a z-score model, the mean is always 0; the standard deviation, 1. In T-score model, the mean is always 50; the standard deviation, 10. Other models are as follows: mean of 100, standard deviation of 20; mean of 500, standard deviation of 100; mean of 5, standard deviation of 2.

is Johnny's "true" score on the test, but we know very well that it is only an obtained score at a particular point in time. If we could estimate how much error there is in assuming that 41 is the true score, we would be able to make a fairer evaluation of his achievement in terms of both the achievement of the other students and the scores of his previous tests.

A measurement error is not difficult to determine, if the teacher can somehow estimate the reliability of the test as a whole. Two rather simple ways to obtain reliability coefficients that attempt to measure the internal consistency of tests are the *Spearman–Brown Prophecy formula* and the *Kuder–Richardson formulas.** The main assumption of the first technique is that when a given test is split (odd–even or first–second halves), the two parts are homogeneous or parallel—that is, they are both measuring the same content or behavioral objectives. With this assumption reasonably certain, the correlation between the halves is then put into a formula to estimate the reliability coefficient of the whole test. The formula is as follows:

$$\text{reliability} = \left[\frac{2 \times \text{correlation of the halves}}{1 + \text{correlation of the halves}}\right].$$

For example, if the correlation between odd–even halves in Johnny's test is found to be .65, the corrected correlation or reliability of the whole test would be $\frac{2 \times .65}{1 + .65}$, or .79. Similarly, using a simplified form of the Kuder–Richardson formula #21,

$$\text{reliability} = 1 - \left[\frac{\text{mean (number of items} - \text{mean)}}{\text{number of items} \times \text{variance}}\right]^{**}$$

---

* The *Spearman–Brown Prophecy formula* permits estimation of the reliability of a test that is lengthened or shortened by any amount, from the known reliability of a test of specified length. Its most common application is in the estimation of reliability of an entire test from the correlation between two halves of the test (*split-half reliability*).

The *Kuder–Richardson formulas* permit estimation of the reliability of a test from information about the individual items in the test, or from the mean score, standard deviation, and number of items in the test. Because the Kuder–Richardson formulas permit estimation of reliability from a single administration of a test, without the labor involved in dividing the test into halves, their use has become common in test development. The Kuder–Richardson formulas are not appropriate for estimating the reliability of speeded tests.

** *Variance* is the square of the standard deviation.

we find that the reliability estimate is

$$1 - \left[\frac{36\,(45 - 36)}{45 \times 25} \right] = .71.$$

The Kuder–Richardson technique has an additional assumption that the items of the test are equally difficult. Of course, these assumptions of homogeneity and equal-item difficulty may not be completely satisfied, but in most tests they are met sufficiently for the teacher to make use of either or both of these methods to estimate test reliability.

Knowing the reliability estimate—the measure of precision or accuracy in the test—we can then determine the amount of error present in the test by finding what is called the *standard error of measurement** (the standard deviation of the distribution of errors in the test). The formula for the standard error measurement is as follows:

$$\text{the standard deviation of the text} \times \sqrt{1 - \text{reliability coefficient}}.$$

In the example cited above, the standard deviation was 5 and the reliability estimate somewhere between .71 and .79. If we assume that the reliability was exactly between the two estimates, or .75, the standard error of measurement would be 2.5. We could take Johnny's score of 41, then, and say that his "true" score is probably somewhere between 38.5 and 43.5—in other words, within a range of 2.5 points on either side of his obtained score. Technically, the probability of Johnny's true score lying within this range is only about 68 percent, however. If we wanted to increase that probability to 95 percent, the range would be approximately doubled, or from 36 to 46 (45, since that was the highest possible score).

The point of all of this discussion and calculation is to help the teacher interpret obtained raw scores more intelligently, which means to think of test scores in terms of *ranges.* This is called the *standard error of difference,* which can be calculated for a single test by the following formula:

$$\sqrt{(\text{standard error of measurement})^2 \times 2}$$

* The *standard error* is an estimate of the magnitude of the "error of measurement" in a score—that is, the amount by which an obtained score differs from a hypothetical true score. The standard error is an amount such that in about two-thirds of the cases the obtained score would not differ by more than one standard error from the true score.

Using the above example, then, we have $\sqrt{6.5 \times 2}$, or 3.6, which means that there would have to be 3.6 (or 4) points between any two test scores before we could be reasonably (68 percent) confident that the two scores were indeed different. With this information, Johnny's score of 41 could not be naively declared as higher than a classmate's score of 38. In other words, the apparent difference of 3 points might only be a chance difference, and a decision to give a higher grade to 41 than to 38 or even 37 would be a serious grading error.

To assist the teacher who is aware of measurement errors but has little time to calculate them for given tests, Educational Testing Service has published a pamphlet entitled *Short-Cut Statistics for Teacher-made Tests* (Diederich, 1964), which contains tables that can be used for quick estimates of both reliability coefficients and measurement errors. These tables are highly recommended as useful guides to test-score interpretations.

As we have noted, guessing is another interfering factor in test-score interpretations. Although it is extremely difficult for a student to bluff an answer in a supply or essay examination, guessing is quite common and even encouraged in true–false and multiple-choice tests. However, it is generally not necessary for the teacher to make any correction for guessing, because research has found that the ranking of scores for all students will remain the same after correction of the scores for the guessing factor. Still, in some situations in which erratic patterns of guessing are expected—that is, where some students are likely to guess on many of the items and others guess on very few—it might be beneficial to correct the scores for guessing. The usual formula for this adjustment is

$$R_c = R - \left[\frac{W}{k-1} \right],$$

in which R_c is the corrected number of right answers, R is the number of correct responses, W is the number of wrong responses, and k is the number of alternative answers possible for each item. In the test cited above, Johnny's corrected score would be

$$41 - \left[\frac{4}{5-1} \right] = 40,$$

assuming that each item in the test had five possible answers.

It is best to tell students in advance whether there is to be a correction for guessing. If nothing is said by the teacher, the more aggressive students may do some guessing and improve their scores while the timid ones will refrain from guessing in fear of hurting their scores. And in these circumstances, the correction for guessing would reward the students who do the guessing (unless, of course, it was done most carelessly).

One additional comment should be made about corrections for guessing. It is important in many classroom situations for the teacher to calculate a *chance score*** (one that could be obtained by pure guesswork) for every test, so that a passing grade will not be given to such a score. Chance scores are calculated by multiplying the probability of guessing the correct answer by the number of items in the test. For example, in a true–false test of 20 items, the probability of guessing the correct answer would be 50–50, or .5, and the chance score would therefore be 10. A score of 10, then should not be considered a passing score. Similarly, in a multiple-choice test of 20 items, with four alternatives for each item, the probability of guessing the correct answer for each item would be .25, and the chance score would therefore be only 5. Such a low score would undoubtedly be considered failing.

CRITERION-REFERENCED VERSUS NORM-REFERENCED MEASUREMENT

Since the publication of Glaser's famous article (1963), which pointed to the inadequacy of existing measurement instruments and the need to develop both theory and tests based on performance, an increasing number of articles by educators have discussed the merits of criterion-referenced measurement instead of norm-referenced measurement. Norm-referenced tests are used to identify a student's performance in relation to the performance of other students on the same test. Criterion-referenced tests are used to identify a student's performance in relation to a specified expectation or standard. Such tests are usually constructed on the basis of specified behavioral objectives and content areas to measure the degree of mastery that has taken place. Although the relatively new criterion-referenced measurement theory is proposed for

---

* A *chance score* is the score that is acquired by chance alone, assuming no knowledge of the subject matter in answering a question or a series of questions. For a single item, the chance score would be the probability (50–50) of guessing it right; for a series of items, the chance score would be the probability of guessing each item correctly multiplied by the number of items in the series.

its ability to evaluate qualities not being measured by traditional norm-referenced measurement techniques, there is still some question as to whether it is the inadequacy of norm-referenced tests to measure outcomes that has promoted the suggested change, or whether it is the new instructional approaches in the schools that, in turn, require new measurement techniques.

Intelligence tests, achievement tests, aptitude tests, and most teacher-made tests are norm-referenced. They have established means and standard deviations, and an individual student's performance is assessed by comparing it to the norm. In criterion-referenced measurement, a performance level is specified for an individual student somewhere on a continuum from no learning to perfect learning. If the learner meets the designated level, he has mastered the task and has met the criterion. Let us consider the following illustration of each measurement technique:

A classroom teacher has specified two behavioral objectives for a teaching–learning task:

1. The student will be able to multiply whole numbers to find distances.
2. The student will be able to find the area of an object.

After learning the relevant concepts (level 6 learning), the students were taught the following two rules (level 7 learning):

a. To find a product, multiply the two factors available; that is, $f \times f = p$.
b. To find area, multiply length times width; that is, $l \times w = A$.

The students were then given the following problem:

A swimming pool is 75 feet long and 40 feet wide. How many square feet are in the swimming pool? How far does Mark travel in swimming twice the length of the pool?

To measure learning outcomes, the teacher will grade the correctness of the two answers computed by each student. Would the teacher use norm-referenced or criterion-referenced measurement? Either may be used, although criterion-referenced technique is preferable. We shall examine a norm-referenced measurement first.

It is very impractical to attempt to grade an assignment with two answers on a norm-referenced basis, so, for illustrative purposes, let us assume that these two rules are to be applied in 20 problems. First, the teacher plots each score to determine the range of student responses within the class of 32:

Total scores	Number of students
19	3
18	2
17	4
16	4
15	6
14	6
13	3
11	2
10	2
	32

The mean score for the class is found to be 15.0, and individual grades could be computed from this figure. But what does this tell the teacher about the learning of each student? One student correctly answered 14 problems, which approximates the mean, and the teacher might then give that student a C and proceed with him to the next learning task. But suppose this student applied rule 1 correctly to all 10 problems representing that rule but used rule 2 correctly only four times. Has the student sufficiently learned? Obviously, the teacher could be satisfied with his learning of rule 1 and its relevant concepts, but what about rule 2? Without such diagnosis, it is easy for the teacher to assume that the student has learned all of the material at an average level and to proceed to the next task, leaving the student inadequately prepared.

Considering this same student's performance using a criterion-referenced measurement, the student's test is analyzed first in reference to his past achievements and not to the entire class. The test is then analyzed in terms of whether the stated performance objectives were met. This second procedure would reveal that rule 1 was sufficiently mastered and rule 2 was not. This analysis tells the teacher not only that the student was unable to find area but also that he may not have learned the necessary prerequisite concepts for formulating the rule. In other words, the reason that the student did not apply rule 2 correctly is that he had not really learned the rule. The instructional implications for the teacher are, of course, to go back over the material and make sure that the student acquires the relevant skills and knowledge and then to remeasure the student's ability.

In using criterion-referenced measurement, the teacher must be cautious not to equate mastery with perfection. Since criterion-based performance is on a continuum, it is logical that teachers specify certain percentages as acceptable for mastering a specified performance objective. If, for instance, the learning of the above rules was the expected performance, the teacher might specify 100 percent mastery. Certainly, the teacher would expect 100 percent mastery of the relevant concepts that went into the rules. On the other hand, if the terminal behavior is to memorize a list of words, the criterion level might be set more realistically at 80 percent (Hackett, 1971). The end product of criterion-referenced measurement is, of course, the same as that of norm-referenced measurement—a score or percentage that must usually be translated into conventional symbols or marks.

Criterion-referenced measurement may be easily accommodated within several current teaching–learning trends:

1. Within Gagné's learning hierarchy, mastery from one level to the next is necessary for advanced learning to occur. Recognition of learning deficiencies at any level provides the teacher with an instructional direction.

2. Within the theory of instruction proposed in this book, behavioral objectives are an important instructional procedure, and behavioral objectives are, in fact, performance objectives, because they specify the desired terminal behavior of the student.

3. Because computer-assisted instruction is highly individualized and based on mastery learning, criterion-referenced feedback is essential to effective computer programming.

4. With all individualized instruction, the student must be at least initially evaluated on some basis other than norm-referenced measurement if individualization is to be meaningful.

MARKING SYSTEMS

A grade or mark is an established symbol that represents the final evaluation of a given set of educational objectives. A marking system, then, remains useful as a means of communication so long as the marks are based on valid evaluation and have real meaning for the persons involved. In the section on scores, there was considerable emphasis given to the problem of interpretation of scores and, specifically, the recognition of errors of measurement; for marks cannot be more accurate than the score data from which they are derived.

The most common method of grading in schools today is the *five-point system,* with letter grades of A, B, C, D, and F. There are variations that involve pluses and minuses and other marks for incompletes and withdrawals, but, essentially, there is only this single set of five marks to measure classroom achievement. Since the various factors that influence the evaluation of achievement are different from teacher to teacher, it is quite likely that if different teachers were to evaluate the same learning experiences in the classroom, there would be a markedly different set of final marks established for the students. In some cases, only test scores would be used to determine grades; in others, student interest, personality, attention, participation, and so on would strongly bias the evaluation. The differences in evaluations would also depend on the teacher's sophistication in norm- and criterion-referenced measurement. The track system now in practice in many high schools is already confronting this problem with terminal students who decide they want to enter college. The point is that the actual (not necessarily stated) educational objectives are different for each teacher in each classroom, and the method of measuring them is likely also to be different. Marks reflect these differences and, therefore, cannot be considered meaningful and valid for comparisons from classroom to classroom, let alone from one institution to another.

In an attempt to resolve this difficulty, many schools have established two or more sets of marks for each course. One set of marks is designed to reflect only the academic achievement of the student; the other(s) reflects the nonintellectual factors that are considered relevant. As helpful as this division of objectives has been, there remain many serious problems. How do teachers prevent nonintellectual behaviors from influencing their evaluations of academic areas? How are ability and aptitude separated from achievement? Is progress or growth during the course more important than the achievement level reached at the end of the course? Is achievement to be measured by comparisons with other student achievement in the same class, all previous classes that the instructor has had, or some ideal class of students conceived by the instructor? Further complications are involved when some students are placed in special curricula, such as honors or remedial. What are the grading standards to be for these situations? If the standards are different, and they usually are, what effect do these marks have when other educational institutions and employers compare the credentials of these students with other students' marks?

As we noted earlier, many professional educators today feel that our present grading system, in fact our whole approach to evaluation in the classroom, needs to be changed. Unfortunately, it is a lot easier to criticize the status quo than to come up with constructive alternatives. Experimental approaches range widely, from one extreme of increased subdivisions in marks, to the other of no evaluative marks at all, just a statement of completion. For example, some colleges are reporting grades by using grade points only. In a 4-point system, in which an A is 4 points, a B, 3 points, and so on, marks such as 3.3 or 2.7 are entered on the grade reports for each course. The rationale is that grade-point marks are more flexible and grade-point averages are more precise. It sounds logical enough, but the main difficulty still remains in the precision or accuracy of the original course mark. Knowing what we do know about measurement errors connected with classroom testing, how can we believe that a grade-point mark is really accurate? Even professional test writers cannot claim such accuracy.

More moderate attempts to gain precision in marking systems are found in the use by many secondary schools and colleges of pluses and minuses on letter grades, so that the number of letter grades can be increased to 15 if F minus is used. The obvious problem with this approach is again one of consistency in interpretation. Are the intervals between all consecutive marks equal, or is B— closer to B than it is to C+? Teachers naturally view these grades differently, so we still have ambiguity. However, even with these problems of accuracy and consistency of meaning, this system has important psychological advantages for both teachers and students. Students usually feel a lot better about earning a C+ rather than just a C, especially if they think they only deserved a C. Similarly, teachers feel they can give a little more meaning to their marks by using the plus and minus. On the other hand, teachers often have a considerable problem in justifying to a student the evaluation process that leads to a C+ rather than a B—.

Recognizing the obvious faults in these attempts to make marking systems more definitive, many schools are going the opposite direction and suggesting the use of only two marks—satisfactory–unsatisfactory or pass–fail. This type of marking, which is new to the secondary and college levels, is a simple approach and takes care of some of the measurement problems mentioned earlier, but it usually does not adequately satisfy students and parents. Students want to know how *well* they passed a course, not just that they passed it, and parents share their concern. What frequently happens, then, is that a third category—high pass or honors—is added to make a three-mark system.

Extending the pass–fail trend somewhat further, a few institutions are initiating the *competency approach*. When a certain competency level of achievement has been reached, the student's academic record will show that he has satisfied that requirement or completed that part of the curriculum. This criterion-referenced approach appears to satisfy all the measurement and scoring problems previously discussed, but, in actuality, it does not. In the classroom, the teacher still has to determine the point at which minimum competence is reached, and the likelihood that all teachers will agree in all classes as to that point of competence is unquestionably remote.

There is enough reason and good in any of these marking systems to justify their continued existence. There is also enough bad to justify continued criticisms. During the next several years, many more evaluation methods and marking systems will undoubtedly be tried in an attempt to solve the basic assessment problems of the classroom. The important elements that must be considered in any new approach are as follows:

1. *The student and his needs.* Evaluation procedures must give not only to educational objectives that are more meaningful to a student's life and society but also to the satisfaction of motivational and reinforcement needs of the student. In one way or another, students will have to be given the means to understand and gain insight into life processes and world problems, as well as to acquire the necessary academic and professional skills to survive in this world and to contribute to its destiny.

2. *Society and its needs.* Education is required in any modern society, and society has to have some way of knowing who can fill what positions to contribute services to its members. School systems have a responsibility, then, not only to train and educate but also to be able to communicate when and to what degree the training and education has been accomplished. Rapid and accurate articulation from school to school and from school to employer is necessary if adequate evaluations of a person's qualifications are to be made. Minimally, this requires accurate reporting of student achievement and progress, multiple levels of qualitative achievement, and consistent and meaningful use of symbols.

3. *Recognition of measurement and evaluation problems.* In addition to the measurement errors associated with test scores and the subjective elements that affect evaluations, there is the big question of what the mark really means. If quantitative techniques are to be used in the assessing process, then educational institutions must modify their methods of communicating evaluations to students, parents, and the outside world. Marking symbols must represent evaluations as accurately as possible and must take any inaccuracies into account.

The science teacher is troubled by the selection of the most appropriate way to assign marks and final grades. *Is there one way of grading that is distinctly preferable?*

Not really. Many educators do feel strongly that raw scores do not really tell the teacher the relative position of a student in a class. To find out how one student stands in relation to all others, the teacher must convert the raw score to a standard score, which reveals the relative position of an individual score to the class average or mean. Assignment of grades also depends on the teacher's philosophy of grading. If a teacher uses norm-referenced measurement, then the scores of every student must be calculated against one another. If criterion-referenced measurement is used, each student is individually measured against selected criteria and not against all other students. The latter is generally preferable if instruction is to be individualized and marking is to be truly evaluative.

If these considerations are taken seriously in the development of improved measurement and evaluation techniques, important strides will be made in solving many of the present problems.

APPENDIX B

Instrumentation of Bloom's and Krathwohl's Taxonomies for the Writing of Educational Objectives

During the past six or eight years an increased amount of attention has been given to the statement of educational objectives in behavioral terms both to facilitate the evaluation of educational programs and to improve the validity of the measures and scales utilized in the evaluation process (Metfessel & Michael, 1967; Michael & Metfessel, 1966). Although set up as a programmed learning text, Mager's (1962) *Preparing Instructional Objectives* has been one of the most useful guides to teachers and specialists in curriculum who sought help in stating the desired outcomes of instruction in behavioral language—in describing the kinds of specific and relatively terminal behaviors which the learner will be capable of exhibiting subsequent to his

From Newton S. Metfessel, W. B. Michael, and D. A. Kirsner, "Instrumentation of Bloom's and Krathwohl's Taxonomies for the Writing of Educational Objectives," *Psychology in the Schools,* 1969, **6** (3), 227–231. Reprinted with permission of the authors and the publisher.

exposure to a program of instruction. Another useful source has been the volume edited by Lindvall (1964) who, in collaboration with Nardozza and Felton (Lindvall, Nardozza, & Felton, 1964) not only prepared his own chapter concerned with the importance of specific objectives in curricular development, but also enlisted the aid of several distinguished educators, e.g., Krathwohl (1964) and Tyler (1964) with specialized interests in evaluation. Such efforts have essentially involved a fusion of curriculum design with the evaluation process in that curricular planning is described in terms of behavioral objectives that are necessary for the construction of valid tests and scales. The taxonomies provide the required model necessary to furnish meaningful evidence regarding the attainment of desired behavioral changes.

Although Krathwohl (1964) related the taxonomy of educational objectives in both the cognitive (Bloom, 1956) and the affective (Krathwohl, Bloom, & Masia, 1964) domains to curriculum building, he was able to present only a limited number of concrete illustrations, some of which Mager would probably challenge because of their relative lack of specificity. Admittedly, Krathwohl has made an important and helpful start in relating objectives to a meaningful and rather well-known conceptual framework. However, the writers believe that there exists a need for an instrumentation of the taxonomy of educational objectives within both the cognitive and affective domains—that is, a more clear-cut description of how the taxonomy can be implemented in the school setting. The approach utilized was the development of *behaviorally oriented* infinitives which, when combined with given objects, would form a basis for meaningful, cohesive, and operational statements.

Thus the essential purpose of this paper was to show how specific behavioral objectives can be formulated within the hierarchy of the major levels and sublevels of the taxonomies of educational objectives as set forth by Bloom (1956) and Krathwohl (1964). Such a framework should furnish a helpful base around which behavioral statements of objectives can be formulated.

DEFINITION

An educational objective consists of a description of the behaviors of an individual (the learner or examinee) in relation to his processing information embodied in subject matter—that is, what the learner must be capable of doing with certain characteristics or properties of subject matter. The behavioral component, which may be described as a process involved at an appropriate level of the taxonomic classification, is usually expressed in the form of a noun "ability" or a verb of being "able" followed by an infinitive such as the "ability to do" or "able to do." The second component of the objective, which consists of the specific content often found in the formal learning experience (e.g., in the curricular or instructional unit), constitutes a direct object of the verb or infinitive form. The terms "subject matter" or "content" are used in a fairly broad sense, as their level of specificity is highly variable, depending upon the characteristics of the curricular unit.

INSTRUMENTATION: COGNITIVE DOMAIN

To facilitate the formulation of statements of specific behavioral objectives within the framework of Bloom's taxonomy, the writers have included a table made up of three columns. The first column contains the taxonomic classification identified by both code number and terminology employed in Bloom's (1956) taxonomy. The entries in the second column consist of appropriate infinitives which the teacher or curriculum worker may consult to achieve a precise or preferred wording of the behavior or activity desired. In the third column somewhat general terms relative to subject matter properties are stated. These direct objects, which may be expanded upon to furnish specificity at a desired level, may be permuted with one or more of the infinitive forms to yield the basic structure of an educational objective—activity (process) followed by content (subject matter property). At the discretion of the reader the words "ability" or "able" can be inserted in front of each of the infinitives.

Although within a given major process level or sublevel of the taxonomy each infinitive cannot in all instances be meaningfully or idiomatically paired with every direct object listed, many useful permutations of infinitives and direct objects that furnish entirely readable statements are possible. Certainly use of these tables should lead to a substantial gain in the clarity and speed with which teachers and curriculum specialists, as well as those involved in construction of achievement tests, may state curricular objectives. The writers have found that these tables have been of considerable help to their students, as well as to personnel in public schools who are concerned with writing objectives prior to curriculum development, constructing test items, or to carrying out evaluation studies. Slight modifications can be made with the entries to meet the requirements of specific learning situations.

INSTRUMENTATION: AFFECTIVE DOMAIN

The instrumentation of the Affective Domain is the same as that of the Cognitive Domain, to wit, the selection of behaviorally oriented infinitives combined with selected direct objects. As in the case of the Cognitive Domain, these are to be conceptualized as examples for the stimulation of other infinitives and objects and, more important, meaningful objectives in a total framework.

TABLE 1.   Instrumentation of the Taxonomy of Educational Objectives: Cognitive Domain

| Taxonomy Classification | Key Words | |
	Examples of Infinitives	Examples of Direct Objects
1.00 Knowledge		
1.10 Knowledge of specifics		
1.11 Knowledge of terminology	to define, to distinguish, to acquire, to identify, to recall, to recognize	vocabulary, terms, terminology, meaning(s), definitions, referents, elements
1.12 Knowledge of specific facts	to recall, to recognize, to acquire, to identify	facts, factual information, (sources), (names), (dates), (events), (persons), (places), (time periods), properties, examples, phenomena
1.20 Knowledge of ways and means of dealing with specifics		
1.21 Knowledge of conventions	to recall, to identify, to recognize, to acquire	form(s), conventions, uses, usage, rules, ways, devices, symbols, representations, style(s), format(s)
1.22 Knowledge of trends, sequences	to recall, to recognize, to acquire, to identify	action(s), processes, movement(s), continuity, development(s), trend(s), sequence(s), causes, relationship(s), forces, influences

TABLE 1 (*continued*)

Taxonomy Classification	Key Words Examples of Infinitives	Examples of Direct Objects
1.23 Knowledge of classifications and categories	to recall, to recognize, to acquire, to identify	area(s), type(s), feature(s), class(es), set(s), division(s), arrangement(s), classification(s), category/categories
1.24 Knowledge of criteria	to recall, to recognize, to acquire, to identify	criteria, basics, elements
1.25 Knowledge of methodology	to recall, to recognize, to acquire, to identify	methods, techniques, approaches, uses, procedures, treatments
1.30 Knowledge of the universals and abstractions in a field		
1.31 Knowledge of principles, generalizations	to recall, to recognize, to acquire, to identify	principle(s), generalization(s), proposition(s), fundamentals, laws, principal elements, implication(s)
1.32 Knowledge of theories and structures	to recall, to recognize, to acquire, to identify	theories, bases, interrelations, structure(s), organization(s), formulation(s)
2.00 Comprehension		
2.10 Translation	to translate, to transform, to give in own words, to illustrate, to prepare, to read, to represent, to change, to rephrase, to restate	meaning(s), sample(s), definitions, abstractions, representations, words, phrases
2.20 Interpretation	to interpret, to reorder, to rearrange, to differentiate, to distinguish, to make, to draw, to explain, to demonstrate	relevancies, relationships, essentials, aspects, new view(s), qualifications, conclusions, methods, theories, abstractions
2.30 Extrapolation	to estimate, to infer, to conclude, to predict, to differentiate, to determine, to extend, to interpolate, to extrapolate, to fill in, to draw	consequences, implications, conclusions, factors, ramifications, meanings, corollaries, effects, probabilities

TABLE 1 (continued)

Taxonomy Classification	Key Words	
	Examples of Infinitives	*Examples of Direct Objects*
3.00 Application	to apply, to generalize, to relate, to choose, to develop, to organize, to use, to employ, to transfer, to restructure, to classify	principles, laws, conclusions, effects, methods, theories, abstractions, situations, generalizations, processes, phenomena, procedures
4.00 Analysis		
4.10 Analysis of elements	to distinguish, to detect, to identify, to classify, to discriminate, to recognize, to categorize, to deduce	elements, hypothesis hypotheses, conclusions, assumptions, statements (of fact), statements (of intent), arguments, particulars
4.20 Analysis of relationships	to analyze, to contrast, to compare, to distinguish, to deduce	relationships, interrelations, relevance, relevancies, themes, evidence, fallacies, arguments, cause–effect(s), consistency/consistencies, parts, ideas, assumptions
4.30 Analysis of organizational principles	to analyze, to distinguish, to detect, to deduce	form(s), pattern(s), purpose(s), point(s) of view, techniques, bias(es), structure(s), theme(s), arrangement(s), organization(s)
5.00 Synthesis		
5.10 Production of a unique communication	to write, to tell, to relate, to produce, to constitute, to transmit, to originate, to modify, to document	structure(s), pattern(s), product(s), performance(s), design(s), work(s), communications, effort(s), specifics, composition(s)
5.20 Production of a plan, or proposed set of operations	to propose, to plan, to produce, to design, to modify, to specify	plan(s), objectives, specification(s), schematic(s), operations, way(s), solution(s), means
5.30 Derivation of a set of abstract relations	to produce, to derive, to develop, to combine, to organize, to synthesize, to classify,	phenomena, taxonomies, concept(s), scheme(s), theories, relationships, abstractions, generaliza-

TABLE 1 (continued)

Taxonomy Classification	Key Words	
	Examples of Infinitives	Examples of Direct Objects
	to deduce, to develop, to formulate, to modify	tions, hypothesis/hypotheses, perceptions, ways, discoveries
6.00 Evaluation		
6.10 Judgments in terms of internal evidence	to judge, to argue, to validate, to assess, to decide	accuracy/accuracies, consistency/consistencies, fallacies, reliability, flaws, errors, precision, exactness
6.20 Judgments in terms of external criteria	to judge, to argue, to consider, to compare, to contrast, to standardize, to appraise	ends, means, efficiency, economy/economies, utility, alternatives, courses of action, standards, theories, generalizations

TABLE 2. *Instrumentation of the Taxonomy of Educational Objectives: Affective Domain*

Taxonomy Classification	Key Words	
	Examples of Infinitives	*Examples of Direct Objects*
1.0 Receiving		
1.1 Awareness	to differentiate, to separate, to set apart, to share	sights, sounds, events, designs, arrangements
1.2 Willingness to receive	to accumulate, to select, to combine, to accept	models, examples, shapes, sizes, meters, cadences
1.3 Controlled or selected attention	to select, to posturally respond to, to listen (for), to control	alternatives, answers, rhythms, nuances
2.0 Responding		
2.1 Acquiescence in responding	to comply (with), to follow, to commend, to approve	directions, instructions, laws, policies, demonstrations
2.2 Willingness to respond	to volunteer, to discuss, to practice, to play	instruments, games, dramatic works, charades, burlesques
2.3 Satisfaction in response	to applaud, to acclaim, to spend leisure time in, to augment	speeches, plays, presentations, writings
3.0 Valuing		
3.1 Acceptance of a value	to increase measured proficiency in, to increase numbers of, to relinquish, to specify	group membership(s), artistic production(s), musical productions, personal friendships
3.2 Preference for a value	to assist, to subsidize, to help, to support	artists, projects, viewpoints, arguments
3.3 Commitment	to deny, to protest, to debate, to argue	deceptions, irrelevancies, abdications, irrationalities
4.0 Organization		
4.1 Conceptualization of a value	to discuss, to theorize (on), to abstract, to compare	parameters, codes, standards, goals
4.2 Organization of a value system	to balance, to organize, to define, to formulate	systems, approaches, criteria, limits

TABLE 2 *(continued)*

	Key Words	
Taxonomy Classification	*Examples of Infinitives*	*Examples of Direct Objects*
5.0 Characterization by value or value complex		
5.1 Generalized set	to revise, to change, to complete, to require	plans, behavior, methods, effort(s)
5.2 Characterization	to be rated high by peers in, to be rated high by superiors in, to be rated high by subordinates in and to avoid, to manage, to resolve, to resist	humanitarianism, ethics, integrity, maturity extravagance(s), excesses, conflicts, exorbitancy/ exorbitancies

ADDITIONAL REFERENCES

Travers, R. M. W. *Essentials of learning.* 3rd Ed. New York: Macmillan, 1972.

Zigler, E. Social reinforcement, environmental conditions, and the child. *American Journal of Orthopsychiatry,* 1963, **33,** 614–623.

Zigler, E., Butterfield, E. C., and Capobianco, F. Institutionalization and social reinforcement. *Developmental Psychology,* 1970, **3,** 255–263.

References

Abrahamson, S., Wolf, R. M., & Denson, J. S. A computer-based patient simulator for training anesthesiologists. *Educational Technology,* 1969, **9** (10), 55–57.

Achilles, E. M. Experimental studies in recall and recognition. *Archives of Psychology,* 1920, **6** (44).

Adorno, T. W., Frenkel-Brunswick, E., Sevenson, D. J., & Sanford, R. N. *The authoritarian personality.* New York: Harper & Row, 1950.

Allen, P. M., Barnes, W. D., Reece, J. L., & Roberson, E. W. *Teacher self-appraisal: A way of looking over your own shoulder.* Worthington, Ohio: Charles A. Jones, 1970.

Amidon, E. J., & Flanders, N. A. The effect of direct and indirect teacher influence on dependent-prone students learning geometry. *Journal of Educational Psychology,* 1961, **52,** 286–291.

Amidon, E. J., & Flanders, N. A. *The role of the teacher in the classroom.* Minneapolis: Amidon and Associates, 1963.

Amidon, E. J., & Hough, J. B. (Eds.) *Interaction analysis: Theory, research, and application.* Reading, Mass.: Addison-Wesley, 1967.

Amidon, E. J., & Hunter, E. *Improving teaching: Analyzing verbal interaction in the classroom.* New York: Holt, Rinehart and Winston, 1966.

Anderson, H. H. The measurement of domination and of socially integrative behavior in teachers' contacts with children. *Child Development,* 1939, **10,** 73–89.

Anderson, H. H., & Brewer, J. E. Studies of teachers' classroom personalities. II. Effects of teachers' dominative and integrative contacts on children's classroom behavior. *Applied Psychology Monographs,* 1946, No. 8.

Armstrong, R. J., Cornell, T. D., Kraner, R. E., & Roberson, E. W. *The development and evaluation of behavioral objectives.* Worthington, Ohio: Charles A. Jones, 1970.

Atkin, J. M. Behavioral objectives in curriculum design: A cautionary note. *Science Teacher,* 1968, **35,** 27–30. (a)

Atkin, J. M. Research styles in science education. *Journal of Research in Science Teaching,* 1968, **5,** 338–345. (b)

Atkinson, J. W. *Motives in fantasy, action, and society.* New York: Van Nostrand Reinhold, 1958.

Atkinson, J. W. *An introduction to motivation.* New York: Van Nostrand Reinhold, 1964.

Atkinson, J. W. The mainsprings of achievement oriented activity. In J. D. Krumboltz (Ed.), *Learning and the educational process.* Chicago: Rand McNally, 1965. Pp. 25–66.

Atkinson, R. C. Computerized instruction and the learning process. Technical Report No. 22, 1967, Stanford University, Institute for Mathematical Studies in the Social Sciences.

Atkinson, R. C., & Hansen, D. N. Computer-assisted instruction in initial reading: The Stanford project. *Reading Research Quarterly,* 1966, **2,** 5–25.

Ausubel, D. P. The use of advance organizers in the learning and retention of meaningful verbal material. *Journal of Educational Psychology,* 1960, **51,** 167–172.

Ausubel, D. P. *Educational psychology: A cognitive view.* New York: Holt, Rinehart and Winston, 1968.

Ausubel, D. P., & Ausubel, P. Ego development among segregated Negro children. In A. H. Passow (Ed.), *Education in depressed areas.* New York: Teachers College, Columbia University, 1963. Pp. 109–141.

Ausubel, D. P., & Ausubel, P. Cognitive development in adolescence. *American Educational Research Journal,* 1966, **3,** 403–413.

Ausubel, D. P., Stager, M., & Gaite, A. J. H. Proactive effects in meaningful verbal learning and retention. *Journal of Educational Psychology,* 1969, **60,** 59–64.

Bales, R. F. *Interaction process analysis.* Reading, Mass.: Addison-Wesley, 1950.

Bandura, A. Social learning through imitation. In M. R. Jones (Ed.), *Nebraska symposium on motivation,* 1962.

Bandura, A. Behavior modification through modeling procedures. In L. P. Ullmann & L. Krasner (Eds.), *Research in behavior modification.* New York: Holt, Rinehart and Winston, 1965. Pp. 310–340. (a)

Bandura, A. Vicarious processes: A case of no-trial learning. *Advances in Experimental Social Psychology,* 1965, **2,** 1–55. (b)

Bandura, A. Behavioral psychotherapy. *Scientific American,* 1967, **216,** 78–86.

Bandura, A. *Principles of behavior modification.* New York: Holt, Rinehart and Winston, 1969.

Bandura, A., Blachard, E. B., & Ritter, B. The relative efficacy of desensitization and modeling approaches for inducing behavioral, affective, and attitudinal changes. Unpublished manuscript, Stanford University, 1968.

Bandura, A., Ross, D., & Ross, S. A. Imitation of film-mediated aggressive models. *Journal of Abnormal and Social Psychology,* 1963, **66,** 3–11.

Bandura, A., & Walters, R. H. *Social learning and personality development.* New York: Holt, Rinehart and Winston, 1963.

Barlow, J. A. *Stimulus and response.* New York: Harper & Row, 1968.

Biddle, B. J. Methods and concepts in classroom research. *Review of Educational Research,* 1967, **37,** 337–357.

Bienbrauer, J. S., & Lawler, J. Token reinforcement for learning. *Mental Retardation,* 1964, **2,** 275–279.

Bigge, M. L., & Hunt, M. P. *Psychological foundations of education.* New York: Harper & Row, 1962.

Bijou, S. W., & Baer, D. M. *Child development I.* New York: Appleton-Century-Crofts, 1961.

Bijou, S. W., & Baer, D. M. *Child development II.* New York: Appleton-Century-Crofts, 1965.

Birch, D., & Veroff, J. *Motivation: A study of action.* Monterey, Calif.: Brooks/Cole, 1966.

Birney, R. C. The reliability of the achievement motive. *Journal of Abnormal and Social Psychology,* 1959, **58,** 266–267.

Bitzer, M. Self-directed inquiry in clinical nursing instruction by means of the Plato simulated laboratory. University of Illinois Coordinated Science Laboratory Report R–184, 1963.

Bloom, B. S. Learning for mastery. *UCLA Evaluative Comment,* 1968, **1** (2), 1–12.

Bloom, B. S., Englehart, M. D., Hill, W. H., Furst, E. J., & Krathwohl, D. R. *Taxonomy of educational objectives: Cognitive domain.* New York: McKay, 1956.

Bodwin, R. F. The relationship between immature self-concepts and certain educational disabilities. *Dissertation Abstracts,* 1957, **17,** 564.

Bogardus, E. S. *Fundamentals of social psychology* (2nd ed.). New York: Appleton-Century-Crofts, 1931.

Bolles, R. C. *Theory of motivation.* New York: Harper & Row, 1967.

Bower, G. H., & Clark, M. C. Narrative stories as mediators for serial learning. *Psychonomic Science,* 1969, **14,** 181–182.

Briggs, L. J. *Handbook of procedures for the design of instruction.* Pittsburgh: American Institute for Research, 1970.

Brookover, W. B., Erickson, E. L., & Joiner, L. M. Self-concept of ability and school achievement. *Sociology of Education,* 1964, **37,** 271–279.

Broudy, H. S. Can research escape the dogma of behavioral objectives? *School Review,* 1970, **79,** 43–56.

Brown, J. Some tests on the decay theory of immediate memory. *Quarterly Journal of Experimental Psychology,* 1958, **10,** 12–24.

Brown, P., & Elliot, R. Control of aggression in a nursery school class. *Journal of Experimental Child Psychology,* 1965, **2,** 103–107.

Bruce, R. W. Conditions of transfer of training. *Journal of Experimental Psychology,* 1933, **16,** 343–361.

Bruner, J. S. Going beyond the information given. In *Contemporary approaches to cognition.* Cambridge, Mass.: Harvard University Press, 1957. Pp. 41–70.

Bruner, J. S. The act of discovery. *Harvard Educational Review,* 1961, **31,** 21–32.

Bruner, J. S. *Toward a theory of instruction.* New York: W. W. Norton, 1966.

Brunner, C. Deprivation—Its effects, its remedies. *Educational Leadership,* 1965, **23,** 103–107.

Bugelski, B. R. *The psychology of learning applied to teaching.* Indianapolis: Bobbs-Merrill, 1964.

Bugelski, B. R., & Scharlock, D. P. An experimental demonstration of unconscious mediated association. *Journal of Experimental Psychology,* 1952, **44,** 334–338.

Bundy, R. F. Computer-assisted instruction—Where are we? *Phi Delta Kappan,* 1968, **49,** 424–430.

Buros, O. K. *Tests in print.* Highland Park, N.J.: Gryphon Press, 1961.

Butler, R. A. The effects of deprivation of visual incentives on visual exploration motivation in monkeys. *Journal of Comparative and Physiological Psychology,* 1957, **50,** 177–179.

Byrne, D. Parental antecedents of authoritarianism. *Journal of Personality and Social Psychology,* 1965, **1,** 369–373.

Carroll, J. B. A model of school learning. *Teachers College Record,* 1963, **64,** 723–733.

Carter, T. P. Negative self-concepts of Mexican-American students. *School and Society,* 1968, **96,** 217–229.

Cattell, R. A culture free intelligence test. *Journal of Educational Psychology,* 1940, **31,** 161–179.

Cattell, R. Theory of fluid and crystallized intelligence: A critical experiment. *Journal of Educational Psychology,* 1963, **54,** 1–22.

Cattell, R. Are IQ tests intelligent? *Psychology Today,* 1968, **1** (10), 56–62.

Cawelti, G. Youth assess the American high school. *PTA Magazine,* 1968, **62,** 16–19.

Ceraso, J. The interference theory of forgetting. *Scientific American,* 1967, **217** (4), 117–124.

Chapman, R. L., & Carpenter, J. T. Computer techniques in instruction. In J. E. Coulson (Ed.), *Programmed learning and computer based instruction.* New York: John Wiley, 1962. Pp. 240–253.

Child, I. L., & Whiting, J. W. M. Determinants of levels of aspiration. Evidence from everyday life. *Journal of Abnormal and Social Psychology,* 1949, **44,** 303–314.

Christie, R. The prevalence of Machiavellian orientation. Paper presented at the meeting of the American Psychological Association, Los Angeles, 1964.

Christie, R., & Lindauer, F. Personality structure. *Annual Review of Psychology,* 1963, **14,** 201–230.

Clark, K. B., & Clark, M. P. Emotional factors in racial identification and preference in Negro children. *Journal of Negro Education,* 1950, **19,** 341–351.

Clifford, M. M. Motivational effects of competition and goal setting in reward and non-reward conditions. *Journal of Experimental Education,* 1971, **39,** 11–16.

Coleman, E. B. The association hierarchy as an indicator of extraexperimental interference. *Journal of Verbal Learning and Verbal Behavior,* 1963, **2,** 417–421.

Coleman, J. S. *The adolescent society.* New York: Free Press, 1961.

Coleman, J. S., Campbell, E. Q., Hobson, C. J., McPartland, J., Mood, A. M., Weinfield, F. D., & York, R. L. *Equality of education opportunity.* Washington, D.C.: Government Printing Office, 1966.

Combs, A. W., & Snygg, D. *Individual behavior.* New York: Harper & Row, 1959.

Congreve, W. J. Independent learning. *North Central Association Quarterly,* 1965, **40,** 222–228.

Cornell, T. D. *A systematic approach to needs assessment.* Tucson: EPIC Evaluation Center, 1970.

Craig, R. C. *The psychology of learning in the classroom.* New York: Macmillan, 1966.

Cronbach, L. J. How can instruction be adapted to individual differences? In R. M. Gagné (Ed.), *Learning and individual differences.* Columbus, Ohio: Charles E. Merrill, 1967. Pp. 23–39.

Crootof, C. Bright underachievers' acceptance of self and their need for achievement. Unpublished doctoral dissertation, New York University, 1963.

Crouse, J. H. Transfer and retroaction in prose learning. *Journal of Educational Psychology,* 1970, **61,** 226–228.

Crowder, N. A. Automatic tutoring by intrinsic programming. In A. A. Lumsdaine & R. Glaser (Eds.), *Teaching machines and programmed learning.* Washington, D.C.: National Education Association, 1960. Pp. 286–298.

Cummings, R., & Gillespie, M. E. Dropouts among the disadvantaged. *Arizona Teacher,* 1971, **59** (3), 12, 21, 29.

Dai, G. Minority group membership and personality development. In J. Masuoka & P. Valien (Eds.), *Race relations: Problems and theory.* Chapel Hill: University of North Carolina Press, 1961. Pp. 181–199.

Dave, R. H. The identification and measurement of environmental process variables that are related to educational achievement. Unpublished doctoral dissertation, University of Chicago, 1963.

DeCecco, J. P. *The psychology of learning and instruction: Educational psychology.* Englewood Cliffs, N.J.: Prentice-Hall, 1968.

Deep, D. The computer can help individualize instruction. *Elementary School Journal,* 1970, **70,** 351–358.

Deese, J., & Hulse, S. H. *The psychology of learning.* New York: McGraw-Hill, 1967.

Diederich, P. B. *Short-cut statistics for teacher-made tests.* Princeton, N.J.: Educational Testing Service, 1964, No. 5.

Dietze, A. G. The relation of several factors to factual memory. *Journal of Applied Psychology,* 1931, **15,** 563–574.

Dietze, A. G., & Janes, H. E. Factual memory of secondary school pupils for a short article which they had read a single time. *Journal of Educational Psychology,* 1931, **22,** 667–676.

Dollard, J., & Miller, N. E. *Personality and psychotherapy.* New York: McGraw-Hill, 1950.

Drever, J. *A dictionary of psychology.* Baltimore: Penguin Books, 1964.

Dumas, W. W. Strengths and weaknesses of student teachers in English. *Journal of Experimental Education,* 1966, **35,** 19–27.

Duncan, A. D. Self-application of behavior modification techniques by teenagers. Research Training Paper No. 11. Kansas City: Bureau of Child Research Laboratory, University of Kansas Medical Center, 1968.

Duncan, C. P. Description of learning to learn in human subjects. *American Journal of Psychology,* 1960, **73,** 108–114.

Duncan, C. P. Learning to learn in response-discovery and in paired-associate lists. *American Journal of Psychology,* 1964, **77,** 367–379.

Ebbinghaus, H. *Memory.* Trans. H. A. Ruger & C. E. Bussenius. New York: Teachers College, Columbia University, 1913. Original work, 1885.

Ebel, R. L. Behavioral objectives: A close look. *Phi Delta Kappan,* 1970, **52,** 171–173.

Ebel, R. L. Command of knowledge should be the primary objective of education. *Today's Education,* 1971, **9,** 36–39.

Edwards, A. J., & Scannell, D. P. *Educational psychology: The teaching-learning process.* Scranton, Pa.: International Textbook, 1968.

Eisner, E. W. Educational objectives: Help or hindrance. *School Review,* 1967, **76,** 250–260.

Elkind, D. Egocentrism in adolescence. *Child Development,* 1967, **38,** 1025–1034.

Ellis, H. *The transfer of learning.* New York: Macmillan, 1965.

English, H. B., & English, A. C. *A comprehensive dictionary of psychological and psychoanalytical terms.* New York: McKay, 1958.

Feather, N. T. Effects of prior success and failure on expectations of success and subsequent performance. *Journal of Personality and Social Psychology,* 1966, **3,** 287–298.

Ferster, C. B., & Skinner, B. F. *Schedules of reinforcement.* New York: Appleton-Century-Crofts, 1957.

Feshback, N. D. Variations in teachers' reinforcement style and imitative behavior of children differing in personality characteristics and social background. In A. Bandura (Ed.), *Principles of behavior modification.* New York: Holt, Rinehart and Winston, 1969. P. 148.

Fitts, W. H. *Manual, Tennessee self-concept scale.* Nashville: Counselor Recordings, 1965.

Flanagan, J. C. Program for learning in accordance with needs. *Psychology in the Schools,* 1969, **6,** 133–136.

Flanagan, J. C., Dailey, J. T., Davis, F. B., Goldberg, I., Heyman, C. A., Jr., Orr, D. B., & Shaycraft, M. F. The American high school student. Cooperative Research Project No. 635. Pittsburgh: University of Pittsburgh, 1964.

Flanders, N. A. Personal-social anxiety as a factor in experimental learning situations. *Journal of Educational Research,* 1951, **45,** 100–110.

Flanders, N. A. Teacher influence, pupil attitudes, and achievement. U.S. Office of Education Cooperative Research Project No. 397. Minneapolis: University of Minnesota, 1960.

Flanders, N. A. Intent, action, and feedback: A preparation for teaching. *Journal of Teacher Education,* 1963, **14,** 251–260.

Flanders, N. A. Teacher influence, pupil attitudes, and achievement. U.S. Office of Education Cooperative Research Monograph No. 12. Ann Arbor: University of Michigan, School of Education, 1965.

Flanders, N. A. *Analyzing teacher behavior.* Reading, Mass.: Addison-Wesley, 1970.

Friesen, D. Academic–athletic–popularity syndrome in the Canadian high school society (1967). *Adolescence,* 1968, **3** (9), 39–52.

Gage, N. L. Theories of teaching. In E. R. Hilgard (Ed.), *Theories of learning and instruction.* Sixty-Third Yearbook of the National Society for the Study of Education. Chicago: National Society for the Study of Education, 1964. Pp. 268–285.

Gage, N. L. An analytical approach to research on instructional methods. *Phi Delta Kappan,* 1968, **49,** 601–606.

Gage, N. L., & Unruh, W. R. Theoretical formulations for research on teaching. *Review of Educational Research,* 1967, **37,** 358–370.

Gagné, R. M. Problem solving. In A. W. Melton (Ed.), *Categories of human learning.* New York: Academic Press, 1964.

Gagné, R. M. *Conditions of learning.* New York: Holt, Rinehart and Winston, 1965.

Gagné, R. M. Contributions of learning to human development. *Psychological Review,* 1968, **75,** 177–191.

Gagné, R. M. Context, isolation, and interference effects on the retention of fact. *Journal of Educational Psychology,* 1969, **60,** 408–414.

Gagné, R. M. *The conditions of learning* (2nd ed.). New York: Holt, Rinehart and Winston, 1970. (a)

Gagné, R. M. Instructional variables and learning outcomes. In M. C. Wittrock & D. E. Wiley (Eds.), *The evaluation of instruction: Issues and problems.* New York: Holt, Rinehart and Winston, 1970. Pp. 105–125. (b)

Gagné, R. M. Some new views of learning and instruction. *Phi Delta Kappan,* 1970, **51,** 468–472. (c)

Gagné, R. M. Domains of learning. President's address, meeting of the American Educational Research Association, New York, 1971. (a)

Gagné, R. M. Instruction based on research in learning. *Engineering Education,* 1971, **61,** 519–523. (b)

Gagné, R. M. Learning outcomes and their varieties. Invited address, University of Arizona, Tucson, Department of Educational Psychology, 1971. (c)

Gagné, R. M. Quality in undergraduate education. Psychology Colloquium, University of Arizona, Tucson, 1971. (d)

Gagné, R. M., & Paradise, N. E. Abilities and learning sets in knowledge acquisition. *Psychological Monographs,* 1961, **75** (14, Whole No. 518).

Galloway, C. M. An exploratory study of observational procedures for determining teacher nonverbal communication. Unpublished doctoral dissertation, University of Florida, 1962.

Gibson, E. J. A systematic application of the concepts of generalization and differentiation to verbal learning. *Psychological Review,* 1940, **47,** 196–229.

Gibson, E. J. Retroactive inhibition as a function of degree of generalization between tasks. *Journal of Experimental Psychology,* 1941, **28,** 93–115.

Gilbert, T. F. Mathetics: The technology of education. *Journal of Mathetics,* 1962, **1,** 7–73.

Gilliland, A. R. The rate of forgetting. *Journal of Educational Psychology,* 1948, **39,** 19–26.

Glaser, R. Psychology and instructional technology. In R. Glaser (Ed.), *Training research and education.* Pittsburgh: University of Pittsburgh Press, 1962. Pp. 1–30.

Glaser, R. Toward a behavioral science base for instructional design. In R. Glaser (Ed.), *Teaching machines and programmed learning.* Vol. 2. Washington, D.C.: National Education Association, 1965. Pp. 771–809.

Glaser, R., & Nitko, A. J. Measurement in learning and instruction. In R. L. Thorndike (Ed.), *Educational measurement* (2nd ed.). Washington, D.C.: American Council on Education, 1971. Pp. 625–670.

Goldberg, M. L. Studies in underachievement in the academically talented. In A. Frazier (Ed.), *Freeing the capacity to learn.* Washington, D.C. American Society for Curriculum Development, 1960. Pp. 56–73.

Goldman, B. A. Effect of classroom experience and videotape self-observation upon undergraduate attitudes toward self and toward teaching. Paper presented at the meeting of the American Psychological Association, Washington, D.C., 1969.

Gough, H. G. Academic achievement in high school as predicted from the California Psychological Inventory. *Journal of Educational Psychology,* 1964, **55,** 174–180.

Gronlund, N. E. *Measurement and evaluation in teaching.* New York: Macmillan, 1965.

Guilford, J. P. Three faces of intellect. *American Psychologist,* 1956, **14,** 469–479.

Guilford, J. P. *The nature of human intelligence.* New York: McGraw-Hill, 1967.

Guthrie, E. R. Association and the law of effect. *Psychological Review,* 1940, **47,** 127–148.

Guthrie, E. R. Conditioning: A theory of learning in terms of stimulus, response, and association. In *Forty-first Yearbook of the National Society for the Study of Education,* Part II. Bloomington, Ind.: Public School Publishing, 1942.

Guthrie, E. R. *The psychology of learning* (Rev. ed.). New York: Harper & Row, 1952.

Guttman, N., & Kalish, H. I. Discriminality and stimulus generalization. *Journal of Experimental Psychology,* 1956, **51,** 79–88.

Hackett, M. G. *Success in the classroom.* New York: Holt, Rinehart and Winston, 1971.

Hall, J. F. *The psychology of learning.* Philadelphia: Lippincott, 1966.

Hall, K. A. Computer-assisted instruction: Problems and performance. *Phi Delta Kappan,* 1971, **51,** 628–631.

Hamilton, C. E. The relationship between length of interval separating two learning tasks and performance on the second task. *Journal of Experimental Psychology,* 1950, **40,** 613–621.

Hamilton, R. J. Retroactive facilitation as a function of degree of similarity between tasks. *Journal of Experimental Psychology,* 1943, **32,** 363–376.

Harlow, H. F. The formation of learning sets. *Psychological Review,* 1949, **56,** 51–65.

Hart, F. W. *Teachers and teaching.* New York: Macmillan, 1934.

Havighurst, R. J., & Moorefield, T. E. The disadvantaged in industrial cities. *The Educationally Retarded and Disadvantaged.* 1967, **66** (Part I), 8–20.

Healy, G. W. Self-concept: A comparison of Negro-, Anglo-, and Spanish-American students across ethnic, sex, and socioeconomic variables. Unpublished doctoral dissertation, New Mexico State University, Las Cruces, 1969.

Hendrickson, G., & Schroeder, W. Transfer of training in learning to hit a submerged target. *Journal of Educational Psychology,* 1941, **32,** 206–213.

Herbart, J. *The science of education.* Trans. H. M. Felkin & E. Felkin. Boston: D. C. Heath, 1904.

Hilgard, E. R. Teaching machines and programmed learning: What support from the psychology of learning? *NEA Journal,* 1961, **50,** 20–21.

Hilgard, E. R., & Bower, G. *Theories of learning* (3rd ed.). New York: Appleton-Century-Crofts, 1966.

Holt, J. *The underachieving school.* New York: Pitman, 1969.

Homme, L. E., de Baca, P. C., Deirue, J. V., Steinhorst, R., & Rickert, E. J. Use of the Premack principle in controlling the behavior of nursery school children. *Journal of the Experimental Analysis of Behavior,* 1963, **6,** 554.

Hough, J. B., & Duncan, J. K. *Teaching: Description and analysis.* Reading, Mass.: Addison-Wesley, 1970.

Hough, J. B., & Ober, R. The effect of training in interaction analysis on the verbal teaching behavior of pre-service teachers. Paper presented at the meeting of the American Educational Research Association, Chicago, 1966.

Hughes, M. M. *Development of the means for the assessment of the quality of teaching in elementary schools.* Salt Lake City: University of Utah Press, 1959.

Hughes, M. M. Teacher behavior and concept of self. *Childhood Education,* 1964, **41** (1), 29–33.

Hull, C. L. The concept of the habit family hierarchy and maze learning. *Psychological Review,* 1934, **41,** 33–54, 134–152.

Hull, C. L. *Principles of behavior.* New York: Appleton-Century-Crofts, 1943.

Hull, C. L. *A behavior system: An introduction to behavior theory concerning the individual organism.* New Haven, Conn.: Yale University Press, 1952.

Hunt, J. McV. *Intelligence and experience.* New York: Ronald Press, 1961.

Institute for Personality and Ability Testing, Information Bulletin No. 9. Champaign, Ill.: *New prediction possibilities for vocational and educational counseling with the 16 PF,* IPAT, 1963.

Irion, A. L. Reminiscence in pursuit-rotor learning as a function of length of rest and amount of pre-rest practice. *Journal of Experimental Psychology,* 1949, **39,** 492–499.

Israel, J. The effect of positive and negative self-evaluation on the attractiveness of a goal. *Human Relations,* 1960, **13,** 33–47.

Jackson, P. W. *Life in classrooms.* New York: Holt, Rinehart and Winston, 1968.

Jackson, P. W., Silberman, M. L., & Wolfson, B. J. Signs of personal involvement in teachers' descriptions of their students. *Journal of Educational Psychology,* 1969, **60,** 22–27.

Jenkins, D. H. Characteristics and functions of leadership in instructional groups. In N. B. Henry (Ed.), *The dynamics of instructional groups.* Part 2. Chicago: National Society for the Study of Education, University of Chicago, 1969. Pp. 164–184.

Jenkins, J. J. Mediated associations: Paradigms and situations. In C. N. Cofer & B. S. Musgrave (Eds.), *Verbal behavior and learning.* New York: McGraw-Hill, 1963. Pp. 210–244.

Jensen, A. R. An empirical theory of the serial-position effect. *Journal of Psychology,* 1962, **53,** 127–142.

Jensen, A. R. How much can we boost IQ and scholastic achievement? *Harvard Educational Review,* 1969, **39,** 1–123.

Jensen, L., & Anderson, D. C. Retroactive inhibition of difficult and unfamiliar prose. *Journal of Educational Psychology,* 1970, **61,** 305–309.

Jersild, A. T. Characteristics of teachers who are "liked best" and "disliked most." *Journal of Experimental Education,* 1940, **9,** 139–151.

Jones, J. C. *Learning.* New York: Harcourt Brace Jovanovich, 1967.

Jones, M. C. A laboratory study of fear. The case of Peter. *Pedagogical Seminary,* 1924, **31,** 308–315.

Judd, C. H. The relation of special training and general intelligence. *Educational Review,* 1908, **36,** 42–48.

Jung, J. Effects of response meaningfulness *(m)* on transfer of training under two different paradigms. *Journal of Experimental Psychology,* 1963, **65,** 377–384.

Kantor, R. E. The affective domain and beyond. *Journal for the Study of Consciousness,* 1970, **3** (1), 20–42.

Katz, D., & Stotland, E. A preliminary statement to a theory of attitude structure and change. In S. Koch (Ed.), *Psychology: A study of a science.* Vol. 3. New York: McGraw-Hill, 1959. Pp. 423–475.

Kendler, H. H. The concept of the concept. In A. W. Melton (Ed.), *Categories of human learning.* New York: Academic Press, 1964. Pp. 212–236.

Kibler, R. J., Barker, L. L., & Miles, D. T. *Behavioral objectives and instruction.* Boston: Allyn and Bacon, 1970.

Kimble, G. A. *Hilgard and Marquis' "Conditioning and learning."* New York: Appleton-Century-Crofts, 1961.

Kirk, J. The effects of teaching the Minnesota system of interaction analysis on the behavior of student teachers. Unpublished doctoral dissertation, Temple University, 1964.

Klausmeier, H. J., Feldhausen, J., & Check, J. An analysis of learning efficiency in arithmetic of mentally retarded children in comparison with children of average and high intelligence. U.S. Office of Education, Research Project No. 153. Madison: University of Wisconsin, 1959.

Klausmeier, H. J., & Ripple, R. E. *Learning and human abilities* (3rd ed.). New York: Harper & Row, 1971.

Klausmeier, H. J., Sorenson, J. S., & Ghatala, E. S. Individually guided motivation: Developing self-direction and prosocial behaviors. *Elementary School Journal,* 1971, **71,** 339–350.

Koffka, K. *The growth of the mind.* New York: Harcourt Brace Jovanovich, 1924.

Kolesnik, W. B. *Educational psychology* (2nd ed.). New York: McGraw-Hill, 1970.

Koppenaal, R. J. Time changes in the strengths of A–B, A–C lists: Spontaneous recovery? *Journal of Verbal Learning and Verbal Behavior,* 1963, **2,** 310–319.

Krathwohl, D. R. The taxonomy of educational objectives—Its use in curriculum building. In C. M. Lindvall (Ed.), *Defining educational objectives.* Pittsburgh: University of Pittsburgh Press, 1964. Pp. 19–36.

Krathwohl, D. R., Bloom, B. S., & Masia, B. B. *Taxonomy of educational objectives: Affective domain.* New York: McKay, 1964.

Kreuger, W. C. F. The effect of overlearning on retention. *Journal of Experimental Psychology,* 1929, **12,** 71–78.

Kuethe, J. L. *The teaching–learning process.* Glenview, Ill.: Scott, Foresman, 1968.

Kuypers, D. S., Becker, W. C., & O'Leary, K. D. How to make a token system fail. *Exceptional Children,* 1968, **35** (2), 101–108.

Leeds, C. H. Teacher behavior liked and disliked by pupils. *Education,* 1954, **75,** 29–36.

Lefrancois, G. *Psychology for teaching.* Belmont, Calif.: Wadsworth, 1972.

Leggett, G., et al. *Prentice-Hall handbook for writers* (3rd ed.). New York: Prentice-Hall, 1954.

Lewin, K., Dembo, T., Festinger, L., & Sears, P. S. Level of aspiration. In J. McV. Hunt (Ed.), *Personality and the behavior disorders.* New York: Ronald Press, 1944. Pp. 333–378.

Lindgren, H. C. *Educational psychology in the classroom* (3rd. ed.). New York: John Wiley, 1967.

Lindvall, C. M. (Ed.), *Defining educational objectives.* Pittsburgh: University of Pittsburgh Press, 1964.

Lindvall, C. M., Nardozza, S., & Felton, M. The importance of specific objectives in curriculum development. In C. M. Lindvall (Ed.), *Defining educational objectives.* Pittsburgh: University of Pittsburgh Press, 1964. Pp. 10–18.

Lipton, A. Cultural heritage and the relationship to self-esteem. *Journal of Educational Sociology,* 1963, **36,** 211–212.

Litvak, S. B. Attitude change by stimulus exposures. *Psychological Reports,* 1969, **25,** 391–396.

Logan, F. A. The Hull–Spence approach. In S. Koch (Ed.), *Psychology: A study of a science.* Vol. 2. New York: McGraw-Hill, 1959. Pp. 293–358.

Logan, F. A. *Fundamentals of learning and motivation.* Dubuque, Iowa: W. C. Brown, 1970.

Long, B. H., & Henderson, E. H. Self social concepts of disadvantaged school beginners. In B. R. McCandless, *Children: Behavior and development.* New York: Holt, Rinehart and Winston, 1967. P. 292.

Loree, M. R. *Psychology of education* (2nd ed.). New York: Ronald Press, 1970.

Lovaas, O. I. A program for the establishment of speech in psychotic children. In J. K. Wing (Ed.), *Early childhood autism.* Elmsford, N.Y.: Pergamon Press, 1966. Pp. 115–144.

Lovell, K. Developmental processes in thought. *Journal of Experimental Education,* 1968, **37,** 14–21.

Lowell, E. L. The effects of need for achievement on learning and speed of performance. *Journal of Psychology,* 1952, **33,** 31–40.

Luchins, A. S. Implications of Gestalt psychology for AV learning. *AV Communications Review,* 1961, **9** (5), 7–31.

Lumpkin, D. D. Relationship of self-concept to achievement in reading. *Dissertation Abstracts,* 1959, **20,** 204–205.

Lyon, D. O. The relation of quickness of learning to retentiveness. *Archives of Psychology,* 1916, **5** (34).

Macdonald, J. B., & Wolfson, B. J. A case against behavioral objectives. *Elementary School Journal,* 1970, **71,** 119–128.

Machiavelli, N. *The prince.* Trans. W. K. Marriott. New York: P. F. Collier, 1910.

Maehr, M. L., & Sjogren, D. D. Atkinson's theory of achievement motivation: First step toward a theory of academic motivation? *Review of Educational Research,* 1971, **41,** 143–161.

Mager, R. F. *Preparing instructional objectives.* Belmont, Calif.: Fearon, 1962.

Manuel, H. T. *Spanish-speaking children of the Southwest.* Austin: University of Texas Press, 1965.

Margolius, G. J., & Sheffield, F. D. Optimum methods of combining practice with filmed demonstration in teaching complex response sequences: Serial learning of a mechanical assembly task. In A. A. Lumsdaine (Ed.), *Student response in programmed instruction.* Washington, D.C.: Academy of Sciences National Research Council, 1961. Pp. 33–35.

Markle, S. M. *A programmed primer on programming.* Vols. 1 & 2. New York: Center for Programmed Instruction, 1961.

Marks, E., & Lindsay, C. A. Machiavellian attitudes: Some measurement and behavioral considerations. *Sociometry,* 1966, **29,** 228–236.

Marlow, D. Relationship among the direct and indirect measures of the achievement motive and overt behavior. *Journal of Consulting Psychology,* 1959, **23,** 329–332.

Marx, M. H., & Tombaugh, T. N. *Motivation.* San Francisco: Chandler, 1967.

Maslow, A. H. A theory of human motivation. *Psychological Review,* 1943, **50,** 370–396.

Maslow, A. H. *Toward a psychology of being.* New York: Van Nostrand Reinhold, 1962.

McClelland, D. C., Atkinson, J. W., Clark, R. A., & Lowell, E. L. *The achievement motive.* New York: Appleton-Century-Crofts, 1953.

McGeoch, J. A. *The psychology of human learning.* London: Longmans, 1942.

McGeoch, J. A., & Whitely, P. L. The recall of observed material. *Journal of Educational Psychology,* 1926, **17,** 419–425.

McKeachie, W. J., & Doyle, C. L. *Psychology* (2nd ed.). Reading, Mass.: Addison-Wesley, 1970.

McKenzie, H., Clark, M., Wolf, M., Kothera, R., & Benson, C. Behavior modification of children with learning disabilities using grades as tokens and allowances as backup reinforcers. *Exceptional Children,* 1968, **34,** 745–753.

McLeod, R. J. Changes in verbal interaction patterns of secondary science student teachers who have had training in interaction analysis and the relationship of these changes to the verbal interaction of their cooperating teachers. U.S. Office of Education Small Contract Project No. 6–8078. Ithaca, N.Y.: Cornell University, 1967.

Medley, D. M., & Mitzel, H. E. Application of analysis of variance to the estimation of the reliability of observations of teachers' classroom behavior. *Journal of Experimental Education,* 1958, **27,** 23–25.

Medley, D. M., & Mitzel, H. E. Measuring classroom behavior by systematic observation. In N. L. Gage (Ed.), *Handbook on research on teaching.* Chicago: Rand McNally, 1963. Pp. 247–328.

Meeker, M. N. *The structure of intellect, its interpretation and uses.* Columbus, Ohio: Charles E. Merrill, 1969.

Metfessel, N. S., & Michael, W. B. A paradigm involving multiple criterion measures for the evaluation of the effectiveness of school programs. *Educational and Psychological Measurement,* 1967, **27** (Part 2), 931–943.

Meux, M., & Smith, B. O. Logical dimensions of teaching behavior. In B. J. Biddle & W. J. Ellena (Eds.), *Contemporary research on teacher effectiveness.* New York: Holt, Rinehart and Winston, 1964. Pp. 127–164.

Michael, W. B., & Metfessel, N. S. A paradigm for developing valid measurable objectives in the evaluation of educational programs in colleges and universities. *Educational and Psychological Measurement,* 1967, **27,** 373–383.

Miller, G. A. The magical number seven: plus or minus two: Some limits on our capacity for processing information. *Psychological Review,* 1956, **63,** 81–97.

Miller, N. E., & Dollard, J. C. *Social learning and imitation.* New Haven, Conn.: Yale University Press, 1941.

Montague, E. J., & Butts, D. P. Behavioral objectives. *Science Teacher,* 1968, **35,** 33–35.

Moore, G. Untitled, unpublished case study, Arizona Center for Early Childhood Education, 1969.

Moore, W. J., & Kennedy, L. D. Evaluation of learning in the language arts. In B. S. Bloom, J. T. Hastings, & G. F. Madaus, *Handbook on formative and summative evaluation of student learning.* New York: McGraw-Hill, 1971. Pp. 399–446.

Mowrer, O. H. *Learning theory and behavior.* New York: John Wiley, 1960.

Mulhall, E. F. Tests of the memories of school children. *Journal of Educational Psychology,* 1917, **8,** 294–302.

Murdock, B. B., Jr. The retention of individual items. *Journal of Experimental Psychology,* 1961, **62,** 618–625.

Murray, H. A. *Explorations in personality.* New York: Oxford University Press, 1938.

Mursetin, B. I. The relationship of grade expectation and grades believed to be deserved to actual grades received. *Journal of Experimental Education,* 1965, **33,** 357–362.

Neel, F. F. The relationship of authoritarian personality to learning: F-scale scores compared to classroom performance. *Journal of Educational Psychology,* 1959, **50,** 195–199.

Nelson, L. Teacher leadership: An empirical approach to analyzing teacher behavior in the classroom. *Journal of Teacher Education,* 1966, **17,** 417–425.

Noble, C. E. Meaningfulness and familiarity. In C. N. Cofer & B. S. Musgrave (Eds.), *Verbal behavior and learning.* New York: McGraw-Hill, 1963.

Ober, R. T. The nature of interaction analysis. *High School Journal,* 1967, **51** (1), 7–16.

Ohanian, V. Educational technology: A critique. *Elementary School Journal,* 1971, **71,** 183–197.

Ojemann, R. H. Who selects the objectives for learning—and why? *Elementary School Journal,* 1971, **71,** 262–273.

O'Leary, K. D., & Becker, W. C. Behavior modification of an adjustment class: A token reinforcement program. *Exceptional Children,* 1967, **33,** 637–642.

Ornstein, A. C. Selected teacher behavior attributes rated as desirable by ninth-grade disadvantaged students and ninth-grade teachers of the disadvantaged. Unpublished doctoral dissertation, New York University, 1970.

Ornstein, A. C. Systematizing teacher behavior research. *Phi Delta Kappan,* 1971, **52,** 551–556.

Page, E. B. Teacher comments and student performance. *Journal of Educational Psychology,* 1958, **49,** 175–181.

Pankratz, R. S. Verbal interaction patterns in the classrooms of selected science teachers. Unpublished doctoral dissertation, Ohio State University, 1966.

Parakh, J. S. A study of teacher–pupil interaction in high school biology classes. Unpublished doctoral dissertation, Cornell University, 1966.

Parke, R. D., & Walters, R. H. Some factors influencing the efficacy of punishment training for inducing response inhibition. *Monographs of the Society for Research in Child Development,* 1967, **32** (1, Serial No. 109).

Pavlov, I. P. *Conditioned reflexes: An investigation of the physiological activity of the cerebral cortex.* Trans. and ed. G. V. Anrep. London: Oxford Press, 1927.

Perkins, H. V. A procedure for assessing the classroom behavior of students and teaching. *American Educational Research Journal,* 1964, **1,** 249–260.

Perkins, H. V. *Human development and learning.* Belmont, Calif.: Wadsworth, 1969.

Phillips, E. L. Achievement place: Token reinforcement procedures in a home-style rehabilitation setting for "pre-delinquent" boys. *Journal of Applied Behavior Analysis,* 1968, **1,** 213–223.

Piaget, J. *The psychology of intelligence.* Trans. M. Percy & D. E. Berlyne. London: Routledge & Kegan Paul, 1950.

Piaget, J. *Play, dreams, and imitation in childhood.* Trans. C. Gattegno & F. M. Hodgson. New York: W. W. Norton, 1951.

Piaget, J. *The origins of intelligence in children.* Trans. M. Cook. New York: International University Press, 1952.

Piaget, J. *The child's conception of physical causality.* Trans. M. Gabain. Totowa, N.J.: Littlefield, Adams, 1960.

Piaget, J., & Inhelder, B. *The growth of logical thinking from childhood to adolescence.* Trans. A. Parsons & S. Seagrin. New York: Basic Books, 1958.

Piaget, J., & Szeminska, A. *The child's conception of number.* Trans. C. Gattegno & F. M. Hodgson. London: Routledge & Kegan Paul, 1952.

Postman, L. The present status of interference theory. In A. W. Melton (Ed.), *Verbal learning and verbal behavior.* New York: McGraw-Hill, 1961. Pp. 145–201.

Postman, L. Rewards and punishments in human learning. In L. Postman (Ed.), *Psychology in the making.* New York: Knopf, 1962.

Poussaint, A. F., & Atkinson, C. O. Negro youth and psychological motivation. *Journal of Negro Education,* 1968, **37,** 241.

Premack, D. Toward empirical laws: Positive reinforcement. *Psychological Review,* 1959, **66,** 219–233.

Pressey, S. L. A simple apparatus which gives tests and scores—and teachers. *School and Society,* 1926, **23,** 373–376.

Raths, L. E., Harmin, M., & Simon, S. B. *Values and teaching.* Columbus, Ohio: Charles E. Merrill, 1966.

Raynor, J. O., & Rubin, I. S. Effects of achievement motivation and future orientation on level of performance. *Journal of Personality and Social Psychology,* 1971, **17,** 36–41.

Razran, G. Experimental semantics. *Transactions of the New York Academy of Sciences,* 1951, **14,** 171–177.

Remmers, H. H. Rating methods in research on training. In N. L. Gage (Ed.), *Handbook of research on teaching.* Chicago: Rand McNally, 1963. Pp. 329–378.

Roberts, E. A., Jr. Middle-class values. *Today's Education,* 1970, **59,** 20–23.

Rogers, C. R. *On becoming a person.* Boston: Houghton Mifflin, 1961.

Romberg, T. A. Current research in mathematics education. *Review of Educational Research,* 1969, **39,** 473–491.

Rosen, B. C., & d'Andrade, R. The psychosocial origins of achievement motivation. *Sociometry,* 1959, **22,** 185–218.

Rosenthal, R. L., Zimmerman, B. J., & Durning, K. Observationally induced changes in children's interrogative classes. *Journal of Personality and Social Psychology,* 1970, **16** (4), 681–688.

Rothkepf, E. Z., & Bisbicos, E. Selective facilitative effects of interspersed questions on learning from written material. *Journal of Educational Psychology,* 1967, **58,** 56–61.

Ryans, D. G. *Characteristics of teachers.* Washington, D.C.: National Council on Education, 1960.

Ryans, D. G. Research on teacher behavior in the context of the teacher characteristics study. In B. J. Biddle & W. J. Ellena (Eds.), *Contemporary research on teacher effectiveness.* New York: Holt, Rinehart and Winston, 1964. Pp. 67–101.

Sanford, N. The approach of the authoritarian personality. In J. L. McCary (Ed.), *Psychology of personality: Six modern approaches.* New York: Grove Press, 1956. Pp. 261–282.

Sarason, S. B., Davidson, K. S., Lighthall, F. F., Waite, R. R., & Ruebush, B. K. *Anxiety in elementary school children.* New York: John Wiley, 1960.

Sarason, S. B., & Mandler, G. Some correlates on test anxiety. *Journal of Abnormal and Social Psychology,* 1952, **47,** 810–817.

Scharf, J. The effects of anxiety, stress instructions, and difficulty on verbal problem solving behavior. Unpublished doctoral dissertation, New York University, 1964.

Sears, P. S. Levels of aspiration in academically successful and unsuccessful children. *Journal of Abnormal and Social Psychology,* 1940, **35,** 498–536.

Shaw, M. C. Motivation in human learning. *Review of Educational Research,* 1967, **37,** 563–582.

Shuell, T. J., & Keppel, G. Learning ability and retention. *Journal of Educational Psychology,* 1970, **61,** 59–65.

Silberman, M. L. Behavioral expression of teachers' attitudes toward elementary school students. *Journal of Educational Psychology,* 1969, **60,** 402–407.

Singer, J. E. The use of manipulative strategies: Machiavellianism and attractiveness. *Sociometry,* 1964, **27,** 128–150.

Skinner, B. F. *The behavior of organisms: An experimental analysis.* New York: Appleton-Century-Crofts, 1938.

Skinner, B. F. Are theories of learning necessary? *Psychological Review,* 1950, **57,** 193–216.

Skinner, B. F. *Science and human behavior.* New York: Free Press, 1953.

Skinner, B. F. Teaching machines. *Science,* 1958, **128,** 969–977.

Skinner, B. F. *The technology of teaching.* New York: Appleton-Century-Crofts, 1968.

Smith, B. O. A concept of teaching. *Teachers College Record,* 1960, **61,** 229–241.

Snider, R. M. A project to study the nature of physics teaching using the Flanders methods of interaction analysis. Cooperative Research Project No. S–280. Ithaca, N.Y.: Cornell University, 1965.

Soar, R. S. Pupil needs and teacher–pupil relationships: Experiences needed for comprehensive reading. In E. J. Amidon & J. B. Hough (Eds.), *Interaction analysis: Theory, research, and application.* Reading, Mass.: Addison-Wesley, 1967. Pp. 243–250.

Solomon, R. L. Punishment. *American Psychologist,* 1964, **19,** 239–253.

Sontag, M. Attitudes toward education and perception of teacher behaviors. *American Educational Research Journal,* 1968, **5,** 385–402.

Spearman, C. *The abilities of man.* New York: Macmillan, 1927.

Spearman, C., & Jones, L. W. *Human ability.* London: Macmillan, 1950.

Spence, K. W. Theoretical interpretations of learning. In S. S. Stevens (Ed.), *Handbook of experimental psychology.* New York: John Wiley, 1951.

Spence, K. W. *Behavior theory and conditioning.* New Haven, Conn.: Yale University Press, 1956.

Spence, K. W., Bergmann, G., & Lippitt, R. A study of simple learning under irrelevant motivational-reward conditions. *Journal of Experimental Psychology,* 1950, **40,** 539–551.

Spence, K. W., & Lippitt, R. "Latent" learning of a simple maze problem with relevant needs satiated. *Psychological Bulletin,* 1940, **37,** 429.

Spence, K. W., & Lippitt, R. An experimental test of the sign-gestalt theory of trial-and-error learning. *Journal of Experimental Psychology,* 1946, **36,** 491–502.

Spielberger, C. D. The effects of anxiety on complex learning and academic achievement. In C. D. Spielberger (Ed.), *Anxiety and behavior.* New York: Academic Press, 1966. Pp. 361–398.

Stampfl, T. G., & Lewis, D. J. Essentials of implosive theory: A learning-theory based psychodynamic behavior theory. *Journal of Abnormal Psychology,* 1967, **72,** 496–503.

Stark, J. R. Educational technology: A communications problem. *Phi Delta Kappan,* 1967, **48,** 194–198.

Steinberg, S. The language of prejudice. *Today's Education,* 1971, **60,** 14–17.

Stephens, J. M. *Educational psychology* (2nd ed.). New York: Holt, Rinehart and Winston, 1956.

Suppes, P. The uses of computers in education. *Scientific American,* 1966, **215** (3), 207–220.

Suppes, P. Computer technology and the future of education. *Phi Delta Kappan,* 1968, **49,** 420–423.

Taba, H. *Thinking in elementary school children.* San Francisco: San Francisco State College, 1964.

Talbert, E. G. Story preferences: A technique for assessing children's motives. Unpublished doctoral dissertation, University of Oklahoma, 1968.

Telford, C. W., & Sawrey, J. M. *Psychology: A concise introduction to the fundamentals of behavior.* Monterey, Calif.: Brooks/Cole, 1968.

Terman, L. M., & Merrill, M. A. *Stanford-Binet intelligence scale, manual* (3rd rev.), Form L-M. Boston: Houghton Mifflin, 1960.

Thornburg, H. D. Single presentation of emotionally loaded words and recall rates. Unpublished data, 1967.

Thornburg, H. D. The effects of authoritarianism and manipulation tendencies on attitudes toward sex. Paper presented at the meeting of the Southwestern Psychological Association, New Orleans, 1968.

Thornburg, H. D. Varying personality traits observed in undergraduate elementary and secondary education students. Paper presented at the meeting of the Southwestern Psychological Association, Austin, 1969.

Thornburg, H. D. Attitudes toward school and self: Indians, Blacks, and Mexican-Americans. Paper presented at the meeting of the Pacific Division, AAAS, San Diego, 1971. (a)

Thornburg, H. D. (Ed.), *Contemporary adolescence: Readings.* Monterey, Calif.: Brooks/Cole, 1971. (b)

Thornburg, H. D. An investigation of attitudes among potential dropouts from minority groups during their freshman year in high school. Final Report, U.S. Department of Health, Education, and Welfare, Office of Education, Bureau of Research, Contract No. OEC–9–71–0002(057), 1971. (c)

Thornburg, H. D. Minority youth families: A comparative analysis of attitude between self and family. Paper presented at the meeting of the Southwestern and Rocky Mountain Division, AAAS, Tempe, Arizona, 1971. (d)

Thorndike, E. L. Animal intelligence: An experimental study of the associative processes in animals. *Psychological Review Monograph Supplement,* 1898, **2,** 1–109.

Thorndike, E. L. *Educational psychology.* New York: Lemcke and Buchner, 1903.

Thorndike, E. L. *Animal intelligence.* New York: Macmillan, 1911.

Thorndike, E. L. *The psychology of learning.* Vol. II. New York: Teachers College Press, 1913.

Thorndike, E. L. *The fundamentals of learning.* New York: Teachers College Press, 1932. (a)

Thorndike, E. L. Reward and punishment in animal learning. *Comparative Psychological Monographs,* 1932, **8** (39). (b)

Thorndike, E. L. *The psychology of wants, interests, and attitudes.* New York: Appleton-Century-Crofts, 1935.

Thorndike, E. L., & Lorge, I. *The teacher's word book of 30,000 words.* New York: Columbia University, Bureau of Publications, Teachers College, 1944.

Thorndike, E. L., & Woodworth, R. S. The influence of improvement in one mental function upon the efficiency of other functions. *Psychological Review,* 1901, **8,** 247–261.

Thurstone, L. L. *Primary mental abilities.* Chicago: University of Chicago Press, 1938.

Tolman, E. C. *Purposive behavior in animals and men.* New York: Appleton-Century-Crofts, 1938.

Travers, J. F. *Learning: Analysis and application.* New York: McKay, 1965.

Travers, J. F. *Fundamentals of educational psychology.* Scranton, Pa.: International Press, 1970.

Turner, R. L. Teaching as problem-solving behavior: A strategy. In B. J. Biddle & W. J. Ellena (Eds.), *Contemporary research on teacher effectiveness.* New York: Holt, Rinehart and Winston, 1964. Pp. 102–126.

Two million youngsters in U.S. learn science with a new curriculum. *AAAS Bulletin,* 1961, **16** (2), 1–2.

Tyler, R. W. Some persistent questions on the defining of objectives. In C. M. Lindvall (Ed.), *Defining educational objectives.* Pittsburgh: University of Pittsburgh Press, 1964. Pp. 77–83.

Underwood, B. J. Retroactive and proactive inhibition after five and forty-eight hours. *Journal of Experimental Psychology,* 1948, **38,** 29–38.

Underwood, B. J. Proactive inhibition as a function of time and degree of prior learning. *Journal of Experimental Psychology,* 1949, **39,** 24–34.

Underwood, B. J. Studies of distributed practice: II. Learning and retention of paired-adjective lists with two levels of intralist similarity. *Journal of Experimental Psychology,* 1951, **42,** 153–161. (a)

Underwood, B. J. Studies of distributed practice: III. The influence of stage of practice in serial learning. *Journal of Experimental Psychology,* 1951, **42,** 291–295. (b)

Underwood, B. J. Studies of distributed practice: VI. The influence of rest-interval activity in serial learning. *Journal of Experimental Psychology,* 1952, **43,** 329–340. (a)

Underwood, B. J. Studies of distributed practice: VII. Learning and retention of serial nonsense lists as a function of intralist similarity. *Journal of Experimental Psychology,* 1952, **44,** 80–87. (b)

Underwood, B. J. Studies of distributed practice: X. The influence of intralist similarity on learning and retention of serial adjective lists. *Journal of Experimental Psychology,* 1953, **45,** 253–259.

Underwood, B. J. Intralist similarity in verbal learning and retention. *Psychological Review,* 1954, **61,** 160–166.

Underwood, B. J. Interference and forgetting. *Psychological Review,* 1957, **64,** 49–60.

Underwood, B. J. Verbal learning and the educative process. *Harvard Educational Review,* 1959, **29,** 107–117.

Underwood, B. J. Degree of learning and the measurement of forgetting. *Journal of Verbal Learning and Verbal Behavior,* 1964, **3,** 112–129. (a)

Underwood, B. J. Laboratory studies of verbal learning. In E. R. Hilgard (Ed.), *Theories of learning and instruction.* Sixty-third Yearbook. Chicago: National Society for the Study of Education, 1964. Pp. 133–152. (b)

Underwood, B. J., & Goad, D. Studies of distributed practice: I. The influence of intralist similarity in serial learning. *Journal of Experimental Psychology,* 1951, **42,** 125–134.

Underwood, B. J., & Hughes, R. H. Gradients of generalized verbal responses. *American Journal of Psychology,* 1950, **63,** 422–430.

U. S. Commission on Civil Rights. *Racial isolation in the public schools.* Vol. 1. Washington, D.C.: U.S. Government Printing Office, 1967.

Veroff, J. Social comparison and the development of achievement motivation. In C. P. Smith (Ed.), *Achievement-related motives in children.* New York: Russell Sage Foundation, 1969.

Walters, R. H., Parke, R. D., & Cane, V. A. Timing of punishment and the observation of consequences to others as determinants of response inhibition. *Journal of Experimental Child Psychology,* 1965, **2,** 10–30.

Watson, J. B. *Behavior, an introduction to comparative psychology.* New York: Holt, Rinehart and Winston, 1914.

Watson, J. B., & Raynor, R. Conditioned emotional reactions. *Journal of Experimental Psychology,* 1920, **3,** 1–14.

Wattenberg, W. W., & Clifford, C. Relationship of self-concepts to beginning achievement in reading. *Child Development,* 1964, **35,** 461–467.

Wechsler, D. *The measurement of adult intelligence.* Baltimore: Williams & Wilkins, 1944.

Wechsler, D. *Wechsler intelligence scale for children, manual.* New York: Psychological Corp., 1949.

Wenrich, W. W. *A primer of behavior modification.* Monterey, Calif.: Brooks/Cole, 1970.

Wheeler, L. Toward a theory of behavioral contagion. *Psychological Review,* 1966, **73,** 179–192.

White, R. W. Motivation reconsidered: The concept of competence. *Psychological Review,* 1959, **66,** 297–333.

Whitely, P. L., & McGeoch, J. A. The curve of retention for poetry. *Journal of Educational Psychology,* 1928, **19,** 471–479.

Wiegand, V. K. A study of subordinate skills in science problem solving. Unpublished doctoral dissertation, University of California, Berkeley, 1969.

Winterbottom, M. R. The relation of need for achievement to learning experiences in independence and mastery. In J. W. Atkinson (Ed.), *Motives in fantasy, action, and society.* New York: Van Nostrand Reinhold, 1958. Pp. 453–478.

Withall, J. The development of a technique for the measurement of social-emotional climate in classrooms. *Journal of Experimental Education,* 1949, **17,** 347–361.

Withall, J. The development of a climate index. *Journal of Educational Research,* 1951, **45,** 93–99.

Wolpe, J. *Psychotherapy by reciprocal inhibition.* Stanford, Calif.: Stanford University Press, 1958.

Wolpe, J. *The practice of behavior therapy.* Elmsford, N.Y.: Pergamon, 1969.

Wolpe, J., & Lazarus, A. A. *Behavior therapy techniques.* Elmsford, N.Y.: Pergamon, 1966.

Wylie, H. H. An experimental study of transfer of response in the white rat. *Behavioral Monographs,* 1919, **3** (16).

Wylie, R. C. *The self-concept: A critical survey of pertinent research literature.* Lincoln: University of Nebraska Press, 1961.

Zajonc, R. B. Attitudinal effects of mere exposure. *Journal of Personality and Social Psychology,* 1968, **9** (Part 2), 1–27.

Zigler, E. Social reinforcement, environmental conditions, and the child. *American Journal of Orthopsychiatry,* 1963, **33,** 614–623.

Zigler, E., Butterfield, E. C., & Capobianco, F. Institutionalization and social reinforcement. *Developmental Psychology,* 1970, **3,** 255–263.

Zigler, E., & Kanzer, P. The effectiveness of two classes of verbal reinforcers on the performance of middle- and lower-class children. *Journal of Personality,* 1962, **30,** 157–163.

Author Index

Subject Index

COMMON PSYCHOLOGICAL TERMS

MAJOR SECTIONS IN THE TEXT*

* Italicized page numbers refer to entire sections.